JERUSHA TANNER LAMPTEY
is a scholar of Islam, theology of religions, and comparative theology. She is currently Assistant Professor of Islam and Ministry at Union Theological Seminary in the City of New York. She previously taught at Georgetown University, where she also received her Ph.D. in Theological and Religious Studies with a focus on religious pluralism in Catholic and Islamic thought. She has published several articles and book chapters on religious pluralism, ecumenical relations, John Paul II, Vatican II, and African traditional religion.

Never Wholly Other

NEVER WHOLLY OTHER

A Muslima *Theology of Religious Pluralism*

JERUSHA TANNER LAMPTEY

OXFORD
UNIVERSITY PRESS

OXFORD
UNIVERSITY PRESS

Oxford University Press is a department of the University of Oxford. It furthers the University's objective of excellence in research, scholarship, and education by publishing worldwide.

Oxford New York
Auckland Cape Town Dar es Salaam Hong Kong Karachi
Kuala Lumpur Madrid Melbourne Mexico City Nairobi
New Delhi Shanghai Taipei Toronto

With offices in
Argentina Austria Brazil Chile Czech Republic France Greece
Guatemala Hungary Italy Japan Poland Portugal Singapore
South Korea Switzerland Thailand Turkey Ukraine Vietnam

Published in the United States of America by
Oxford University Press
198 Madison Avenue, New York, NY 10016

Library of Congress Cataloging-in-Publication Data
Lamptey, Jerusha Tanner.
Never wholly other : a *Muslima* theology of religious pluralism /
Jerusha Tanner Lamptey.
pages cm
Includes bibliographical references and index.
ISBN 978–0–19–936278–3 (cloth : alk. paper) 1. Qur'an—Hermeneutics.
2. Qur'an—Feminist criticism. 3. Religious pluralism—Islam.
4. Qur'an—Criticism, interpretatation, etc. I. Title.
BP 130.2.L36 2014
297.2082—dc23
2013031835

1 3 5 7 9 8 6 4 2
Printed in the United States of America
on acid-free paper

To Jalilah,
my āyat Allah
may you always be filled with light
may you always fill others with light

Contents

Acknowledgments

I AM PROFOUNDLY grateful to the many people who inspired this book and guided me throughout its development. To begin, I must acknowledge my indebtedness to Asghar Ali Engineer, Abdulaziz Sachedina, Mahmut Aydin, Seyyed Hossein Nasr, Reza Shah-Kazemi, Muhammad Legenhausen, Tim Winter, Amina Wadud, Asma Barlas, Riffat Hassan, Farid Esack, Ismāʿīl al-Fārūqī, and Toshihiko Izutsu. These scholars provoked my investigation into Islamic views of religious pluralism and provided a critical foundation for this book.

I also recognize the encouragement, assistance, and opportunities provided by Daniel A. Madigan, S.J., Jeannine Hill Fletcher, Yvonne Haddad, Michael Mason, Taha Jabir al-Alwani, Louis Cantori, Mona Abul Fadl, Paul Knitter, Mohammad Hassan Khalil, John Esposito, and Cynthia Read. From the earliest stages, Madigan offered invaluable insights and guidance on this project. Hill Fletcher, in addition to reading earlier versions, introduced me to the complex and fascinating interconnections between feminist theology, identity, and religious pluralism. Knitter created vital opportunities for me to share my research and offered generous support before and after I joined the faculty of Union Theological Seminary. Khalil encouraged my work, provided important occasions for scholarly dialogue, and freely proffered advice. Esposito graciously recommended this book to Oxford University Press. Read, and everyone at Oxford University Press, supported this project and expertly guided me through the publication process.

I am also very thankful for my colleagues at Georgetown University with whom I learned and worked while writing the majority of this book. In particular, my gratitude is extended to Peter C. Phan, John W O'Malley, S.J., Stephen Fields, S.J., John Borelli, Chester Gillis, Theresa Sanders, Tod Linafelt, Terrence Reynolds, Erika Seamon, Maureen Walsh, and Anh

Tran. I am likewise grateful for the inspiration and encouragement of my new colleagues at Union Theological Seminary in the City of New York.

My deep appreciation is extended to my family and friends, especially my mother, Mary Rhodes; my sister, Molly Naughton; Victoria Curtis; and Bethany Black. Their support and confidence have been unfailing. I am also grateful to my daughter, my heart, Jalilah Odaaley, who walked through every moment of this book with me, providing balance, challenge, and laughter. In all, my ultimate gratitude rests with God, *alḥamdulillah*.

Note on Transliteration, Translation, and Gendered Language

I HAVE UTILIZED the transliteration system of the *International Journal of Middle Eastern Studies* (IJMES) to render Arabic terms into English. Where transliterations appear in quotations and titles of other works, I have retained the original transliteration despite minor inconsistencies with the IJMES system. I have included approximate English translations of the transliterated Arabic terms at each first occurrence and elsewhere when necessary for clarity. A glossary of these terms is provided.

References to Qur'ānic verses follow a chapter (*sūra*): verse (*āya*) format. For example, 4:1 refers to the fourth chapter of the Qur'ān and the first verse in that chapter. The numbering of verses follows the standard Royal Egyptian edition. An index of Qur'ānic verses is also provided.

In rendering translations of the Qur'ān, I have consulted major English translations, including those of M. A. S. Abdel-Haleem, Muhammad Asad, Abdullah Yusuf Ali, Muhammad Marmaduke Pickthall, Arthur Arberry, Yahiya Emerick, Muhammad Muhsin Khan, and Tarif Khalidi. For accessibility and flow, I have aimed to use contemporary English constructions and phrasing.

With translation of the Qur'ān, I have also paid special attention to the manner in which gendered language is employed. This involves using inclusive language (humankind instead of mankind, and humanity/human instead of man) but also consciously considering the broader implications of other gendered translations. It is common practice, for example, to utilize masculine personal pronouns (He, His) when translating verses related to God. This is a literal translation of the Arabic, in which all words are grammatically gendered and in which the Arabic word for God happens to be masculine. The transfer of masculine personal pronouns into English—a language with no grammatical but only biological gendering—has unintended and problematic theological implications. While there have been some historical Islamic debates over the application of anthropomorphic language in reference to God, there has been widespread consensus that God is neither human nor male. Utilization of masculine pronouns—for example, "He created" and "His power"—obscures these central theological tenets and also inherently privileges male normativity. I have therefore avoided these pronouns by using "God" in all such places (e.g., "God creates" and "God's power"). While at times stylistically cumbersome, it is nonetheless more theologically sound.

Never Wholly Other

Introduction

The Qur'ān and the Religious Other

How does the Qur'ān depict the religious Other? This succinct question forms the heart of this book. While seemingly straightforward, it is in fact a profound and pressing question with significant theological and practical implications.

Theologically, it is directly connected to the understanding of God and God's action in the world. If the Qur'ān is seen to be the Word of God, to be God's speech—as it is by Muslims—then the content of that speech will necessarily reveal much about the Speaker. What kind of God is this? What does God communicate to humanity? The question about the Qur'ānic depiction of the religious Other is also intertwined with the general understanding of humankind and the purpose of human creation. In many ways, this question defines the theological nexus between God and humankind. What does God require of humankind? What kinds of relationships between God and humanity are sought? What kinds of relationships are disdained? How does humankind live up to—or struggle to live up to—this requirement? Moreover, in defining this nexus between God and humankind, the Qur'ān's depiction of the religious Other is also and always a depiction of the religious self.

Practically, the depiction of the religious Other assumes great importance in light of the uniqueness and pervasiveness of the modern experience of religious plurality. In today's world, we encounter diversity—of all sorts—in a more intimate and intricate manner than in the past. Such encounters frequently prompt inquiry into convergences and divergences in belief and practice and discussions of appropriate forms of inter-religious interaction. Furthermore, ongoing waves of religious violence and oppression force us to ask difficult questions about the relationship between depictions of religious Others, intolerance, and oppression.

While there is not always a necessary connection between negative depictions of religious Others and intolerant actions, at the very least negative depictions can be used as fuel for already kindled fires.

The question of the Qur'ān's depiction of the religious Other is also crucial due to another increasingly common phenomenon. In the United States, interreligious interaction and cooperation have grown substantially in the last decade. While not triggered by September 11, 2001, the horrific tragedy and resultant trauma of that day certainly increased awareness of the necessity and value of interreligious cooperation and involvement. This has led to extensive interfaith dialogues aimed at learning about diverse traditions. It has also led to many interreligious efforts that focus on social justice and community welfare, including disaster relief, youth projects, food banks and community health service programs. The tide of interreligious engagement shows no sides of ebbing; it is not a passing fad. By all accounts, it is the new norm of mainstream religious communities, including American Muslims. Whereas in the past some reticence may have been expressed toward participation in such activities, interreligious cooperation today is commonplace and widely valued.

However, the embrace of interreligious engagement—that is, the practical embrace of the religious Other—has not necessarily been accompanied by a theological embrace of the religious Other. In fact, there frequently exists a pronounced bifurcation between practical action and theological understandings of religious Others. Many Muslims, for example, are fully committed to interreligious engagement and devote their lives to such work yet still harbor theological commitments to the finality, uniqueness, and superiority of the religion of Islam. Though from an Islamic standpoint this does not mean that other religions are completely devoid of divine guidance or value, it nevertheless does imply that the ideal relationship with God is actualized only within the specific tradition of Islam. Bifurcation between the practical and theological is problematic because the two topics are treated as if they do not come into contact with or inform one another. Questions of how we act—or should act—in this world in relation to other humans become severed from questions of how we should act in relation to God and vice versa. Ultimately, this is an unrealistic—and therefore unstable—partitioning.

Eventually, inquiries into the relationship between practice and theology always arise. Is there any theological justification for practical interreligious engagement? Is it necessary to affirm the value of the religious Other to affirm the value of interreligious engagement? Is there only one possible theological view of religious Others? Or are there multiple possible views? While these questions arise in response to particular experiences in a particular context, they cannot be answered in relation to practical experience alone. In seeking to answer these questions, and in seeking to uncover new legitimate possibilities, all of these questions necessarily redirect Muslims back to the central and most authoritative source for religious knowledge in the Islamic tradition: the Qur'ān. Although the Qur'ān is not the only religious source, it is the primary starting point, the primary touchstone for such questions.

Redirection to the Qur'ān, however, does not automatically reveal an unequivocal perspective on the religious Other. This is due partially to the role of interpretation and interpreters in mediating the text but also due to the fact that the Qur'ānic discourse on the religious Other, or religious difference, is inherently complex. The Qur'ān explicitly and extensively discusses the topic of religious difference, sometimes referencing specific groups and at other times utilizing a more general terminology, such as believers, hypocrites, disbelievers, and submitters. In this discourse, moreover, the Qur'ān does not consistently depict religious otherness as acceptable or unacceptable. In some places, otherness is positively evaluated, and elsewhere it is blatantly scorned. The extensive—and seemingly ambivalent—discussion of religious Otherness is also tangled together with repeated Qur'ānic affirmations of continuity and commonality (or sameness) between religious communities, revelations, and prophets.

These facets of the Qur'ānic discourse on religious Otherness have prompted the articulation of a variety of hermeneutical approaches and interpretations, all of which aim to address—or make sense of—this complexity. While one such approach could be to deem the text inconsistent and thereby account for the apparent mixed messages, this strategy has not been employed by most historical or contemporary Islamic scholars, who largely view the Qur'ān as the inerrant Word of God. Rather, Islamic scholars have preferred hermeneutical strategies that rely upon notions such as chronology, progressive revelation, textual and prophetic abrogation, distinctions between particular and universal Qur'ānic verses (*āyāt*), and prioritization of Qur'ānic ethical principles. These strategies, with varying degrees of authority, have and continue to result in diverse depictions of the overarching Qur'ānic view of the religious Other.

In the context of the United States, the rise of pointed questions about the relationship between practical and theological views of the religious Other and the resultant redirection to the Qur'ān to explore theological possibilities are evident. A number of contemporary Islamic scholars writing in and for the US context have begun to grapple with the Qur'ān's depiction of the religious Other and to offer provocative commentaries on the existence, value, and function of religious plurality. This contemporary discourse does manifest hermeneutical diversity but also reveals two prominent trends. First, some scholars prioritize the message of religious commonality, downplaying—even ignoring—Qur'ānic discussions of difference or Otherness. And second, other scholars aim to account simultaneously for religious sameness and Otherness but are able to do so only through interpretations that depict religious communities as isolated or hierarchically ranked. In both of these trends, there are significant shared presuppositions and, as a result, significant shared shortcomings. Foremost among these is a prevailing view of religious difference as that which unambiguously divides humanity through the erection of clear and static boundaries. In other words, religious communities are conceived of as being wholly discrete, clearly defined, and unchanging entities. This particular view of Otherness has led to an interpretative gridlock; it has placed severe restrictions on the discourse and has resulted in inability to perceive—and engage—other invaluable Qur'ānic possibilities.

This book arises in response to the gridlock. It endeavors to illuminate new pathways within the Qur'ānic discourse that have been obscured due to the dominant, shared conception of difference. In addition to deconstructing, and thereby revealing the limitations of, the contemporary Islamic discourse, in this book I also construct an alternative conceptual and methodological approach to the subject matter. I then use that alternative approach to articulate a novel—yet theologically, contextually, and practically sound—reinterpretation of the Qur'ānic discourse on the religious Other.

Theology of Religions and Islamic Contributions

In this study, I focus on contemporary Islamic scholarly discourse written in and for the US context. While there are, of course, many other voices beyond the scholarly and the US contexts, I have chosen this particular focus as it is to this discourse and these contexts that I endeavor to make a constructive contribution. In addition to being an engagement with the existing contemporary Islamic discourse, this book is also intended to be a contribution to the specific field of theology of religions. While a few of the contemporary Islamic scholars I examine do explicitly engage this field, Islamic contributions are generally nascent and rare. Therefore, it is necessary to briefly introduce this field—a field spearheaded by Christian theologians—and to highlight some significant convergences and divergences between the field and the existing Islamic discourse.

Theology of religions is generally defined as a "discipline of theological studies which attempts to account theologically for the meaning and value of other religions."[1] As a theological enterprise, it attempts to work within and through the parameters of one religion—using the distinctive theological methods and sources of that tradition—to theorize about the meaning of religious diversity in general and to assess the value of specific religions and their role, if any, in relation to the tradition. Theology of religions does draw upon other resources and methods as well, but it is primarily concerned with accounting for the religious Other from the theological standpoint; it is primarily concerned with critically exploring particular traditions' possibilities and obstacles in respect to embracing the religious Other.

The field of theology of religions, as indicated, has largely been developed by Christian theologians. As a result, many of the central questions and theoretical underpinnings have a distinctive Christian character. This is evident from the fact that the foremost question of the field has been salvation and the (in)accessibility of salvation to individuals who align themselves with religions other than Christianity. In some circumstances, this question has arisen from the attempt to negotiate two affirmations: first, that God desires the universal salvation of all people; and, second, that Jesus Christ is the unique locus of salvation. Various Christian perspectives in theology of religions "reflect a sorting out and struggling with these two foundational affirmations."[2] Thus, some perspectives emphasize only one affirmation, while others diversely attempt to balance or maintain both affirmations simultaneously. Although the central question in theology of religions has been salvation, Christian theology of religions has also explored other issues, such as the presence of revelation in other religions[3] and the moral and ethical value of other religions.[4]

Some contemporary Islamic scholars have begun to contribute to the field of theology of religions. These contributions include Islamic articulations of the soteriological status of religious Others; examinations of Islamic perspectives toward specific religious groups; and attempts to formulate overarching accounts of the origin, value and purpose of religious diversity.[5] Nevertheless, Islamic theology of religions remains an emergent field because not all of these articulations explicitly or consciously attempt to grapple with the theoretical underpinnings of the larger field of theology of religions. The discussion of religious diversity from an Islamic perspective is not new. However, the deliberate attempt to engage the central questions and theories of theology of religions is.

Such engagement requires, for instance, an evaluation of the relevance of the central question of salvation. As noted, this question frequently arises from the tensive convergence between two distinctive Christian affirmations. While it is tempting simply to substitute the defining feature of the Islamic tradition—that is, the Qur'ānic revelation—in the place of Jesus in these affirmations, to do so would be to assume structural and theological parity. A general concept of salvation certainly plays a role in the Islamic tradition, but it arises out of distinct conceptions of human anthropology (the situation, purpose, and goal of humankind), divine ontology, and the relationship between God and humankind. In recognition of this, a few contemporary Islamic scholars have endeavored to shift the central focus from the question of salvation. Muhammad Legenhausen, for example, has—in lieu of the salvation question—emphasized the deontological question of correct religion, that is, the question of what God commands in terms of practice.[6]

Islamic contributions to the field of theology of religions also must examine the suitability of the standard tripartite typology of exclusivism, inclusivism, and pluralism to the Islamic tradition. In this typology, exclusivism denotes the perspective that explicit adherence to one particular religious tradition is necessary for salvation or a correct relationship with God. Inclusivism denotes the perspective that the particulars of one tradition—for example, Jesus—lead to salvation but that salvation is also possible in some manner outside of the particular tradition. And, finally, pluralism denotes the perspective that salvation or a correct relationship with God is possible in many, if not all, religions. Legenhausen and Reza Shah-Kazemi[7] have both offered explicit critiques of this typology. While they have attempted, as I will discuss in detail in Chapter 2, to affirm the value of other religions to some degree, they have done so through the introduction of the alternative models of non-reductive pluralism and universalism. Legenhausen's non-reductive pluralism is a critical response to the pluralism of John Hick,[8] a pluralism that Legenhausen deems unsuitable for religious traditions that emphasize law and social praxis. Shah-Kazemi's universalism aims to affirm religious pluralism as the intentional creation of God. Both of these alternatives hint at the fact that Islamic contributions to theology of religions will most likely result in tweaks to the standard typology, tweaks that allow for the introduction of particular Islamic theological concerns and contentions. Some such major concerns and contentions relate to supersession, to the status and content of other revelations, to issues of ethics and justice, and to the depiction of religious diversity within various Islamic sources. In the following two chapters on the historical and contemporary discourses, I aim to explicate the intricacies of many of these particular Islamic concerns. Then, in my constructive interpretation, I aim to articulate an Islamic theology of religions that integrates these concerns and contributes to the broader field of theology of religions.

Muslima *Theology?*

I have termed the alternative conceptual and methodological approach to religious difference that I outline in this book a *Muslima* theology of religious pluralism. This unique label is intended to capture many vital facets of my particular approach, including my personal and theoretical positioning, my use of foundational insights drawn from Muslim women interpreters of the Qurʾān, and my critical and comparative engagement with feminist theology.

In Arabic, the term *Muslima* means a female Muslim, or a female who submits to and is devoted to God. This indicates that my approach arises out of my positioning as a believing and practicing Muslim. More importantly, it indicates that I endeavor to articulate a theology of religions through a critical reappraisal and revisiting of the central Islamic sources, primarily the Qurʾān. This theology of religions is rooted in the Islamic tradition while simultaneously probing and testing the bounds of that tradition.

The term *Muslima* also indicates an interconnection with my positioning as a woman. Part of this relates to my individual experiences as a woman. However, another aspect of it arises from a deliberate choice to align myself with—and draw pointed insights from—scholarly reflections on women's experience. It is, therefore, not only an experiential but also a theoretical positioning.

This theoretical positioning is evident in the fact that I cull the foundational insights—both conceptual and hermeneutical—of *Muslima* theology from the work of Muslim women interpreters of the Qurʾān, specifically Amina Wadud, Asma Barlas, and Riffat Hassan. While these scholars are focused primarily on examining sexual (meaning biological) difference in the Qur'ān, their approaches are invaluable in that they display a new way of understanding difference and a specific hermeneutical strategy. In *Muslima* theology, I aim to extend their insights from one genre of human difference, that is, sexual difference, to another genre of human difference, that is, religious difference.

To do so—and this is another aspect of my theoretical positioning as a woman embodied in the term *Muslima*—I critically and comparatively engage feminist theological contributions to the field of theology of religions that emerge from other traditions. The unique—albeit in many cases emergent—perspectives manifest in these contributions are the direct result of a conscious endeavor to apply the foundational theories and insights of feminist reflections on sexual difference, gender, and androcentrism to the topic of religious difference. It is this conscious endeavor that makes their work of great value to my articulation of *Muslima* theology. Of particular relevance are their critiques of the standard typologies of theology of religions, their desire to affirm particularity without necessarily resorting to hierarchical evaluation, and their incorporation of identity theory into the discussion of religious diversity.[9]

Another important facet of my approach captured by the term *Muslima* theology is that my approach is theological. It endeavors to engage in textual interpretation but also to consciously and explicitly go beyond exegetical work to formulate a theological model of religious Otherness based upon that exegesis. Therefore, while I carry out a close and detailed reading of the Qur'ānic text, I am also interested in weaving together elements of this exegetical enterprise into an integrated and comprehensive model of religious pluralism, a model that aims to account for not just religious difference but also religious sameness, divine ontology, human anthropology, and human relationality.

Finally, the term *Muslima* theology is deliberately intended to carve out a new intellectual space and to partially circumvent recurring discussions of the validity—and even referent—of the label *Islamic feminism*. There have been extensive debates over the compatibility of Islam and feminism, and two dominant positions have emerged. The first refers to Islamic feminism as a misnomer and dismisses the search within the Islamic tradition for resources that support egalitarianism and women's rights as limited and compromised; the core ideas of feminism and the basic principles of Islam are seen as being in diametric opposition.[10] The second position affirms the validity of searching within the Islamic tradition for egalitarian resources while simultaneously encompassing various opinions on the label Islamic feminism itself.[11] While scholars who support the second position agree that Islamic sources, especially the Qur'ān, contain liberative messages, they do not all adopt the label *feminism*. The ambivalence expressed toward the term feminism arises in part from a historical affiliation of feminism with colonialism and secularism and the related secular feminist critique of most religions as oppressive, backward, and androcentric. Additionally, in reaction to colonialism, feminism has been depicted by various Islamic authorities as a foreign, "un-Islamic," and therefore illegitimate transplantation into the Islamic tradition.[12]

Contemporary scholars who attempt to use the Islamic tradition as a basis for affirming women's rights and human equality—myself included—often find themselves contending with the residual impact of these dual historical circumscriptions. From the secular side, the religious approach is depicted as traditional and backward and perhaps even as manifesting a false consciousness. From the religious side, our feminism is depicted as modern, Western, and thus un-Islamic. This has contributed to the reticence of many scholars to identify their work as Islamic feminism.

However, discomfort with the label Islamic feminism is not simply a product of competing historical contentions; it is also tied intimately to the desire of Muslim women scholars to effect change and assert authority. To do so, we must be aware of and responsive to common—albeit naive—communal assessments of Islam and feminism. For Muslim women scholars working in academia, our faith commitment can be seen as compromising objectivity and serious intellectual engagement. This is exacerbated by the fact that most research on Muslim women is not carried out by Muslim women themselves. While some "confessional" Muslim women scholars have garnered academic acceptance, others have continued to feel that that acceptance is marginal or token rather than based upon appreciation of the rigor and insight of their specific scholarly contributions. Conversely, within Muslim communities, scholars' academic affiliations and conclusions on gender can be depicted as diverging from traditional methods and knowledge and, thus, as being of little value and of great risk. In short, what these tensions reveal is that the debate over the label Islamic feminism is indicative of a multifaceted and complex struggle for power and authority. Moreover, a central component of this is the struggle for self-identification, the struggle to define and redefine one's self and one's work rather than being corralled into a predetermined and defined box.

It is in response to these struggles that I have chosen not to apply the label Islamic feminism to the scholars I explore in this book. While they are engaged in work many would describe as Islamic feminism, I have opted to refer to them with the descriptive—albeit somewhat unwieldy—phrase *Muslim women interpreters of the Qur'ān*. In my own constructive theology, I have adopted the label *Muslima* theology to provocatively indicate a reaction to these debates as well as a deliberate assertion of experiential and scholarly self-identity. While I do not apply this designation to the work of other scholars, I leave open the possibility that it may be applicable to similar efforts.

Qur'ān Only?

The *Muslima* theology of religious pluralism that I articulate in this book is the result of not only a new conception of difference but also a specific hermeneutical method. This method derives in part from the hermeneutical insights of Muslim women interpreters of the Qur'ān as well as from the method of semantic analysis put forth by Toshihiko Izutsu. While I will explore the particulars of my approach in Chapters 3 and 5, at this juncture it is important to directly address one facet of this methodology: the focus on the Qur'ān.

As is already evident in the central question of this work—how does the Qur'ān depict the religious Other?—and as will become increasingly evident, I deliberately focus *primarily* and *initially* on the Qur'ān itself. In adopting the Qur'ān as the primary focus, I thoroughly acknowledge the existence, validity, and traditional function of other interpretative sources, including the *sunna* (practice of Muḥammad), *aḥādīth* (narrations of the sayings, actions, and tacit approval of Muḥammad), and *'ijmā'* (consensus of scholars). However, I also assert that the Qur'ān—due to its unique stature within the Islamic tradition—is the main standard for theological reinterpretation. I do not unequivocally dismiss other sources, nor do I advocate a Qur'ān-only approach. Rather, I contend that other sources must be subjected to a hermeneutic of suspicion that gives precedence to the Qur'ānic message and the Qur'ānic ethos, a hermeneutic that prioritizes the Qur'ān and uses it to critically assess the other sources.

In reference to the initial focus on the Qur'ān, I contend that it is vital to give voice to the complexities, interconnections, and nuances of the Qur'ānic discourse prior to engaging in the legitimate enterprise of utilizing other sources to explicate the text itself. This is an intentional hermeneutical choice designed to facilitate the exposure of—and not necessarily to resolve—relational intricacies within the Qur'ān. Frequently, a single Qur'ānic concept is analyzed by tracing its meaning through multiple interpretative planes: the Qur'ān, the *aḥadīth*, exegesis, law, and other sources. This is a viable and valuable method. However, this study aims to focus on Qur'ānic unity and the relationships among multiple concepts within that unity. To get at this unity and relationality, substantial, integrated exegetical work must be first carried out on the Qur'ānic plane. This initial step forms a foundation upon which to carry out further examinations of the depiction of religious difference in other sources.

Overview of Chapters

In the first part of this book, I explore historical and contemporary Islamic discourse on religious difference. Chapter 1 examines various genres of the historical discourse—including the apologetic, polemical, exegetical, juridical, and Sufi—in an effort to highlight the complex and diverse processes of self-identification, boundary creation, and Othering that are woven throughout Islamic history. This chapter provides a foundation upon which to better understand the contemporary Islamic discourse that, in addition to being a nascent engagement with the modern field of theology of religions, is also a continuation—and in some ways an amalgamation—of various historical preoccupations.

Chapter 2 critically explores contemporary Islamic discussions of religious difference that feature prominently in English scholarly discourse in the United States. Therein, I further highlight the two dominant trends (the prioritization of sameness and the attempt to simultaneously affirm both sameness and difference) and the shared, underlying conception of difference as that which discretely and statically divides. I also detail the implications of this conception of difference for understanding the proximate religious Other, the Other-who-can-never-be-wholly-other.

In Part 2, I construct the conceptual and hermeneutical infrastructure of a *Muslima* theology of religious pluralism by drawing foundational insights from three sources: contemporary Muslim women's interpretation of the Qur'ān; feminist approaches to religious pluralism; and Toshihiko Izutsu's semantic analysis of the Qur'ān. In Chapter 3, I examine the conceptual and hermeneutical contributions of select Muslim women interpreters of the Qur'ān and argue that some elements of these scholars' conception of sexual difference can be generalized and connected to an innovative and integrated conception of religious difference.

In Chapter 4, I provide an overview of feminist contributions to theology of religions with the goal of identifying various elements that are consistent with—and thus capable of guiding the extension of—the conception of difference drawn from Muslim women interpreters of the Qur'ān. I probe the ways various feminist theologians have attempted to extend their methods, sources, and norms to the topic of religious diversity, critically co-opting aspects of their approaches, including the endeavor to account for and value sameness and difference without resorting to hierarchical evaluation.

In Chapter 5, I critically engage the hermeneutical approach of Toshihiko Izutsu, focusing primarily on his intra-Qur'ānic and synchronic semantic methodology. I argue that Izutsu's method of semantic analysis provides the ideal extension to the hermeneutical approach drawn from Muslim women interpreters of the Qur'ān. With its emphasis on relational meaning, overlapping semantic fields, and multifaceted interconnections, it is well suited to explicating the complex relationality that exists in the Qur'ānic discourse on the religious Other.

In Part 3, I use the infrastructure developed in Part 2 to reevaluate, reinterpret, and reenvision the Qur'ānic discourse on the religious Other, thereby articulating a *Muslima* theology of religious pluralism. In Chapter 6, I distinguish between hierarchical and lateral religious difference in the Qur'ān—between the semantic fields of *taqwā* (God consciousness) and *umma* (community)—and argue against the static and holistic alignment of the two genres of difference, which results in automatic ascription of a particular evaluation to a particular religious community.

In Chapter 7, I focus on the genre of hierarchical religious difference—that is, the semantic field of *taqwā*—in greater detail. I explore the hierarchical, value-laden concepts of *īmān* (belief), *islām* (submission, devotion), *ḥanīf* (nonconfessional monotheist), *kufr* (disbelief), *shirk* (ascribing partners to God), and *nifāq* (hypocrisy) in reference to *taqwā* to illuminate similarities, differences, overlaps, and gradations in the Qur'ānic discourse. Based on this exploration, I contend that the Qur'ānic discourse on hierarchical religious difference is characterized by dynamism, ambiguous boundaries, and relational complexity.

In Chapter 8, I articulate an integrated model of Qur'ānic religious difference, a model that aims to reweave creation, revelation, nonevaluated religious difference, and evaluated religious difference into a coherent—although complex and at times ambiguous—narrative. I also argue for the necessity of reenvisioning the Qur'ānic discourse as provocative guidance rather than as taxonomy of difference.

1

Historical and Contemporary Approaches to Religious Otherness

1

Self and Other in Historical Islamic Discourse

IN *BORDER LINES: The Partition of Judaeo-Christianity*, Daniel Boyarin argues that the historical division between Judaism and Christianity was the result not of a "natural parting of ways" but rather an intentional project—heresiology—that focused on "anatomizing, pinning down, making taxonomies of Christians" who were not "in."[1] The discourse of orthodoxy and heresy, moreover, was not simply a descriptive enterprise that highlighted extant distinctions. On the contrary, it was a deliberately prescriptive enterprise designed to "eradicate the fuzziness of the borders, semantic and social" and thereby to clearly establish boundaries and threshold criteria by which membership in either one or another community could be determined and enforced.

Drawing upon the theory of interpellation, Boyarin also contends that heresiology was concerned not only with voicing a negative assessment of the Other but also—and perhaps more significantly—with creating the Other as a subject.[2] By erecting borders—between heretical and orthodox Christians and ultimately between Judaism and Christianity as religions[3] —the Other was called into existence and became the necessary counterpoint for a community's delineation of its own identity. Borders, then, according to Boyarin, are as much about identifying the Other as they are about identifying or proclaiming the uniqueness of the self.

While the historical relationship between Islam and other religions does not exactly parallel the historical relationship between Judaism and Christianity, a similar process of Othering is readily discernible within Islamic history. In particular, the themes of utilizing the Other as a counterpoint for articulating self-identity; of creating taxonomies of internal difference; and of defining and defending discrete boundaries are all present in historical Islamic writings on religious difference. Due to this overlap, Boyarin's central contention about identity and the deliberate construction and enforcement of borders provides a valuable analytical lens for examining historical Islamic discussions of intra- and interreligious difference.

In the present chapter, I explore representative examples of various genres of this historical discourse in an effort to highlight the complex and diverse processes of self-identification, boundary creation, and Othering that are woven throughout Islamic history and that, thus, form the backdrop of contemporary Islamic discourse. Many of the historical preoccupations—such as the status of previous divine revelations and the definition of faith, *īmān*—retain central significance in contemporary discussions, as do many historical scholars. In recognition of the latter, this chapter is not a comprehensive survey of historical discourse but rather a survey of selected scholars who are centrally representative of the various genres (e.g., Abū ʿĪsā al-Warrāq and al-Bāqillānī), are frequently cited by contemporary scholars in their construction of Islamic approaches to religious diversity (e.g., Ibn al-ʿArabī), or are common points of reference in more general "Western" discussions of Islamic thought (e.g., Ibn Taymiyya and Ibn Kathīr).

Rejecting the Other and Projecting the Self: Polemical and Apologetic Trends

One of the most evident genres of historical Islamic discourse on religious difference is the polemical refutation of Christianity and Judaism. While it is tempting to lump these writings into a monolithic body of work concerned primarily with undercutting the legitimacy of Judaism and Christianity, there are in fact important nuances worthy of illumination.

An early example of this genre is the 3rd *h*/9th century[4] *Kitāb al-radd ʿalā l-thalāth firaq min al-Naṣārā* (Refutation of Three Christian Sects) written by Abū ʿĪsā Muḥammad b. Hārūn al-Warrāq (d. 247/861).[5] Abū ʿĪsā lived and wrote in the context of the religiously pluralistic culture of Baghdad under Abbasid rule. While this was a context of religious diversity and religious interaction, it was simultaneously a context of legal separation between religions in general and uneasiness with and mere toleration of Christianity in particular. Abū ʿĪsā is associated early on with Muʿtazilite thought but later was accused of various unorthodox views, including Manichean and Shīʿa sympathies. Despite these accusations of heresy, his writing on religions and sects has served as an invaluable source for many prominent, later scholars, some of whom draw upon him explicitly and others who do so anonymously (e.g., al-Bāqillānī and al-Jabbār).[6]

In the *Radd*, Abū ʿĪsā details the beliefs and doctrines of three Christian sects: the Nestorians; Monophysites/Jacobites; and Chalcedonians/ Melkites. He then proceeds to refute each sect's position on the specific doctrines of the Trinity and the Incarnation. Three characteristics of his treatise are of particular interest. The first is the amount of effort that Abū ʿĪsā devotes to detailing the intricacies of various Christian sects. While many other polemicists attacked Christianity on similar subjects and even with similar argumentation, the degree and nuance of his description are distinctive. In addition to the level of detail, David Thomas maintains that Abū ʿĪsā, in the *Radd* and an earlier (lost) descriptive account of various religions within Muslim society, *Kitāb al-maqālāt*, seems to have had a somewhat objective approach toward and interest in other religions.[7] This interest in describing other religions, however, is not a necessary component in the polemical and heresiological enterprise that Boyarin describes as being aimed at asserting self-identity in contrast to the Other. In fact, excessive description can be counterproductive to the goal of erecting clear, simple borders between groups. While Abū ʿĪsā does ultimately carry through on the polemical project ("projection"), his emphasis on description—coupled with his willingness to critique aspects of Islamic belief[8] and his affiliation with various liminal Muslim communities—no doubt contributed to his allegiances being called into question and to him ultimately being labeled as a heretic, that is, as one who blurs the boundaries.

The second notable characteristic of the *Radd* is the criteria by which Abū ʿĪsā assesses the doctrines of the Christian sects. Abū ʿĪsā bases his refutation on two criteria: coherence with the Christian system of belief and coherence with human reason or logic. Rather than explicitly subjecting the Christian doctrines to Islamic norms, such as those dictated by the Qurʾān, he adopts "forms of argument . . . based exclusively upon principles which Christians would sanction and presumably employ themselves."[9] The criteria are highlighted throughout the treatise with almost every section ending with statements such as "This is contrary to your principles" and "It is accepted both by us and others—and so none of them can disdain its rationality or entertain any possibility of doubt."[10]

While the aim is certainly to show the shortcomings of Christianity, Abū ʿĪsā, through his knowledge of the Other, is able to base his critique upon what he envisions to be a common ground of discourse.

A striking third aspect of the *Radd* is that, despite his extensive description and knowledge of Christian beliefs, his refutation focuses only on the doctrines of the Trinity and the Incarnation. Abū ʿĪsā targets "the two doctrines that most challenged the Muslim doctrine of *tawḥīd*... irrespective of the beliefs and doctrines that Christians themselves emphasized."[11] His selection of these doctrines and his treatment of them in isolation from other aspects of Christian belief are thus a clear projection of Muslim self-identity onto the Christian Other. The doctrines of the Trinity and the Incarnation are refuted not only because they are deemed "illogical" or "incoherent" within the Christian worldview but also because they present a golden opportunity to espouse and define the distinctiveness of Muslim self-identity and the defining role of the doctrine of divine unity, *tawḥīd*, in that identity. Furthermore, this move clearly indicates that Abū ʿĪsā's *Radd* specifically and other polemical works more generally are in fact equally apologetic; they are as much about promoting the self as devaluing the Other.

The integration of polemical and apologetic objectives is perhaps best illustrated in the later writings of Abū Bakr Muḥammad b. al-Ṭayyib al-Bāqillānī (d. 403/1013), the Ashʿarī and Maliki jurisprudent who was born in Basra but spent most of his life in Baghdad. In his *Kitāb al-tamhīd* (Introduction),[12] which was written upon request of the *amīr*, al-Bāqillānī offers refutations of both Christian and Jewish doctrines. While his argumentation in both instances is intriguing in and of itself, what is most remarkable about this work is its structure. The refutations of Christian and Jewish doctrines are woven into an overarching framework designed positively to outline central Islamic doctrines. The refutation of Christianity follows positive articulations on the nature of knowledge and the nature of God.[13] Intriguingly, the refutation of Judaism is not grouped with refutations of Christianity but rather follows a discussion of the prophethood of Muḥammad. Each group is deliberately addressed in reference to the central Islamic doctrine from which they vary. As with Abū ʿĪsā, the Christian doctrines of the Trinity and the Incarnation challenge—and in doing so, perhaps, highlight the uniqueness of—the Islamic conception of God. With Judaism, the central contention resides not with the conception of God but with the refusal to recognize the prophethood of Muḥammad and the abrogating nature of the Qurʾān. This topical juxtaposition aims not only to invalidate Christian and Jewish doctrines but also to bolster and glorify the Islamic doctrines. As David Thomas clarifies:

> Each group is thus held up as a counterexample to Muslim orthodoxy, and the weakness of its position, as al-Bāqillānī amasses arguments successively to demolish it, serves to prove that alternatives to the Islamic teachings are not viable. Thus, refutations of non-Muslim groups ... contribute towards building the case of the total coherence of Islam and the rational absurdity of pursuing any alternative.[14]

Al-Bāqillānī's *Kitāb al-tamhīd* also indicates another important shift within the polemical and apologetic discourse. While, like Abū ʿĪsā, he relies primarily upon logic and knowledge of other traditions to refute many doctrines, he also explicitly invokes Islamic norms—for example the prophethood of Muḥammad, the necessity of accepting Muḥammad as a universal prophet, and the abrogating nature of the Qurʾān—as definitive criteria. This is a notable departure from Abū ʿĪsā's "elaborate efforts to meet his opponents on their own ground,"[15] a departure that indicates a change in audience and context. Christians are no longer the primary interlocutors, and Christian ideas are no longer perceived to be as imminent of a threat as they were in the time of Abū ʿĪsā. The primary objective for al-Bāqillānī—as evinced in the structure of his work and the explicit use of Islamic norms—is to clarify and correct beliefs and practices within the Muslim community. The Other is thus silenced and used to illuminate and reassure the faith of the self.[16]

Another example of the foregrounding of Islamic norms is found in the concept of *taḥrīf*, or scriptural falsification, which emerges as a central evaluative criterion in many other refutations of Christianity and Judaism. This criterion was derived directly from Qurʾānic accusations:

> So can you hope that such people will believe you, when some of them used to hear the words of God and then deliberately twist (*yuḥarrifūnahu*) them, even when they understood them? (2:75)
>
> ... They distort (*yuḥarrifūna*) the meaning of [revealed] words and have forgotten some of what they were told to remember ... (5:13, excerpt)

It was also intimately tied to justifications for the necessity of the prophethood of Muḥammad and the reiteration of God's message in the Qur'ān. Accordingly, the concept of *taḥrīf* was employed as a twofold critique of religious Others. It was a critique of their treatment of their own scriptures and also a critique of their receptivity—or lack thereof—to Muḥammad and the Qur'ān.[17]

While such criticism abounded within Islamic discourse, its holistic application was impeded by another current of thought: the polemical argument that earlier scriptures foretold the coming of Muḥammad.[18] The dilemma should be clear: How could one argue for the falsification of earlier scriptures and revelations while simultaneously calling Jews and Christians to acknowledge that those same scriptures predicted the prophethood of Muḥammad? In response to this tension, a variety of formulations to *taḥrīf* were espoused.

Ghulām Ḥaider Āasī identifies three primary views: first, that the extant scriptures were corruptions and in no way identifiable with the revelations referred to in the Qur'ān as the *Zabūr* (usually identified as the Psalms), *Tawrāt* (Torah), and *Injīl* (Gospel); second, that corruption was found not in the scriptures but in the interpretation of the scriptures; and third, that *taḥrīf* was a combination of both corruption stemming from misinterpretation and corruption of some aspects of the text itself.

An example of the first formulation of *taḥrīf* is found in Abū Muḥammad 'Alī b. Aḥmad ibn Ḥazm's (d. 456/1064) *Kitāb al-fiṣal fī al-milal wa al-ahwā' wa al-niḥal* (Book on Religious Traditions, Ideologies, and Sects).[19] Born in Cordova in Muslim Andalus, Ibn Ḥazm was a historian, poet, jurist, theologian, and philosopher and is attributed with the codification of Ẓāhirī methodology and doctrine. Although Ibn Ḥazm's life began in relative economic and social comfort, it was colored by ongoing political struggles between the Slavs, Berbers, and Andalusians. In these struggles, he was not simply a passive bystander; rather, he was actively involved, being subjected to expulsion and imprisonment, engaging in military campaigns, and voicing harsh critiques of the political establishment and other schools of thought. In *Kitāb al-fiṣal fī al-milal,* Ibn Ḥazm presents a critique of non-Muslim religions as well as a critique of Muslims sects. Through the application of Islamic norms and close textual criticism of biblical scripture, he contends—in reference to Jews and Christians—that they have lost the complete revelation that they were initially granted and that their scriptures are "rife with lies and errors and therefore untrustworthy."[20] Ibn Ḥazm is able to push this critique as far as he does precisely because he shows little interest in arguing for proofs of Muḥammad's prophethood based upon earlier scriptures.

In contrast to Ibn Ḥazm, the earlier work of ʿĀli b. Rabbān al-Ṭabarī (d. 250/864), *Kitāb al-dīn wa al-dawla* (The Book of Religion and Empire), provides an example of the second approach. Born in Ṭabaristān (present-day Iran), al-Ṭabarī was a convert from Christianity, who utilized knowledge of his former tradition in his polemical writings. In highlighting biblical texts that he views as referring to Muḥammad, al-Ṭabarī implicitly accepts the validity of the scripture itself but challenges the normative interpretations of the text within the Jewish and Christian communities.

The third approach—an emphasis on corruption in interpretation and in parts of the text itself—is apparent in Shāfiʿī, Muʿtazilite theologian ʿAbd al-Jabbār ibn Aḥmad al-Hamadhānī's (d. 415/1025) *Tathbīt dalāʾil al-nubuwwa* (The Confirmation of the Proofs of Prophethood). In the section of this work that Gabriel Said Reynolds entitles the "Critique of Christian Origins," ʿAbd al-Jabbār's central contention is that Christianity is a "deviation from the religion of Christ."[21] Using a variety of sources, including biblical texts, Christian liturgies, creeds, and exegeses, ʿAbd al-Jabbār discusses the composition of the Bible, the contents of the Bible, Christian history, and Christian practice. While he acknowledges that there are parts of the Bible with authentic teachings, he nevertheless presents Christianity as a deliberate fabrication and a betrayal of Christ.[22] What is notable in the "Critique" is that beyond textual criticism and eventual negative assessment ʿAbd al-Jabbār endeavors to present a specific, historical explanation of the falsification and corruption he envisions within Christianity. Moreover, as a contemporary of al-Bāqillānī, ʿAbd al-Jabbār wrote in a context of Muslim ascendency. His "Critique" thus evinces a similar concern for his Muslim audience and a similar depiction of Christian voices as "muted and monotone."[23]

The concept of *taḥrīf*—in all of its three formulations—is not a means of positive valuation. It is most surely a projected criterion by which the Other is measured as deficient in reference to the self. This projection derives not only from the fact that *taḥrīf* is a Qurʾānic accusation but also from the underlying Islamic worldview. While part of *taḥrīf* implies invention, the main thrust of this concept relates to the idea of corruption or deliberate change. Unpacking the logical implications of this, a group cannot corrupt something if they do not have that "something" to begin with. In other words, a group cannot corrupt or alter revelation if that group did not at one time have true revelation. Therefore, while *taḥrīf* is a negative assessment, it is also an acknowledgment of the very real contact that God has had with these other communities. This continuity of contact is central to the Islamic worldview and Muslim self-identity. Islamic views on divine unity, unity of religion, and unity of guidance coalesce and present Islamic thinkers with a distinct challenge: how to understand the Other who can never be wholly Other.

Appeals to *taḥrīf* are also closely tied to the concepts of scriptural abrogation (*naskh*) and prophetic supersession. Scriptural abrogation within the historical and contemporary discourse arises in response to apparent contradictions within the Qur'ānic corpus, including apparent contradictions in the assessment of religious Others. To resolve these apparent contradictions, verses that were revealed chronologically later—according to actual *ḥadīth* reports or thematic inference—are depicted as rendering earlier verses null and void.[24] Prophetic supersession makes similar claims, albeit in relation to prophets and revelation; later prophets and revelations render earlier, divinely sent and revealed prophets and revelations defunct. *Taḥrīf*, abrogation, and supersession all highlight the Islamic attempt to grapple simultaneously with issues of continuity and discontinuity between self and Other.

The challenge presented by the Other-who-can-never-be-wholly-other is also manifest in another characteristic of numerous polemical and apologetic writings. As indicated in reference to Ibn Ḥazm's *Kitāb al-fiṣal fī al-milal wa al-ahwā' wa al-niḥal*, many such works contain critiques of other religions as well as critiques of "heretical" sects within the Muslim community. Additionally, both types of critiques are frequently and purposefully intermingled to highlight similarities between the groups. For example, in *Kitāb al-fiṣal*, Ibn Ḥazm compares the Jewish view that Isaac's blessing for Esau could be effective for Jacob, to the Shī'a view that Gabriel's revelation to Muḥammad was actually intended for 'Alī.[25] Elsewhere, he links Christians with Manicheans, Jews, Shī'a, and other Muslim heretics.[26] By drawing connections between various "objectionable" groups, Ibn Ḥazm intends to encourage disdain for all such groups. Similar polemical associations are also present in 'Abd al-Jabbār's *Critique of Christian Origins*. Therein, critiques of validity of Rāfiḍa (Shī'ī), atheist, and dualist claims are placed within the section of *Tathbīt dalā'il al-nubuwwa* that deals primarily with Christianity.[27]

Throughout his expansive corpus of polemical and apologetic writings,[28] Aḥmad ibn 'Abd al-Ḥalīm ibn Taymiyya (d. 728/1328) also underscores the connections between the errors of other religions and the errors of heretical Muslim sects. An intensely polemical and political Ḥanbalī theologian and jurist, Ibn Taymiyya was born in Ḥarrān (present-day Turkey) and died in Damascus. He was appointed by various rulers to exhort individuals to partake in armed struggle and was himself engaged in expeditions against other groups. However, throughout his life his zealous critiques of innovation and other Muslim groups resulted in multiple imprisonments. Ibn Taymiyya had a very broad definition of innovation (*bidʿa*), wherein anything that did not derive directly from the Qurʾān, the *Sunna*, or the righteous ancestors (*salaf*) was excluded. This definition of innovation is directly tied to his redefinition of Qurʾānic exegesis, a redefinition that would have a major impact on later scholars, including Ibn Kathīr.[29]

In connecting the errors of other religions and the errors of heretical Muslim sects, Ibn Taymiyya goes beyond mere comparison of similar indiscretions to contend that intra-Muslim corruption is actually *caused* by contact with other religions. In *Jawāb al-ṣaḥīḥ li-man baddala dīn al-Masīḥ* (The Correct Reply to Those Who Have Altered Christ's Religion),[30] a response to a revised letter originally issued by Paul of Antioch,[31] he argues that "the heterodox Muslim groups were not only culpable of the same fundamental errors, but also directly tainted by Christian teachings."[32] A similar perspective on the "corrupting influence"[33] of other religions is evident in *Kitāb iqtiḍāʾ aṣ-ṣirāṭ al-mustaqīm mukhālafat aṣḥāb al-Jaḥīm* (Book on the Necessity of the Straight Path, Opposing the Companions of the Fire), in which Ibn Taymiyya endeavors to show that various features of popular religion such as festivals, intercession, and visiting graves are borrowed from Christianity, Judaism, Sabianism, Zoroastrianism, and Arab paganism.[34]

To combat the dire threat of such "foreign transplantations"[35] to the "pure" Islamic community, Ibn Taymiyya states that it is necessary to establish complete distinction through limitations on interaction and assimilation. He advocates for the same eradication of fuzziness on the borders that is stressed by Boyarin. Heretical sects in particular are targeted by Ibn Taymiyya because they are transgressors of borders; they are "hybrids." Through stringent emphasis on dissimilarity in actions and beliefs and clear separation between communities, including his "pure" Islamic community and heretical Muslim sects, Ibn Taymiyya aims to reestablish distinct borders between Others of all sorts and the small "beleaguered community of righteous within Islam."[36] Furthermore, Ibn Taymiyya links the desire to be distinct to divine command and an advanced understanding of Islam.[37] Ultimately, however, as Boyarin observes, establishing borders is not the end of the story; once defined, borders must be policed. Ibn Taymiyya is equally cognizant of and committed to this secondary endeavor. For him, the polemical enterprise is not only about scriptural or dogmatic sparring. As evident in his political *fatāwa*, his military campaigns, and his pronouncements of *takfir* (labeling another as a disbeliever), it is also about practical and concrete action in response to the immediate threat presented by the Other.

Delineations of Qur'ānic Difference: Exegetical and Juridical Trends

Just as Qur'ānic teachings served as a basis upon which to evaluate Others in polemical and apologetic writings, the Qur'ān also gave rise to another genre of discourse aimed at explicating religious difference. Mostly found in exegetical and juridical works, this discourse aimed to clarify the meaning of and boundaries between central Qur'ānic concepts, including *islām* (submission or devotion), *īmān* (faith), and *kufr* (disbelief).[38]

Such clarification was of the utmost importance due to the divine evaluations—both positive and negative, in reference to this world and the next—associated with each concept. If *islām* and *īmān* were divinely praised traits, then it was vital to understand what each entailed and who could legitimately be referred to as a *muslim* (a submitter) and a *mu'min* (a believer). Equally was the case for the divinely condemned trait of *kufr*. Centered on a small number of recurring themes and questions, this discourse spurned feverish debates throughout Islamic history.

The discussion of the Qur'ānic concept of *islām* centered on three verses (*āyāt*) in *Sūrat āl-ʿimrān* and *Sūrat al-mā'ida*, the third and fifth chapters of the Qur'ān:

> True religion (*al-dīn*), in God's eyes, is *al-islām* ... (3:19, excerpt)
>
> If anyone seeks a religion (*al-dīn*) other than *al-islām*, it will not be accepted from the person: he or she will be one of the losers in the Hereafter. (3:85)
>
> ... Today I have perfected your religion (*dīnakum*) for you, completed My blessing upon you, and chosen as your religion (*dīnakum*) *al-islām* ... (5:3, excerpt)

Unmistakably *al-islām* was something important, but the primary question that provoked great exegetical efforts was "What precisely is *al-islām*?" Was it an action, a personal response to God? Was it an entity, a system, or perhaps a group? Jane Smith has written an extensive comparative survey of exegeses related specifically to the Qur'ānic concept of *islām*.[39] Tracing the interpretations of fourteen historical and modern interpreters, she argues that early exegesis of the Qur'ān was characterized by both *tafsīr bi'l-ma'thūr* (exegesis carried out with primary reference to prophetic *aḥadīth*) and *tafsīr bi'l-ra'y* (exegesis based on personal opinion). In both of these genres, and in the frequent combination of the two, exegetes expressed a variety of understandings of *islām*, many of which emphasized *islām* as an affirmation of *tawḥīd* (the unicity of God). In reference to one of the earliest exegetes—the first generation Companion of Muḥammad and "father" of Qur'ānic exegesis—'Abd Allāh ibn 'Abbās (d. 68/687), Smith draws attention to Ibn 'Abbās's linking of the concepts of religion (*dīn*) and *islām*, which results in an interpretation of *islām* as worship of God based on the recognition of God's oneness and uniqueness. This general interpretation is further explicated in reference to Qur'ān 3:85, and Ibn 'Abbās indicates that *al-islām*, as worship based on *tawḥīd*, is the shared message and teaching of all prophets that have been sent by God.

Smith notes a similar emphasis on *tawḥīd* in the Qur'ānic commentary of the immensely influential historian and exegete Abū Ja'far Muḥammad ibn Jarīr al-Ṭabarī (d. 310/923). In *Jāmi' al-bayān 'an ta'wīl āyāt al-Qur'ān*,[40] al-Ṭabarī also explores the meaning of the interrelated concept of *dīn* and depicts *islām* as humble submission and obedience to God.[41] Smith astutely highlights that al-Ṭabarī emphasizes *islām* as an action; *islām* is seen as "man's response to God by humbling himself and entering into a state whereby he is in complete readiness to accept and fulfill the commands and desires of his Lord."[42] More specifically, according to al-Ṭabarī *islām* is a personal—or individual—action performed with sincerity in verbal affirmation and sincerity of the heart.[43] As we will come to see, this multifaceted view of *islām* as involving actions, verbal profession, and sincerity of the heart was debated by other exegetes, especially in light of Qur'ān 49:14.

Representing another interpretative approach more indicative of the genre of exegesis based on personal opinion (*tafsīr bi'l-ra'y*), Abū 'Abd Allāh Muḥammad ibn 'Umar ibn al-Ḥusayn al-Rāzi (d. 606/1209)—the Ash'arī theologian and Shāfi'ī jurist commonly known as Fakhr al-Dīn al-Rāzi—approaches the concept of *islām* from a linguistic perspective. Al-Rāzi identifies various meanings of the term, including submitting/becoming a *muslim*, becoming secure or whole, and expressing sincerity in devotion.[44] Similar to al-Ṭabarī, in all three of these possible interpretations al-Rāzi emphasizes *islām* as an active and individual approach. According to Smith, al-Rāzī's interpretation of *al-islām* focuses on a person's response to God and offers "no instance in which *al-islām* might have even a possible group reference."[45]

However, by the seventh century of the Islamic calendar, the enterprise of *tafsīr* came to be defined primarily by the "solidification of traditionalism," or by the prioritization of repetition of earlier exegeses and a "dwindling of individual interpretation."[46] This solidification affected *tafsīr* in general but also had a noticeable impact on interpretations of the concept of *islām* specifically. Perhaps one of the best examples of this is found in Ismāʿīl ibn ʿUmar ibn Kathīr's (d. 774/1373) *Tafsīr al-Qurʾān al-ʿaẓīm*.[47] Ibn Kathīr, a Shāfiʿī scholar and student of Ibn Taymiyya who lived mostly in Damascus, reiterates earlier interpretations of *islām* as a recognition of *tawḥīd* and a sincere response to that recognition.[48] Where Ibn Kathīr diverges, however—and is thereby indicative of solidification—is in his further specification of the content of the *dīn* of *al-islām*. For Ibn Kathīr, *al-islām* is the specific, historical path of Muḥammad. Therefore, in reference to Qurʾān 3:19 and 5:3, he acknowledges *al-islām* as the religion of earlier messengers but then stresses the role of Muḥammad in "sealing," finalizing, and perfecting earlier prophetic commissions. Therefore, all other paths, except for the path of Muḥammad, are closed and unnecessary.[49] Ibn Kathīr thus presents "a very specific emphasis on Muḥammad and the clear understanding that the *dīn* which he has made incumbent (*sharaʿa*) is the only acceptable one."[50] In intentionally and unequivocally linking *al-islām* with a historical community, Ibn Kathīr marks a pivotal move toward a more reified depiction of *islām*. It is vital to note that the solidification or reification evident in Ibn Kathīr is connected in many ways with his interpretative methodology. While not comprehensively implemented, Ibn Kathīr's *tafsīr* aimed to apply the hermeneutical approach outlined by his teacher Ibn Taymiyya, an approach that prioritized the Qurʾān, the prophetic traditions, and the traditions of the *salaf* (righteous ancestors). This methodology, which largely excluded personal reflection or debate on possible meanings and depended primarily on the previous historical interpretations of the *salaf*, seems to incline necessarily toward historical reification. Furthermore, with this as his underlying methodology, it is not shocking to find a similar trend toward reification—or the association of Qur'ānic categories with specific historical communities—reflected throughout his *tafsīr*. For example, in his exegesis of *Sūrat al-kāfirūn* (Qur'ān 109:1–6), he acknowledges that *al-kāfirūn* (disbelievers) refers to all disbelievers but emphasizes it as a specific address to the disbelievers among the Quraysh. Also in *Sūrat al-bayyina* (Qur'ān 98:1–8), he specifies *ahl al-kitāb* (people of the Scripture) as being Jews and Christians only.

The interpretation of the Qur'ānic concept of *islām* was made more complex by the existence of numerous other verses that enjoin *īmān* (belief) and promise rewards for those who are *mu'min* (believers). If the "true religion in the sight of God was *al-islām*" and elsewhere God praised *īmān*, what exactly was the relationship between the two concepts? Were *islām* and *īmān* the same thing? Or did they differ in some way? Al-Rāzi asserts that *īmān* is synonymous with *islām*. He develops this position in response to Qur'ān 3:83, which indicates that no other religion will be accepted by God except *islām*. As a result, if *īmān* and *islām* were not the same, then by implication *īmān* would not be accepted by God, a conclusion inconsistent with other Qur'ānic statements on *īmān*.

While correspondence between *islām* and *īmān* seems obvious, explorations into the relationship between these two concepts were forced to account for another Qur'ānic *āya* in *Sūrat al-ḥujarāt* that appears to associate *islām* with submission in actions only and *īmān* with true conviction in the heart:

> The Arabs say, "We have faith (*āmannā*)." Tell them, "You do not have faith (*tu'minū*). What you should say instead is, "We have submitted (*'aslamnā*)," for *al-īmān* has not yet entered your hearts." If you obey God and God's Messenger, God will not diminish any of your deeds. God is most forgiving and most merciful. (49:14)

In attempting to interpret this *āya*, many exegetes cited a well-known *ḥadīth* in which Muḥammad defines *islām*, *īmān*, and *iḥsān* (excellence):

> On the authority of Umar . . . who said: One day while we were sitting with the Messenger of Allah . . . there appeared before us a man whose clothes were exceedingly white and whose hair was exceedingly black; no signs of journeying were to be seen on him and none of us knew him. He walked up and sat down by

> the Prophet ... Resting his knees against his and placing the palms of his hands on his thighs, he said: O Muhammad, tell me about *islām*. The Messenger of Allah ... said: *islām* is to testify that there is no god but Allah and Muhammad is the Messenger of Allah, to perform the prayers, to pay the *zakat*, to fast in Ramadan, and to make the pilgrimage to the House if you are able to do so. He said: You have spoken rightly, and we were amazed at him asking him and saying that he had spoken rightly. He said: Then tell me about *īmān*. He said: It is to believe in Allah, God's angels, God's books, God's messengers, and the Last Day, and to believe in divine destiny, both the good and the evil thereof. He said: You have spoken rightly. He said: Then tell me about *iḥsān*. He said: It is to worship Allah as though you are seeing God, and while you see God not yet truly God sees you. He said: Then tell me about the Hour. He said: The one questioned about it knows no better than the questioner. He said: Then tell me about its signs. He said: That the slave-girl will give birth to her mistress and that you will see the barefooted, naked, destitute herdsmen competing in constructing lofty buildings. Then he took himself off and stayed for a time. Then he said: O Umar, do you know who the questioner was? I said: Allah and God's Messenger know best. He said: It was Gabriel, who came to you to teach you your religion.[51]

Indicative of the debates that had taken place before him, the exegesis of this *ḥadīth* offered by the eminent *ḥadīth* commentator and Shāfiʿī jurist Yaḥyā ibn Sharaf Muḥyī al-Dīn al-Nawawī (d. 676/1277)[52] illustrates some of the complexity involved in the attempt to delineate between the two concepts. Al-Nawawī defines *īmān* as "assent" to the various tenets of belief explicated in the *ḥadīth* and *islām* as the externals of practice outlined in the *ḥadīth*. He then utilizes this definition of *islām* to interpret Qurʾān 49:14 and contends that the Arabs mentioned in this verse—the ones who are told not to say they have *īmān* but rather *islām*—were hypocrites and liars. Despite this, God acknowledged their external practices, which aligned with those required by God. Returning to the concept of *īmān*, al-Nawawī clarifies that assent means that one's tongue—literally what one professes or says—is aligned with what resides in one's heart. While al-Nawawī seems to have drawn a fairly clear line between *islām* as external actions, regardless of assent, and *īmān* as assent in tongue and heart, his distinction is not maintained. In the very next section of his commentary, he asserts that *īmān* is the "condition of validity" for the external acts of *islām*. However, if the hypocrites did not have *īmān* yet God recognized their actions and called them *islām*, then how can having *īmān* be a precondition for the validity of *islām*? This undercuts the neat distinction he initially articulates.

While a clear-cut delineation between *islām* and *īmān* was appealing in its simplicity, it raised a series of new questions. Did this mean that the "true religion in the sight of God" consisted in actions alone? Furthermore, did *īmān* involve not actions but only conviction in the heart? Could a person be a believer (*muʾmin*) and not perform any of the obligatory actions? Could a person be a *muʾmin* and sin? Ibn Taymiyya indicates a possible alternative interpretation of the same *ḥadīth* about *islām, īmān*, and *iḥsān* in his *Kitāb al-īmān*.[53] In his interpretation, Ibn Taymiyya does not depict *islām* and *īmān* as mutually exclusive categories, with the former referring to actions alone and the latter referring to profession and assent. Rather, he argues that *islām, īmān*, and *iḥsān* are three hierarchical ranks (*darajāt/marātib*) within the religion sent to Muḥammad. Thus, *iḥsān* is the apex that encompasses all elements of belief, action, and profession included in the lower ranks of *īmān* and *islām*. Likewise, *īmān* encompasses all that is included in the lower rank of *islām*. According to Ibn Taymiyya:

> *Iḥsān* is a more inclusive concept than *Īmān*, but it also has a more specific sense than *Īmān*. *Īmān*, in turn, is a more inclusive concept than *Islām*. Thus, *Iḥsān* includes *Īmān*, which in turn, includes *Islām*. Consequently, *al-muḥsinūn*, the people of *Iḥsān*, are more distinguished than *al-muʾminūn*, the believers, and the believers are more distinguished than the Muslims.[54]

In placing the three in this hierarchy, Ibn Taymiyya is able to maintain the centrality of actions to *īmān*, something with which al-Nawawī is less successful due to his delineation between *islām* and *īmān*. Ibn Taymiyya also expounds further on *īmān*, arguing that it is holistically composed of verbal profession, actions, sincerity, and alignment with the prophetic Sunna. He then defines *īmān* without actions as being *kufr* (disbelief); profession and actions without sincerity as *nifāq* (hypocrisy); and—keeping in line with his polemic against innovation and internal diversity within the Muslim community—profession, actions, and sincerity without alignment with the Sunna as *bidʿa* (innovation). The reprehensible status of each of these three options—disbelief, hypocrisy, and innovation—served to underscore his insistence of the complexity of *īmān*.[55]

The importance of actions to *īmān*, however, was not a novel position by Ibn Taymiyya's time; since early in Islamic history, many scholars had focused specifically on the concept of *īmān*, striving to understand its relationship to the verbal profession of faith (*shahāda/iqrār*), conviction of the heart (*taṣdīq*), and physical actions. In his *Kitāb al-īmān*,[56] Abū ʿUbayd al-Qāsim ibn Sallām (d. 224/838)—the grammarian, Qurʾānic scholar and jurist who wrote largely on the *gharīb* (difficult linguistic passages) in the Qurʾān and *ḥadīth*—outlines two dominant positions with regard to the meaning of *īmān*. The first is that *īmān* consists of conviction of the heart, verbal profession, and physical actions. The second is that *īmān* consists of conviction of the heart and verbal profession only. In assessing these two positions, Abū ʿUbayd depicts a progressive stage-by-stage elaboration of the concept of *īmān*. At the beginning of Muḥammad's prophethood and the revelation of the Qurʾān, *īmān* was composed only of witnessing, or verbal profession (*iqrār*). There were no specific actions required of people who made this profession. After the migration to Medina, however, specific commands and prohibitions began to be revealed. Abū ʿUbayd contends that "whenever a law was revealed, it became a part of what had already been established before. All of them became a part of what was called 'faith [*īmān*]' and those who followed them were called 'people of faith' [*muʾmin*]."[57] With each such revelation, the definition of *īmān* was continuously expanded to encompass the required actions. To support this position, Abū ʿUbayd cites *aḥadīth* about the progressive increase in precepts of faith and Qurʾānic verses about the interconnection between the concept of *īmān* and actions. Abū ʿUbayd, moreover, argues that *īmān* (as sincerity, profession, and action together) has levels, meaning that it is possible for a person to have more or less *īmān*. Since multiple components comprise the category of *īmān*, it is both feasible and probable that a person would not embody every single component or every single component to the same degree.

In line with the views of Abū ʿUbayd, a historical consensus developed that *īmān* involved conviction, profession, and action and was a multifaceted concept with various internal levels and degrees. Furthermore, *īmān*, as manifest in individuals, could fluctuate based upon an individual's knowledge, conviction, and performance of actions. With this consensus, however, the question became at what point does one cease to be a member of the category? In other words, where is the border, or the threshold, that distinguishes the *mu'min*, the person with *īmān*, from the person without *īmān*?

While exegetes and jurists embraced the internal complexity and dynamism of *īmān*, they remained vigilantly committed to defining the border between it and the Qur'ānic concept of disbelief (*kufr*), which was largely presented as its antithesis. In defining this border, scholars proffered various criteria. Abū 'Ubayd contends that the threshold criterion—that is, the border between *īmān* and not-*īmān*—is the *shahāda*, the verbal profession of belief: "the beginnings of it and the highest point of it are the verbal utterance of the *shahāda*." [58] Therefore, by verbally articulating the *shahāda*, a person enters into faith (*īmān*) and can accurately be referred to as a believer (*mu'min*).

Emphasis on the *shahāda* as a threshold criterion is also apparent in the official creed promulgated by the Abbasid Caliphs al-Qādir bi'llāh and al-Qā'im bi-Amr Allāh in Baghdad in 430/1039. Caliph al-Qādir espoused a Ḥanbalī-inspired perspective and was primarily concerned with "any doctrines deemed pernicious and especially those which constituted a danger to the caliphate."[59] Specifically, he sought to condemn Shī'ism, Mu'tazilism, and even aspects of Ash'arism, and to reassert the obligatory status of venerating the Companions of Muḥammad. Recorded in 'Abd al-Raḥman Ibn al-Jawzī's (d. 597/1200) *al-Muntaẓam fī ta'rīkh al-mulūk wa al-umam*,[60] the Qādrī creed discusses various aspects of correct belief regarding the nature of God and the Qur'ān and reiterates of a view of *īmān* similar to that advocated by Abū 'Ubayd. *Īmān*, therein, is described as being a combination of speech, action, and intention, which "increases by obedience and decreases by sin, and... may be divided into parts and portions."[61] The creed acknowledges the primacy of the *shahāda* as a marker of *īmān*, but it also presents another criterion by which the boundary between *īmān* and disbelief (*kufr*) is illuminated. Citing a well-known *ḥadīth* ("What lies between a person and disbelief is the abandonment of prayer."),[62] it states that *kufr* is "not associated with the omission of any of the required acts other than prescribed prayer."[63] Thus, a person could neglect—and even reject the obligation of—other prescribed actions, including *zakāt* (obligatory charity/alms), *ḥajj* (pilgrimage to Mecca), and *sawm* (fasting) and still remain within the borders of *īmān*. With these dual threshold criteria, the *shahāda* appears to be the prerequisite criterion for entry into the category of *īmān*, and the lack of prayer appears to be the exit criterion from the category of *īmān*. Thus, the *explicit* profession of faith would be required to be classified as a *mu'min*, and similarly, after the profession, the *explicit* lack of prayer would be required to be declassified as a *muʾmin* and reclassified as a *kāfir* (disbeliever).

What is remarkable about this is that both criteria are observable, and frequently public, actions. The political relevance and expediency of such criteria cannot be overlooked. Clear, publicly observable criteria for delimiting the boundaries of *īmān* and *kufr* are amenable to political enforcement of responsibilities, obligations, and consequences. The creed aims not only to mark the boundaries but also to apply tangible consequences to those who transgress and lie outside of the boundaries, to the *kāfirūn*/*kuffār* (disbelievers). This demarcation illuminates juridical practicalities in reference to religious difference in an Islamic society, and it is reminiscent of Boyarin's contentions about the intentional establishment and utility of clear and enforceable delineations.

While the dual threshold criteria of Caliph al-Qādir biʾllāh's creed are designed to assist in the delineation and enforcement of a particular version of orthodoxy, other scholars, such as Abū Ḥāmid Muḥammad ibn Muḥammad al-Ghazālī (d. 505/1111), employed threshold criteria to promote ecumenical tolerance. Born in Ṭūs (present-day Iran), al-Ghazālī became an influential teacher and lecturer in Baghdad and authored notable works on Ashʿarī dogmatics, philosophy, and the religious sciences. Ultimately abandoning his role in Baghdad to live as an ascetic mystic, al-Ghazālī was troubled by the fact that scholars of his day used religious knowledge to secure worldly advancement. He was also deeply concerned, as is evident in his *Fayṣal al-tafriqa bayna al-islām wa al-zandaqa* (The Decisive Criterion for Distinguishing Islam from Masked Infidelity),[64] about "the atmosphere of intolerance, mutual suspicion, and psychological intimidation engendered by narrow and underinclusive definitions of orthodoxy manufactured and brandished with reckless abandon."[65] Narrow and arbitrary definitions of orthodoxy fostered rampant intracommunal labeling of groups as disbelievers (*kāfirūn*), a phenomenon that in al-Ghazālī's view weakens the Muslim community. In response to this "veritable cyclone of charges and counter-charges of Unbelief [*kufr*],"[66] al-Ghazālī proffers a new threshold criterion for decisively distinguishing between *īmān* and *kufr*: "'Unbelief (*kufr*)' is to deem anything the Prophet brought to be a lie. And 'faith (*īmān*)' is to deem everything he brought to be true."[67] In articulating this criterion, he is cognizant of the fact that many charges of *kufr* are based upon the view that another group has attributed untruths to Muḥammad. Al-Ghazālī, therefore, clarifies by stating that "deeming to be true" means "acknowledging the existence of everything whose existence the Prophet informed us of."[68] He, then, explicates five different levels of existence: ontological, sensory, conceptual, noetic, and analogous. According to al-Ghazālī, an interpretation that is formulated at any of these levels conforms to the criterion of "deeming to be true." He does, however, outline a Rule for Figurative Interpretation, which states that although acceptable interpretation can be based on any of these levels it must commence with the first (ontological) and have a logical reason for progressing to the next level of interpretation. Al-Ghazālī also contends that much of the debate between various Islamic schools is based not on commitment to the scripture but rather on conflicting opinions about when to move between the various levels of interpretation.[69] Overall, his recognition of multiple, legitimate levels makes his criterion more inclusive of internal community diversity, especially diversity in interpretation, while simultaneously safeguarding the foundational beliefs in God, the prophethood of Muḥammad, and the Hereafter.

In light of his minimalist yet inclusive criterion, al-Ghazālī advises that it is best to refrain from judging individuals who have professed the *shahāda*, unless they explicitly claim Muḥammad espoused untruths. Such an explicit claim would quality as *kufr* and would necessitate condemnation. He is keen to note, however, that *kufr* only designates the rejection of the truthfulness of Muḥammad; it "reveals, *in and of itself*, virtually nothing about a person's moral or religious constitution."[70] To be a disbeliever (*kāfir*), therefore, is not necessarily to be immoral, irreligious, or devoid of worldly reward for positive deeds. This implies that one could be a *kāfir*, while professing the *shahāda*, doing righteous and obligatory actions, and having some degree of sincerity in the heart. Al-Ghazālī's singular criterion therefore could be seen as a reduction of Abū ʿUbayd's conception of *īmān* as sincerity, profession, and action combined.

There is nonetheless a notable parallel between al-Ghazālī's description of various levels of "existence" and Abū ʿUbayd's (among others) view of *īmān* as having degrees and levels. In both of these approaches, the internal makeup of *īmān* becomes increasingly intricate. It is dynamic, multifaceted, and comprised of various components. In contrast, however, the border between *īmān* and *kufr* is demarcated by increasingly simplified criteria. Both al-Ghazālī and Abū ʿUbayd permit complexity within the category of *īmān*, but they are simultaneously committed to clearly and simply defining the threshold between *īmān* and *kufr*. While there are many elements involved in *īmān* itself, only one element—the attribution of untruths to Muḥammad or the *shahāda*—marks the boundaries.

The combination of internal complexity and threshold simplification certainly serves a practical—whether positive or negative—role in human society. Delineations between *īmān* and *kufr*, though, are not only of import to social interaction and legal governance. They are also connected to soteriological endpoints in the Hereafter, as indicated in numerous Qur'ānic *verses* that describe believers (*mu'minūn*) as receiving rewards and Paradise and *kāfirūn* as receiving punishments and Hellfire. Therefore, in the historical discourse, questions arose about the correspondence of worldly delineations to soteriological delineations. Were worldly definitions and threshold criteria relevant to the topic of soteriology? Should other factors be considered? Could an individual be classified as a disbeliever in one context yet not in another?

In reference to this world, al-Ghazālī's criterion for distinguishing between *īmān* and *kufr* is centered upon an individual's response to the prophethood of Muḥammad. While the centrality of Muḥammad's prophethood remains when he moves to the discussion of soteriology, he does make an intriguing distinction between the legal and the actual status (comprehensive status in relationship to God) of individuals.[71] Legal status—as *mu'min* or *kāfir*—is based upon his previously discussed criterion. Actual status, however, is based not only upon response to but also upon *exposure to* the message of Muḥammad. It is one's actual status that determines soteriological ends. With the *mu'min*, this distinction indicates that a person could be deemed a legal *mu'min* without simultaneously being an actual *mu'min*; a person could fulfill the legal criterion of truthfulness while being deficient, for example, in terms of actions and sincere commitment. In reference to the *kāfir*, Al-Ghazālī's distinction highlights the fact that some individuals legally classified as *kāfirūn* have never been exposed to the message. He identifies three primary groups that are legally classified in such a fashion: those with no knowledge of Muḥammad or his message; those with knowledge of Muḥammad, his message and character, who nonetheless reject the message; and those with knowledge of Muḥammad, who have been misinformed as to his character and the message.[72] It is al-Ghazālī's view that divine mercy will be extended to the first and third groups and that the second is the only group that truly—meaning actually and thus soteriologically—can be classified as *kāfirūn*. Notably, al-Ghazālī also includes within this group individuals who have minimal exposure to Muḥammad and do not take the initiative to investigate further.[73] Thus, conscious rejection and lack of inquiry warrant ascription as *kāfir*, whereas the unconscious rejection of the others makes them candidates for divine mercy. His taxonomy is further complexified through the discussion of an apparent fourth category, "sincere truth-seekers."[74] These individuals have been appropriately exposed to the message and have investigated the message yet remain outside of the community of Muḥammad. Al-Ghazālī nonetheless envisions them as potential candidates for divine mercy due to the earnestness and perhaps continuousness of their investigation of the message. The prominent role of divine mercy in his soteriology permits a degree of flexibility in the boundaries between the righteous self and the condemned Other, a flexibility not present in his legal distinctions.

A consideration of the implications of exposure to the message of Muḥammad also appears in the writings of Ibn Taymiyya.[75] Ibn Taymiyya's one precondition for the obligation of believing in and following Muḥammad is that the message must have been presented. Following Muḥammad is obligatory therefore "only to 'everyone it [the Message] reaches (Qur'ān 6:19),' rather than to absolutely everyone."[76] Unlike al-Ghazālī, Ibn Taymiyya does not show any leniency to those who know of the message, investigate it, but fail to convert to Islam. In fact, for him the message itself is inherently appealing and capable of being affirmed based upon reason (*'aql*).[77] Exposure, in and of itself, is sufficient to render its recipients culpable for any lack of belief. It is for this reason that Ibn Taymiyya—in contrast with al-Ghazālī—does not present a taxonomy of various types of exposure to Muḥammad's message.

Ibn Taymiyya does, however, identify multiple conditions that make an individual soteriologically accountable: receipt of the message from a Messenger and knowledge that the acts one is performing are detestable or evil. In reference to the latter, he contends that the human intellect can ascertain general categories of good and evil without revelation. He ultimately prioritizes the former, though, and argues that no soteriological punishment could take place until the message was sent. The human capacity to distinguish good and evil is thus secondary to the primary threshold criterion of exposure. After exposure to revelation, human capacity can better or worsen an individual's position, but it is not an independent criterion; human capacity alone cannot determine soteriological ends. Intriguingly, Ibn Taymiyya invokes the notion of a "Messenger of Resurrection" that will appear in the Hereafter to test people who were not exposed to the message in the world.[78] Due to this, he is not compelled to invoke the concept of divine mercy in the same fashion as al-Ghazālī. Ibn Taymiyya does foreground divine mercy in relation to the nature and purpose of Hell, arguing that the punishment of Hell is a form of divine compassion aimed at purifying the residents of Hell. He connects this to his views on the noneternal nature of Hell and ultimate universal salvation.[79] Ibn Taymiyya's emphasis on divine mercy in these areas, though, does not override or complicate his blunt insistence on clear-cut criterion and boundaries in the world and in the Hereafter. Residents of Hell are not mercifully exempted from punishment based upon divine prerogative; rather, they are "mercifully" subjected to punishment as an opportunity to be purified—and thus qualified—for the Garden.

In sum, both al-Ghazālī and Ibn Taymiyya focus on the issue of exposure to the message, recognizing it as a central consideration in soteriology. However, they each adopt a different method for accommodating this consideration. Al-Ghazālī acknowledges an incongruity between "legal" and "actual" assessment of individuals. This acknowledgement implies that the legal criteria for distinguishing *īmān* and *kufr* cannot be applied holistically to actual and soteriological assessment, which will necessarily involve a complex consideration of multiple criteria, including response and exposure to the message (i.e., reception of revelation), divine ontology (i.e., divine mercy), and human capacity (i.e., what an individual could know without revelation). Ibn Taymiyya, in distinction, recognizes the issue of lack of exposure but seeks to resolve this issue through the introduction of the Messenger of Resurrection, a concept that guarantees universal exposure. Universal exposure permits Ibn Taymiyya to utilize the same criteria in reference to worldly and soteriological delineations. Exposure to and acceptance of the message remain the primary criteria in this world and the next. Furthermore, through the Messenger of Resurrection and universal exposure, he is able to maintain unambiguous distinctions between the *mu'min* and the *kāfir*; everyone will be exposed, everyone will decide, and everyone will be either a believer or disbeliever.

Theocentric Oneness and Differentiated Multiplicity: Mystical and Sufi Trends

As seen in the preceding historical genres, divine ontology plays a central and recurring role in conceptions of the Muslim self and the non-Muslim Other. Divine oneness determines many aspects of the polemical and apologetic discourse, and divine mercy is an essential component in soteriological discussions. The centrality of divine ontology continues in mystical or Sufi approaches to religious difference. This is exemplified in the writings of al-Shaykh al-Akbar Muḥyī al-Dīn ibn al-ʿArabī (d. 638/1240), the Sufi mystic and philosopher, who was born in Andalus and is deemed to be the most prolific and systematized of Sufi writers; and Jalāl al-Dīn Rūmī (d. 672/1273), the Persian poet and founder of the Mawlawiyya order of dervishes, who was born in Balkh (present-day Afghanistan) and died in Konya (present-day Turkey). In the Sufi genre, the conception of divine ontology, particularly the doctrine of *waḥdat al-wujūd* (oneness of being), defines both human anthropology and the role of revelation and consequently forms the foundation upon which religious difference is understood and evaluated.

The doctrine of *waḥdat al-wujūd* is frequently linked with Ibn al-ʿArabī. Although he does not use this terminology himself, the essential components of the doctrine originated with his teachings. *Waḥdat al-wujūd* expresses the affirmation that nothing truly and necessarily exists except *wujūd*, or Being/God; "*wujūd* is the absolute and nondelimited reality of God, the 'Necessary Being' (*wājib al-wujūd*) that cannot not exist."[80] While indefinable in its true essence, *wujūd* does manifest in the created world. Utilizing the analogy of Light, Ibn al-ʿArabī describes *wujūd* as pure Light, which is invisible in and of itself but which makes everything else visible. Disclosure in the created world establishes a vital relationship between the one *wujūd* and the many created entities. As William C. Chittick notes, this explains why Ibn al-ʿArabī also and equally stresses the "manyness" of existence as being real. Multiplicity in creation is not an illusion, but it is also not independent from the *wujūd*.[81] On the basis of the same light analogy, the multiplicity of creation is comparable to the various colors produced when the one Light passes through a prism. The colors are real in that they manifest the one Light, but they do so in a delimited fashion contingent upon the properties and characteristics of the prism.

Rūmī also invokes this same analogy, describing the divine as Light that is "only lent to created forms and beings."[82] God is the only thing that has true existence and can therefore manifest that existence in the created order. Rūmī highlights the irony of the fact that the "world of nonexistence appears as existent things, and that world of Existence is exceedingly hidden."[83] This observation is connected to a distinction he draws between the created form (*ṣūrat*), or outward appearance, and the meaning (*maʿnā*), the inward reality. The distinction, however, implies not a lack of real relationship between the two but rather that distortions can easily result from ascribing excessive importance to the "form and not understanding that it derives its existence and significance from meaning."[84] There is always a danger in paying isolated attention to shadows rather than in giving priority to the source, the Light itself: "Form is the shadow, meaning the Sun."[85]

For both Ibn al-ʿArabī and Rūmī, the very purpose of creation is to manifest the divine essence. According to Ibn al-ʿArabī, every created entity displays some aspect—however delimited—of *wujūd*. Although God remains perpetually free from the creation, God manifests the divine names and attributes in the created world. Rūmī, quoting a well-known *ḥadīth qudsī* (a special class of *ḥadīth* that refers to non-Qurʾānic yet divinely revealed content), expresses a similar position: "God says, 'I was a Hidden Treasure, so I wanted to be known.' In other words, 'I created the whole of the universe, and the goal in all of it is to make Myself manifest, sometimes through Gentleness and sometimes through Severity.'"[86] The concluding reference to two prominent divine attributes—gentleness (i.e., mercy) and severity (i.e., wrath)—accentuates another key element of this perspective. God not only manifests in what is typically deemed from a human perspective to be positive qualities but also in both positive and negative ways, in opposites, for example, good and evil or belief and unbelief. According to Rūmī these opposites are relative—nothing is absolutely good or absolutely evil—but also uniquely designed to disclose further the complex divine essence. As such, both opposites are affirmed as "good" and "perfect" in reference to the performance of the singular task of manifesting God.

The manifestation of divine names and attributes in the created order is directly linked to anthropology, or the situation, purpose, and goal of humankind in relation to God. While other created entities manifest particular attributes or names, the human being is the only creation that has the potential to manifest all of the divine names and attributes. Thus, Ibn al-ʿArabī describes the apex of the Sufi path, the "perfect man" (*al-insān al-kāmil*), as "the complete and total human being who has actualized all the potentialities latent in the form of God."[87] In fully actualizing the divine potentialities, *al-insān al-kāmil* is not only the highest form a human can achieve but also the only "proper" form, the only true expression of humanity created in the form of God. Depicting Adam as the prototype of spiritual perfection, Rūmī describes humankind as the potential "mirror of all things," the mirror of all attributes of God. The earthly charge is therefore "to cleanse his heart, polish it, and make it a perfect mirror reflecting God."[88] The goal is the annihilation of the human ego (*fanāʾ*)

to actualize the full manifestation of divine attributes and to "subsist" in God (*baqā'*).

Ibn al-ʿArabī devotes significant effort to outlining the process whereby such actualization is realized. He argues that the divine attributes are part of human nature (*fiṭra*) and are given to all at the time of creation. In the majority of individuals, though, the attributes exist in a state of disequilibrium, with some dominating others. To actualize the divine attributes fully and holistically, a state of balance or equilibrium is required. How can such a state be achieved? Ibn al-ʿArabī offers an unequivocal response: equilibrium, and therefore full actualization, can be achieved only by following divine revelation and the examples of the prophets. While rational inquiry can reveal insights into the incomparability of God, positive knowledge of God can come only from God's self through revelation. Hence, Ibn al-ʿArabī adamantly proclaims the requirement of following revealed religion and law (*sharīʿa*): "The Shariah provides the necessary concrete guidelines for achieving equilibrium among the names and character traits. Having reached this equilibrium, human beings will have actualized the form in which they were created."[89]

Sharīʿa also features prominently in Rūmī's understanding of the process by which the human "mirror" is polished to perfection. Simultaneously stressing the importance of Law, Way, and Reality (*sharīʿa, ṭarīqa,* and *ḥaqīqa*), he argues that the only source of the first two is revelation and prophetic example. Since God does not communicate directly with every individual, it is necessary to have guidelines and a "guide" to imitate:

> God does not speak to everyone, just as the kings of this world do not speak to every weaver. They appoint ministers and representatives so that through them people may find the way to them. In the same way God has singled out certain servants, so that everyone who seeks God may find God within them. All the prophets have come for this reason. Only they are the Way.[90]

Significantly, Rūmī here broaches the topic of other prophets. In doing so, he acknowledges the diversity of prophetic examples while stressing that they have all been sent for the same purpose: to guide others to the Way.

Ibn al-ʿArabī voices a related view of the shared purpose of prophets, but he also endeavors to provide an explanation for the particularities of each revealed law (*sharīʿa*), an explanation of the "ontological roots of religious diversity."[91] He asserts that while revelations are all based on the essential message of divine unicity and oneness (*tawḥīd*), their particularities result from the fact that to have any impact revelation must resonate with the diverse dispositions of the people who receive it. In stating this, he recognizes the role of individual and group context in the delivery and reception of the message; for a message to have relevance to a particular audience, it must be comprehensible within an existential and temporal context.

If all prophets serve the same function and all differences represent responsiveness to context broadly construed, does this indicate that it is acceptable to follow the *sharīʿa* of any prophet, to follow any revealed religion and law? Or is one better than another? Ibn al-ʿArabī's reply is found in his comparison of the relationship between the revealed religion of Muḥammad and that of other prophets to the relationship between the sun and stars:

> All the revealed religions (*sharāʾiʿ*) are lights. Among these religions, the revealed religion of Muhammad is like the light of the sun among the light of the stars. When the sun appears, the lights of the stars are hidden, and their lights are included in the light of the sun. Their being hidden is like the abrogation of the other revealed religions that takes place through Muhammad's revealed religion. Nevertheless, they do in fact exist . . . This explains why we have been required in our all-inclusive religion to have faith in the truth of all the messengers and all the revealed religions. They are not rendered null [*bāṭil*] . . . .[92]

This excerpt foregrounds a number of essential points. The first is that all revealed religions reflect the divine light and that this light is never negated; rather, the lights of the "stars" are outshone by the light of the "sun." Other revealed religions remain true, but the religion of Muḥammad is "all-inclusive," embodying all of the guidance previously granted. In reference to the last statement in this excerpt, Ibn al-ʿArabī elsewhere distinguishes between having "faith" in other prophets, that is, believing them to be truthful, and having "faith" in the specific religion of Muḥammad, that is, implementing his model in practice.[93]

Rūmī also utilizes the analogy of the sun to characterize the relationship among prophets. Castigating those who would deny any prophets, he describes prophets as a "single light shining from a single sun."[94] Yet he continues by stating that although a single sun, the "sun of yesterday" (i.e., previous prophets) is not the same as the "sun of today" (i.e., Muḥammad) because previous suns no longer have the capacity to test humanity. Rūmī thereby introduces an aspect of context similar to Ibn al-ʿArabī: the prophetic message must resonate with and provoke its audience. For Rūmī, the message of Muḥammad—the sun of today—is the one best suited to do so. His privileging of Muḥammad is also evinced in other descriptions of him as "king of the prophets," as the one who achieved the highest possible state of perfection, and evocatively even as the sun itself.

The revealed religion of Muḥammad is further extolled in Ibn al-ʿArabī's description of a variety of "Paths." The first is the "Path of God," which refers to the mere relationship of every existing thing to the nondelimited *wujūd*; it refers to the fact that everything is created by and will return to God. It is "the general path upon which all things walk, and it takes them to God. It includes every divinely revealed religion and every construction of the rational faculty. It takes to God, and it embraces both wretched and felicitous."[95] The second is the "Straight Path of the Blessing-Giver," the path revealed to and modeled by all prophets. It is a path that leads not only to God—as did the first path, and as do all paths—but also to felicity. The third path is the specific "Path of Muḥammad," which Ibn al-ʿArabī refers to as "God's firm cord and all-comprehensive Law."[96] Even though he recognizes and affirms the validity of the diverse revealed Laws and their potential for leading to some form of felicity, he reiterates the previous description of the Path of Muḥammad as being all-inclusive: "the property of all the revealed religions has been transformed to his revealed religion. His revealed religion embraces them, but they do not embrace it."[97] As a result, the Path of Muḥammad promises a unique and more comprehensive form of mercy and felicity. This aligns with Ibn al-ʿArabī's depiction of the Muḥammadan friends of God (the term for saints in Sufism) in juxtaposition with other friends of God. While he acknowledges friends of God who follow other prophets, he asserts that Muḥammadan friends of God "will inherit the totality of the prophetic works, states, and sciences, a totality realized by Muhammad alone among the prophets."[98] This unique inheritance places them in the Station of No Station, the highest of all human stations, characterized by the actualization of all perfections of the *wujūd*. Whereas other friends inhabit particular stations (*maqāmāt*) of spiritual development, Muḥammadan friends have knowledge of all the stations and thus simultaneously "stand with Muhammad in every station and in no station."[99]

Ibn al-ʿArabī's delineation of the various paths is also based upon differentiation between what Chittick terms the engendering command and the prescriptive command.[100] The former is the creative command, the connection of all creation to *wujūd*. The prescriptive command of God, in contrast, refers to the specific and restrictive instructions God provides on how to achieve felicity. Whereas all paths relate to the engendering command—"all paths lead to God"—only the paths of the Blessing-Giver and Muḥammad, the paths of revealed religion, relate to the prescriptive command. For this reason, Ibn al-ʿArabī is able to simultaneously affirm the "truth" of all paths and the necessity of following revealed religion and prophetic examples. All paths are "true" because they correspond in some manner to the reality of *wujūd*, but not all paths have a positive impact on human becoming or balanced actualization of the divine attributes.

This is analogous to Rūmī's view on the manifestation of divine attributes in creation in the form of opposites. When he contends that both opposites perform "one task," he is speaking in reference to the engendering command. Like Ibn al-ʿArabī, he is quick to note that the goodness or perfection of opposites is in relation only to God, not to human beings. Rūmī emphasizes this by differentiating between what God "wills" and what God "approves" or commands. All created things will return to God due to the former, the ontological will of God. Only some, however, will return to—or gain proximity to—God based upon their response to the latter, the deontological will of God.[101] In regard to the deontological path of return, Rūmī does recognize the existence of Heaven and Hell, but he asserts that, similar to other opposites, the purpose of Heaven and Hell is to manifest God. With death, resurrection, and the Day of Judgment, manifestation will be complete, and therefore the need for opposition will dwindle. In the eschatological state, divine gentleness (mercy) will dominate and color divine severity (wrath). As part of this mercy, every person will be made completely aware of the nature or his or her spirit—of the "meaning" of his or her "form"—and the character of death will be determined by that nature: "Everyone's death . . . is the same color as himself."[102] The correspondence of eschatological status to worldly status also implies that some will reside in Hell and others in Heaven but that, consistent with the multiplicity of ranks and degrees of spiritual actualization in this world, there will also be a number of ranks and degrees in the next. Moreover, Rūmī also describes inhabitants of Hell as happy due to their newfound awareness: "The inhabitants of hell are happier in hell than they were in this world, since in hell they are aware of God but in this world they were not. And nothing is sweeter than awareness of God."[103]

Ibn al-ʿArabī's conception of eschatology has many parallels with that of Rūmī. In a similar manner, he contends that the primary function of Heaven and Hell is to manifest the divine attributes and names. He also describes an extensive range of possible destinies, each tied intimately to worldly status. Rather than stressing a binary conception of Heaven and Hell, he emphasizes that the posthumous realities will be determined individually and distinctly based upon a complex assessment of works, ideas, and thoughts. This assessment could result in a multitude of ends, reflecting various degrees of human equilibrium and disequilibrium in the world. Furthermore, Ibn al-ʿArabī in no way confines paradise, or Heaven, to Muslims. This aligns with his view that followers of other prophetic paths can achieve felicity and become friends of God. As with Rūmī, the divine attribute of mercy is seen as taking precedence over divine wrath, and Ibn al-ʿArabī states that there will be a "cooling of the Fire" of Hell; "Hell's chastisement must disappear because in the end... mercy will show its precedence and priority."[104] This "cooling" will result in the inhabitants of Hell experiencing felicity. The felicity of the inhabitants of Hell, however, will differ from the felicity of the inhabitants of Heaven in that the former will be veiled (*maḥjūb*) from God, and the latter will have a vision (*ruʾya*) of God.

What are the implications of the Sufi approach for understanding religious difference and religious identity? The first is that in this discourse human identity is not defined primarily in reference to the human Other. It is theocentrically defined in reference to *wujūd* or God. The only Other that can serve as a counterpoint for articulating identity is the *wujūd* itself, as its nondelimited nature illuminates the delimited nature of all humans and all "forms." Divine oneness (*tawḥīd*) also played a role in polemical and apologetic delineations of self and Other. However, therein, divine oneness was a tenet to which people ascribed or did not ascribe. In the Sufi approach, identity is not defined based on ascription to a tenet but rather identity is defined by "oneness" itself.

Sufi approaches also emphasize a universal human purpose defined in reference to *wujūd*. Humankind is created by God to manifest God and is judged in reference to the actualization of that manifestation. The achievement of perfect actualization is connected to annihilation of the ego, or effacement of self-identity (*fanāʾ*). On this level, the ultimate goal is not to solidify membership in a particular group or to establish discrete boundaries that define that group. The goal, in contrast, is to eradicate such delimited conceptions of self and formal boundaries, all of which impede recognition of the reality of *waḥdat al-wujūd*. One intriguing aspect of this, however, is that to eradicate delimited conceptions of self and Other—to recognize the ontological reality that there is only really *wujūd*—one must adopt a delimited deontological path; one must follow the path of a revealed religion. The deontological command—and particularly the emphasis on the specific Path of Muḥammad—asserts that there is only one way to full actualization. One must follow the delimited path to reach the nondelimited reality. According to Ibn al-ʿArabī, all beliefs, including the beliefs of revealed religion, are delimited representations of *wujūd*, or "knots." Revealed knots, however, are providential because they disclose new perspectives and insights directly from the divine source. One must therefore utilize the revealed knots to gain an awareness of the existence of knots (delimitation), to untie detrimental knots (beliefs not based on revelation), and to acknowledge of the possibility of untying all knots (of achieving *fanāʾ* and *baqāʾ*). This approach thereby presents an ongoing oscillation between universalism and particularism, between undifferentiated oneness and specificity. Both are asserted, and neither can be negated.

Another example of this oscillation is evident in the dual emphases on egalitarianism and hierarchy. While the view of humankind in potential form and in ontological reference to the *wujūd* is egalitarian through and through, the path of authentic actualization is exceedingly hierarchical. Only very few ever reach the goal of perfection, and most linger in intermediate states of spiritual development. Significantly, the hierarchy of actualization depicted in this approach is not a linear hierarchy, meaning it is not a hierarchy accessible only through one path. With the exception of the uppermost echelon of actualization (the Station of No Station), the hierarchy is not confined to or affiliated with only one religious identity. Individuals do not have to follow the Path of Muḥammad to embark upon and progress in actualization; the other Paths of the Blessing-Givers also enable degrees of actualization. Complexification of the hierarchy, however, should not be misconstrued as an obliteration of all boundaries. The boundaries remain in the deontological frame of reference, although the threshold is pushed back to allow partial inclusion of other prophetic paths. While actualization is not confined to one religion, it is still confined to revealed religion and prophetic examples. This again underscores the oscillation of the ontological and deontological relationship between humans and God. Ontologically, all paths—all ways of life, belief, unbelief, good and evil—return to God. Deontologically, only some open the way to actualization and "unveiled" proximity to God.

Selves and Others

The historical Islamic discourse on religious difference displays an array of approaches to identifying the Muslim self and the non-Muslim—or heretical—Other. More specifically, the historical discourse is characterized by repeated attempts to grapple with an Other-who-can-never-be-wholly-other, an Other who is different yet somehow always connected. In his exploration of the Qur'ānic definition of Christianity, Francis Peters refers to this as a situation of "problematic continuity,"[105] in which self-identity is simultaneously defined by distinguishing self from Other and establishing a correlation between self and Other. Moreover, the diverse strands of the historical discourse have resulted from the fact that the dialectical articulation of otherness and self-identity is never finalized or fixed; rather, it is a process whereby self and Other are continuously and contextually "assembled and reassembled."[106]

In this complex dialectical process of constructing, clarifying, and enforcing otherness and self-identity, the genres surveyed converge around a number of central themes. These themes include the implications of divine ontology (e.g., primarily divine oneness and mercy) for assessing the human Other, the depiction of created anthropology (e.g., the status of humans without revelation and the purpose of humanity), the relationship between various revelations and prophets (e.g., issues of *taḥrīf*, supersession, completion, and the necessity of affirming Muḥammad), and the legal and soteriological explication of Qur'ānic categories (e.g., definition of threshold criteria and internal composition).

While largely centered on recurring questions and concerns, the historical discourse is not monolithic or homogeneous. It is characterized by intense debate and diversity of interpretation. The primary concerns are clear, but conclusions have varied based upon numerous factors, including intended audience, historical and political context, and experiences of religious diversity. With regard to the topic of audience, it is notable that, with the possible exception of Abū ʿĪsā, the majority of the perspectives surveyed are not directed to the religious Other. The religious Other—in the form of other religions or other Islamic groups—is used as a means of articulating the particularities of the religious self. As a result, there is little evidence of complex or dialogical engagement with the Other. Intriguingly, scholars that did present more nuanced information on the Other were subjected to accusations of heresy (as with Abū ʿĪsā) or had a more limited impact within the historical discourse as a whole (as with al-Ṭabarī).

The historical discourse should not be construed as a simple intellectual exercise. It reveals responsiveness to particular contextual issues, especially political issues related to governance and religious orthodoxy. Many of the scholars were political appointees or affiliates of various rulers. They were appointed to establish a basis upon which religious difference could be assessed, and they were frequently responsible for enforcing that assessment. Therefore, their intellectual efforts had to be amenable to practical implementation, as seen, for example, in Abū ʿUbayd's dual threshold criteria. Even scholars that periodically found themselves at odds with the administrative authority, such as Ibn Taymiyya, were still invested in the relationship between political authority and the faith. The intimate historical relationship between the discourse on religious difference and political power is especially significant because the perspectives of historical scholars such as Ibn Taymiyya and Ibn Kathīr are widely invoked in the contemporary context of the United States, where the Islamic faith is not linked with political power. More specifically, their perspectives are invoked without due consideration of the divergent political and power contexts.

One concluding observation about the historical discourse is essential. In these genres, it appears that the tangible existence of religious diversity seems to have done little to promote appreciation for such diversity. In most cases, the immediate presence of religious diversity actually fostered more fervent theological and physical aggression. Moreover, some of the more inclusive perspectives on religious diversity emanate from the Sufi scholars, but there exists debate over the extent of these scholars' actual knowledge of and interaction with other traditions. The fact that immediate experience of diversity does not necessarily lend itself to appreciation is another especially pertinent consideration in reference to the contemporary appropriation of historical ideas, since the contemporary discourse is generally based on the reverse assumption, that is, that greater interaction and exposure leads to—or at least necessitates—greater understanding and appreciation.

2

Sameness and Difference in Contemporary Islamic Approaches to Religious Diversity

THE CONTEMPORARY ISLAMIC discourse on religious diversity within the United States raises many provocative and pointed questions about the existence, value, and functionality of religious difference. What does the Qurʾān say about Judaism, Christianity, and other religions? Is Islam the only "valid" religion in the present time? Are all religions particular expressions of an ineffable Divine unity? Is Islam the only acceptable and salvifically effective path? Or are there multiple paths? Are non-Muslims capable of achieving salvation, however defined? If so, do they achieve salvation because of or in spite of their religion? Is salvation even the central issue? In responding to these specific questions and offering more general explications of religious difference, contemporary scholars unsurprisingly refer to many of the same themes identified in the historical discourse: divine ontology; created anthropology; revelation; and Qurʾānic categories.

However, in addition to the sometimes explicit and sometimes implicit continuation of historical themes, the contemporary discourse is also responsive to unique contemporary concerns, especially those that arise in relation to the fact that religions—or religious individuals—intermingle and live side by side to an extent less common in earlier contexts. This lived reality provokes new and pressing questions about the status of and interaction with the Other. In the context of the United States, the Other-who-can-never-be-wholly-other in theological terms has now, more than ever, become the Other-who-can-never-be-wholly-other in physical and practical terms as well. Thus, in the contemporary discourse, practical and theological concerns converge with scholars aiming to provide a road map for a world permeated with religious diversity, a roadmap that simultaneously remains faithful to the self-understandings of the Islamic tradition and enables productive and practical coexistence. This has resulted in Islamic (re)articulations of the soteriological status of religious Others, (re)examinations of Islamic perspectives toward specific religious groups, and attempts to formulate overarching accounts of the origin, value, and purpose of religious diversity.

This chapter focuses selectively on the latter, that is, on attempts to formulate overarching accounts. More specifically, I explore contemporary approaches written in English, which feature prominently in scholarly discourse in the United States. These include the writings of Asghar Ali Engineer, Abdulaziz Sachedina, Mahmut Aydin, Seyyed Hossein Nasr, Reza Shah-Kazemi, Muhammad Legenhausen, Tim Winter, Farid Esack, and Ismāʿīl al-Fārūqī. Although not all of these scholars are physically located within the United States, their writings on religious diversity have shaped US scholarly discourse. Their work has also necessarily been influenced by their diverse backgrounds and specific contexts. Some of these scholars, such as Engineer and Esack, have been compelled to write on religious diversity due to their firsthand experience of religious intolerance. Others, such as Sachedina, Nasr, and al-Fārūqī, have written in the context of religious plurality and academic discussions thereof within the United States. These scholars also represent various philosophical and theological perspectives, including Shīʿism (Engineer, Sachedina, Shah-Kazemi, Nasr, and Legenhausen), Sunnism (Aydin, Winter, Esack, and al-Fārūqī), Sufism (Aydin, Nasr, and Shah-Kazemi), and Perennial Philosophy (Nasr and Shah-Kazemi). This diversity is another distinctive feature of the US discourse. In all of their contextual, theological, and philosophical diversity, these scholarly perspectives form the backdrop to my endeavor to construct an alternative Islamic theology of religions that is relevant and responsive to the contemporary American context, and that builds upon the strengths of existing approaches while attempting to overcome some of their notable shortcomings.

Prioritization of Sameness

The existing contemporary Islamic discourse on religious diversity is largely dominated by two distinct trends: the prioritization of religious sameness; and the attempt to account simultaneously for both religious sameness and difference. While distinct, these trends are both premised upon a shared, underlying conception of difference: they envision difference in the same fashion. This shared conception dictates the manner in which these scholars are able to account for religious difference, and as such it has profound implications—in fact, limitations—with regards to understanding the religious self and the religious Other.

The first prevailing trend—the prioritization of religious sameness over religious difference—is apparent, for example, in Asghar Ali Engineer's contribution to Paul Knitter's edited volume *The Myth of Religious Superiority: A Multifaith Exploration.*[1] Asghar Ali Engineer (d. 2013) was an Indian activist; the chairman of the Centre for Study of Society and Secularism, which he also founded; and the general secretary of the Progressive Dawoodi Bohra Movement, an organization aimed at bringing reform to this branch of Ismāʿīlī Shīʿa Islam, based in India. Engineer received a traditional religious education from his father and also obtained a degree in civil engineering. His writing and scholarship center on liberation theology, gender issues, and ethnic violence.

While a public intellectual working primarily in the Indian context, Engineer's inclusion as one of only two Islamic contributions to Knitter's pivotal volume pushed him to the center of American scholarly discussions. In his essay and other works,[2] Engineer's aim is to explore Islam's attitude to religious pluralism from a "theological perspective" to answer important questions about pluralistic civil society. For Engineer, the unique contemporary context of modernization, liberalization, and globalization requires a unique Islamic response that provides a solid rationale upon which to affirm universal human rights and freedoms. The pressing connection between theological and practical concerns is here made explicit.

Engineer's attempt to formulate such a rationale revolves around four central assertions. The first is that the Qurʾān "not only accepts the legitimacy of religious pluralism but considers it central to its system of beliefs."[3] He highlights Qurʾān 5:48:

> We sent to you (Muḥammad) the Scripture with the truth, confirming the Scriptures that came before it, and with final authority over them. So judge between them according to what God has sent down. Do not follow their whims, which deviate from the truth that has come to you. We have assigned a law and a path to each of you. If God had so willed, God would have made you one community,

> but God wanted to test you through that which God has given you, so race to do good. You will all return to God and God will make clear to you the matters you differed about.

Based upon this, he argues that every religious community has been given its own laws through its own prophets, scriptures, and revelations and that it is in adhering to those laws that each community achieves spiritual growth. The one God did not wish to impose one law on all people but rather to create multiple diverse communities that would work together to enrich the larger human civilization. Diversity therefore is a divinely intended asset that should be used to foster "peace and harmony among all communities."[4] Although Engineer proposes this optimistic intention, he notes that more often than not religious diversity leads to conflict and aggression, especially when individuals or communities attempt to assume the divine prerogative of judging other humans. He does not clarify, however, the precise means by which diversity can be rechanneled into more productive and humane engagements.

In reference to Qur'ān 5:48, Engineer also invokes the concept of *wahdat-e-din* (unity of religion). This concept implies that the *dīn*—defined by Engineer as the divine origin or essence or truth of all revelations and religions—is affirmed, despite differences that occur in law, practice, or beliefs. Moreover, the differences in the latter are secondary and can in no way override the "thoroughly pluralistic approach to the religious 'other' " entailed in the former.[5] Engineer thus acknowledges difference but prioritizes sameness.

Engineer's second assertion confirms his prioritization of sameness over difference. He maintains that the Qur'ān emphasizes general "good deeds" rather than specific "dogmas."[6] Ironically, to support this claim, he cites Qur'ān 2:177:

> True goodness does not consist in turning your face towards East or West. The truly good are those who believe in God and the Last Day, in the angels, the Scripture, and the prophets; who give away some of their wealth, however much they cherish it, to their relatives, to orphans, the needy, travelers and beggars, and to liberate those in bondage; those who keep up the prayer and pay the prescribed alms; who keep pledges whenever they make them; who are steadfast in misfortune, adversity, and times of danger. These are the ones who are true, and it is they who are conscious of God.

Engineer interprets this *āya* (verse) as a clear illustration of the Qur'ānic deemphasis of particular beliefs and modes of worship and the Qur'ānic elevation of a general ethical criterion of judgment. Whereas the importance of the ethical criterion cannot be debated, it is difficult to see how an exhortation to believe in God, the Last Day, all the revelations and prophets; to perform prayer (*ṣalāt*); and to pay charity (*zakāt*) is *not* concerned with particular beliefs and practices.

Engineer's third assertion is that the Qur'ān promotes freedom of conscience and freedom from compulsion in respect to religion and belief. He links these freedoms with another prominent Qur'ānic theme, the unity of humanity, as expressed in Qur'ān 2:213:

> Humankind was a single community, then God sent prophets to bring good news and warning, and with them God sent the Scripture with the Truth to judge between people in their disagreements. It was only those to whom it was given who disagreed about it after clear signs had come to them because of rivalry between them. So by God's leave God guided the believers to the truth they had differed about. God guides whoever God will to a straight path.

Although he translates the first phrase of this *āya* imprecisely as "Humankind *is* a single nation" rather than "Humankind *was* a single nation," Engineer uses it to introduce the principal importance of a universal, shared creation: from the Qur'ānic perspective, all of humankind was created by God. By pairing these two concepts—freedom and unity—Engineer argues that humanity is one but that God sends different revelations to guide people, thus resulting in the appearance of religious and cultural diversity that should be allowed to exist freely. Humans should not argue over or become envious of each other's particularities, as doing so would permit human difference to undermine the divinely intended unity. Engineer obviously acknowledges the reality and value of difference. However, difference for him is something that should be extolled or engaged, never evaluated; evaluation threatens—or complicates—the prioritization of sameness.

The final assertion that Engineer makes is that the Constitution of Medina (*Ṣaḥīfat al-Madīna* or *Mithāq al-Madīna*) provides a concrete, historical example of the "pluralistic vision" of the Qur'ān. In allowing for multiple religious communities to be united under one charter while maintaining autonomy in all religious affairs and the majority of other matters, Engineer envisions the constitution as an alternative to other more authoritarian Islamic political models, an alternative that embodies the idea that "no nation can become a strong, stable, prosperous, and violence-free society unless religious diversity or pluralism is accepted as legitimate, indeed beneficial, ingredient in the organization and functioning of nation and state."[7] In drawing on this example, Engineer clearly reveals his primary concern for sociopolitical harmony. He is rightly concerned with providing an Islamic justification for tolerant interaction and a positive valuation of religious diversity. Nonetheless, in the process of articulating his justification he ignores—even devalues—other aspects of Islamic belief and practice.

While sameness, unity, and respect in the face of diversity are core aspects of the Qur'ān, they do not exist in isolation. Engineer does not probe their relationship to more "pluralism-ambivalent" aspects of the Qur'ān, such as the piercing evaluations the Qur'ān makes of some forms of difference, such as *shirk* (ascribing partners to God).[8] Rather, he employs a selective textual methodology that prioritizes sameness and fails to substantially engage difference. Notably, the selective textual methodology (proof texting) that Engineer employs to affirm religious pluralism and stress sameness is the same methodological approach used by other historical and contemporary scholars to arrive at an exclusivist reading of the text that prioritizes difference. In both cases, only aspects of the Qur'ān that bolster the respective positions—that is, pluralism or exclusivism—are acknowledged, and all other aspects of the text that run counter to or complexify these conclusions are ignored or summarily dismissed.

Abdulaziz Sachedina articulates a similar concern for sociopolitical pluralism.[9] Of Indian descent and born in Tanzania, Sachedina is the Professor and IIIT Chair in Islamic Studies at George Mason University in Fairfax, Virginia. He earned his Ph.D. from the University of Toronto, and his writing focuses on Islamic theology, ethics, law, and interfaith relations. Like Engineer, Sachedina grounds his discussion of pluralism in the Qur'ān, citing 2:213 and deducing three main conclusions: the unity of all humanity under one God; the particularities of the religions brought by prophets; and revelation's role in resolving differences among various religious communities.[10] While Sachedina later expounds upon his initial two conclusions, he does not explain exactly how revelation resolves difference. In fact, a large portion of his work is devoted to illuminating the various ways the particularities of each revelation have led to conflict, exclusivism, and claims of uniqueness.

Sachedina also contends that at its core Islam is a religion primarily concerned with the public realm and that, while the Qur'ān does speak of private faith, the main principles in that arena are individual freedom of conscience and nonintervention. With regard to the public projection of that faith, Sachedina argues that the overriding Qur'ānic principle is coexistence, or the establishment of an "ethical public order" to "protect the divinely ordained right of each and every person to determine his or her spiritual destiny without coercion."[11]

Sachedina stresses that the main concern of the Qur'ān is ethical, public, and aimed at coexistence but also offers an insightful account of the interweaving of history and the interpretation of the Qur'ān, which has largely resulted in an exclusivist interpretation of the text that privileges the specifics of Islam over all other religions. Sachedina highlights, in particular, the impact of political and identity dynamics on the hermeneutical process: "From the standpoint of political organization, exclusivist claims, were effective in providing a legitimating and integrative discourse that could furnish members of the community with a reliable means to assert their collective and political identity."[12] The hermeneutical inclination toward exclusivism, though, was also impelled by perceived tensions or contradictions within the Qur'ān itself, especially between those verses that affirmed the salvific value of other religions and those that seemed to imply that Islam was the only religion capable of leading to salvation. Classical scholars, according to Sachedina, thus concocted a variety of terminological and methodological "stratagems to circumscribe those verses of the Qur'ān which underscored its ecumenical thrust by extending salvific authenticity and adequacy to other monotheistic traditions."[13] These stratagems included selective citation of the Qur'ānic text, *naskh* (abrogation of some Qur'ānic verses by others), supersession (abrogation of previous revelations by the revelation to Muḥammad), and the soteriological prerequisite of recognizing and adhering to the religion revealed to Muḥammad.

Based on this assessment, Sachedina considers whether modern scholars should adhere to such exclusivist readings that elevate Islam above all other religions and that primarily focus on difference. His response to this question is to reiterate notions of divine unity, unity of humankind, and God as the source of all revelations, which despite different external forms contain the same message. In addition to this obvious elevation of sameness over the differences, intricacies, and conundrums introduced through various revelations, he also states that there is historical precedent for avoiding exclusivism. This is the theological position (commonly associated with the Mu'tazilite thought) that the unaided human intellect, or reason, is "capable of attaining a godly life by choosing from among an array of prophets and their messages."[14] For Sachedina, this approach—in contrast to exclusivism, which requires explicit exposure to Muḥammad's message—is the desirable choice in the modern context. It is also a choice that he sees as centering upon a common human capacity, the universal human *fiṭra* (defined by him as primordial nature). *Fiṭra*, thus conceived, serves as a sort of moral compass that universally directs all humans in the development of a common moral ground and a consensus of ethical values and goals. Responding to the Qur'ānic exhortation to "compete with one another in good works" or "race to do good" (5:48), the development of a moral consensus furthermore transcends mere tolerance, requiring active engagement and understanding despite differences. While Sachedina does note a correlation between the epistemes of reason and revelation, he emphasizes that the innate disposition and faculties were created before the prophets and revelations. In other words, in origin and purpose, the sameness manifest in *fiṭra* takes precedence over and reduces the importance of the external differences introduced by revelation.

The prioritization of sameness over difference is also apparent in the approach of Mahmut Aydin, a professor in the Faculty of Theology at University of Ondokuz Mayis in Turkey, who teaches on history of religions and interreligious dialogue and earned his Ph.D. from the Centre for the Study of Islam and Christian–Muslim Relations at the University of Birmingham. Aydin highlights that the contemporary context raises new questions about Muslim claims of uniqueness and universality.[15] In a world of religious diversity, such claims—specifically those about the singular truth of Islam, the Qur'ān as the absolute Word of God, and Muḥammad as the most superior and final prophet—are increasingly challenged by and increasingly present a challenge to interreligious interaction and dialogue. He thus argues that it is imperative to "reconstruct" Muslim theology both in light of the contemporary context and in dialogue with other religions: "New developments demand that Muslim theology be reconstructed—not in isolation but in relation with other religions and theological visions—because these new developments make it clear that only an Islam that sees itself in the context of the world religions will make sense in the twenty-first century."[16] Perceptively noting that such a reconstruction will entail reevaluation of a number of interconnected and core Islamic theological categories, he defines the goal as a pluralist Muslim theology of religions that allows for individuals to achieve salvation through their respective religious traditions, not just through explicit adherence to the ways of Muḥammad.

In articulating his pluralist theology, Aydin reexamines the central Qur'ānic concepts of *dīn* and *islām* with explicit reference to historical exegetical debates. He eventually concludes that these terms are synonymous and refer to general belief and faith characterized by submission and self-surrender to God. Aydin draws upon W. C. Smith's distinction between faith and belief in further elucidating his position. Faith is *dīn* and *islām*, which is shared across all traditions. Belief refers to that which is specific to particular traditions.[17] Notably, he states that Islam's specifics or beliefs are defined by the Qur'ānic category of *īmān* (belief). However, he does not explore this statement in detail and thus presents no account for Qur'ānic references to *īmān* as something present in other particular religious groups. According to Aydin, the particularities of traditions, the "established structures such as revelation, a sacred book, prophethood, sacred places, the religious community, and law (*sharī'ah*) are not religion *per se* but its concrete forms."[18] Aydin contends that these concrete forms are bound to time and place. They are wholly dependent upon context. His inclusive reinterpretation of *dīn* and *islām* permits Aydin to argue that all individuals who have general faith—despite all particularities of practice or dogma—are eligible for salvation. Faith or sameness—not context-specific difference—is tied to salvation.

To bolster this position, Aydin briefly alludes to the universality of revelation, to the view that revelations "confirm" rather than "negate" one another, and to the view that God is God equally to all of humanity. These are central aspects of Islamic theology, but Aydin does not thoroughly weave them into his overarching pluralist theology or explore them in any depth. Do revelations really confirm each other when they oblige humans to perform different practices? If God is in the same relationship to all of humankind, what precisely is the relationship? How is it affected by disobedience or disbelief? Aydin's position may be correct, but some intricacies need to be explored and integrated into his overall position. Yet since he prioritizes sameness, these rich areas of exploration are simply offered as uninvestigated corroborations of his pluralist stance.

In more recent work, Aydin revisits another historical genre—mystical approaches—and proffers an interpretation of Jalāl al-Dīn Rūmī as an Islamic exemplar of Knitter's "religious–mystical bridge" to affirming pluralism.[19] Aydin presents a number of excerpts from Rūmī's poetry to stress the ineffability of the Divine, the partial nature of the experience of that Divine in each religious tradition, the dialectic of inner unity and external diversity, and the notion that multiple paths are equally equipped to achieve the ultimate goal of a movement away from egocentrism. Although many of these assertions feature prominently in Rūmī's writings, Aydin's effort to emphasize the unity, shared origin and goal, and effectiveness of every religion oversimplifies Rūmī's understanding of the complex relationship between unity and diversity. This simplification is evident in the parallel Aydin draws between John Hick's employment of the Kantian distinction between noumenon and phenomena and Rūmī's distinction between meaning and forms.[20] Both Kant and Rūmī do aim to account simultaneously for the existence of One Real/God and for the multiplicity of religions. Aydin, though, overlooks a vital dissimilarity between the two. For Hick, the phenomena are human projections or human responses defined in light of "limited cultural and psychological categories."[21] For Rūmī, in contrast, the multiplicity of forms is the divinely intended result of divine self-disclosure; it is a result of the manifestation of divine attributes and names in the world. Both models depict the Real/God as greater than any one religion (phenomenon or form), but for Rūmī there is an authentic connection between the two. The forms, although delimited, are real manifestations of *wujūd* (Being/God) rather than human projections.[22]

Oversimplification is also apparent in the fact that Aydin does not clearly define what counts in Rūmī's mind as an acceptable religion. Aydin appears to argue for the acceptability and salvific efficacy of all religions, but he quotes Rūmī as saying, "Is not the origin of the law or revelation the same?"[23] This refers to what is very clear in the examination of Rūmī in Chapter 1: Rūmī insists upon the necessity of following the teachings and practices of revealed religion in general and preferably the specific teachings and practices of Muḥammad. While a case could be made that Rūmī has a more universal definition of what religions are the products of divine revelation communicated through prophets, Aydin does not make such an argument. On the other hand, Aydin does not wish to affirm every manifestation of religion; there is corruption and contamination. Since he cannot distinguish between distorted and undistorted revelation based upon any prioritization of external forms, he is forced, like Hick, to avoid relativism through the invocation of an amorphous ethical criterion, "ethical fruits."

Aydin also does not address the distinction Rūmī draws between the ontological and deontological commands of God: between what God wills and what God approves or commands. He implicitly favors the ontological command when he states that "the reality of religious diversity was rooted in the reality of God."[24] Based on this in isolation, he is able to interpret Rūmī's poetry as an unequivocal assertion of the shared origin and goal, the equal validity, and the equal effectiveness of all religious paths, despite their differences.[25] As in his earlier work, Aydin acknowledges the existence of difference but prioritizes sameness: the "lamps are different but the Light is the same"; and religions are "different vehicles" headed in the "same direction."[26] He is able to stress the general message rather than the established system of particular religions. However, the ontological command, which arises from the very nature of God, is only one aspect of Rūmī's complex position on the relationship between oneness and multiplicity. The other component is the deontological command, whereby God commands human beings to follow only certain paths. Though Rūmī definitely emphasizes sameness and oneness, difference—in the form of the established systems of revealed religions—is never negated and, in fact, is the precise means by which one comes to a full appreciation of sameness. The full appreciation of sameness is thus the end product of following a distinctive path. Strikingly, Aydin concludes his examination by asking whether Rūmī's example "suggests that the deeper the holiness of a Muslim, the greater the likelihood that that Muslim will be a pluralist."[27] Unintentionally perhaps, this question summarizes precisely what Aydin loses sight of in prioritizing sameness to the degree that he does: the most complete understanding of sameness, according to Rūmī, is achieved through adherence to a specific manifestation of formal difference, that is, to a specific religious tradition.

What then is the role of difference according to Aydin? It is perhaps indicative of his overall emphasis on sameness that Aydin's most extensive discussion of difference comes in a footnote. In it, he states that difference in general is divinely intended so that humans can strive to know one another and compete with each other in good deeds. Difference "affirmed by both the Qur'an and Rumi, in no way is meant to lead to either relativism or chaos. It is, rather, a diversity grounded in, and productive of, unity."[28] He also characterizes difference as a test that humans must accept. Despite the divine intention, this test, when manifest in various external forms, is more frequently than not the source of discord among humanity. In line with this observation, Aydin himself refers to these forms as "combustible materials" and quotes Rūmī as referring to them as "obstacles" and "roadblocks" that must be "looked beyond."[29] In Aydin's estimation, an emphasis on particularities, while potentially beneficial in a utopian scenario, in the real world leads to conflict.

Simultaneous Affirmation of Sameness and Difference

An apparently similar approach to that of Aydin is found in the writings of Seyyed Hossein Nasr, an Iranian philosopher who is currently university professor of Islamic studies at George Washington University. He received his Ph.D. from Harvard University, was the president of the Imperial Iranian Academy of Philosophy (the first academic institution to be founded upon the principles of philosophical Traditionalism), and was the first Muslim to give the Gifford Lectures ("Knowledge and the Sacred," 1980–1981). His research and writing focus on a wide variety of subjects, including Perennial Philosophy, Sufism, comparative religion, and metaphysics.[30] Examining the topic of religious diversity from the perspectives of both Perennial Philosophy (the philosophical perspective that religious truth derives from a single divine reality) and Sufism, Nasr reiterates many of the central contentions of Aydin's Sufi interpretation, including the notions of inner unity, external diversity, and divine ineffability. Beyond these similarities, though, Nasr's approach diverges significantly from Aydin's and thus reveals the second prominent trend in contemporary Islamic discourse on religious diversity: the attempt to affirm and value both religious sameness and religious difference simultaneously.

Nasr's approach is grounded in a particular understanding of the modern context in juxtaposition with the "traditional" context.[31] Traditional civilizations, according to Nasr, were homogeneous wholes structured in every arena by principles of transcendent origin. This traditional context is the only normal, natural, and meaningful context for humans. Nasr asserts that humankind "has been created to live in a homogeneous religious tradition, one in which the values of his religion are for him *the* values, absolute and binding."[32] In such a context, other religions were "alien worlds" that did not provoke concern; there was no need to "take cognizance of the metaphysical significance of other traditions."[33] Nasr does acknowledge that the homogeneity of the traditional context has been "broken" in the majority of the modern world and hence depicts modern humanity as faced with "abnormal conditions" [34] and the unique dilemma of wanting to simultaneously maintain faith in one's own religion while accepting the validity of others'. The dual affronts of secular philosophies and contact with other traditions have made the existence of other religions into an urgent metaphysical and theological concern.

Nasr promotes Perennial Philosophy and Sufism as the only effective ways to grapple with this modern concern. These approaches, which have some similarities, are the keys because they avoid the common pitfalls of other modern attempts to comprehend religious diversity. Some such pitfalls include historicism, phenomenology, lowest common denominator ecumenism, and relativism.[35] Nasr argues that each of these fails to engage in serious discussion of metaphysical and theological topics. Although such topics may not readily lend themselves to resolution or reconciliation, they must be studied, elaborated, and better understood: "It is too late for diplomatic platitudes and the kind of relativization which in the name of ecumenical understanding belittles issues of major theological concern, creating so-called human accord at the expense of truncating, reducing, or distorting the Divine Message."[36] Nasr is thus obviously concerned with avoiding an approach that depicts all religions as the same through neglect of their distinct—and potentially conflicting—particularities.

How, then, does Perennial Philosophy portray religious diversity? Nasr states that the foundational contention is the existence of a single ineffable divine reality that is the "source of the teachings of each authentic faith."[37] He utilizes the analogy of a spring that gushes forth water to depict the manner in which the one Divine manifests in the world. The spring issues many cascades of water that descend through various levels of reality, passing over and through various terrains. No cascades are the same, although some are similar and some come into contact. Moreover, "only at the Spring Itself are all the cascades one and nowhere else should complete unity be sought among them."[38] There exists a transcendent unity in that the source of all revelations is the same but in the world religions are characterized by various degrees and forms of difference.

Similar to other scholars writing from a Sufi or mystical perspective, Nasr explains the simultaneous existence of unity and diversity—or sameness and difference—by drawing a distinction between the esoteric and exoteric, or the meaning (*maʿnā*) and the form (*sūra*). While the two are distinct, they are nonetheless integrally connected. Therefore, he does not permit the reduction or devaluation of the exoteric forms of religions, which for Nasr include particular dogmas, rites, and law. The forms are "necessary," "sacrosanct," and the "gateways" to the esoteric. According to Nasr, traditional esotericism, unlike modern Western ecumenism, "emphasizes the basic distinction between transcending forms from above and rejecting forms by falling below them, thereby forfeiting the very possibility of ever reaching the world of the Formless."[39] In other words, one can reach the world of the Formless or gain an understanding of the inner meaning only through the forms.[40] Nasr, thus, diverges from Aydin in stressing the importance of both the *message* and the *system* as well as in explicitly rejecting the severing of noumenon and phenomena characteristic of Immanuel Kant and John Hick.

To maintain the simultaneous value of both sameness and difference, Nasr asserts that both the meaning and the forms are absolute: the former as the Absolute in Itself and the latter as what Frithjof Schuon calls "the relatively absolute." Nasr clarifies this through the analogy of suns and their solar systems, in which each manifestation of the Divine Logos represents the sun in a planetary system. Echoing other descriptions of a traditional context, he states that every sun is actually one star among many, but to those in the planetary system it is the only sun and seems to be of a completely different nature than the many other stars. Nasr also reiterates in this context that the formal expressions of the religious systems derive relatively absolute status from the manifestation of the one Divine Logos. More significantly, he argues that in such a model, "the fact that these elements (forms) within a particular religious universe might differ from or even contradict elements belonging to another universe does not prove their falsity or destroy their absoluteness within the universe to which they belong."[41] Nasr's analogy is effective in validating the integrity of particular religious universes and in suggesting a model for understanding how the existence of other particular religious universes does not falsify one's own universe. However, it also vividly highlights one of the foremost limitations of Nasr's approach. He assigns value to both sameness and difference, but he does not effectively address the topic of interaction or conflict between religions. While he does introduce the notion of "crossing religious frontiers,"[42] he describes this as simply recognizing and appreciating the aforementioned reality. Other examples of such crossing, specifically missionary activity and Islamic fundamentalism, serve as indications that such interactions have bred hostility and created tension.[43] Thus, the analogy of relatively absolute religious universes fails to address the fact that contemporary religious universes do not exist in isolation and are not typically homogeneous wholes. Religious universes collide, cross orbits, have internal systematic tensions, and are frequently not defined by clear boundaries. This is the very reality of the modern context as Nasr describes it. Therefore, it is striking that his method of understanding that new—albeit in Nasr's estimation abnormal—context is to superimpose the traditional model upon it to reassure people confused by the discovery of relativity that everyone's absolutes are still in place.[44]

Reza Shah-Kazemi also utilizes the Sufi approach as the basis of his model of the relationship between Islam and other religions. The founding editor of the *Islamic World Report*, Shah-Kazemi is a research fellow in the Department of Academic Research and Publications at the Institute of Ismaili Studies. He earned his Ph.D. in comparative religion from the University of Kent, and his writing focuses on mysticism, Islam, Sufism, and Shīʿism.[45] Building upon Nasr's approach and coupling it with a Sufi hermeneutic developed from Ibn al-ʿArabī,[46] he reasserts the familiar themes of the transcendent unity of all religion, the necessity of the One manifesting in the many, and the notion of Divine self-disclosure through created diversity.

A novel aspect of Shah-Kazemi's approach is his introduction of the category of universalism in response to what he sees as shortcomings in the general classifications of exclusivism, inclusivism, and pluralism common to Christian theology of religions. Like pluralism, Shah-Kazemi's universalism recognizes diverse religious traditions as salvifically effective. Unlike pluralism, however, it sees those various paths as divinely ordained and authored rather than humanly constructed, and it refuses to deny the uniqueness of each religion to subsume them under one "global theology." With respect to inclusivism, his universalism shares the assertion of a single religious essence but again insists that "the very otherness of the other is rigorously maintained and respected, rather than being domesticated and appropriated as part of one's formal religion."[47] Finally, although his universalism does not deny the validity of other religions, it does echo the exclusivist view that one's religion is normative and binding. Shah-Kazemi's universalism, therefore, serves as a reiteration of Nasr's contention that the forms of religions—their particularities—are important and integrally tied to the meaning. If the various paths or forms are divinely ordained and intended, they cannot be abolished, reduced, or ignored. Furthermore, when Shah-Kazemi asserts that difference is simultaneously upheld and transcended, he echoes Nasr's distinction between transcending forms from above rather than rejecting them from below through negating of the importance of forms. For both Nasr and Shah-Kazemi, differences in formal religious expressions must be upheld and followed in this world; they are transcended only on the "supra-phenomenal plane of the divine Principle itself."[48]

Another concern for Shah-Kazemi is the development of a model for interreligious dialogue that is appealing and open to other religions as well as to more exclusivist perspectives within the Muslim community. In this regard, he cites Qur'ān 16:125:

> Call to the way of your Lord with wisdom and good teaching. Argue with them in the most courteous way, for your Lord knows best who has strayed from God's way and who is rightly guided.

Based upon this he then formulates his conception of dialogue as the "most beautiful discourse," built upon the twin principles of the universality of revelation and the connection of that revelation to the unique Absolute. In the context of dialogue he does state that what is shared between all believers (defined as those who believe in the absolute and in revelation) is "of infinitely greater value than that which differentiates them," but he simultaneously fends off an isolated emphasis on sameness by asserting that unity does not entail uniformity and that there can be "no question of bland leveling out of formal differences."[49]

Shah-Kazemi's struggle to account equally for sameness and difference is again obvious in his definition of Islam as both quintessential, universal submission and as an institutional, reified religion that possesses normativity, completeness, and finality. In fact, he states that one of the main goals of his approach is to reconcile these "apparently contradictory positions."[50] He acknowledges that the insistence on the normativity of institutional Islam—an insistence upheld by the historical scholars cited by Shah-Kazemi—could lead to "arrogance and chauvinism," but he contends that the universal and institutional definitions of Islam can be integrated through his metaphysical Sufi universalism. Since Shah-Kazemi is concerned with practical interaction, primarily in the form of inclusive dialogue, he is unable to affirm both sameness and difference by isolating the two as in Nasr. Rather, he affirms both by appealing to a hierarchy of evaluation between particular traditions, with Islam—more precisely Sufism—being the normative apex.

Central to this second trend, the concern to avoid reduction of difference assumes its most explicit expression in the work of Muhammad Legenhausen. Legenhausen, an American philosopher, received his

Ph.D. from Rice University and currently teaches at the Imam Khomeini Education and Research Institute in Iran. He is also a founding member of the advisory board of the Shīʿite Studies Center in Qom and serves on the scientific board of the Human Rights Center of Mofid University, Qom. In addition to his own works, he has translated a number of books into Persian and Arabic. Legenhausen criticizes the views of John Hick and other scholars, whom he describes as advocating a "reductive pluralism" that affirms religious diversity based upon a lowest common denominator conception of sameness.[51] This type of pluralism, according to Legenhausen, emphasizes private faith over the public enactment of religion and thus neglects the "practical dimensions" of religions: "Religions have important practical dimensions, not only because of the moral codes they promote, but also because of their ritual and aesthetic dimensions. Even if the doctrinal conflict among religions could be reconciled along the lines suggested by Hick, the practical conflicts would remain."[52]

While reductive pluralists emphasize freedom of religion, Legenhausen states that their freedom relates only to doctrine or beliefs, not rituals, ethics, and laws. Furthermore, even on the doctrinal side, reductive pluralism downplays differences, resulting in the reduction of religious imperative to a question of preference or personal taste. This form of pluralism, according to Legenhausen, is therefore unsuitable for Islamic discussions because of the emphasis Islam places on social and legalist piety and absolute monotheism.

Laying the foundation for his articulation of a non-reductive alternative, Legenhausen defines pluralism as "a doctrine according to which *some sort* of favorable attribution is ascribed to a plurality of religions."[53] He then identifies a "plurality of pluralisms," explicating an array of different *sorts* and *scopes*. The sorts of religious pluralism he outlines include soteriological (pertaining to salvation), normative (pertaining to treatment of adherents of other religions), epistemological (pertaining to the logical justification of beliefs), alethic (pertaining to the truth of beliefs), ethical (pertaining to moral obligations and systems), deontological (pertaining to religious obligations based on God's command), and hermetic (pertaining to esoteric unity). In terms of scope, Legenhausen distinguishes between equality pluralism and degree pluralism. The former implies that the favorable attribution is present equally in all religions, while the latter implies that the positive attribution is present in different religions to different degrees. In exposing the complexity of religious pluralism, he intends not only to extend his critique of reductive pluralism but also to introduce the possibility that different sorts of pluralism may be the central focus in theologies of religions formulated within different religious traditions. This reiterates his critique of the essentially Christian development of theology of religions, which has primarily focused upon the topic of salvation. Thus, for Legenhausen, reduction of difference is a concern with regard not only to the assessment of religions but also to the complexity of the field itself.

The explication of a plurality of pluralisms also forms the basis of his distinction between the concepts of "correct religion" and "salvation."[54] Whereas in other traditions the two are directly linked, Legenhausen draws a division between them, contending that correct religion comprises those beliefs and actions that are "divinely ordained" in the present era and that salvation is ultimately contingent upon God's Mercy rather than belief or works alone. Legenhausen is not primarily interested in salvation, as in many ways all humans stand in the same situation of need with respect to God's Mercy. Rather, he is concerned with the question of correct religion, that is, with the question of God's deontological command in relationship to various religions. Legenhausen argues that Islam—the religion revealed to Muḥammad—is the only correct religion in this specific sense. Other religions and revelations are neither wholly incorrect nor completely devoid of guidance. However, appealing to the ideas of supersession, superiority, and perfection, he claims that Islam is the only divinely ordained religion in contemporary times. Conceding that this position may sound exclusivist, he describes it as a degree pluralism that acknowledges degrees of truth in other religions and the possibility of religious others achieving salvation. Thus, similar to Shah-Kazemi, Legenhausen accommodates both sameness and difference by invoking rigid hierarchical evaluation: other religions have some truth and ability to guide, but Islam is comprehensive and unsurpassed.

Prioritization of Difference

The prioritization of sameness and the attempt to simultaneously affirm both sameness and difference emerge clearly as the two dominant trends in contemporary Islamic scholarly discourse. There is, however, another possible approach: the prioritization of religious difference. The prioritization of religious difference is the inverse of the prioritization of religious sameness. In this approach, while sameness may be acknowledged, it is treated as negligible. In contrast, difference and the supposed clear-cut divisions between religions are emphasized.

An example of this approach is found in the writings of Tim Winter, who is the Shaykh Zayed Lecturer in Islamic Studies in the Faculty of Divinity at Cambridge University and the director of studies in theology at Wolfson College. He has written and translated a number of works on Islamic theology, Muslim–Christian relations, and political theology. In his writings on religious pluralism, he focuses primarily on the soteriological implications of classical Sunni speculative theology (*kalām*) and proffers a critique of the validity of contemporary Islamic pluralistic formulations.[55]

His critique targets pluralism in general and Islamic pluralism specifically. Generally, he argues that pluralism violates the "law of non-contradiction;" it requires simultaneous affirmation of contradictory statements, beliefs, or doctrines.[56] God cannot simultaneously exist and not exist. Monotheism and dualism cannot be simultaneously affirmed. Winter argues that Islam (like many other religions) asserts certain propositions and claims that are envisioned as truth and thus rule out or negate the validity of other contradictory propositions and claims. He also challenges the Islamic relevance of a pluralism based on the model of Hick and premised upon the Kantian distinction between noumenon and phenomena. While he inaccurately presents most contemporary Islamic pluralists as co-opting this model,[57] his critique of this particular brand of pluralism as being inconsistent with Islamic conceptions of God, revelation, and knowledge of God is voiced by other scholars, including Legenhausen.

With specific reference to Islam, Winter's critique targets what he presents as contemporary Islamic pluralists' deviation from the content and hermeneutical approach of traditional Muslim interpretations. The approaches of Islamic pluralists, according to Winter, conflict with the "self-understanding of the primordial Muslim community" and "relinquish fundamental methodological principles which for centuries have overlaid the texts with a unifying exegetical template, including such features as the belief in abrogation of certain Koranic passages, the centrality of the canonical hadith discourse and the theory of scholarly consensus (*ijmāʿ*) as a transhistorical expression of God's will."[58] Winter may be accurate in highlighting the wide-ranging implications of the challenges raised by pluralists (something about which many of these scholars are scrupulously aware), but his critique is primarily illuminative of his own insistence on defining boundaries through a projection of intra-tradition, at least intra-Sunni, homogeneity. The mirror image of this projection is, as seen in the historical discourse, the attempt to assert stark delineation from other traditions. The Islamic tradition is unified and monolithic and has agreed upon norms, according to Winter. It is thus distinguishable and distinctive. Pluralists are critiqued because they do not "properly" adhere to the highlighted norms, nor do they confirm the depiction of Islam as unified, static, and unambiguously distinct.

Winter's claim to internal homogeneity is the stepping stone to his larger argument that revelation is a supersessionist event and that all other religions, besides Islam, have been abrogated. Exploring Qur'ānic verses and elements of the *Sunna*, he highlights arguments directed against other religious groups, including paganism, Judaism, and Christianity. He does acknowledge, in reference to the latter two communities, that the critiques are somewhat less straightforward due to the view that the founders of these religions and the original messages had divine authorization. There is sameness at the origin.

Turning to Qur'ān 5:48—frequently cited by pluralists as evidence of continuing divine sanction of multiple religious communities—Winter offers a different interpretation that conforms with his prioritization of difference through the emphasis on supersession and abrogation. Qur'ān 5:48 through his lens has two objectives: "Firstly, to affirm the Judeo-Christian line of prophecy in order to proclaim Muhammad's triumphant succession to it, and secondly, to make of his religion a 'guardian' (*muhaymin*) over the surviving advocates of earlier versions of faith."[59] In other words, God's current covenant is with Prophet Muḥammad and the people of Islam only, but other communities should be tolerated in this world. Worldly toleration, though, is not mandated as a result of the legitimacy of the beliefs and practices of these communities; the originally valid revelations have been corrupted, leaving only "distorted remnants."[60] This seemingly comprehensive distortion thus necessitates abrogation by a new, universal, and final revelation: Islam. Underscoring his conception of consensus and unity within Sunni Islam, Winter cites a number of classical scholars who agree that other religions have been "trumped" by Islam and rendered invalid (*bāṭil*). Thus, worldly toleration does not extend to soteriological pluralism; the other traditions are accommodated, not affirmed as salvifically effective.

While asserting the soteriological singularity and primacy of the Islamic path, Winter notes that this does not mean that all non-Muslim monotheists are subjected to eternal damnation. As discussed in the historical survey, ignorance of and lack of exposure to the message brought by Muḥammad were frequently seen as mitigating factors in soteriological evaluation. In the discussion of ignorance and exposure, Winter also explores the topics of eschatological prophetic intercession and divine mercy. With the former, he contends that it presents another vehicle for limiting the negative soteriological outcomes of non-Muslims, even when knowledge of the Islamic message was present. According to Winter, Muḥammad's ability, in particular, to intercede on behalf of non-Muslim Others reiterates Islam's restricted affirmation of and primacy over other prophets and religions. Eschatological intercession of all forms, however, is always an expression of divine mercy, not an expression of validation of Otherness.

Ultimately labeling his overall presentation of Islam's relationship to other religions as "non-categoric supersession," he maintains that this perspective need not lead to "a triumphalist assurance that Muslims alone will be saved or to a worldview that endangers rather than reinforces ethics."[61] Rather, non-categoric supersession could foster humility, responsibility toward others, and honest dialogue on difference. This approach, unlike his view of Hickian pluralism, does not foster tolerance through the denial of the validity or permissibility of all exclusive or particular claims.

In addition to the similar critique of pluralism, Winter's approach also overlaps with that of Legenhausen in another fashion. Both scholars construct their approaches by focusing on notions of supersession, salvation, divine mercy, and tolerance. However, they do so in strikingly different ways, and these divergences vividly accentuate their respective engagements with religious sameness and religious difference. For example, both present Islam as superseding prior religious traditions, but they differ on the cause of this supersession and the resulting implications. Winter describes corruption of the prior messages and traditions as the raison d'être for the Qurʾānic revelation.[62] Although he discusses ambiguity related to the affirmation of the divine origin of these traditions, there is no such ambiguity about their current validity. They are invalid, and Islam is valid. The two are clearly distinguished. Legenhausen, though, does not directly connect supersession to corruption. While he does not rule out the possibility of corruption, he acknowledges truth and goodness within other traditions. Those traditions are superseded not because they are invalid but because God has commanded something new and more.

This distinction leads to differing presentations of salvation and divine mercy. According to Winter, there is a direct connection (albeit with some mitigating factors) between following Islam and achieving salvation. Islam is the only salvifically effective religious path. While divine mercy can extend the "circle of hope" related to salvation, religious traditions are plainly different and two different paths cannot be simultaneously legitimate. Legenhausen, in comparison, unhinges the question of salvation from the status of Islam and the status of other religions. The question of salvation for him is holistically a question of divine mercy. Divine mercy is not an add-on to a salvifically effective religious path, but divine mercy is *the* primary vehicle of all salvation. His unhinging of the question of salvation relates closely to his critique of the Christocentric nature of the excessive focus on soteriology in theology of religions. It also relates to the complexity of his attempt to simultaneously affirm sameness and difference.

A final comment is required on Winter's and Legenhausen's shared invocation of the need for tolerance, despite what may appear in their approaches as outright and pseudo-exclusivism. Various assessments of the practicality of this call for tolerance can be proffered, but what is significant is that the call for tolerance is a recognition of the reality of and need for engagement with the Other. While both utilize the term tolerance, it assumes a particular flavor in their respective approaches. Winter advocates for a tolerance that is humble, worldly, and paternalistic, a tolerance that recognizes valid origins but makes no pretense about legitimacy. Legenhausen advocates for a tolerance that rests upon some degree of recognition of truth and guidance in other traditions, and recognition that salvation is connected to divine mercy alone. The need to explicitly make this caveat about tolerance while promoting an exclusive theology is provocative. It could be argued that the idea that religious exclusivism—or an emphasis on difference—leads to intolerant action is a modern intellectual construct, but aspects of the Sunni majority discourse that Winter heavily references have been implicated in intolerant action. This does not substantiate a necessary connection. However, it does compel Winter's categorical statement about tolerance as well as his call for the "disconnection" of supersessionist theological claims from "purported legal entailments"[63] that have not been uniformly tolerant or respectful toward non-Muslims, especially non-Muslim minorities.

In reflecting more broadly on the prioritization of difference approach, there are three critical observations. First, the majority of contemporary scholars who engage in the discourse of theology of religions do not promote this view. Second, the relative absence of this trend, which is notable in and of itself, is related to the inherent grappling with the Other-who-can-never-be-wholly-other. Most contemporary scholars acknowledge at least a degree of irreducible sameness, and as such they must contend with this particular type of Other. Contrary to the oversimplified presentation of some scholars who prioritize difference, this grappling with the complex religious Other has not resulted in a monolithic, unqualified, or relativistic affirmation of pluralism. Third, although this perspective is not common within the discourse of theology of religions, it is more common within general contemporary Islamic discussions. Moreover, when voiced, it is frequently voiced—with varying degrees of specification and accuracy—as a verbatim reiteration of the historical discourse, drawing upon the ideas and writings of scholars, such as Ibn Taymiyya and Ibn Kathīr. This is of great significance because it indicates a gulf between the majority of the discourse examined herein and more general discussions. This gulf is perpetuated in part by the fact that the writings of historical scholars who prioritize difference are widely available and widely referenced. Ibn Kathīr's *Tafsīr*, for example, is translated into more languages than any other *tafsīr*, and it is also widely available on the Internet. The fact that difference is prioritized in more general discourse is also significant because it coexists tensively with increasing interreligious engagement and as such highlights the bifurcation between praxis and theology.

Proximity and Otherness: The Prevailing Conception of Difference and Beyond

While the preceding approaches illuminate various theological concerns and offer a plethora of valuable insights, they all revolve around a singular pivotal concern: the identification and evaluation of religious difference. Perhaps more significantly, these scholarly approaches manifest a shared conception of religious difference. In this conception, religious difference is depicted as dividing humanity through the erection of clear, static, and impermeable boundaries.

In the first trend, the prioritization of religious sameness, such boundaries are seen as impediments to the ultimate goal of tolerant interaction; boundaries and difference create conflict. Thus difference is devalued and downplayed, while sameness is emphasized. Deeds are stressed over dogmas (Engineer), ethical *fiṭra* over revelation (Sachedina), and the message and meaning over the system and form (Aydin). In the second trend, the attempt to simultaneously affirm religious sameness and religious difference, divisions and boundaries are upheld in an effort to maintain the value and divine intentionality of difference. Religions are therefore depicted as bounded wholes that either do not—or ideally would not—interact at all (Nasr) or are related only through some sort of evaluative hierarchy (Shah-Kazemi and Legenhausen). Separation and hierarchical evaluation maintain boundaries and difference, and although sameness is acknowledged it is not permitted to eradicate or blur such boundaries. Nasr, for example, envisions all religions as being connected to the Absolute in Itself, but religions ideally and under normal conditions remain discrete universes or frontiers. Likewise in Legenhausen, divine revelation is acknowledged in respect to other religions, but divine revelation also creates bounded communities that are deontologically commanded in successive and linear order without any overlap. The prioritization of religious difference, although not as common, is an extreme example of this particular conception of the difference. As seen in the historical discourse, especially with Ibn Taymiyya and Ibn Kathīr, and in Winter this approach manifests a fixation on defining and enforcing distinct and fixed boundaries between various segments of humanity.

To gain a better understanding of the nuances and implications of this particular conception of religious difference, it is useful to briefly revisit Boyarin. In addition to explicating the deliberateness of Othering and the enforcement of boundaries demarcating difference, he also describes the end product of such processes. The result of "fetishizing borders and boundaries"[64] is a depiction of religions as "separate, hermetically sealed compartments."[65] Such rigid and static compartments do serve a cognitive function, but they are also a gross simplification of religious identity and interaction. They present religions fully purged of all fuzziness, complexity, and hybridity.

The theories of Jonathan Z. Smith also help to clarify the implications of the shared conception of religious difference in contemporary Islamic discourse. Smith intricately probes the construction of the Other, describing the most basic view of the Other as the binary opposition WE/THEY or IN/OUT.[66] Similar to Boyarin, Smith states that this stark dualism is characterized by a preoccupation with clearly defined and impenetrable boundaries, limits, thresholds, and pollution. Therefore, the primary mode of interaction depicted by this binary opposition is a dual process of containment, that is, keeping in and keeping out. The threshold or boundary consequently assumes great prominence as the symbol and marker of the division between insiders and outsiders.

Smith, however, contends that Othering is much more complex than this basic and clearly defined binary opposition. It actually involves four possible alternative stances to the Other: like us; not like us; too much like us; and we are not like them. The deepest intellectual issues surround the third stance, which Smith terms the proximate Other in distinction from the distant Other. Distant Others (not like us) are so clearly distinguished that they are insignificant and voiceless. Since they are easily defined and contained, they require no exegetical effort. The proximate Other, however, is much more complex and amorphous. It is the Other who claims to be you. It is the Other-who-can-never-be-wholly-other. As a result, the proximate Other presents a direct and perpetual challenge to the worldview and self-identity of the initial group, forcing ongoing modification, reconsideration, and redrawing of boundaries. For Smith, therefore, the Other, the different, is not wholly distinct or discretely bounded. Difference—at least meaningful and meaning-making difference—is always relational, dynamic, and provocative.

Neither dominant trend in contemporary Islamic discourse effectively accounts for the complexity of this proximate Other. The trend of prioritizing religious sameness partially addresses proximity as defined by Smith but neglects Otherness by devaluing difference. Conversely, the attempt to affirm both religious sameness and religious difference neglects the full complexity of proximity by establishing clearly defined and distinct (even when related) religious wholes. However, Farid Esack and Ismāʿīl al-Fārūqī are two other contemporary Islamic scholars who begin to indicate alternatives to the shared conception of difference and thus begin to better account for the proximate religious Other.

Esack, a South African scholar and activist, is a professor in the study of Islam and head of the Department of Religious Studies at the University of Johannesburg. He earned his Ph.D. from the University of Birmingham, completed *Darsi Nizami* (a traditional Islamic studies program) in Pakistan, and previously served as the national commissioner on gender equality (appointed by Nelson Mandela). His scholarship and activism focus on interfaith relations, gender issues, hermeneutics, liberation theology, and Islam and AIDS. In his writing, Esack explicitly addresses the topic of identity and argues that the majority of interreligious thought and interaction is premised upon the notion of a stable self or stable religious community that adheres to a "package of essential and unchanging values, principles and beliefs which stand in contrast with the other equally stable, even if invariably 'lesser', other."[67] Like Boyarin, Esack maintains that this depiction—or distortion—masks that fact that identity is multiple and continually undergoing transformation. Esack, moreover, argues that the "insistence on viewing identity as stable, static, or monolithic" is reflective of an insecurity or fear about the fuzziness that may emerge if identity of self and Other were truly examined.[68] Despite the potential risks, he contends that it is essential to carry out such an examination:

> There is, however, only one way to live; through discovering what the self and other and their ever changing nature are really about, to understand how much of the other is really reflected in us and to find out what it is that we have in common in the struggle to a world of justice and dignity for all the inhabitants of the earth. To do so requires transcending theological categories of self and other that were shaped in and intended for another era and context.[69]

According to Esack, clinging to theological categories that were developed in another era, in another context, leads to injustice. He therefore seeks to transcend those categories through critical and selective reinterpretation and recontextualization of the Qur'ānic categories related to the religious self and the religious Other.[70]

Working from within his specific context—apartheid and post-apartheid South Africa—and utilizing a set of intertwined and dialectically related hermeneutical keys, Esack articulates a Qur'ānic theology of liberation grounded in an analysis of the Qur'ānic usage of categories, such as *īmān* (belief), *islām* (submission), *kufr* (disbelief), *ahl al-kitāb* (People of the Scripture), and *mushrikūn* (those who ascribe partners to God). His analysis uncovers an interpretative trend toward reification: terms that appear as dynamic qualities in the Qur'ānic text have been interpreted as "entrenched" labels that designate particular groups.[71] Rather than avoid such terms due to traditional and exclusivist interpretations, Esack aims to redefine them. His examination of the Qur'ān, however, is not aimed at introducing a new set of static delineations. On the whole, his reinterpretation is more concerned with demonstrating the nuances, dynamism, and exceptions related to such categories. For instance, he emphasizes the degrees and fluctuation of *īmān*, the active and conscious nature of *kufr*, and the exceptions related to negative evaluations of the *mushrikūn*. As these examples indicate, rather than eliminating fuzziness and complexity Esack is illuminating it and demonstrating that neat divisions are more problematic than most scholars admit.[72] The illumination of complexity, though, is not simply a postmodern indulgence. It is not, as some critics have contended, a dissolution of all distinction between the self and Other;[73] in contrast, it is an assertion that such distinction is dynamic, is in flux, and does not correspond to static designations of socioreligious communities. His illumination of complexity also is designed to facilitate his ultimate goal of advocating interaction, engagement, and practical cooperation across religious groups, based upon defined principles, and in the quest to fulfill the specific objectives of human liberation and justice.

Ismāʿīl al-Fārūqī (d. 1986) was born in Palestine, received his Ph.D. from Indiana University, and also studied at al-Azhar University in Egypt. He taught Islam and comparative religion at various universities, including Temple, McGill, al-Azhar, and Syracuse. At the time of his death in 1986, he was a professor in the Department of Religion at Temple University. al-Fārūqī founded many university Islamic studies programs, the Islamic Studies Group of the American Academy of Religion, and the International Institute of Islamic Thought.[74] Unlike Esack, al-Fārūqī does not explicitly address identity from a theoretical perspective. In his description of the relationship between Islam and other religions, however, he outlines a multifaceted and integrated approach that accommodates sameness and difference without resorting to isolation or to hierarchical evaluation of static, bounded categories.

Al-Fārūqī begins with an examination of the worldview inherent in the concept of *tawḥīd* (divine unicity or oneness). Based on this examination, he outlines five principles: that God and creation are utterly and absolutely distinct; that despite this distinction they are related and relevant to each other; that creation is teleological; that humankind is endowed with the natural capacities necessary to fulfill the divinely intended purpose; that creation is malleable to permit humankind to realize the will of God; and that due to humanity's capacity and creation's malleability humankind stands in a position of moral responsibility and accountability to God.[75] These principles, according to al-Fārūqī, are the common core of all revelations sent from God and delivered by prophets. Significantly, they are also "built by God in the very fabric of human nature, constituting the unerring natural religion or natural conscience upon which human acquired knowledge rests."[76] Al-Fārūqī thus presents a scenario in which knowledge of *tawḥīd* is accessible via two avenues: divine revelation and human nature (human reason).

He explicates the implications of these principles in terms of the theories of God, revelation, humankind, works and moral action, and society. Before even entering into the details of these theories, it is important to note that the sheer comprehensiveness of his approach is indicative of the fact that he is not aiming to reduce complexity or create neat compartments of difference.

In respect to God, al-Fārūqī stresses that every member of humanity is God's creature and vicegerent and that God did not "give any special status to any person or group."[77] All of humanity stands in the same relationship to God, with the same responsibilities and the same accountability. This illustrates a unique aspect of his approach. He is not simply presenting a more egalitarian model that allows the Other to be valued; rather, he is presenting an approach that both values the Other and holds the Other accountable to God.[78]

With revelation, al-Fārūqī contends that the divine will is knowable through a variety of sources, including revelation, science, the *sensus numinis*, and human nature (*fiṭra*). In his model, revelation has been given to all people—it is universal—and the other capacities have been instilled in all people through creation. The only distinction he draws between these sources of knowledge is that revelation provides certainty, whereas the other sources require humans to utilize and develop their innate faculties. He also states that while all of humankind has been "the object and subject of revelation," revelation can be lost, changed, or confused. This, though, does not render a person incapable of knowing the divine will, nor does it sever the relationship with God.[79]

His theory of humankind centers on the depiction of humanity as capable, innocent, and endowed with "innate perfections." Al-Fārūqī argues that, based upon human nature (*fiṭra*), every person—Muslim and non-Muslim alike—possesses *dīn al-fiṭra* (natural religion), and through this humans naturally arrive at a recognition of the principles of *tawḥīd*. While all historical religious traditions emerge out of *dīn al-fiṭra, dīn al-fiṭra* must be perpetually distinguished from them all. This is vital for al-Fārūqī because *dīn al-fiṭra* becomes a sort of measuring rod against which all historical traditions can be assessed and creatively reformed. Religions are therefore not compared with Islam, but all religions—including Islam—are to be compared with *dīn al-fiṭra*.

In terms of accountability to God, al-Fārūqī claims that good works are the most vital component and that the "lowest premium" is placed on self-identification with a particular religion. This follows necessarily from his emphasis on *dīn al-fiṭra*. Using the example of the *ḥanīf*, which he defines as a person who has *dīn al-fiṭra* without belonging to a particular religion, he argues that the explicit profession of faith is secondary. In fact, he contends that faith is just another "good work." There is value in it, but it is not a *prerequisite* for good works to be accepted by God. Finally, in relation to society, al-Fārūqī urges Muslims to mimic God's relationship with all of humanity, envisioning all others both as objects of concern and as moral subjects actively involved in fulfilling the divine will.

Through these theories, al-Fārūqī avoids simplistic and common delineations among religious groups. He acknowledges historical religious traditions in the institutional and reified sense, but he provokes essential questions about the value attributed to the discrete borders drawn between such traditions. He also draws upon similar ideas expressed by other contemporary scholars—especially Sachedina—but is unique in seeking to unite and integrate various components into an overarching, egalitarian, yet principled system.

Two Shortcomings

By and large the individual assertions of contemporary scholars are valid and valuable; however, the discourse manifests two crucial shortcomings. The first is the noted conception of religious difference as dividing humanity through the erection of clear, static, and impermeable boundaries. This conception results in the need to either neglect difference, isolate it, or rank it hierarchically. The first two, neglect and isolation, are not viable options in the contemporary era. The third, hierarchical assessment, is practically problematic as well. Moreover, it is conceptually insufficient in light of an understanding of the religious Other as the proximate Other that blurs boundaries and compels ongoing, complex consideration.

The second and directly related shortcoming in the contemporary discourse is the failure to integrate—rather than prioritize—a number of diverse topics including religious sameness, religious difference, interaction, dynamic relationality, and the teleological value of religious difference. The writings of Esack and al-Fārūqī, though, indicate potential ways to overcome each of these shortcomings. Esack provides an explicit articulation of dynamic religious identity upon which he bases his subsequent interpretation of the Qur'ān, and al-Fārūqī constructs an elaborate and integrated model of religious difference that aims to account for many of the aforementioned topics. Drawing upon these contributions and responding to the perceived shortcomings in the broader contemporary discourse, the remainder of this book focuses on the constructive articulation of an alternative conception of religious difference and of an integrated model of religious pluralism. It is this alternative conception and model that I have termed *Muslima* theology of religious pluralism.

2

Conceptual and Hermeneutical Foundations of Muslima *Theology*

3

Contemporary Muslim Women Interpreters of the Qur'ān: Hermeneutical Approach and Conception of Difference

IN OUTLINING HIS hermeneutical approach, Farid Esack argues that it is imperative to "center" Muslim minorities in contemporary Islamic discourse. Referring primarily to Muslims who do not live under Muslim rule, he states that minority perspectives are uniquely equipped to offer significant contributions to the discourse on pluralism and diversity. Minority perspectives, however, have been largely marginalized and ignored in efforts to articulate the relevance of Islam to contemporary challenges, such as religious diversity. In this chapter, I foreground the perspectives of a particular Muslim minority: Muslim women interpreters of the Qur'ān working in the context of the United States. These scholars are minorities in the sense that Muslims in the United States do not comprise a majority or live under Muslim political rule. More significantly, Muslim women interpreters are a minority in terms of their interpretative contributions and authority. Muslim women—whether silent, silenced, or unheard—have generally suffered from interpretative "voicelessness" within Islamic history; the Islamic interpretative tradition has historically been dominated and controlled by men. Thus, the mere inclusion of a largely excluded voice has the potential to offer new insights. However, this group of scholars is an essential resource in the construction of a *Muslima* theology of religious pluralism for another fundamental reason. The central interpretative task of these scholars is the elucidation of a

Qur'ānic conception of human difference, specifically sexual (i.e., biological) difference as distinguished from gender (the socially and culturally constructed roles of, for example, masculinity and femininity).[1] This conception of sexual difference is partially hermeneutical and partially theoretical; it is arrived at through a combination of insights revealed through a particular hermeneutical method and insights derived from the application of identity theory. As such, elements of this specific conception of sexual difference can be generalized and used as a guide in articulating other conceptions of human, particularly religious, difference.

In this chapter, I focus on the writings and scholarship of Amina Wadud, Asma Barlas, and Riffat Hassan. Amina Wadud, who received her Ph.D. in Arabic and Islamic studies from the University of Michigan, is an African American scholar of Islam, gender, and the Qur'ān. Prior to her early retirement, she was a full professor at Virginia Commonwealth University, and currently she is a research scholar at the Starr King School for the Ministry in California and a consultant at the International Centre for Islam and Pluralism in Indonesia. Asma Barlas, born in Pakistan, is currently the director of the Center for the Study of Culture, Race, and Ethnicity and a professor in the Department of Politics at Ithaca College. She received her Ph.D. in international studies from the University of Denver, and her scholarship focuses on the ideologies, epistemologies, and practices of violence; Muslim sexual/textual politics; and patriarchal interpretations of the Qur'ān. Pakistani American scholar and activist Riffat Hassan, who received her Ph.D. at Durham University in England, is widely recognized as a pioneer in the fields of Muslim women's reinterpretations of Islamic sources and the Islamic discourse on women's rights. She is a professor emerita in the religious studies department at the University of Louisville, from which she retired in 2009.

In addressing central issues related to women, biological sex, and gender, such as marriage, divorce, violence, and custody, these scholars share much in common with other Muslim women scholars. As a whole, though, contemporary Muslim women interpreters of the Qur'ān by no means form a monolithic or homogeneous group. While central areas of concern may be shared, interpretative approaches, conclusions, and contexts vary widely. I have specifically selected Wadud, Barlas, and Hassan from among this group due to their explicit emphasis on hermeneutical approach; their attempts to articulate an underlying framework upon which sexual (biological) difference is to be understood; and their situatedness within the context of the United States.

Qur'ān-Centered Hermeneutical Approach

The hermeneutical approach of Amina Wadud, Asma Barlas and Riffat Hassan is rooted in the relationship between their self-identification as Muslim women and the manner in which such identification influences their choice of interpretative sources, methods, and concerns. Many—including many Muslim women—have addressed the topics of gender, women, and Islam by drawing upon "an amalgam of Islamic modernist, secular nationalist, and humanitarian (and later human rights) discourses"[2] to advocate for gender equality. While recognizing similar inequalities and injustices in reference to women, Wadud, Barlas, and Hassan adopt a different approach. They aim to ameliorate the conditions of women and to redefine their status by returning to the Islamic sources themselves and reinterpreting them. This does not mean that they are inherently opposed to the use of extra-Islamic ideas and insights but rather that they begin with a positive valuation of the primary Islamic source—the Qur'ān—and with the conviction that the Qur'ān does not promote injustice or inequity. The return to and reinterpretation of the Qur'ān is seen as an effective and necessary weapon in combating injustice and reconceptualizing women's roles and status.

Thus, the central defining feature in the hermeneutical approaches of Wadud, Barlas, and Hassan is the focus on and prioritization of the Qur'ān. From a faith-based perspective, they view the Qur'ān as the "inimitable, inviolate, inerrant, and incontrovertible"[3] Word of God. As such, the Qur'ān's content and order are held to be unified, intentional, and purposeful. The Qur'ān is not simply a compilation of various verses revealed throughout the course of twenty-two years to Muḥammad; rather, it is a unified whole that expresses a divinely intended worldview and coherent moral ethos.

Underlying this view of the Qur'ān is a staunch critique of what Wadud refers to as traditional *tafsīr*, a genre of exegesis—whether classical or modern—that largely utilizes an atomistic methodology, working through the Qur'ān in a linear fashion making minimal effort "to recognize themes and to discuss the relationship of the Qur'an to itself, thematically."[4] In challenging this primarily male and largely androcentric interpretative approach, Wadud and Barlas advocate a hermeneutic that emphasizes textual holism, textual unity, and an overarching Qur'ānic worldview, or Weltanschauung. The exegetical task therefore involves a continual interpretative struggle to understand the Qur'ānic Weltanschauung, to derive central hermeneutical principles from it, and to interpret verses with constant reference to that worldview and those principles. To do so, these scholars mainly advocate *tafsīr al-Qur'ān bil-Qur'ān* (exegesis of the Qur'ān with primary reference to other parts of the Qur'ān). Through close intratextual reading; cross referencing of grammar, syntax, terminology, and structure; contextualization and recontextualization; and elucidation of larger Qur'ānic themes, the Qur'ān becomes the principal source of its own intratextual explication.

While Wadud, Barlas, and Hassan all discuss other interpretative sources, including the *sunna* (practice of Muḥammad), *aḥādīth* (narrations of the sayings, actions, and tacit approval of Muḥammad), *'ijmā'* (consensus of scholars), and *qiyās* (analogical reasoning), they hold the Qur'ān to be the main standard for theological reinterpretation and reform. Other sources are not wholly dismissed, but they are subjected to hermeneutical suspicion or "skepticism"[5] and are evaluated in light of the message and principles of the Qur'ān. This is especially important since all three of these scholars claim that it is from extra-Qur'ānic sources that the majority of patriarchal, androcentric, and unjust ideas about women have arisen and been legitimated. Their approach is intentionally designed to facilitate the unreading of such ideas.

Wadud, Barlas, and Hassan are also adamant about highlighting the fact that every encounter with the Qur'ānic text, including their own, is an act of human interpretation.[6] It is not possible simply to read the text and uncover its singular meaning. Rather, interpretation is an encounter between the text itself and the interpreter's prior text, meaning their historical and cultural situatedness, the context they bring to the reading of the text. There exists a dialectical interplay between these various elements, in which "every 'reading' reflects, in part, the intentions of the text, as well as the 'prior text' of the one who makes the 'reading.'"[7]

Invoking Fazlur Rahman's notion of a "double movement,"[8] the interpretative goal is defined as understanding the text by comprehending the original context and then extracting general principles or a general worldview, which can then be reapplied to the contemporary context. Barlas demonstrates, however, that the topic of context is not confined to questions of historical situatedness. Contextualization is an issue that arises within the Qur'ān itself (i.e., intratextually), between the Qur'ān and other Islamic sources (i.e., intertextually), and between the Qur'ān and historical context (i.e., extratextually). Barlas thus highlights the need for a multifaceted exploration of context, an exploration not only in terms of the text in history but also and initially in terms of the text within and in reference to itself.

Barlas is also concerned with the implications of the historical conflation and even overshadowing of the text with interpretation. This conflation misconstrues the role of the interpreter, presenting interpreters as receptive vessels without any impact or influence on the meaning. It is also directly tied to an obsession with textual monovalency or monosemy, the notion that the text has only one—or more accurately, only one *correct*—meaning. Contrary to this view, Barlas argues that the Qur'ānic text is in fact polysemic, open to multiple readings or interpretations. The polysemy of the text is not seen as a weakness or something to be overcome, even if overcoming it were possible, which she contends it is not. Rather, it is the essential nature of a universal, divine text.

Describing the Qur'ān as a "catalyst affecting behavior in society,"[9] Wadud similarly claims that interpretative subjectivity does not impede universal relevance of the Qur'ān. On the contrary, universal relevance is impeded "when one individual reader with a particular world-view and specific prior text asserts that his or her reading is the only possible or permissible one."[10] Such an assertion prevents readers in various contexts from forming "their own *relationship* to the text."[11] Wadud's use of the word relationship is worth considering in more depth, as it implies an ongoing interplay between text and context. The act of interpretation or reading is not monovalent, where the text disseminates a fixed meaning to all people in all times. Nor is it a situation in which the interpreter has completely free reign over the interpretation. These scholars conceive of interpretation as an ongoing relationship, engagement, and encounter with divine discourse and with the Divine itself. If either extreme—monovalency or complete relativism—is privileged, the universal message is lost.

Polysemy therefore does not equate to hermeneutical relativism. While the Qur'ān does say multiple things, it does not say everything; the Qur'ān does not permit every possible interpretation. There will never be one final interpretation of the Qur'ān, but there will always be convergences in interpretation based upon the fact that the text and principles are unchangeable. Moreover, despite the inevitability of polysemy, there remains an imperative and an ability to evaluate various interpretations. Barlas invokes the idea of "best precepts"[12] and derives methodological criteria from the Qur'ān for interpreting and assessing interpretations including intratextual holism, reading for best meanings, and using analytical reasoning. Although in keeping with the notion of polysemy she frankly admits that it is difficult to identify the best reading, she argues that is feasible to outline a field of possible interpretations and thus to discount many that fall clearly outside of that field.

Another central aspect of the interpretive approaches of Wadud, Barlas, and Hassan is the significance they attribute to textual silence. In outlining the main principles of her intratextual Qur'ānic method of analysis, Wadud, for example, describes attentiveness to "Qur'anic ellipses and textual silences" as the second most important principle of reinterpretation.[13] These are meaningful, and an effort should be made to interpret them in holistic reference to the entire Qur'ān. Barlas, likewise, describes Qur'ānic silence as "symbolically suggestive" and argues that it should not automatically be construed legalistically as consent to everything that remains unmentioned. [14] Other possible meanings—such as opposition, resistance, and indifference—should be considered in relation to Qur'ānic themes.

Hassan provides a vivid illustration of the emphasis on silence in her exploration of three fundamental assumptions and attitudes related to the creation and status of women: that man is God's primary creation; that woman was the cause of the Fall of humankind; and that woman was "created not only *from* man but also *for* man." [15] Hassan's methodology for examining these assumptions involves not only identifying extra-Qur'ānic sources of these ideas but also returning to the Qur'ān, examining what it *does* say on a particular topic, and emphasizing what it *does not* say. When she tackles the second assumption, for example, her analysis begins by discussing collective disobedience but then moves to focus chiefly on the absence of a notion of the Fall of humanity in the Qur'ān. If the Qur'ān, as the Word of God, is silent on a topic, this silence should be an important consideration in exegetical efforts. It therefore is not a carte blanche to fill in the blanks with information derived from other sources or cultural norms, especially when that information is inconsistent with the overarching Qur'ānic Weltanschauung.

The preceding example from Hassan also touches on the theological implications of certain interpretations. Even though many continue to be ready and willing to accept the notion that woman was responsible for the Fall of humanity, ironically, when isolated from the discussion of woman's culpability or status very few are inclined to accept the concept of the Fall itself. The Fall is widely held to be inconsistent with the Qur'ānic account of Adam and Eve and with Islamic theological anthropology. Muslim women interpreters, in advocating a unified, holistic approach to interpretation, stress the necessity of exposing such interconnections and implications and then using them as a system of exegetical checks and balances.

While Hassan employs theological implications to deconstruct extant interpretations, Barlas draws out theological interconnections and implications to construct the central principles of her hermeneutical approach. Highlighting the connection between divine ontology and divine disclosure (or speech), she states that any attempt to comprehend divine speech—that is, the Qur'ān—must be connected to or guided by an understanding of the divine "Being," of God. She then selects three theological principles to guide her interpretation: divine unity; divine justness; and divine incomparability.[16] By crafting her hermeneutical approach in this manner, Barlas underscores that no one topic of interpretation exists in isolation or is compartmentalized; all are intertwined with and have direct implications for other aspects of theology.

Interpretation should consider theological as well as social, moral, and ethical implications. Hassan holds that the real-life oppression of women is rooted in theological interpretation and that to overcome such oppression androcentric and misogynist theological foundations must be "demolished."[17] Wadud similarly connects interpretation and practical implications when she critiques "careless and restrictive" interpretations that have comprehensively and adversely impacted the lives of women.[18] Interpretation is not simply a game of meaning for these scholars; it is an endeavor that has immediate implications for the real lives of human beings. Interpretation of the Qur'ān defines practice, potentially changes practice, and at the very least legitimizes practice. Thus, the goal should be to articulate interpretations that are simultaneously theologically, contextually, and practically sound.[19] The goal is to formulate interpretations that highlight theological interconnections, consider historical and contemporary contexts, and undermine—or at very least do not perpetuate—injustice and oppression.

(Re)Conception of Difference

In addition to their unique hermeneutical approach, Wadud, Barlas, and Hassan also outline a novel conception of human difference. While focusing specifically on one genre of difference—sexual difference—they nevertheless proffer a general framework upon which to understand other forms of human sameness, difference, and the relationship between the two.

In returning to and rereading the Qur'ān, Muslim women interpreters endeavor to garner a more comprehensive understanding of the Qur'ānic discourse on men and women. This reinterpretation is largely impelled by the social and historical realities of women and the related patriarchal interpretations of Islamic sources. Such patriarchal interpretations, according to Barlas, are grounded in a binary conception of sexual differentiation, which presents man as the primary subject and woman as wholly and completely Other.[20] This conception is based upon the extension of sexual difference (i.e., biological difference) to an all-encompassing category that determines all aspects of human ontology and establishes a "gender dualism" in which biology (sex) is confused with "its social meanings (gender)."[21] This conception is problematic for two main reasons. First, it depicts one trait (biology) as determinative of all aspects—moral, social, ontological—of a specific group. Second, it not only conceives of the groups—men and women—as wholly distinct but more specifically also depicts the groups as being in opposition. Thus, in this patriarchal conception that emphasizes difference only, men are the central human subjects, and women are everything that men are not. Difference is pervasive and situated in a static hierarchy.

Responding to this difference-only conception, Muslim women interpreters begin their exploration by focusing on human sameness rather than human difference. Wadud, Barlas and Hassan all commence with a discussion of the Qur'ānic discourse on the origin and nature of human creation, in the hope of undermining the "notions of radical difference and hierarchy"[22] that characterize the exclusive focus on sexual difference. According to Hassan, the idea that it is considered "self-evident that women are not equal to men who are 'above' women or have a 'degree of advantage' over them"[23] is intimately related to certain pervasive theological assumptions about creation. As discussed in relation to her hermeneutical method, these assumptions include that man is God's primary creation, that woman was the cause of the Fall of humankind, and that woman was created from and for man. In an effort to understand the foundations of these assumptions and deconstruct them, she formulates three probing questions: How was woman created? Was woman responsible for the Fall? Why was woman created? These questions guide her analysis, leading her to emphasize undifferentiated humanity, the lack of a concept of the Fall in the Qur'ān, and equal status and responsibility for both men and women. Hassan summarizes her analysis: "Not only does the Qur'ān make it clear that man and woman stand absolutely equal in the sight of God, but also that they are 'members' and 'protectors' of each other. In other words, the Qur'ān does not create a hierarchy in which men are placed above women, nor does it pit men against women in an adversary relationship."[24] Wadud is concerned with similar assumptions and consequently explores four creation-related Qur'ānic words or concepts—*āya* (sign), *min* (among, from), *nafs* (soul, self), and *zawj* (pair, spouse)—as well as the Qur'ānic discourse on the Garden of Eden and the Hereafter.[25] Based upon this, she confirms Hassan's analysis, arguing that there is no distinction between men and women in regard to their creation, their status as subjects of divine guidance, or their status as recipients of rewards or punishments. In other words, every individual is created in the same manner. At the time of creation, every individual is placed into the same direct and intimate relationship with God. And every individual has the same potential for reaping rewards or punishments in the Hereafter. In surveying the ontology of a Single Self (*nafs*), Barlas arrives at a similar conclusion: "men and women originate in the same Self, at the same time, and in the same way; that is, they are ontologically coeval and coequal."[26]

By focusing initially on human sameness as manifest in creation, Wadud, Barlas, and Hassan advance three main conclusions. First, there is no inherent hierarchy in the human creation; the *nafs*, or humanity, was created as one without differentiation. Second, difference, as embodied in concept of the intentional *zawj* (pair) does not imply derivative status or an oppositional relationship. In contrast, a pair is conceived of as two equally essential forms of "a single reality...two congruent parts formed to fit together."[27] Third, women are not responsible for a rift between humanity and God, as no such collective rift is discussed within the Qur'ān, and human culpability is assessed only on an individual basis. Furthermore, women do not exist in a collective, mediated or indirect relationship with God.

Wadud, Barlas, and Hassan all initiate their reinterpretations by focusing on sameness, but they do not aim to replace the difference-only approach with one based upon sameness only. In fact, an exclusive emphasis on human sameness is deemed to be as "equally phallocentric"[28] as the emphasis on human biological difference alone. As with difference, if sameness is considered in isolation, it is extended to all aspects of human ontology, thus obliterating or ignoring vital and valuable difference.

Additionally, a sameness-only focus extends one norm to all individuals and groups. According to Barlas, even in a sameness-only approach man remains the normative subject and woman remains the Other. Thus, the male norm is generalized and presented as a universal human norm, as a "paradigm to define women."[29] The affirmation of a shared egalitarian humanity, therefore, does not result in an understanding of humanity as homogeneous. These scholars acknowledge differences between men and women; they are not interested in denying or reducing difference. What they are interested in is contesting the "pervasive (and oftentimes perverse) tendency to view differences as evidence of inequality"[30] and the resultant hierarchy, which has customarily depicted women as inferior, derivative, and in an indirect relationship with God.

They are also interested in articulating a new framework for simultaneously affirming both sameness and difference without resorting to a partitioned view of human existence. As Barlas clarifies, some interpreters of the Qurʾān willingly concede the equality or sameness of men and women in the moral realm of worship (*ʿibāda*). However, this is not extended to the social realm. Thus, while women may be created with equal capacity for righteousness and may be held equally responsible before God, they are not equal in the context of human-to-human encounters. Sameness characterizes human nature and potentially even the relationship of an individual to God; hierarchical difference reigns in social interaction. Barlas denounces this, arguing that such a division of the moral and social realms fails to account for the fact that "the Qurʾān defines moral personality in terms not only of *ʿIbadah*, but also in terms of responsibility to the *ummah* [community] and the two are connected and inseparable."[31]

The novel approach articulated by Muslim women interpreters thus aims to affirm sameness and to "think of difference itself differently so as to de-link it from biology and also from social hierarchies and inequalities."[32] This rethinking of difference, in contrast to the difference-only approach, does not ascribe sexual difference to essential human nature. As should be readily apparent from the discussion of human creation, the essential human nature is universal in men and women. This being said, difference is not depicted as degeneration from an original and perfect state of unity and sameness. As expounded upon by Wadud in her analysis of the fourth chapter of the Qurʾān, *Sūrat al-nisāʾ*, God created the undifferentiated *nafs* (soul, self) and then the *zawj* (pair).[33] This indicates that difference was also divinely intended. If difference is not a result of degeneration but is divinely intended, then it should not be eradicated: "by representing differences as an expression of God's Will... the Qur'ān... establishes the inappropriateness of trying to erase or obliterate them."[34]

Divine intentionality also implies value and purposefulness, and for these scholars the value or purpose of human difference is defined in terms of functionality, mutuality, and complementarity.[35] Difference is not viewed as something that divides or establishes bounded groups. On the contrary—through the examination of the Qur'ānic themes of divinely intended dualism and diversity in creation—difference is interpreted as the impetus toward a unique form of relationality in which neither particularity (maleness or femaleness) is automatically privileged but where the two are ideally engaged in a relationship of mutual benefit and functionality.

While functionality is stressed, it is not monolithically defined or fixed, except in reference to childbearing.[36] Wadud, for example, is keen to distinguish childbearing (the biological process of becoming pregnant, carrying the child, and giving birth) from childrearing, the socialization and care of the child. She states that only the former is confined to women. These interpreters judiciously emphasize that although difference exists and prompts relationships there is not one set model of relationship for all times and places for either male or female. The Qur'ān "does not strictly delineate the roles of women and the roles of man to such an extent as to propose only a single possibility for each gender."[37] Biological functions remain, but culturally determined roles are diverse and dynamic. Wadud underlines this flexibility through the Qur'ānic concept of *ma'rūf* (well-known, customary, equitable), which is often invoked in Qur'ānic verses detailing proper relationships between men and women. Based upon this, she argues that it implies a contextual sensitivity and flexibility. Barlas reiterates the same flexibility and dynamism by adamantly differentiating between biological sexual difference and the concept of gender. According to Barlas, the Qur'ān acknowledges the former but "does not even use the concept of gender to speak about humans."[38] Gender is a reified concept of static, rigid roles that is superimposed upon the text.

Barlas also argues that sexual difference has a functional and relational purpose but never serves as the basis for hierarchical differentiation between people. Sexual difference differentiates "laterally"—meaning it distinguishes individuals without ascribing value—but it does not differentiate "hierarchically."[39] Individuals are not assessed on the basis of their biology: in evaluation, "sex is irrelevant."[40] Wadud and Barlas maintain that the only basis for differentiating hierarchically between individuals is *taqwā* (piety, God consciousness), which is manifested and assessed on the individual level rather than based on affiliation with a particular group, that is, men or women. This, however, does not mean that an individual can strive for or achieve *taqwā* in isolation. It is always defined in the context of multiple relationships. Every individual is capable and responsible for himself or herself, but capacity and responsibility can be actualized only in relation to God, oneself, and other humans. The importance of this relationality is reflected in the structure of Wadud's reinterpretation. She begins with human origins and creation (the relation of human to God), moves to discuss women as individuals (human to self) and in the Hereafter (human to God), and ends with the rights and roles of women in the social context (human to human).

Wadud's discussion of *taqwā* also provides a concise summary of the overall conception of difference espoused by these Muslim women interpreters of Qur'ān. In reference to *Sūrat al-ḥujurāt*, 49:13:

> People, We created you all from a single man and a single woman, and made you into races and tribes so that you should know one another. In God's eyes, the most honored of you are the ones most mindful of God [those who manifest the most *taqwā*]. God is all knowing, all aware.

Wadud states, "It begins with creation. Then, it acknowledges the pair: male and female. These are then incorporated into larger and smaller groups…'that you may know one another.'…The culmination of this verse and its central aspect for this discussion is…*taqwā*."[41] In sum, their unique conception of difference begins with sameness, acknowledges intentional difference, conceives of the relationship between sameness and difference as purposeful, and concludes with the assertion that evaluative differentiation is possible only on the basis of individual *taqwā* (God consciousness) as manifest in a multifaceted series of relationships.

Forays into Religious Difference

Wadud, Barlas, and Hassan have not engaged extensively in the field of theology of religions, but they have all drawn general connections between oppression based upon sexual difference and oppression based upon other forms of difference, including religious difference. Moreover, both

Hassan and Barlas have specifically, yet somewhat cursorily, addressed the topic of religious diversity.

The general correlation between various forms of oppression is apparent in Wadud's critique of men "who require a level of human dignity and respect for themselves while denying that level to another human, *for whatever reasons.*"[42] She echoes this same concern with an explicit reference to religious difference when she argues that the contradiction between the intention of the Qur'ānic discourse and the historical development of Islamic civilization has resulted in a lack of social justice "particularly for women and non-Muslim minorities."[43]

Hassan voices similar sentiments to those expressed by Wadud, but she also writes explicitly on the Qur'ānic perspective on religious pluralism. In line with many of the previously discussed contemporary Islamic approaches, Hassan identifies *tawḥīd* (divine unicity or oneness) as the central defining principle in the Qur'ānic view of religious diversity; since God is one, God creates and cares for all of humanity.[44] Hassan also emphasizes what she refers to as the nonexclusive spirit of Islam by presenting Muḥammad's prophethood as universal, the Qur'ān as affirming previous revelations, and the Qur'ān as granting rights to all of humanity irrespective of belief. Addressing the intentional nature of religious diversity, she contends that "one of the basic purposes of diversity is to encourage dialogue among different peoples and also that a person's ultimate worth is determined not by what group he or she belongs to but how God-conscious he or she is."[45] She concludes her explication of the Qur'ānic perspective on religious pluralism by briefly touching upon the importance of tolerance and ethical action.

Hassan's approach to religious difference is clearly an example of the first trend presented in Chapter 2, that is, the prioritization of religious sameness. She acknowledges difference, but like Engineer does not mention or contend with any pluralism-ambivalent aspects of the Qur'ānic text. This is especially intriguing in light of the hermeneutical approach and conception of difference that I have outlined in this chapter. Hermeneutically, with reference to religious diversity, Hassan does focus on the Qur'ān, but not in a holistic fashion. Conceptually, she reiterates the notions of a shared, universal humanity and *taqwā* rather than religious group affiliation as the basis of God's ultimate judgment. These are the first and last components—the bookends—in the novel conception of difference outlined in relation to sex and gender. Hassan, however, does not grapple with the complexity of the intervening elements, including the purpose of diversity, the implications of that purpose for understanding divine ontology and human anthropology, and the different forms of diversity.

In her writing on sexual difference and gender, Barlas presents religious diversity as an example of the "necessary, and ... necessarily moral-social, function" served by difference. Moreover, she cites Qur'ān 5:48 and 30:22 as evidence of the divine intentionality of religious, racial, and linguistic difference:

> ... We have assigned a law and a path to each of you. If God had so willed, God would have made you one community, but God wanted to test you through that which God has given you, so race to do good. You will all return to God and God will make clear to you the matters you differed about. (5:48, excerpt)[46]
>
> Among God's signs is the creation of the heavens and earth, and the diversity of your languages and colors. There truly are signs in this for those who know. (30:22)

As divinely intended, no one of these forms of difference should be eradicated. Barlas, then, discusses *taqwā* as the only basis of hierarchical differentiation in the Qur'ān, stating that the evaluation of *taqwā* aims to "differentiate between belief and unbelief."[47] Although she does not apply the terminology herself, Barlas's juxtaposition of *taqwā* and belief/unbelief suggests that religions are divinely ordained forms of "lateral" difference, whereas belief and unbelief are hierarchical differentiations that do not automatically correspond with specific religions. Just as hierarchical differentiation is not carried out on the basis of sexual difference—or linguistic and racial difference—neither is it carried out on the basis of communal religious difference. *Taqwā* hence becomes a characteristic that is not automatically affiliated with one religion.

This depiction of difference is mostly reiterated in her work on Islamic universalism, tolerance, and religious diversity. Exploring the Qur'ān and the perspectives of al-Ghazālī and Ibn al-ʿArabī, she aims to demonstrate that "the principles of mutual recognition, tolerance, and respect for difference, which are necessary for peace and reconciliation, are integral to Islam."[48] She maintains that the Qur'ān does not make any ontological or epistemological distinctions based upon difference and that difference is divinely intended to encourage mutual recognition.[49] Further explicating the purpose of difference, Barlas describes mutual recognition as an ongoing process of dialogue by which individuals gain self-awareness and moral consciousness.[50] However, she is quick to clarify that "this does not mean that the Other serves as a mere foil for the self against which the self must construct itself oppositionally."[51] Based upon this view of the intentionality and purpose of difference, she concludes that difference is never presented in the Qur'ān as justification for violence. While human fear of both distant ("those who we think are wholly *different* from ourselves") and proximate ("those who we fear are too much *like* ourselves") Others has led to violence, this is not the Qur'ānic perspective. Even the "paradigmatic" and "special" status granted to Islam through the Qur'ānic assertion that Islam is the "culmination and perfection of religion,"[52] in Barlas's view, does not legitimate violence toward other religions.

Barlas's reflections on religious diversity are more extensive and complex than those presented by Hassan. Especially in reference to the construction of self and Other, Barlas demonstrates unique insight into the potential danger of the self being defined in opposition to, rather than in dynamic relation with, the Other. Some aspects of Barlas's approach, however, reduce complexity. One such aspect is her concern to demonstrate that Islam is consistent with tolerance and that it does not advocate violence on the basis of religious difference. These are laudable aims, but tolerance and lack of violence are not the same as a positive valuation of religious difference. Barlas intends to affirm difference as purposeful and valuable in and of itself, but her primary focus on tolerance does not compel her to thoroughly unpack the theological implications of purposeful and valuable difference. This is evident, for example, in the fact that she does not at all challenge the depiction of Islam as the perfection and culmination of all revelation. Rather, she simply asserts that this should not be used a license for violence or intolerance. As exemplified by Legenhausen, it is possible to construct a model of religious difference that integrates a belief in the perfection of Islam and also in the (limited) value of other religions. Barlas, however, does not attempt to explicitly outline such a model.

Trajectories of Analysis

The hermeneutical approach and complex conception of sexual difference outlined by Wadud, Barlas, and Hassan are capable of revealing unique and pivotal insights into religious difference. While this is not necessarily evident in their own nascent writings on religious diversity, it is my goal to co-opt significant elements of their hermeneutical approach and their conception of difference as the foundations for *Muslima* theology of religious pluralism. I articulate more specific aspects of this theology in later chapters, but at this juncture it is valuable to highlight some basic yet fundamental trajectories of analysis that arise from the preceding examination.

As with the discussion of sexual difference, in the discussion of religious difference a difference-only approach that emphasizes the oppositional definition of bounded groups will be inadequate. The attempt to understand religious difference must begin by focusing on and understanding the complexity of human sameness, or theological anthropology. However, a focus on sameness alone will be equally inadequate due to its neglect of vital differences—especially in terms of the social and practical manifestations of religion—and its attempt to present a particular religious norm as an all-inclusive universal norm. As with nonreductive efforts such as those of Nasr, Shah-Kazemi and Legenhausen, both sameness and difference must be affirmed, but a new understanding of the connection between the two—an alternative to both isolation and hierarchical evaluation—is essential. This new understanding will emerge in part from an attempt to discriminate between various genres of religious difference, from an examination of the purpose and value of divinely intended religious difference, and from a comparative examination of the Qur'ānic discourse on religious difference, including the concept of *taqwā* (God consciousness) in relation to the reified definition of religion.

Although certain elements from these scholars' conception of sexual difference can readily be generalized and embraced in a novel, complex, and integrated conception of religious difference, any attempt to do so must acknowledge that the categories of sexual difference and religious difference are not of the same genre. It is, for instance, possible to argue that biological sex is given at the time of creation, whereas religious difference develops later and involves some element of choice. This being said, choice in religion may be more a theoretical postulate than a reality, as many people retain the religion of their birth. Religion thus assumes an inherited and socialized dimension that complexifies any discussion of religion as individually chosen. Nonetheless, the concept of religion cannot simply be plugged in or substituted for biological sex, and the question of what other aspects and theories can appropriately be extended to the topic of religious difference must be critically and deliberately explored.

4

From Sexual Difference to Religious Difference: Feminist Theological Approaches to Religious Difference

ONE RESOURCE FOR this critical and deliberate exploration is the existing discourse on religious difference written by feminist theologians from other religious traditions. Even though it remains true that "the distinct perspective of feminist thought has not yet fully engaged the issues of religious pluralism,"[1] in the last three decades a small number of feminist theologians have made important contributions to the field of theology of religions. These scholars have not simply taken up religious difference as a novel and distinct subject matter. Rather, they have approached theology of religions as another example of a discourse in which the universalization of a particular norm has resulted in the oppression and marginalization of individuals and groups that do not conform to that norm. Their unique perspectives are thus the direct result of a conscious endeavor to apply the foundational theories and insights of their feminist reflections on sexual difference, gender, and androcentrism to the topic of religious difference.

It is this conscious endeavor to apply conceptual insights to religious difference that makes their contributions of great value in constructing a *Muslima* theology of religious pluralism. Of particular relevance are the critique of the standard typologies of theology of religions, the struggle to affirm particularity without necessarily resorting to hierarchical evaluation, and the incorporation of identity theory into the discussion of religious diversity. These various components not only resonate with the basic conceptual model I outlined at the end the preceding chapter but also offer insights into how to overcome the shortcomings highlighted in respect to the majority of contemporary Islamic approaches to religious difference. Consequently, my examination of these contributions aims to identify various elements that are consistent with and thus capable of guiding the extension of the conception of difference extracted from the work of Muslim women interpreters of the Qur'ān. Since these feminist theologians come from various religious traditions, though, it is necessary to explore their perspectives critically and comparatively—rather than adopt them in toto—to avoid flattening out fundamental epistemic differences or universalizing a particular feminist theological perspective to all women.[2]

In line with this critical eye to interreligious convergences and divergences, it is helpful to begin by briefly probing some of the core methodologies, sources, and norms of feminist theology, as articulated by Rosemary Radford Ruether. Professor emerita at Pacific School of Religion, Graduate Theological Union, and Garrett Evangelical Theological Seminary, Ruether received her Ph.D. in classics and patristics from Claremont Graduate School. She is recognized as an early pioneer and an innovator in Christian feminist theology, and she has also taught and written extensively on Catholic thought and practice, eco-feminism, and social justice issues.

While Ruether explicitly acknowledges that her perspective is necessarily particular—she refers to it as *a* feminist theology rather than *the* feminist theology—it provides a starting point for comparative analysis and dialogical engagement. Ruether herself recognizes that different religions and cultural groups will create other paradigms of feminist theology, but she nonetheless hopes that her general model can serve as a working paradigm to stimulate dialogue amid diversity. Moreover, Ruether's overview of feminist theological insights on sexual difference demonstrates meaningful overlap with the theological approaches and concerns of Muslim women interpreters. Meaningful overlap in reference to sexual difference indicates the possibility of meaningful overlap in reference to religious difference as well.

Dialogue amid Diversity

Ruether defines feminist theology as an approach that aims to apply feminist critiques and reconstructions of gender to theological discussions. On the critical level, this involves questioning and challenging theological formulations that present justifications for male dominance and female subordination. These theological formulations, according to Ruether, include "exclusive male language for God, the view that males are more like God than females, that only males can represent God as leaders in church and society, or that women are created by God to be subordinate to males and thus sin by rejecting subordination."[3] Feminist theology, though, is concerned not only with critiquing and deconstructing dominant theological formulations but also with formulating egalitarian and gender-inclusive versions of "the basic symbols of God, humanity, male and female, creation, sin and redemption, and the church."[4] Reconstruction involves reclaiming and developing egalitarian themes within the tradition and can be effective only when theological symbols are recognized to be socially constructed rather than eternal and unchangeable.

Although the targets of critique and the sources of development differ, Muslim women interpreters are similarly engaged in the processes of criticizing, deconstructing, and reconstructing theological formulations and interpretations. However, to claim authority and in line with their view of the Qur'ānic text, Muslim women interpreters typically position their reconstructive efforts as an uncovering or reiteration of what is actually present in the text but has been obscured through patriarchal interpretation. Another interesting divergence in these processes is the degree to which Muslim women interpreters do or do not explicitly bring feminist theories to bear on theology and interpretation. Whereas Asma Barlas is quite explicit and detailed in her use of theoretical insights related to sex and gender, Amina Wadud and Riffat Hassan premise their critiques primarily upon a negative evaluation of social oppression. Barlas, of course, recognizes this oppression as well, but she is more specific about the underlying assumptions and structures of oppression. The reticence of some Muslim women interpreters to explicitly engage feminist theory is, not surprisingly, an extension of the complex relationship between Islam and feminism.

Ruether further explains the social construction of theological formulations and symbols by highlighting the centrality of human experience in the process of interpretation. Although she maintains that the role of human experience has been downplayed in classical theologies, she contends that human experience has always been and will always be the "starting point and the ending point of the hermeneutical circle."[5] In drawing attention to the role of experience in interpretation, feminist theology exposes the fact that, despite the facade of objectivity, classical theology has been based upon male experience not universal human experience.

The hermeneutical role of human experience also indicates that every revelatory experience gains meaning only through social mediation. Mediation takes place in specific social and cultural settings: "the hand of the divine does not write on a cultural *tabula rasa*."[6] Even though meaning-producing mediation is an ongoing process, it has historically been subjected to channeling and control, through which a dominant group identifies a correct interpretation and marginalizes and suppresses all other interpretations. According to Ruether, this is the process whereby an orthodox interpretation and a canon are established. However, human experience continues to play a role despite the reification of the tradition; the institutionalized orthodoxy and canon remain vital as long as they continue to resonate with contemporary human experience. When resonance dwindles or ceases, a crisis of tradition ensues: "religious traditions fall into crisis when the received interpretations of the redemptive paradigms contradict experience in significant ways."[7]

Ruether's views on human experience and social mediation align well with the stress Wadud, Barlas and Hassan place upon context and ongoing interpretation. Wadud, for instance, discusses the interplay between prior text (the cultural situatedness of an interpreter) and the text (the Qur'ān) to highlight the active role of the interpreter and the interpreter's context in the process of ascribing meaning to revelation. Barlas similarly invokes the concept of polysemy to argue that interpretation of revelation takes place within and in relation to context. It is an ongoing process, despite the rhetoric of monosemy and monovalency that has periodically characterized Islamic discourse. To shed light on these tendencies, Barlas carries out an extensive multitextual examination: she explores the intratextual elements of the Qur'ān, the intertextual relationship of the Qur'ān to other Islamic sources, and extratextual relationships in sociopolitical contexts. Furthermore, in adopting the approach of Fazlur Rahman, these Muslim women interpreters again acknowledge that all revelation occurs within a specific context and that for the message to retain its universal relevancy it must be recontextualized within each new context. It is precisely when recontextualization does not take place that the relevancy is jeopardized. While they do not utilize the terminology of crisis, it is in fact a fitting description.

Ruether argues that crises of tradition can be experienced at various levels and to various degrees and thus can evoke various responses. The least radical level results in exegetical criticism, in which the traditional methods of transmitting knowledge are affirmed but new interpretations are formulated. She describes the second type of crisis as more drastic in that it depicts institutional structures as corrupt. As a result, it aims to go behind the historical tradition to access the authentic original revelation, original founder, and early stages of tradition: "The original revelation, and the foundational stages of its formulation, are not challenged but held as all the more authoritative to set them as normative against later traditions."[8] Ruether astutely recognizes that this return to origins is impossible, but she presents it as a more comprehensive strategy for opening up interpretative possibilities in an effort to account for contemporary experience. The third type of crisis—the most radical—deems the entire religious heritage, including the original revelation and founder, corrupt and thus moves outside of the heritage to seek alternative sources of truth.

Wadud, Barlas, and Hassan are most aligned with Ruether's second type of response to crisis. It is clear that they have prioritized the original revelation and that they are seeking to reinterpret that revelation to bypass the historical legacy of patriarchal and androcentric interpretation. They have set the Qur'ān as the standard against which all secondary sources and exegetical efforts must be judged. They do, however, not completely dismiss the traditional methods, and therefore there is some overlap with the first type of response as well. The primary method of *tafsīr al-Qur'ān bil-Qur'ān* (exegesis of the Qur'ān with primary reference to other parts of the Qur'ān), for example, is a classical methodology that has been employed throughout Islamic history, although with divergent conclusions. While other Muslim women scholars have certainly taken the third route—deeming the entire tradition to be corrupt—this is not the approach of Wadud, Barlas, and Hassan. Nor is it the approach of *Muslima* theology.

One interesting observation, which Ruether does not mention but with which she may agree, is that there is another possible response to crisis, which is often voiced by those interested in maintaining the established tradition despite the experience of crisis. In this response, the crisis is attributed to deviation or degradation in the social or cultural context. Its cause is seen not as a failure to socially mediate revelation and theological formulations but rather as an increasing gulf between "true" theological formulations and a "corrupt" society. The burden in such a scenario falls on society, not theology; society must be brought back in line with the formulations and interpretations. Neither the formulations or the interpretations need to be changed. This perspective has certainly been voiced within the Islamic tradition as an outcome of the pervasive tendency to equate universal relevance with interpretative monovalency. If only one interpretation is correct, then only one interpretation is required regardless of time or context. Therefore, if there is tension between the interpretation and the context, it must be due to a problem in the context. This response to crisis is not favored by most feminist theologians or Muslim women interpreters, but it is one with which they must contend in exerting their interpretative authority.

Another key feature in Ruether's articulation of feminist theology is her assertion that the critical principle of feminist theology is the "the promotion of the full humanity of women":

> Whatever denies, diminishes, or distorts the full humanity of women is, therefore, appraised as not redemptive. Theologically speaking, whatever diminishes or denies the full humanity of women must be presumed not to reflect the divine or an authentic relation to the divine, or to reflect the authentic nature of things, or to be the message or work of an authentic redeemer or a community of redemption.[9]

This principle is largely based upon her assessment of the implications of androcentrism and the oppression of women for the pivotal theological paradigm of *imago dei* (image of God), which asserts that humans are created in the image of God and thus have inherent value. When men are presented as the norm of authentic humanity—as the true or complete *imago dei*—women are subjected to scapegoating and marginalization. With scapegoating, women are negatively evaluated as the oppositional inverse of the ideal male norm. With marginalization, women are presented as an incomplete or inferior version of the ideal male norm. For Ruether, both depictions distort and contradict the *imago dei*, and the paradigm becomes an instrument of sin rather than something that discloses the divine or grace.[10] Ruether, however, is quick to indicate that the same sort of distortion or corruption would result from a simple reversal of norms, that is, from presenting women as the ideal. Hence, the goal is to search for a more inclusive—yet not homogenizing—depiction of universal humanity.[11]

Promotion of the full humanity of women is undoubtedly the objective of Muslim women interpreters of the Qur'ān as well. Hassan, for example, criticizes traditions that depict women as being created from and for man and as being responsible for the Fall. In dismissing these traditions due to conflict with the Qur'ān, she aims to re-present women as much more than derivative, secondary, or blameworthy. In a move similar to Ruether's description of scapegoating and marginalization, Barlas argues against dualistic depictions of men and women and against bifurcated depictions of women as being morally but not socially equal to men.

While *imago dei* is a distinctively Christian theological paradigm, Muslim women interpreters also attempt to connect views of women's status with conceptualizations of the divine. Barlas contends that interpretations promoting injustice or patriarchy not only depict women and thus affect them negatively but also misrepresent God, who is described in the Qur'ān as the most just and incomparable. This strategy highlights the importance of assessing the validity of interpretations and theological paradigms in light of their implications for and interrelationships with other aspects of the theological worldview.

Theology of Religions: Feminist Theological Critiques and Contributions

Ruether has also written explicitly on the topic of religious diversity, and, notably, her perspectives on this topic grow directly out of her reflections on sexual and gender difference. Consequently, she argues that the rejection of androcentrism—the presentation of a particular human norm as a universal human norm—necessitates the criticism of all forms of chauvinism, including the presentation of Christians as the norm of humanity. She clarifies by stating:

> This is not a question of sameness but of recognition of value, which at the same time affirms genuine variety and particularity. It reaches for a new mode of relationship, neither a hierarchical model that diminishes the potential of the "other" nor an "equality" defined by a ruling norm drawn from the dominant groups; rather a mutuality that allows us to affirm different ways of being.[12]

Just as Ruether contends that men are not the norm for all of humanity, she similarly argues that Judeo-Christian theological reflections do not have an automatically privileged relation to God, truth, or authentic humanity. This means not that all theological reflections or religions are the same—difference as well as sameness is important—but that the norms are not drawn from one specific tradition.

Exploring various Jewish and Christian perspectives on universalism and particularism, Ruether further opines that the view that one religion has "a monopoly on religious truth is an outrageous and absurd religious chauvinism."[13] In contrast to this exclusive view, she posits a universal Divine Being and the existence of true revelation and a true relationship with the Divine in all religions. Feminism's specific challenge to the notion of one universal faith, according to Ruether, is its illumination of a history of male domination, marginalization of women, and rampant androcentrism within virtually all religious traditions. In light of this history and the resultant exclusion of women "from defining their meaning or being recognized as fonts of authority for the traditions,"[14] feminists simultaneously offer an incisive critique and search for more inclusive and representative alternatives. Similar to her general framework of feminist theology, she notes that the search for alternatives may take many forms but can be divided into two primary trends. First is the search within the tradition for critical and more inclusive perspectives that facilitate development of the tradition. The second is the creation of new models. Noting the hostility with which many retrievals have been met, she concludes that the second trend is the only sufficient response: "Feminist theology cannot just rely on exegesis of past tradition, however ingeniously redefined to appear inclusive. It is engaged in a primal re-encounter with divine reality and, in this re-encounter, new stories will grow and be told as new foundations of our identity."[15] As a result, she encourages the writing of new stories, the creation of a feminist midrash, and the development of interfeminist dialogue.

Marjorie Hewitt Suchocki, like Ruether, also discusses universal norms. Suchocki is a professor emerita at the Claremont School of Theology and co-director of the Center for Process Studies. She received her Ph.D. in religion from Claremont Graduate School, and her scholarship focuses on process theology, feminist thought, and critical interpretation of Christianity. Suchocki argues that the identification and application of norms, when combined with power, permits and encourages exploitation and distorts the perspectives of those falling outside of the norm. This general depiction of normativeness applies to religion as well, and Suchocki contends that universalization of religious norms leads to judgment, oppression, and injustice. In her view, feminists cannot accept these outcomes, and therefore they must "radically affirm religious pluralism."[16] Acceptance of religious pluralism by feminists, however, does not mean relativism. While feminists "accept the uniqueness and self-naming quality of each religion,"[17] they nevertheless distinguish between religions by employing the ethical criterion of justice. The invocation of justice is tied to another key element of her feminist perspective on religious pluralism: the notion that discussions of religious diversity and justice should be premised upon ethical, rather than ideological grounds. For Suchocki, justice is a necessary criterion as "the norm for judging the value of an alternative form . . . could not simply be doctrinal, but historical and ethical."[18]

Perhaps Suchocki's most significant contribution, though, is her discussion of the correlation between religious imperialism and sexism. She observes that feminists have critiqued sexism on two accounts: the universalization of male experience; and the attribution of negative or problematic qualities to women. She equates these two forms with religious inclusivism, in which a religious norm (e.g., Jesus Christ) is extended to all religions, and religious exclusivism, in which reprehensible qualities are assigned to other religions and their value is negated entirely. This parallel, for Suchocki, confirms her view that feminists must necessarily affirm religious pluralism.

The writing and research of Judith Plaskow, a professor of religious studies at Manhattan College who received her Ph.D. from Yale University, focuses on contemporary religious thought, Judaism, and feminist theology. These interests are evident in her pivotal work *Standing Again at Sinai*. In this book, she is primarily concerned with articulating a feminist perspective on Judaism, but couched in the larger argument is an important discussion of the general manner in which Judaism approaches difference. Plaskow argues that Judaism valorizes difference, assessing it in a dualistic and hierarchical manner. For Jewish females, this results in their depiction as simultaneously Other and inferior. Echoing Suchocki, she equates the internal depiction of women with the external distinction between Jew and non-Jew. Here, the concept of *chosenness* takes center stage, defining and valuing all other religions in terms of Judaism. From these insights, Plaskow advocates a two-pronged hermeneutic of suspicion and remembrance, which is capable of fostering a "thorough reconceptualization of the way that difference is understood and portrayed"[19] within Judaism. Chosenness must be replaced with distinctiveness, in which hierarchical dualisms are absent.[20] Drawing connections between chosenness and the traditional Jewish conception of God, she also advocates a corrective employment of a plurality of images for God to give voice to those who have been excluded and a simultaneous recognition of the limitations of all human language about God.

Concerned with the equally "shaky foundations" of exclusivist, inclusivist, and pluralist mainstream Christian approaches to theology of religions, Kate McCarthy asserts that feminist theology offers "exciting and timely" resources for developing a new approach.[21] Currently associate professor of religious studies at California State University–Chico, McCarthy received her Ph.D. from Graduate Theological Union, and her work centers on Latin American liberation theology, interfaith dialogue, Third World feminist theology, and American religion. She identifies the central challenge of religious pluralism as the ability to encounter the Otherness of religious Others without subsuming that Otherness or sacrificing the distinctiveness of one's own religious identity. In response to this challenge, feminist theology and women's experience offer three primary resources. The first is women's immediate experience of Otherness; women have been the Other within religious and interpretative communities. While this has not always been a positive experience, feminist theologians have used their sensitivity to particularities to resist the totalizing impulses of most mainstream theology. The second resource is plurality of social location. McCarthy here draws upon the idea that women have a "consciously plural identity"; they inhabit multiple social locations in multiple communities.[22] Such plurality is not unique to women—in fact, it is a condition of all human experience—but she argues that women are especially aware of particularity, multiplicity, and the impossibility of a universal perspective. As a result, feminist theologians have attempted not to subsume difference under a universal norm but rather to affirm difference, to live the "riddles of difference" by holding together the plurality of identities in dynamic and creative tension.[23] The third resource that McCarthy highlights is embodied spirituality, the reliance on bodily experience, and analogical theology to imagine possibilities beyond formal theological doctrine.

After indicating these three potential resources, McCarthy endeavors to highlight their theological implications in reference to religious pluralism. The first implication relates to the hermeneutical audacity of feminist theologians, who approach scripture and tradition in a highly critical and selective manner. She contends that this is well suited to opening up new avenues, to thinking the unthinkable, in theology of religions. The second implication relates to the doctrine of God. Describing feminist conceptions of God as relational, fluid, and integrated—rather than reified and static—she envisions an alternative to both relativism and exclusivism, which "can condemn as error that which isolates and breaks away from such relationality but endorse and indeed depend upon diverse manifestations of the divine relationship."[24] The final implication she highlights is the reorientation of Christology toward life-centered soteriology rather than metaphysical questions. This permits the depiction of dialogue and cooperation with other religions in the quest for a just worldly society as salvific.

Like McCarthy, Ursula King notes the parallel between the Otherness of women and the Otherness of religious traditions, between the "full and equal participation of women and that of the full and equal dignity and respect accorded to all religions."[25] King, who received her Ph.D. from King's College, University of London, is professor emerita of theology and religious studies and senior research fellow at the Institute for Advanced Studies at the University of Bristol. In her scholarship, she examines women and spirituality, gender issues in world religions, Pierre Teilhard de Chardin, and interfaith dialogue.

In addition to the parallel between sexual and religious Otherness, King also discusses the marginalization, exclusion and invisibility of women in general discussions of religious pluralism, as well as in interreligious dialogue. Despite this lack of representation, she holds that the challenge of feminism could develop into a challenge in theology of religions if feminist theologians examined the standard classifications. The classifications of exclusivism, inclusivism, and pluralism lack nuance and are "much too narrow, static and insufficiently differentiated to capture the organic, fluid and dynamic reality of religion ... nor ... the subtleties and existential commitment of faith."[26] Moreover, King contends that the categories are thoroughly androcentric in that they are intended to be universally and comprehensively applicable. Feminist theologians, however, have widely neglected theoretical analysis of these categories and other linguistic and conceptual aspects of theology of religions. King encourages such investigation, arguing that the inclusion of feminist perspectives and voices will necessitate radical transformation and potentially foster "fuller disclosure of the powers of the Spirit whose oneness embraces and transcends all differences."[27]

Buddhist practitioner and feminist theologian Rita Gross is a retired professor of comparative studies in religion at the University of Wisconsin–Eau Claire. She received her Ph.D. in history of religions from the University of Chicago, and her research and writing focus on patriarchy and religion, Buddhism, social justice, feminism, and religious diversity. In her work focused explicitly on the relationship between the latter two, she draws attention to the lack of an articulated feminist theology of religions. Exploring the question of what feminism *could* bring to the development of theologies of religions, however, she specifies two trajectories: the ethical necessity of inclusivity, that is, the hearing of heretofore excluded voices; and the epistemological quest to "widen the canon," that is, "rejecting the binding authority of the past and... searching for new traditions."[28] Ethically, she believes that feminists must inevitably accept religious pluralism over exclusivism and inclusivism: it is the only "suitable" option.[29] Having suffered exclusion, it is inconceivable for a feminist to exclude others. In this, Gross reiterates the parallel between sexism and religious exclusivism; "exclusive truth claims in religion function as the religious equivalent of biased statements regarding race, gender, class, sexual orientation, or culture..."[30] The epistemological quest presents a greater challenge in its focus on learning *about* and *from* other religions. Here, Gross introduces the concept of the comparative mirror, which critically reveals strengths and weaknesses in our own tradition and presents us with alternatives—a wider canon—that would be difficult to arrive at solely within the context of our own religion.

In more recent work, Gross utilizes the Buddhist metaphor of "fingers pointing to the moon" to emphasize that religious teachings are neither absolute nor ultimate truth. She also reiterates Suchocki's view that ethical considerations are more important than doctrine and that theologies of religious pluralism should be concerned with ethics rather than metaphysics.[31] For Gross, difference, including the existence of conflicting truth claims, is unproblematic in and of itself; difference is problematized only when it assumes the unethical form of imposition.

The most intricate and extensive feminist discussion of religious pluralism comes from Jeannine Hill Fletcher in her book *Monopoly on Salvation?: A Feminist Approach to Religious Pluralism*. Associate professor of theology at Fordham University and co-chair of the Roman Catholic studies group of the American Academy of Religion, Hill Fletcher received her Th.D. from Harvard Divinity School, and her research is concerned with systematic theology, theologies of religious pluralism, global Christianities, and feminist and postcolonial thought. Searching for theological resources with which to formulate a Christian conception of other religions, Hill Fletcher highlights a central and creative tension in Christian thought between making affirmations about the divine and holding that God is ultimately incomprehensible, between "God as known and unknown, God as hidden and revealed, God as spoken and unspoken."[32] Following Karl Rahner, in reference to incomprehensibility, she advocates an understanding of divine mystery as "overabundance" rather than "absence." This forms her starting point in reflecting on religious diversity and leads her to argue that other religions may "have insights to be affirmed of this mysterious overabundance as well."[33] While no religion—not even Christianity—captures the whole of the divine reality, each may communicate something real. Hill Fletcher clearly asserts that both affirmation and incomprehensibility are vital; "the tradition of affirmations must be held in balance with the tradition of incomprehensibility."[34] This notion of balance is precisely what preserves the creative tension, a tension that deepens and continues the ongoing process of knowing God. Hill Fletcher, though, contends that historically this tension has been diffused through a disproportionate emphasis on affirmation or an assertion of the particularities of revelation in Jesus Christ and salvation.

Examining contemporary Christian theologies of religions, Hill Fletcher outlines three criteria for a Christian theology of religious pluralism: it must offer strategies for communication across and among faiths; it must maintain continuity with the affirmed tradition in Jesus; and it must be attentive to material and practical consequences. Based on these criteria, she argues that the typology of exclusivism, inclusivism, and pluralism is "tired" and that the "discourse on religious pluralism seems to be in desperate need of fresh insights and alternative ways of thinking in order to keep the conversation moving in new directions."[35] Standard typologies and approaches to theologies of religions have reached an "impasse of sameness and difference."[36]

Specifically, she describes exclusivism as promoting an affirmation-heavy, God's-eye view that, while not directly tied to physical violence, can foster antagonism and discourage communication. Inclusivism embraces the notion of incomprehensibility absent in exclusivism but nonetheless problematically extends a Christian norm to all religions. This limits blatant dismissal of other traditions but simultaneously impedes the sincere motivation to learn about the distinctive affirmations of religious Others. She critiques pluralism for explicitly seeking sameness while implicitly privileging Christian ideals and norms. As a result, in pluralism, "the distinctiveness of any given community is dissolved under the now universalized qualities of singular human fulfillment,"[37] that is, salvation.

In addition to critiquing the standard tripartite typology as a quest for sameness, Hill Fletcher also sees significant shortcomings in those approaches, for example, George Lindbeck's cultural-linguistic model and S. Mark Heim's model of multiple salvations, which emphasize difference in this world and in the eschaton. Such models depict religions as incommensurable and not only discourage communication but also promote the idea that true understanding is impossible. In sum, exclusivism, inclusivism, pluralism, and the particularism of Lindbeck and Heim arrive at an impasse due to the fact that they all function to distance Otherness. Exclusivism and particularism defend difference but promote incommensurability, thereby inhibiting the possibility of interconnections across religions. Inclusivism and pluralism highlight sameness, thereby "erasing" Otherness and ignoring significant differences.

Hill Fletcher contends that this impasse is the direct result of a particular view of Christian identity as collectively shared, wholly distinct, static, and internally homogeneous. Drawing upon Iris Young's logic of identity, she argues that emphasis on a single identity feature leads to a fixation with defining static boundaries, with defining in and out, pure and impure. She further expounds upon this conception of identity using Ulrich Beck's container theory, in which religions are depicted as facts to be studied in a taxonomic manner: religions are separated, placed within a limited set of containers, and ordered for comparison.[38] Hill Fletcher states that although inclusivism, pluralism, and particularism, respectively, promote hierarchy, parity, and radical difference, they all nonetheless operate on the same conception of religions as distinct and discrete entities. This depiction of identity, however, is a conceptual tool capable of accounting only for total sameness or radical difference, not the actual diversity and dynamic relationships that exist among and within religious groups.

In response to this homogenizing perspective, she proffers an alternative view of identity. Drawing on feminist identity theory, she asserts that identity is neither based on one feature nor static or homogeneous; it is hybrid and always embedded in a complex web of dynamic, intersecting relations.[39] Hill Fletcher reconceives of religious identity as a verb, not something that is simply ascribed by the label *religion*. As a verb, identity is relational and is reconfigured continuously based upon our interactions. Identity is not constructed abstractly in isolation, and it is never fixed.

Rather, it is formed precisely at the points of interaction with diversity, at the contact zones of fluid cultural traffic that engender not static religious identities over against one another but hybridities that dissolve the boundaries between "us" and "them."

Consequently, hybridity also challenges the logic of identity and the container theory by demonstrating that borders and boundaries between the discrete religions are an imposed theoretical construction. Borders are actually dynamic and in flux, and as a result religious homogeneity—or purity—is an illusion. This depiction destabilizes the two central emphases on sameness universalism or hierarchical Otherness that Hill Fletcher identified in relation to categories of exclusivism, inclusivism, pluralism, and particularism. As an alternative, she depicts persons and religious identities as interwoven across religions.

Based on this reconceptualization of identity, she opines that religious distinctiveness is not an insurmountable obstacle that prevents communication, understanding, or cooperative action. On the contrary, the "overlap in our webs of identity" creates relationships in which we can "retell" and "reweave" our various stories.[40] Diversity thus becomes a gift, an opportunity to learn more about God. And as a gift it should not be erased or distanced; it should be valued for its transformative potential, its illumination of the complexity and overabundance of God, and its enabling of us to partake in the complex Divine mystery.

Another unique perspective on theology of religions comes from Kwok Pui Lan, who earned her Th.D. from Harvard Divinity School and is the William F. Cole Professor of Christian Theology and Spirituality at Episcopal Divinity School and former president of the American Academy of Religion. Building upon her broader research interests in Christian theological reflection and practice in the postcolonial world, feminist theology, and women and Christianity in global contexts, Kwok argues that theology of religions must be examined in relation to contemporary political interests and American imperialism. Echoing the views of Hill Fletcher, she criticizes the typology of exclusivism, inclusivism, and pluralism as all being explicitly or implicitly based upon Christian norms. She examines pluralism in greater depth, focusing specifically on the models proposed by John Hick, George Lindbeck, and feminist theologians.[41] Hick's pluralism, according to Kwok, is based upon liberal, Western political ideals and is patronizing in the manner in which it glosses over religious differences. She connects Lindbeck's emphasis on incommensurable difference with American foreign policy and clash of civilizations rhetoric.

She also underscores that Lindbeck presents a view of religion as "narrowly constructed and tightly bound."[42] Referring to feminist theologians, including McCarthy, King, and Gross, she praises their intentions, but argues that they largely speak from a 'white' context and therefore ignore contributions from other feminist theologians throughout the world.

On a more general level, Kwok states that it is vital to scrutinize two underlying assumptions that enable pluralistic models of theology of religions: "an uncritical use of the category of 'religion' and the problematic construction of 'world religions.'"[43] These two assumptions are ideological constructions of Western and Christian thought, and, as such, they are impositions upon other traditions, which impede Western comprehension of other faiths and that can be employed to obscure meaningful difference.

As an alternative to pluralism, she advocates the development of a "postcolonial theology of religious difference" that questions the utility of the reified and bounded conception of religion.[44] She contends that it should focus not on truth claims in isolation but rather on multiple and complex intrareligious and interreligious networks. Similar to Boyarin, she draws upon the work of David Chidester and contends that, when the focus is shifted from reified religion to complex, contested relations, the central issue is no longer "religious diversity, but religious difference as it is constituted and produced in concrete situations, often with significant power differentials."[45]

Kathleen McGarvey, an Irish nun and member of the Missionary Sisters of Our Lady of Apostles, also addresses theology of religions from a feminist perspective. She received her Ph.D. in missiology from the Pontifical Gregorian University in Rome, and her writing and activism focus on women's interfaith efforts, interreligious dialogue, ecumenism, and conflict resolution. As general coordinator of the Interfaith Council of Muslim and Christian Women's Associations in Nigeria, she examines the relations between and discourses of Muslim and Christian women in Northern Nigeria. As part of this endeavor, she evaluates the standard paradigms of theology of religions, highlights areas of commonality between feminist theology and theology of religions, and constructs a feminist-ethical response to religious pluralism.

Like many of the feminist theologians discussed herein, she holds that pluralistic approaches to theology of religions have highlighted either sameness or difference, with a resultant neglect of the necessity and importance of dialogue, which is central in her study of the Northern

Nigerian context. By focusing on sameness or difference alone, "there is no room or need for dialogue. Either there is no Other to dialogue with, or else the Other is so much Other that dialogue is impossible."[46] In addition to this general criticism, she specifically argues against John Hick's universal phenomenalist pluralism because it lacks attention to the fact that diverse religious paths actually come into conflict over both what and how they see. Raimon Pannikar's particularist phenomenalist pluralism, which focuses on a singular mystical approach giving rise to diverse doctrinal expressions, is similarly ill equipped to address pressing issues related to social harmony. With the particularist approach of S. Mark Heim, McGarvey highlights that an emphasis on different paths and salvations leads to a lack of relationality and mutual responsibility. Finally, in reference to the soteriocentric-ethical pluralism promoted by scholars such as Paul Knitter, she supports its ethical focus but problematizes its other basic assumptions, including that there exists a shared view of justice, that praxis must precede doctrinal discussions, and that rules for dialogue can be outlined prior to dialoguing.

Like McCarthy, McGarvey states that feminist theology has much to contribute to the discourse of theology of religions. Since feminist theology grapples with issues of sameness, difference, and Otherness in concrete and diverse contexts, it could potentially provide the foundations for a new paradigm that overcomes the perceived weaknesses. McGarvey highlights certain similarities between feminist theology and theology of religions to justify this perspective including recognition that the Other has frequently been depicted in an essentialized and negative manner, that a universal norm for all of humanity is problematic, and that there is a need to distinguish critically between timeless truths and historical prejudices.

In light of this overlap, she indicates specific contributions that feminist theology could make to theology of religions. Two are of particular import. The first is her challenge to the assumption, which is made by most feminist theologians involved in theology of religions, that a feminist approach would necessarily be pluralistic. McGarvey contends that this is not the case, since pluralistic models generally attribute equal value to all religions. Feminist theologians do not assign equal value to every religion or religious practice, especially those that oppress or marginalize women, and therefore "it would be incoherent for feminist theologians to say that one religion, opinion or belief is automatically as good as another."[47] She argues that a feminist approach would not automatically give equal value to all religions, nor would it automatically require the denial of unique truth claims. Rather, it would be an inclusivist approach that sought to "purify" truth claims of historical prejudices.

The second contribution she indicates is a focus on ethics, but with a reconceptualization of the criterion of justice as something that is created in the process of dialogue, not universally affirmed. According to McGarvey, this overcomes many of the shortcomings of other approaches to theology of religions as it recognizes particularities and gives them a voice in the process of dialogue, does not apply a theoretical universal norm, allows for context-specific variations, and retains a sense ethical responsibility.

Based upon these areas of contribution, McGarvey articulates her feminist-ethical response to religious pluralism. Like Kwok's postcolonial theology of religious difference, this response focuses on the complexity of human existence rather than isolated truth claims. Although her response begins with praxis, she redefines praxis not only as social action but also as a shared examination and discussion of lived realities and the role that religious doctrines play in those realities. Such praxis may lead toward doctrinal reformulation, but only on a context-specific rather than universal basis. As an inclusive model, the goal is not to deny truth claims but to reexamine them and have them grow in meaning through the process of dialogue over shared concerns and in recognition of mutual solidarity and global responsibility. In her feminist-ethical response to religious pluralism, McGarvey clarifies, the ultimate goal is that "adherents of each religion will seek to include the other and be responsible for the other, but will not impose on the other."[48]

Insights and Extensions: Toward a Muslima *Theology of Religious Pluralism*

As is evident in the preceding survey, feminist theologians have proposed a wide variety of distinctive and intricate insights into religious pluralism and theology of religions. Some of those insights are particularly appropriate for extending the general conception of difference drawn from Muslim women interpreters of the Qur᾽ān to the specific topic of religious difference, thereby forming the conceptual basis of a *Muslima* theology of religious pluralism.

Before endeavoring to illuminate these extensions, however, certain theories that have been widely promoted within this emergent field must be subjected to critical scrutiny. One of the most glaring is the direct equation of sexual difference and religious difference. As noted in my discussion of Muslim women interpreters of the Qur'ān, the direct equation of the two is an oversimplification because religious difference involves an element of choice that is not present with sexual difference. It is clear that both sexism and religious exclusivism have promoted unfavorable depictions and oppression of their respective Others. Nevertheless, these objectionable outcomes should not obscure the nuances of each form of difference. Many feminist theologians seemingly overlook the significance of this distinction.

Another critique arises in reference to the discussion of norms and the sources from which norms are derived. The majority of these feminist theologians veer away from the blatant extension of a particular religious norm to all other religions, and they aim to affirm the particularity of the religious Other. Yet with varying degrees of success they simultaneously wish to avoid relativism. Therefore, many of them turn to ethical principles, such as justice (Suchocki) or the promotion of the full humanity of women (Ruether), as substitute criteria by which religions or religious practices can be assessed. While I will discuss this form of evaluation in greater detail later in this chapter, the assumption that such ethical criteria are not premised upon particular norms is in itself tenuous, as McGarvey notes.

Additionally, as seen with McCarthy, the notion that women are somehow especially aware of particularity, multiplicity, and the impossibility of universalizing norms comes dangerously close to essentialism. Awareness of particularity, multiplicity, and universal norms is not something that is inherently linked with female biology; rather, such awareness is linked with the experience of Otherness, especially the experience of being the powerless Other. This is why similar insights, even the use of identity theory, appear in the work of male scholars, such as Farid Esack, who are writing in light of their experiences with other forms of oppression and exclusion.

Despite these critiques, there are many valuable and relevant insights and extensions. The first is related to the standard typology of theology of religions: exclusivism; inclusivism; pluralism; and sometimes particularism. Many of the feminist theologians explicitly support the model of religious pluralism over and against inclusivism or exclusivism, the latter of which is characterized as outrageous and absurd. Religious pluralism is deemed to be the only possible option. While Gross's fairly simple argument is that women's experience of exclusion makes it inconceivable for feminists to exclude other Others, Suchocki presents a more complex rationale for her selection of pluralism, equating exclusivism with the assignment of negative attributes to the religious Other and inclusivism with the extension of one specific norm to all religions. Suchocki's depiction of exclusivism and inclusivism aligns with Ruether's depiction of scapegoating and marginalization. Convergences have already been highlighted between Ruether's depiction and Muslim women interpreters' conception of difference. As a result, it is fairly clear that in their most standard definitions exclusivism and inclusivism will not be viable models for *Muslima* theology. The question of whether pluralism in its stock formulation would be the ideal alternative, however, remains.

While Gross contends that the suitability of pluralism is not "a controversial point among feminist theologians,"[49] a number of the scholars surveyed disagree and highlight deficiencies in all three models of the standard typology. King, for example, describes the typology as a whole as narrow, static, and lacking nuance. Hill Fletcher depicts the models and theology of religions more broadly as having reached an impasse of sameness and difference, a stalemate resulting from a focus on either sameness universalism or hierarchical Otherness, from the universalization of Christian norms, and from a particular conception of religions and religious identity. McGarvey and Kwok voice similar criticisms, although they are focused primarily on pluralistic models. McGarvey notes the inability of pluralism to deal simultaneously with sameness and difference, which results in either a singular focus on sameness (as if there is no Other) or a singular focus on difference (as if the Other is too Other). Kwok's critique of pluralism, moreover, underscores the problematic nature of the reified concept of *religion*, describing it as a Western and Christian imposition. Significantly, in his critique of reductive pluralism, Legenhausen uncovers some of the same deficiencies that feminist theologians identified. Even though his nonreductive alternative has some limitations, his evaluation of the focus on sameness alone and the implicit universalization of Christian norms underscores the inadequacy of a standard pluralistic model.

The evaluations offered by King, Hill Fletcher, McGarvey and Kwok of pluralism specifically and of the entire typology also have much in common with my assessment of the two major shortcomings in the contemporary

Islamic discourse on religious diversity: the conception of difference as dividing humanity through the erection of clear, static, and impermeable boundaries; and the lack of a model that integrates diverse considerations including sameness, difference, and interaction. Hill Fletcher's discussion of the logic of identity and Kwok's critique of the category of reified religion echo the shortcomings identified with a bounded, static, discrete view of religious difference. McGarvey's explanation of the focus on either sameness or difference raises the issue of accounting for the proximate Other. Based upon these convergences, in this *Muslima* theology I will follow these scholars in attempting to move beyond all of the standard models and to construct a new model.

For feminist theologians, the central issue at stake in the construction of a new model is difference. This is not to imply that the feminist theologians focus only on difference; rather, it indicates that issues surrounding difference have been the foremost sticking points in theologies of religions. Frequently, difference has been rejected, ignored, and downplayed. When acknowledged, it has raised questions about the relationship between various "differents," which have been answered primarily through hierarchical evaluation or relativism. Feminist theologians are thus faced with a difficult dilemma in that none of these options is acceptable. Their experiences of diversity and Otherness, their sensitivity to the presentation of a particular norm as a universal norm, and their inability to affirm relativism all necessitate that they develop a novel way by which to conceive of difference differently.

Ruether, for instance, states that religious differences or particularities must be considered and valued. Valuing, however, should be based not upon hierarchical assessment or application of a universal norm but upon recognition of a new type of relationship: mutuality. Plaskow similarly argues that the Jewish concept of chosenness should be reconceived as distinctiveness so that the relationship between Jewish and non-Jewish religious communities can be understood in a nonhierarchical fashion. If acknowledging and valuing difference is required—which is evident with feminist theologians—what is the alternative to hierarchical evaluation?

As was seen with Seyyed Hossein Nasr's depiction of religious universes, one alternative is to adopt a view of different religions existing in isolation. This, of course, is a difficult strategy to apply in the actual contemporary world. Akin to my assessment of Nasr's approach, McGarvey criticizes a number of pluralistic models based precisely upon their inability to account for the fact that different religions and religious communities interact and conflict in the real world. Furthermore, the preceding allusions to Ruether and Plaskow demonstrate that for many feminist theologians the acknowledgment and valuing of difference is connected to relationality. Notably, the conception of difference drawn from Muslim women interpreters involves a similar linking of difference and relationality; the telos of divinely intended difference is to facilitate certain relationships, relationships described variously as mutual, complementary, or functional but never hierarchical. It is in light of this that Wadud describes attempts to ignore or eliminate difference as spiritually, morally and socially counterproductive. A model that values difference based upon isolation therefore is an unacceptable alternative for both feminist theologians and *Muslima* theology. The question thus becomes how to account for and value difference *with* relationality but *without* hierarchical evaluation.

Before exploring the strategies feminist theologians adopt to achieve this, an important clarification must be made. Feminist theologians all seem to voice an unequivocally negative assessment of hierarchical evaluation. In reality, however, they do not reject all hierarchical assessment. Ruether, McCarthy, Suchocki, and McGarvey, for example, dismiss relativism as a model of religious pluralism. If this occurs, then they must adopt some standard for comparative evaluation. For Ruether, the standard is the promotion of the full humanity of women. For Suchocki, the standard is justice. These standards are not based (or not supposed to be based) on the exclusive norm of one religious tradition, but they are nonetheless standards of evaluation that rank religious practices and teachings according to various degrees of value, that is, in a hierarchical fashion. The real contention of these scholars therefore is not that all hierarchical evaluation is problematic. What is at issue is hierarchical evaluation that describes something as automatically good or automatically bad based *only* upon affiliation or nonaffiliation with a particular religious community. A strong parallel exists between this more nuanced explication of feminist theologians' perspectives on hierarchical evaluation and the differentiation Barlas draws between lateral and hierarchical difference. Lateral difference, with which she associates sexual, cultural, linguistic, and communal religious variation, can never be the subject of evaluation. Hierarchical difference, which is associated with variations in *taqwā* (God consciousness) alone, is the only locus of evaluation.

Returning to the question of how feminist theologians account for and value difference with relationality but without *illegitimate* hierarchical evaluation, it is notable that McCarthy, Hill Fletcher, Kwok, and McGarvey all adopt the same strategy: they utilize insights drawn from identity theory to reconceptualize difference. Whereas standard models of theology of religions all operate from a shared conception of religions as clearly distinct entities, identity theory challenges these assumptions, presenting individual and group identity as multifaceted, embedded, and dynamic. McCarthy draws upon notions of multiple identity and multiple social locations. Hill Fletcher offers a complex reinterpretation of religious difference in her critique of the logic of identity and the container theory and in her introduction of the concepts of hybrid identity and a web of relationality. Kwok struggles with the reified conception of religion because it is a Western, Christian imposition but also because it in no way accounts for complex, ongoing, and contested relations. A similar emphasis on the construction of identity through interactions and relationality is put forth by McGarvey and defines her description of and emphasis on dialogue.

The Muslim women interpreters I have examined do not utilize identity theory in the same explicit manner. Barlas, however, does differentiate between sexual (biological) difference and the reified concept of gender, arguing that while the Qur'ānic text discusses the former it never mentions the latter. Wadud makes an analogous contention when she states that the Qur'ān does not dictate any particular, fixed social roles outside of the biological act of childbearing. The aversion to the reified concept of gender is connected to the desire to account for the complexity within the Qur'ānic text, to contextualize it, and to ensure its enduring relevance. Therefore, while Muslim women interpreters are focused on the Qur'ānic text and interpretation, they are asserting the same concern for dynamic and complex relationality. The more explicit application of identity theory, therefore, would support and further explicate this concern in relation to both sexual and religious difference.

The appropriateness of this extension to the topic of religious difference is supported by the use of identity theory in Esack's work. His approach is capable of accounting for the proximate Other—capable of overcoming one of two main shortcomings identified in contemporary Islamic discourse—precisely because he employs insights drawn from identity theory to argue against the notion of a stable self. Recognizing that religious identity is complex and dynamic, he embarks upon an exploration of the Qur'ānic discourse in which he illuminates the complexity and dynamism of central categories that denote religious difference. Esack also raises a challenge to reification through the focus of his analysis. While the Qur'ān does mention certain historical religious communities (e.g., the Jews and Children of Israel), Esack primarily focuses not on these historical groups but rather on the Qur'ānic categories of *īmān* (belief), *islām* (submission), *kufr* (disbelief), *ahl al-kitāb* (People of the Scripture), and *mushrikūn* (those who ascribe partners to God) and argues that they are complex, fluid, and not aligned in a fixed fashion with any particular historical community.

Notably, the application of identity theory to the Qur'ānic text diverges significantly from the perspective of some feminist theologians, who argue for the prioritization of ethics over doctrine in discussions of religious diversity. Suchocki, in employing the liberative concept of justice, advocates the sidelining of doctrinal and ideological concerns. Likewise, Gross argues that the focus should be placed on ethical rather than metaphysical questions. However, it is not as easy to quarantine doctrinal and metaphysical questions as Suchocki and Gross suggest. McGarvey, for instance, perceptively contends that a universal concept of justice does not exist, and therefore an operative concept of justice must be developed in the process of dialogue. Moreover, she argues that doctrinal formulations have a direct bearing on ethical perspectives and must be discussed in the context of dialogue and social action.

Muslim women interpreters of the Qur'ān concur with McGarvey about the interconnections between ethical and doctrinal formulations. In fact, their entire reinterpretative enterprise is premised upon the notion that the Qur'ān is an invaluable source of ethical guidance, which can help to unravel some of the historical formulations and interpretations that have led to less than just circumstances. In many ways, there exists an ongoing dialectic between doctrine and ethics. Certain doctrinal formulations are viewed as unethical and thus as contradictory to the Qur'ānic text. Therefore, they return to the Qur'ānic text to illuminate alternative doctrinal possibilities. In turn, those doctrinal reformulations are used to present a necessary and invaluable challenge to other formulations that legitimate oppression, exclusion, and injustice. This process continues in various contexts and in response to various circumstances. Muslim women interpreters, in fact, define Qur'ānic universality in terms of the ongoing capacity of the Qur'ān to provide the foundations for contextually responsive and ethical doctrinal possibilities.

In articulating a *Muslima* theology in Part 3 of this book, like Esack I will apply insights garnered from identity theory to illuminate the Qur'ānic discourse on religious difference by stressing complexity, fluidity, and multiplicity. However, I will push beyond Esack's approach and retain the emphasis on relationality that is so essential to feminist theologians. This means that instead of focusing primarily on the dynamism within individual Qur'ānic categories my analysis will pay particular attention to the interconnections, points of contact, and border zones among Qur'ānic categories of religious difference. Moreover, in contrast to the historical tendency to seek clarity through the forced reduction of Qur'ānic complexity and the enforcement of static boundaries between these categories, I will explore the dynamic intersections among categories in an effort to illuminate guidance that arises out of the complexity.

Bringing together the approach to difference drawn from Muslim women interpreters and the extensions drawn from feminist theologians, the conceptual outline of a *Muslima* theology of religious pluralism emerges. *Muslima* theology will diverge from standard models of theology of religions (including exclusivism, inclusivism, and pluralism) that are based on difference or sameness alone and aim to articulate an integrated, multifaceted alternative. It will target both religious sameness and difference as well as the relationship between the two. In reference to religious difference, *Muslima* theology will challenge the fixation with viewing difference as dividing humanity through the erection of clear, static, and impermeable boundaries. In contrast, it will utilize the insights of identity theory to explore the complex and dynamic web of relationality that exists within the Qur'ānic discourse on the religious Other.

5

From Holistic Interpretation to Relational Hermeneutics: Toshihiko Izutsu's Semantic Analysis of the Qur'ān

THE QUESTION NOW arises as to whether or not the hermeneutical model of Muslim women interpreters is capable of providing the necessary methodological infrastructure for carrying out this project. Many elements of *Muslima* theology are drawn directly from the conceptual framework of Muslim women interpreters. However, significant conceptual extensions result from insights drawn from identity theory and the primary emphasis placed on relationality. Is the hermeneutical method of Muslim women interpreters suited to explicating dynamic and complex relationality within the Qur'ān? Or, as was the case with their basic conception of difference, do some hermeneutical extensions need to be made when moving from a discussion of sexual difference to a discussion of religious difference?

Certainly, the primary focus upon and representation of the Qur'ān is appropriate. So too is the emphasis placed upon polysemy, as it allows the dynamism inherent in the text to be retained. If there is no pretense to having uncovered the one and only meaning of the text, then complexity and dynamism are not seen as something that must be contained or simplified. Furthermore, the multifaceted consideration of theological, contextual, and practical implications remains vital in reference to the new topic of religious difference.

With regard to exploring the Qur'ānic discourse on religious difference, the main shortcoming in the hermeneutical approach of Muslim women interpreters relates to the manner in which they carry out *tafsīr al-Qurʾān bil-Qurʾān* (exegesis of the Qurʾān with primary reference to other parts of the Qurʾān). While they do emphasize textual holism and unity, they have primarily depended upon cross-referencing, retranslation, and thematic and historical contextualization of *individual* terms and concepts. For instance, Amina Wadud's reinterpretation of the term *zawj* (mate, spouse, pair)[1] as two equally essential and intentional parts of a larger whole is formulated by citing other verses that use the term in relation to plants and animals and other verses indicating that pairing is a universal aspect of all of creation. She also discusses the term *zawj* in relation to the Hereafter, focusing on verses such as Qurʾān 37:21–22: " 'This is the Day of Decision, which you used to deny. Gather together those who did wrong, and others like them (*ʾazwājahum*), as well as whatever they worshipped.' " The plural of *zawj*, *ʾazwāj*, is commonly translated as "wives" or "spouses." Wadud critiques this translation and invokes thematic and historical contextualization to argue that the Qurʾānic theme of individual responsibility rules out any interpretation depicting the *zawj*'s fate as contingent upon another person. Likewise, she critiques the conflation of *zawj* with *ḥūr* (companions in Paradise), stating that it reduces the "Qurʾanic depiction of the highest reality to a single ethnocentric world-view."[2] The value and novelty of Wadud's method and interpretative conclusions are not to be dismissed, but these strategies alone are not sufficient to illuminate the dynamic relationships and overlap among multiple Qurʾānic terms and concepts. As a result, it is necessary to supplement the hermeneutical approach drawn from Muslim women interpreters of the Qurʾān with insights that are consistent with their approach but are capable of elucidating relationships and complexities in the Qurʾānic discourse.

A highly suitable resource for such supplementation is the method of semantic analysis proposed by Toshihiko Izutsu (d. 1993), who taught at Keio University in Tokyo (also his alma mater), McGill, and the Royal Institute of the Study of Philosophy in Tehran. In addition to the works discussed in this chapter, he also published widely on Islamic Sufism, Hindu Advaita Vedanta, Mahayana Buddhism (particularly Zen), and Philosophical Taoism.[3] Similar to Muslim women interpreters, Izutsu's semantic analysis focuses principally on the Qurʾānic text, conceiving of it as a unified whole with a distinctive worldview. Izutsu's method, however, ascribes great significance to the intratextual relational context in determining the meaning of key Qurʾānic concepts. This attentiveness to relational context is capable of providing insights necessary for exploring—without reductionism—the Qur'ānic discourse on religious difference.

Relational Meaning and the Semantic Weltanschauung: Toshihiko Izutsu's Method of Analysis

Toshihiko Izutsu defines semantics as the analysis of a language's key terms to eventually arrive at "a conceptual grasp of the *weltanschauung* or world-view of the people who use that language as a tool not only of speaking and thinking, but, more important still, of conceptualizing and interpreting the world that surrounds them."[4] Based upon this definition, he clarifies that his application of semantic analysis to the Qur'ān is in fact an endeavor to explicate the distinctive Qur'ānic Weltanschauung, an endeavor to investigate "how, in the view of the Scripture, the world of Being is structured, what are the major constituents of the world, and how they are related to each other."[5] As the preceding quote indicates, Izutsu's primary focus is not on individual Qur'ānic concepts. While analysis of individual concepts has value, a central premise of his semantic approach is that the various concepts comprising the Qur'ānic—or for that matter any—worldview do not stand in isolation from one another; rather, they are "closely interdependent and derive their concrete meanings precisely from the entire system of relations."[6] Individual concepts are woven together into a complex conceptual system (worldview), and therefore what is most vital is to garner an understanding of the relationships and interconnections between concepts.

Consistent with this emphasis, Izutsu distinguishes between what he calls the basic and relational meaning of words. He defines basic meaning as the meaning or conceptual content an individual word has and retains outside of the Qur'ānic context. Izutsu states that although the basic meaning perpetually inheres in the word it does not exhaust the meaning of the term.[7] In the context of the Qur'ān, every word also has a relational meaning, a connotative meaning defined by its complex and particular relations to other Qur'ānic words and concepts. The relational meaning is determined by "the word's having taken a particular position in a particular field, standing in diverse relations to all other important words in that system."[8] Since he is interested in elucidating the overarching worldview, Izutsu emphasizes the primacy of relational meaning over basic meaning.

The structure of the whole conceptual system, or the semantic Weltanschauung, is closely knit and determined by a number of important words or concepts, which Izutsu refers to as key terms. Acknowledging a degree of arbitrariness in the identification of key terms within the Qur'ān, he nevertheless contends that they constitute the general pattern of the conceptual vocabulary through their diverse and multiple relations with each other. Underscoring the fact that concepts do not exist in isolation and that the conceptual vocabulary is never a haphazard collection, Izutsu states that the diverse and multiple relations between individual concepts result in a multitude of overlapping areas or semantic fields. Each semantic field is composed of multiple key terms that cluster around one focus word, aparticularly important key term.

His depiction of the semantic relations in the Qur'ān is further complexified by the fact that key terms and even focus words are not restricted to only one semantic field; they normally have a "multiple relationship to many other words that properly belong to other fields."[9] A key term in one field may be a key term in another; it may be the connecting link between two systems. In fact, this is virtually universal since the semantic fields of the Qur'ān are largely overlapping. Moreover, a key term may be the focus word of another semantic field, and inversely a focus word may be a key term in a different field. The overlapping focus words, key terms, and semantic fields thus form countless associative interconnections that define the distinctive character of the organized and unified semantic Weltanschauung. In light of this depiction, Izutsu describes the process of semantic analysis as being initially focused on "trying to isolate major conceptual spheres of the Qur'an, then... engaged in discovering how these various spheres or semantic fields, large and small, are delimited by their neighbors, how they are related with one another, how they are internally structured, and how they are organized and integrated into the largest multi-strata system, i.e., that of the whole Qur'an."[10] Semantic analysis of the Qur'ān can be carried out in synchronic and diachronic fashions. In the synchronic approach, the Qur'ān is treated as a complete vocabulary, and the goal is to illuminate the distinctive aspects of that vocabulary. Diachronic semantic analysis aims to compare vocabularies at different historical intervals. Izutsu, for example, compares the Qur'ānic Weltanschauung to both the pre-Qur'ānic (*Jahili*) worldview and various post-Qur'ānic worldviews.[11] In diachronic analysis, he emphasizes that regardless of the fact that different vocabularies may share many of the same words the words are structured according to different patterning

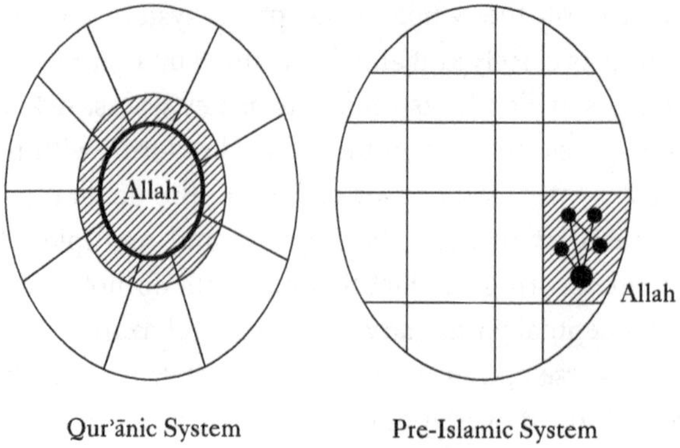

FIGURE 5.1 Reproduced with permission from Toshihiko Izutsu, *God and Man in the Koran: Semantics of the Koranic Weltanschauung* (Tokyo: Keio University, 1964).

principles; they are understood and situated in different conceptual relationships. For example, he discusses how the Qur'ān utilizes some of the same concepts that were prevalent in pre-Qur'ānic discourse. The Qur'ān, however, transposed them into a different network, configuring them into different relations with other concepts, and thus modifying old meanings and producing new meanings. One prominent example of this phenomenon, according to Izutsu, is the concept of Allāh, God (Figure 5.1).[12]

In the Qur'ānic system, the concept of Allāh presides over the entire vocabulary and over all semantic fields; it is the supreme focus word. By contrast, in the pre-Islamic system the concept of Allāh was situated in only one semantic field, side by side with other concepts such as *āliha* (gods/divinities) and without significant contrast to them. As is evident in this example, a change to any one concept in an integrated Weltanschauung reverberates throughout the entire system. The transposition of the concept of Allāh reflects not only a change in the meaning of that one concept but also a worldview that has been totally restructured in a theocentric fashion.

The Qur'ānic Weltanschauung: Conceptual Opposition and a Basic Moral Dichotomy

Despite the focus on complexity and nuance in his semantic method, Izutsu nonetheless describes the overarching Qur'ānic Weltanschauung as a large multistrata system built upon conceptual opposition.[13] He states that conceptual opposition—and the resultant aura of strain and tension—pervades the Qur'ānic system, manifesting in a series of specific oppositions, the first of which is the opposition of God and humankind.[14] Although he recognizes that nothing can truly stand in opposition to God, who as Creator is the center of all being, Izutsu describes the Qur'ān, God's Word, as primarily concerned with the problem of human salvation. It is because of this "problem" that God has revealed the Qur'ān; thus, humans form the second major pole in the Qur'ānic Weltanschauung. The basic confrontation that exists between these two major poles—God and humankind—is the most significant conceptual opposition in the system. Despite his somewhat tenuous characterization of the relationship between God and humankind as confrontational, Izutsu simultaneously, and more perceptively, describes the relationship as multiple, bilateral, and reciprocal. Moreover, he explicates four primary aspects of the human–divine relationship: the ontological relationship of Creator to creature; the verbal and nonverbal communicative relationship; the Lord–servant relationship; and the ethical relationship. He then analyzes each of these in detail.

The second conceptual opposition is that of the Muslim community and non-Muslim Others. Izutsu defines the Muslim community as groups that acknowledge the preceding relationships between God and humankind and choose the positive manifestations of those relationships. In other words, Muslims are those who recognize God as the Creator, respond willingly and comprehensively to the divine call, behave toward God as true servants, and manifest gratitude and fear toward God. Furthermore, he contends that this community (*umma*) introduced a new idea of social unity founded upon common religious belief. In the pre-Islamic society that up until that the time of revelation had been organized on the basis of blood kinship, this notion of *umma* presented a unique challenge that resulted in societal disturbance and change.

In his explication of the conceptual opposition of the Muslim community and non-Muslim Others, Izutsu introduces the Qur'ānic categories of *kuffār* (same as *kāfirūn*, disbelievers), *munāfiqūn* (hypocrites), and *ahl al-kitāb* (People of the Scripture). He describes the *kuffār* as individuals who openly refuse to affirm the various relationships between God and humankind. *Munāfiqūn* are a subgroup of the *kuffār*, and they outwardly pretend to belong to the Muslim community. In regard to *ahl al-kitāb*, Izutsu acknowledges a more complex and close relationship. Nevertheless, he ultimately disregards this complexity and depicts the

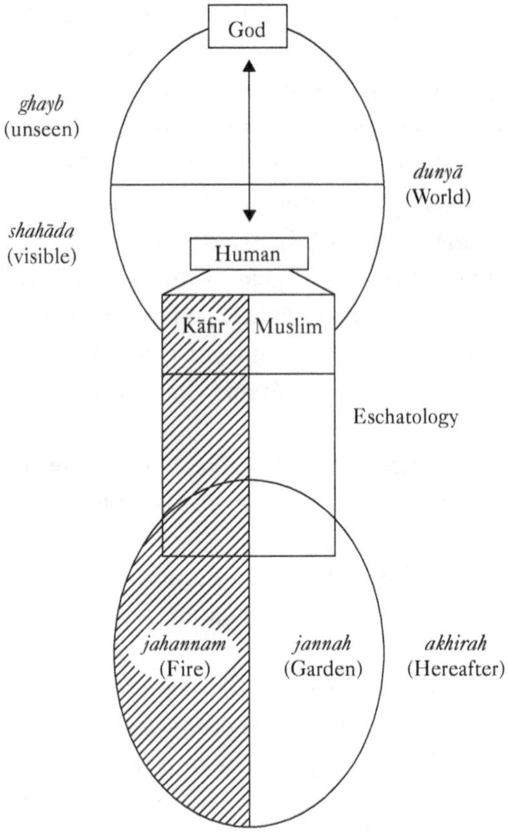

The Qur'ānic *Weltanschauung*

FIGURE 5.2 Reproduced with permission from Toshihiko Izutsu, *God and Man in the Koran: Semantics of the Koranic Weltanschauung* (Tokyo: Keio University, 1964).

Muslim community and *ahl al-kitāb* as also standing in conceptual opposition, a conceptual opposition that is "no less sharp than that of the Islamic *ummah* and the idolatrous *Kāfirs*."[15]

The remaining Qur'ānic conceptual oppositions that Izutsu emphasizes are the unseen (*ghayb*) and visible (*shahāda*) world; the present world (*al-dunyā*) and the Hereafter (*al-ākhira*); and the Garden (*al-janna*) and the Fire (*al-jahannam*) in the Hereafter. He also notes a series of eschatological concepts such as the Last Day, the Day of Judgment, and Resurrection that act as a transition between *al-dunyā* and *al-ākhira*.

After outlining these foundational oppositions, Izutsu provides a comprehensive schematization of the Qur'ānic Weltanschauung (Figure 5.2).[16]

This diagram clearly reiterates his emphasis on conceptual opposition in its oversimplification and establishment of clear-cut borders and endpoints. For example, while Izutsu acknowledges multiple groups of non-Muslim Others—*kuffār*, *munāfiqūn*, and *ahl al-kitāb*—and the particularities of each group, in this final diagram all non-Muslim communities have been subsumed under the heading of *kāfir* (disbeliever). This permits Izutsu to underscore the basic conceptual opposition between the Muslim community and all others. These two clearly delineated categories are then directly and unambiguously connected with two distinct endpoints: the Garden (*al-janna*) and Hellfire (*al-jahannam*). This not only maintains the forced neatness of his thesis of conceptual opposition but also underscores his contention that salvation is the primary concern of the Qur'ān.

Izutsu revisits the notion of conceptual opposition in his more extensive semantic analysis of the categories of *īmān* (belief), *islām* (submission/devotion to God), and *kufr* (disbelief). He describes *islām* and *kufr* as opposites that exist in the semantic field of *īmān*; "in this... field, *kāfir* (or, to use the correspondingly nominal form, *kufr*) stands opposed to *īmān* contradictorily, while *Islām* (the nominal form correspondingly to *muslim*) and *īmān* are complementary concepts."[17] He does acknowledge, though, that there is one place in the Qur'ān where the concepts of *īmān* and *islām* stand in sharp contrast:

> The desert Arabs say, "We have faith." Tell them, "You do not have faith. What you should say instead is, 'We have submitted,' for faith has not yet entered your hearts." If you obey God and God's Messenger, God will not diminish any of your deeds: God is most forgiving and most merciful. The true believers are the ones who have faith in God and God's Messenger and leave all doubt behind, the ones who have struggled with their possessions and their persons in God's way. They are the ones who are true. (49:14–15)

He argues that this is an exceptional depiction applicable only to the Bedouin Arabs, not "ordinary Muslims" for whom *islām* is the ultimate religious act of complete surrender. Therefore, he states that the terms *mu'min* (believer) and *muslim* (one who submits or is devoted to God) may be used interchangeably as they denote the same type of individual. He also contends that the most important issue in the Qur'ān is not the relationship between *īmān* and *islām* but the fundamental conceptual opposition that exists between the *īmān*/*islām* and *kufr*.

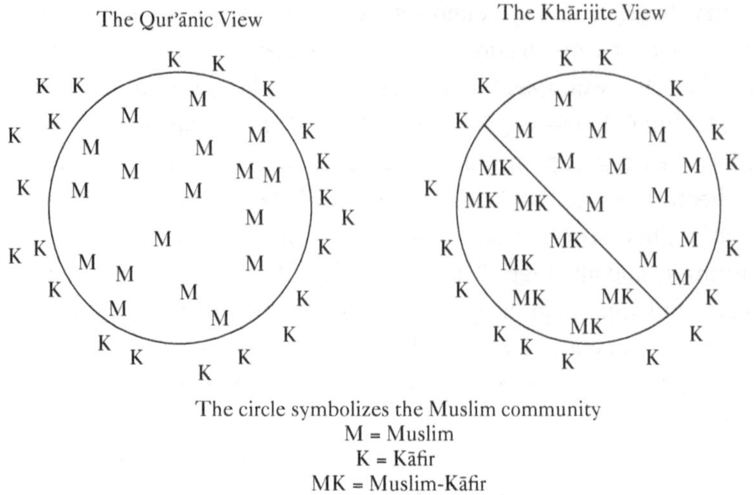

FIGURE 5.3 Reproduced with permission from Toshihiko Izutsu, *The Concept of Belief in Islamic Theology: A Semantic Analysis of* Īmān *and* Islām (Tokyo: Keio University, 1965).

As indicated in his depiction of the Qur'ānic Weltanschauung, Izutsu conceives of *īmān* and *kufr* as being "radically opposed" and forming a basic and essential moral dichotomy.[18] *Īmān* is the center of all positive moral properties, and conversely *kufr* is the pivot around which all negative moral properties revolve. Thus, despite some revealing insights into their semantic nuances, he describes the Qur'ānic concepts of *islām* and *ḥanīf* (which Izutsu defines as a nondenominational monotheist) as aspects of *īmān* and the Qur'ānic concepts of *shirk* (ascribing partners to God) and *nifāq* (hypocrisy) as aspects of *kufr*.

The dichotomization of *īmān* and *kufr* is made even clearer in his diachronic analysis of the Qur'ānic worldview in relation to the post-Qur'ānic worldview of the Khārijites, an early sect within Islam that were noted for their willingness to label other members of the Muslim community as *kuffār* (Figure 5.3).[19]

Therein, he describes the Qur'ānic position as "a very simple structure based on a clearcut distinction between Muslims and *Kāfirs*."[20] In this simple Qur'ānic view, there is no confusion or ambiguity—that is, the borders are clear—between the groups, and the two represent contrasting and static categories.

In the Khārijite worldview, the relational contextualization of *kufr* changes. *Kufr* is no longer something that exists only outside of the Muslim community; it becomes something that is equally prevalent "within the wall."[21] As a result, the concept of *kufr* loses "its denotative stability and fixedness, and become something mobile, ready to be applied even to a pious Muslim if he happens to do this or that."[22] Izutsu argues that this leads to an emphasis on and complexification of the concept of *kufr*; the *kāfir* is no longer simply an "unbeliever" but now also a "wrong believer" (indicated in Figure 5.3 by Muslim–*Kāfir*, or MK).[23] Furthermore, according to Izutsu, the main concern becomes the *kāfirūn* that exist "inside of the wall," whereas non-Muslim *kāfirūn* are neglected or even almost forgotten.

Insights: Toward a Muslima *Hermeneutic of Relationality*

Izutsu's focus on the Qur'ān and depiction of the Qur'ān as a unified whole echo the central defining feature of the hermeneutical approaches of Muslim women interpreters: the prioritization of the Qur'ān. In addition, Izutsu describes his approach as "a method which will let the Qur'anic terms explain themselves."[24] The concern for listening to the Qur'ān's self-explication is also evident in Muslim women interpreters, both in their emphasis of *tafsīr al-Qur'ān bil-Qur'ān* and in their critiques of heavy historical reliance upon and even prioritization of other sources over the Qur'ānic text.

Another convergence between Izutsu's method and the hermeneutical approach of Muslim women interpreters is related to the topic of polysemy. Muslim women interpreters argue that the Qur'ān is polysemic, that is, open to multiple interpretations. Polysemy is a middle position between monovalency (the idea that the Qur'ān has only one correct interpretation) and relativism (the idea that the Qur'ān is open to any interpretation). While Izutsu does offer one specific depiction of the Qur'ānic worldview, he nonetheless expresses an awareness of other interpretative possibilities. When introducing the particularity of his semantic method, for example, he acknowledges that the "Qur'an is capable of being approached from a number of different points of view."[25]

Izutsu also recognizes a degree of arbitrariness in the selection of key terms and focus words; there is a possibility that other interpreters would identify different concepts as key terms and focus words. Variances in the selection of terms and words could lead to different configurations of semantic fields. For instance, Izutsu designates *nifāq* (hypocrisy) as a key term in the semantic field of *kufr*. However, it would be possible to take *nifāq* itself as a focus word in its own separate semantic field. This designation as a focus word, however, would not result in it is being disconnected from the concept of *kufr*. A particular concept may be prioritized differently by different interpreters, but it is never removed from its relational context. Since it is not removed from its context, the degree of fluctuation in meaning is confined to a limited, though not monovalent, field of possibilities. Although Izutsu depicts the Qurʾānic worldview as static and fixed when comparing it with the Khārijite worldview, in the introduction of his interpretative process he ironically yet aptly describes the Qurʾānic worldview as a "living dynamic ontology."[26] Such a depiction parallels Muslim women interpreters' emphasis on the polysemic and dynamic nature of the Qurʾānic text.

Beyond these convergences, the two most significant insights that Izutsu offers are his elevation of relational meaning over basic meaning, and his description of the process by which relational meaning is illuminated. In his definition of relational meaning as contextual, complex, and multiple, he provides an invaluable alternative to approaches that attempt to interpret the Qurʾān by focusing on individual concepts in isolation and approaches that aim to establish clear-cut delineations between various concepts. Isolation and clear-cut delineations are unable to fully grasp the intricacies of relational meaning and are therefore unable to situate the meaning of any one concept within the larger integrated whole of the Qurʾānic worldview. At best, such methods are limited and at worst misrepresentative.

In his description of the method of semantic analysis, he provides a lucid guide for identifying, explicating and integrating the various nuances of and relationships among Qurʾānic concepts. Moreover, since the goal of this type of analysis is to describe semantic fields and the overlap among semantic fields, there is no need to attempt to reduce the complexity of Qurʾānic categories or to attempt to define them based upon singular criterion. This obsession with identifying threshold criteria dominated much historical Islamic discourse on religious diversity. Izutsu presents a process through which one is also able to avoid the common exegetical devices of *naskh* (scriptural abrogation) and chronological ordering, by which later verses are taken to be authoritative over earlier verses. Since concepts have multiple facets, and since they intersect and overlap, he is not compelled to resort to these tactics.[27]

Izutsu thus provides an alternative hermeneutical strategy that allows both commonalities (overlaps) and distinctions to be illuminated. In other words, he provides a method that allows for complex and simultaneous consideration of aspects of sameness and aspects of difference between Qur'ānic concepts. This is precisely what other historical and contemporary hermeneutical approaches to religious difference have failed to do, and it is precisely what I aim to do with *Muslima* theology of religious pluralism.

It is worth noting that Izutsu's method not only extends the hermeneutical approach drawn from Muslim women interpreters but also aligns with *Muslima* theology's conception of difference. Izutsu's approach steers away from both isolation and hierarchy. Isolation, as already discussed, is an ineffective hermeneutical method when relational meaning is prioritized. Izutsu also avoids hierarchy through relational emphasis and through his depiction of the structure of the Qur'ānic worldview. Although he does identify Allāh as the "supreme" focus word in the Qur'ānic Weltanschauung, he constructs a system in which Allāh is situated centrally rather than hierarchically (see Figure 5.1). Furthermore, Izutsu's description of the Qur'ānic vocabulary as "an extremely tangled web of semantic groups" resonates with Hill Fletcher's emphasis on the web of dynamic relationality.[28] Although he presents his task as "disentangling" that web—something that would seem to be impossible and counter to his other assertions—his invocation of the analogy of the web reemphasizes the suitability of his method to illuminating the alternative conception of difference of *Muslima* theology.

My analysis of religious difference in Chapters 6 and 7 has significant overlap with Izutsu's own analysis, since he examines key concepts such as *īmān*, *islām*, and *kufr* as part of his articulation of the overriding Qur'ānic Weltanschauung. While his hermeneutical approach is invaluable to my analysis, some of his conclusions manifest glaring inadequacies. Many of these are problematic not only because they diverge from the central assumptions of *Muslima* theology but also because they diverge from, even contradict, the basic tenets of Izutsu's own method of semantic analysis.

The first major divergence relates to Izutsu's portrayal of the overarching Qur'ānic Weltanschauung as being characterized by conceptual opposition. The idea of conceptual opposition is problematic in that it emphasizes radical difference only. Such an emphasis is clear in Izutsu's description of *kufr* (or the *kāfir*) as the "exact antithesis" of *īmān* (or the *mu'min*).[29] The focus on conceptual opposition is not only incongruent with the foundational conception of difference of *Muslima* theology but also appears to be incongruent with Izutsu's own method.

Izutsu describes semantic analysis as analysis of the relational context of terms and concepts, analysis of overlaps, interconnections, and differences. This is why he prioritizes relational meaning and the notion of interlocking semantic fields. Yet in his schematization of the Qurʾānic worldview (see Figure 5.2), he presents the oppositional pairs as wholly distinct. Izutsu even acknowledges some weaknesses in this schematization when he notes that nothing can really stand in opposition to God. Another indication of the limitations of his conception is found in the opposition of the concepts of *ghayb* (unseen) and *shahāda* (visible). It is difficult to understand how these two concepts can be conceived of as oppositional: different, yes, but not standing in opposition.

One way to explain Izutsu's focus on conceptual opposition is to recognize it as a byproduct of his perspective that the Qurʾān is primarily concerned with salvation, eschatology, and status in the Hereafter. In one of his more valid conceptual oppositions, he divides the Hereafter into *al-janna* (the Garden) and *al-jahannam* (the Fire). While Izutsu is certainly neglecting some nuances in these two opposed categories, he appears to utilize them as a means of arguing back to his presentation of humankind in the world. He states that salvation is the main issue in the Qurʾān, and in his view of salvation there are two distinct endpoints. Based on these two distinct endpoints, he divides humanity into two distinct groups: Muslims (i.e., those who will go to the Garden); and *kuffār* (i.e., those who will go to the Fire). Thus, all nuances or differences among groups of people are collapsed and reduced; the only characteristic that is considered is the description of their respective endpoints.

As an illustration of this, in Izutsu's analysis of *nifāq* (hypocrisy) in relation to *kufr*, he cites Qurʾān 66:9: "Prophet, strive hard against the disbelievers and the hypocrites. Deal with them sternly. Hell will be their home, an evil destination!" Then, he states, "This last point, that is, the decree of God that the final abode of the *munāfiq* should be the Hell Fire, is very significant in that it discloses the *essential* connection of *nifāq* and *kufr*, for the common punishment suggests that the two are equal in the *degree* and *nature* of sinfulness."[30] What makes his reductionist lumping together even more striking is that it appears in the very midst of an insightful analysis of the nuances of the concept of *nifāq*. He notes that some historical scholars have divided humanity into three groups (*muʾmin*, *kāfir*, and *munāfiq*), rather than two only (*muʾmin* and *kāfir*). His response to this is not a reassertion of his binary conceptual opposition between *īmān* and *kufr*. Rather, he responds by arguing that *nifāq* is not a tightly bound category; *nifāq* is something mobile, something that overlaps with and can be born out of either *īmān* (belief) or *kufr* (disbelief). For Izutsu, "*Nifāq* is in no way a water-tight compartment situated between *kufr* and *īmān*, but rather an extensive range of meaning with uncertain boundaries. It is, so to speak, a category of a conspicuously dynamic nature, that may extend with elasticity towards either direction to shade off almost imperceptibly into *kufr* and *īmān*."[31] This description appears to blatantly challenge his reduction of *nifāq* to a subset of *kufr*, as manifest in his schematization of the Qur'ānic Weltanschauung (see Figure 5.2).

Significantly, Izutsu's analysis of the semantic structure of other concepts is as equally insightful as his analysis of *nifāq*. When he describes *īmān*, for example, he transcends a simple focus on belief, or even belief and action, to highlight aspects such as gratitude, humility, response to divine guidance, and fear of God (one aspect of *taqwā*). The complexity of his analysis of *īmān* is also evident in his description of the *mu'min* (believer) as someone who positively affirms the four primary relationships with God. As these examples illustrate, for Izutsu, *īmān* is a complex and multifaceted concept.

The complexity of his analysis of *nifāq* and *īmān* also raises intriguing questions about his comparison between the Qur'ānic worldview and the Khārijite worldview (see Figure 5.3). In this comparison, he describes the Qur'ānic worldview as simple, static, and clear-cut. However, one wonders how this could be the case if, based on Izutsu's own analysis, *nifāq* (hypocrisy) is a concept that is dynamic and overlaps with both *īmān* (belief) and *kufr* (disbelief). This would necessarily call into question his static and clearly defined presentation of the Qur'ānic worldview. If we concede Izutsu's contention that *nifāq* is a genre of *kufr* and we accept his semantic analysis that depicts *nifāq* as being born out of *īmān* or *kufr*, then this implies that *kufr* can exist within the sphere of *īmān*. If this is the case, Izutsu's diagram begins to look very much like the Khārijite worldview; the stability of and clear-cut delineation between the borders of *īmān* and *kufr* are called into question.

Another provocative question that arises is whether *īmān* (belief) is always confined within the wall of the historical and explicitly professed Muslim community. In both his diagrams of the Qur'ānic and Khārijite worldviews, Izutsu assumes that all that exists outside of the wall is *kufr* (disbelief). However, if *kufr* can lose "its denotative stability and fixedness, and become something mobile,"[32] is it not possible that *īmān* can do the same? This question naturally arises from Izutsu's own semantic analysis, which highlights relational meaning, overlaps, and interconnections between Qur'ānic concepts. It is a question I endeavor to answer through my own analysis of the Qur'ānic discourse.

In that analysis, I do not adopt Izutsu's model of conceptual opposition. This model is not only inherently weak but also in direct conflict with my central objective, that is, the attempt to conceive of difference as relational rather than as something that divides humanity through the erection of clear, static, and impermeable boundaries. Likewise, I do not follow Izutsu in his ultimate reduction of complexity and his subsumption of various Qur'ānic concepts under other Qur'ānic concepts. Rather, I aim to explore and explicate—not disentangle—the Qur'ān's complex, relational web. In carrying out this exploration and explication, however, I do draw upon many of his insights into the structure of individual Qur'ānic categories. Moreover, I also adopt his general method of semantic analysis, with its emphasis on relational meaning, overlapping semantic fields, and multifaceted interconnections, applying it in a synchronic fashion to the specific topic of religious difference.

3

A Muslima *Theology of Religious Pluralism*

6

Lateral and Hierarchical Religious Difference in the Qur'ān

THROUGHOUT THIS BOOK, I have aimed to highlight the nature and source of two prominent shortcomings in the contemporary Islamic discourse on religious difference: the inability to account effectively for both the proximity and the Otherness of the Other-who-can-never-be-wholly-other and the failure to offer integrated models for understanding religious difference. To begin to address these shortcomings, I have constructed an alternative conceptual and hermeneutical infrastructure, which I utilize throughout the remaining chapters to reevaluate, reinterpret, and reenvision the Qur'ānic discourse on religious difference.

Whether it be the shared conception of difference evident in contemporary Islamic approaches or the presentation of difference critiqued by Muslim women interpreters and feminist theologians, difference is always the central issue, the central problematic. Therefore, to move the discourse in new directions, it is necessary to start by re-evaluating difference itself. In this chapter, I do so by distinguishing between hierarchical and lateral religious difference in the Qur'ān and thereby challenging the static and holistic alignment of the two distinct genres of difference.

Defining Characteristics of Hierarchical and Lateral Difference

Asma Barlas draws a distinction between two types of difference: one that differentiates laterally and the other that differentiates hierarchically. Her main contention is that sexual difference must be acknowledged—not ignored or downplayed—but that it never serves as the basis of hierarchical evaluation. In other words, for Barlas sexual difference is lateral difference; it distinguishes groups without attaching an evaluative measure to that distinction. Moreover, she states that in the Qur'ān lateral difference is conceived of as divinely intended and therefore purposeful. Apart from this nonevaluative form of difference, Barlas identifies another genre of difference, hierarchical, which *is* associated with evaluation and assessment. According to Barlas and Amina Wadud, hierarchical difference is evaluated only with respect to the concept of *taqwā* (piety or God consciousness).[1] While *taqwā* is something that must be actualized in social and relational contexts, it is assessed on an individual basis. In arguing for the distinction between these two genres of difference, Barlas aims to illuminate and dismiss the pervasive conflation and static linking of the two; lateral and hierarchical difference are not the same, and no particular hierarchical assessment of *taqwā* is permanently ascribed to a lateral group as a whole.

On the basis of Barlas's distinction, it is possible to outline defining characteristics for both genres of difference. First, hierarchical difference is connected with accountability, judgment, rewards, and punishments. Second, evaluation of this genre of difference is carried out only on the basis of conformity or non-conformity with the concept of *taqwā*. Third, the evaluation of *taqwā*—and therefore of hierarchical difference—is assessed on the individual level. It is, however, always connected to social and relational manifestations. Every person is assessed individually, but assessment is integrally related to the individual's interactions with divine and human others.

There are also three defining characteristics of lateral difference. First, it is a group phenomenon. It primarily refers not to individual particularities but rather to patterns and trends of difference at the group level. The fact that lateral difference is a group phenomenon, though, does not mean that lateral groups are completely discrete; groupings that denote lateral difference can overlap, intersect, and even be inclusive of other lateral groups. Second, lateral difference is divinely intended. As such, it is not the result of degeneration, human error, or corruption but is willed by God for a teleological purpose and thus should not be targeted for eradication or homogenization. Third, lateral difference never serves as the basis of evaluation. Evaluation is not tied to difference that is divinely intended. Moreover, it is not conducted at the group level. It is important to clarify that this does not imply that there will be no evaluation whatsoever within groups of lateral difference; rather, it implies that a singular evaluation will not be uniformly ascribed to an entire group solely on the basis of membership in that group. As a result, in seeking to identify groups of lateral religious difference, the goal is to find groups that are partially and diversely evaluated, rather than never evaluated.

Hierarchical Religious Difference: The Semantic Field of Taqwā

As is apparent in Toshihiko Izutsu's analysis of the central concepts of the Islamic worldview, as well as in other historical and contemporary approaches discussed in this study, the concepts of *īmān* (faith), *islām* (submission), *kufr* (disbelief), and *nifāq* (hypocrisy)[2] undeniably play a central role in the Qur'ānic discourse on religious difference. Furthermore, while Izutsu's depiction of the Qur'ānic worldview is compromised due to its oversimplification, he does illustrate that these concepts are connected to notions of accountability, judgment, rewards, and punishments. The Qur'ān provides extensive descriptions of the *mu'min* (believer) and the *muslim* (submitter) as those who will be rewarded with Paradise:

> But as for those who believe (*āmanū*) and do good deeds, their Lord will guide them because of their faith. Streams will flow at their feet in the Gardens of Bliss. Their prayer in them will be, "Glory be to You, God!" Their greeting, "Peace." And the last part of their prayer, "Praise be to God, Lord of the Worlds." (10:9-10)
>
> In fact, any who submit (*'aslama*) themselves wholly to God and do good will have their reward with their Lord: no fear for them, nor will they grieve. (2:112)

In contrast, there are equally as many, if not more, Qur'ānic descriptions of the *kāfir* (disbeliever) and *munāfiq* (hypocrite) as those who will be punished with the Fire of Hell:

> We shall send those who reject Our revelations (*kafarū*) to the Fire. When their skins have been burned away, We shall replace them with new ones so that they may continue to feel the pain: God is mighty and wise. (4:56)
>
> The hypocrites (*munāfiqīn*) will be in the lowest depths of Hell, and you will find no one to help them. (4:145)

> God will punish the hypocrites and those that ascribe partners to God, both men and women, (*munāfiqūn/munāfiqāt* and *mushrikīn/mushrikāt*) and turn with mercy to the believers, both men and women (*mu'minīn* and *mu'mināt*): God is most forgiving, most merciful. (33:73)

The direct association of these concepts—along with other similar concepts, including *shirk* (ascribing partners to God, *mushrik*)—with ultimate judgment is enough to indicate that these concepts denote forms of hierarchical religious difference. Their status as forms of hierarchical difference, though, is further confirmed by the fact that they are consistently praised or critiqued even without explicit reference to rewards and punishment:

> The believers, both men and women (*mu'minūn* and *mu'mināt*), support each other; they order what is right and forbid what is wrong; they keep up the prayer and pay the prescribed alms; they obey God and God's Messenger. God will grant mercy to such people. God is almighty and wise. (9:71)

> Who could be better in religion than those who submit (*'aslama*) themselves wholly to God, do good, and follow the religion of Abraham, who was true in faith (*ḥanīf*)? . . . (4:125, excerpt)

> The worst creatures in the sight of God are those who reject (*kafarū*) God and will not believe. (8:55)

> The hypocrites, both men and women (*munāfiqūn* and *munāfiqāt*), are all the same: they order what is wrong and forbid what is right; they are tight-fisted. They have ignored God, so God has ignored them. The hypocrites are the disobedient ones. (9:67)

> Say, "Do you order me to worship someone other than God, you foolish people?" It has already been revealed to you and to those before you: "If you ascribe any partner (*'ashrakta*) to God, all your work will come to nothing: you will be one if the losers. No! Worship God alone and be one of those who are grateful to God." (39:64–66)

In his analysis of these concepts, Izutsu depicts *īmān* and *kufr* as the focus words of two intersecting semantic fields. Consequently, *kufr* acts as a negative key term in the semantic field of *īmān*, and *īmān* likewise acts as a negative (meaning opposite) key term in the semantic field of *kufr*.[3] Izutsu states that these concepts form the "two pillars of Qur'anic ethics"[4] around which all other concepts, positive and negative, revolve. There is certainly much to be garnered from his presentation of the semantic situatedness of these concepts. Even the limited Qur'ānic verses (*āyāt*) presented so far in this chapter indicate that *īmān* and *kufr* are central and, in many ways, antithetical concepts. However, as with his conception of the overarching Qur'ānic worldview, his analysis of *īmān* and *kufr*—not to mention all of the other concepts that are subsumed under these two—is constrained by the fact that he depicts them as exact opposites and wholly antithetical. *Kufr* therefore becomes simply what *īmān* is not, and *īmān* becomes what *kufr* is not. This is evident when, after carrying out his analysis of the inner structure and semantic field of *kufr*, he states:

> As for the semantic structure of "belief" itself, it may be admitted that we know already all the essential points, for, by trying to analyze semantically the principal terms of negative valuation, we have also been describing the characteristic features of the true "believer" in the Islamic sense from the reverse side, as it were. So our main task ... will consist simply in re-examining briefly all that has been said about *kufr* and its various aspects from the opposite angle.[5]

While there is a degree of oppositional overlap between these concepts, they are not simply the inverse of one another, and their depiction as such impedes examination of the nuances and complexities of each. Izutsu's schema of conceptual opposition is far too neat to explicate these in a sustained fashion.

In light of this, and in line with Barlas's definition of the central characteristics of hierarchical difference, I propose that *īmān* and *kufr* should be reconceived as two concepts, among others, that define the semantic field of *taqwā* (God consciousness) (Figure 6.1).

This reconceptualization of the semantic relationship of these two concepts is not intended to dismiss the majority of Izutsu's analysis of these concepts, nor does it imply that these terms are no longer focus words. Both *īmān* and *kufr* remain focus words of their own highly significant semantic fields as well as key terms within other fields. This reconceptualization, however, is intended to deconstruct the absolute oppositional characterization of the concepts. *Īmān* and *kufr* are no longer primarily understood through inverse comparison; the complexity of these concepts

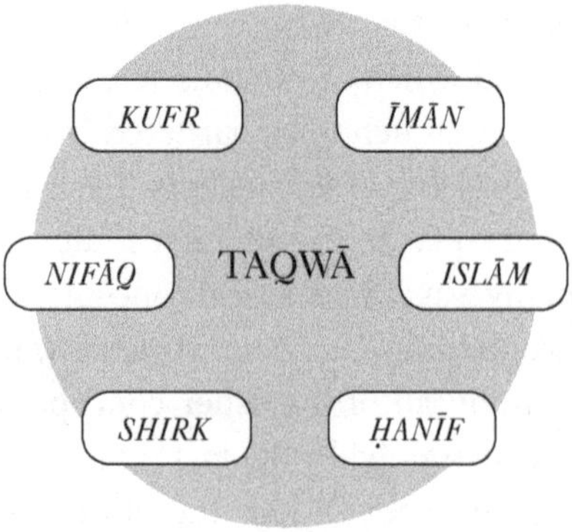

FIGURE 6.1 Hierarchical Religious Difference: Semantic Field of *Taqwā*

is now illuminated through reference to and comparison with a third core concept, *taqwā*. Additionally, other concepts denoting hierarchical religious difference—such as *islām* (submission), *ḥanīf* (commonly translated as non-denominational monotheist), *nifāq* (hypocrisy), and *shirk* (ascribing partners to God)—are no longer subsumed in a secondary status under the dual pillars of *īmān* and *kufr*. These concepts unquestionably retain a direct relationship with the former pillars, but they now are also interpreted directly in relation to *taqwā* and represent focus words of their own semantic fields.

Notably, this *taqwā*-centric reconceptualization is also tied to the difference in focus between this *Muslima* theology and Izutsu's work. I have magnified and ascribed greater significance to certain concepts due to their pivotal role in the Qur'ānic discourse on religious difference. In Izutsu's analysis, for example, the concept of *ḥanīf* warrants very limited consideration as a facet of *īmān*.[6] Yet in my analysis despite *ḥanīf*'s limited use within the Qur'ānic text[7] it is a pivotal concept and so is treated as a focus word in its own right.

While the exploration of the complex web of relationships formed by the semantic field of *taqwā* is the subject of the next chapter, I will here focus on the inner structure of the concept of *taqwā* itself and its central role in the Qur'ānic discourse. What is *taqwā*, and why is it important? Additionally, does *taqwā*—and by extension the concepts that inhabit its semantic field—fulfill Barlas's third defining characteristic of hierarchical difference; that is, does it evaluate on the individual level in reference to social relationships?

Up until this point, I have translated *taqwā* as piety and God consciousness. However, this translation falls short in that it does not convey many of the key intricacies of the concept or its paramount significance. *Taqwā* is piety, but piety is devotion to God, awe of God, mindfulness or consciousness of God, worship of God, and even fear of God. Highlighting the importance of *taqwā* within the Qurʾānic worldview, the second chapter of the Qurʾān, *Sūrat al-baqara*, begins by offering a sketch of the *muttaqūn* (those who manifest *taqwā*):

> That is the Scripture in which there is no doubt, containing guidance for those who are mindful of God (*muttaqīn*), who believe in the unseen, keep up the prayer, and give, those who believe in the revelation sent down to you [Muḥammad], and in what was sent before you, those who have firm faith in the Hereafter. Such people are following their Lord's guidance and it is they who will prosper. (2:2–5)

The divine scripture (*kitāb*) is guidance for the *muttaqūn*, and the *muttaqūn* are those who believe in God, in what they cannot know from their own experience, in revelation, and in the Hereafter. With regard to the Hereafter and other eschatological realities, *taqwā* conveys a sense of fear of God.[8] In this capacity, the Qurʾān links *taqwā* with the term *khashiya* (fear) and describes the *muttaqūn* as those whose hearts tremble when they reflect on God's eschatological plan:

> ...Those who are mindful of God (*muttaqīn*), those who stand in awe (*yakhshawna*) of their Lord, though God is unseen, and who fear the Hour. (21:48–49, excerpt)
>
> Those who stand in awe (*khashyati*) of their Lord, who believe in God's messages, who do not ascribe partners to God, who always give with hearts that tremble at the thought that they must return to God, are the ones who race toward good things, and they will be the first to get them. We do not burden any soul with more than it can bear. We have a Record that tells the truth. They will not be wronged. (23:57–62)

As the preceding *āyāt* indicate, *taqwā* is not only about belief; the *muttaqūn* also perform actions. They pray, give, and race toward good things. Therefore, as Wadud states, *taqwā* is both attitude and action; it is "a pious manner of behavior which observes constraints...and 'consciousness of Allah,' that is, observing that manner of behavior because of one's reverence towards Allah."[9]

The seemingly routine activities of praying and giving also draw attention to another fundamental feature of *taqwā*. *Taqwā* is manifest, whether in belief or action, in relationship not only to God but also to other humans. *Taqwā* is manifest socially; it involves "both responsibility to God and to humankind."[10] As such, it denotes an integral connection between the vertical relationship of humans to God and the horizontal relationship of humans to humans. The connection between these two relationships is also evident in the common association of *taqwā* with *birr* (goodness, piety):[11]

> ...Goodness (*al-birr*) does not consist of entering houses by the back; the truly good person (*al-birr*) is the one who is mindful of God (*'ittaqā*). So enter your houses by their doors and be mindful (*'attaqū*) of God so that you may prosper. (2:189, excerpt)

At first encounter, this *āya* is somewhat jarring in its repetition of the concepts of *birr* and *taqwā* in the middle of a discussion of proper social etiquette, but it is precisely this intimate connection that defines the character of *taqwā*. *Taqwā* is an orientation toward God, a constant awareness of God, that colors every facet of how one acts in the world. This intimate connection between the relationship with God and social relationships is confirmed in another *āya* from *Sūrat al-baqara*:

> True goodness (*al-birr*) does not consist in turning your face towards East or West. The truly good are those who believe in God and the Last Day, in the angels, the Scripture, and the prophets; who give away some of their wealth, however much they cherish it, to their relatives, to orphans, the needy, travelers and beggars, and to liberate those in bondage; those who establish and maintain the prayer and pay the prescribed alms; who keep pledges whenever they make them; who are steadfast in misfortune, adversity, and times of danger. These are the ones who are true, and it is they who are aware of God (*muttaqūn*). (2:177)

There also exists a particularly close connection between *taqwā* and familial or kinship relationships:

> People, be mindful (*ʾittaqū*) of your Lord, who created you from a single soul, and from the same essence created its mate, and from the pair of them spread countless men and women far and wide; be mindful (*ʾittaqū*) of God, in whose name you make requests of one another. Beware of severing the ties of kinship. God is always watching over you. (4:1)

In other *āyāt* that do not specifically reference *taqwā* but relate to the command of God, a similar motif is evident. Moreover, these verses link the reverence due to parents and due to God with *shukr* (gratitude). Humans are commanded to respect and obey their parents as an acknowledgment of the favors that God has bestowed upon them:

> We have commanded the human to be good to his parents: his mother struggled to carry him and struggled to give birth to him—his bearing and weaning took a full thirty months. When he has grown to manhood and reached the age of forty he [may] say, "Lord, help me to be truly grateful (*ʾashkura*) for Your favors to me and to my parents. Help me to do good work that pleases You. Make my offspring good. I turn to You. I am one of those who devote themselves to You." (46:15)

The Qurʾān, however, makes an important caveat with regard to the intertwining of *taqwā* with social and familial relations. One should show gratitude and endeavor to maintain proper relations, but in situations where social or familial ties threaten to or actually interfere with one's relationship with God, the relationship with God takes precedence:

> We have commanded people to be good to their parents. Their mothers carried them, with strain upon strain, and it takes two years to wean them. Give thanks to Me and to your parents. All will return to Me. If they strive to make you associate with Me anything about which you have no knowledge, then do not obey them. Yet keep their company in this life according to what is right, and follow the path of those who turn to Me. You will all return to Me in the end, and I will tell you everything that you have done. (31:14–15)

> We have commanded people to be good to their parents, but do not obey them if they strive to make you serve, beside Me, anything of

which you have no knowledge. You will all return to Me, and I shall inform you of what you have done. (29:8)

Taqwā is the interconnection between the vertical and horizontal relationships, but it is the vertical relationship between humans and God that is the defining relationship. When the opposite occurs—when the horizontal relationship between humans begins to define or impact the vertical relationship—the Qur'ān reasserts the preeminence of the vertical relationship. It is vital to note that these *āyāt* do not advocate the complete severing of relationships. A person can and should still show gratitude and kindness toward their family, but they should not obey them with respect to beliefs or practice that run contrary to *taqwā*.

Another central trait of *taqwā* is that it is not simply something that can be achieved once and for all; rather, it is an active quality. It is something that must be constantly striven for and sustained, not simply achieved or professed. This is corroborated by the sheer volume of Qur'ānic exhortations to have *taqwā*, to be mindful or conscious of God. The status of *taqwā* as an active and dynamic quality is also confirmed by the fact that many of these exhortations are made in reference to those who believe, to the *mu'minūn*. The Qur'ān constantly invokes the imperative, reminding them to be conscious of God:

> You who believe (*āmanū*), fasting is prescribed for you, as it was prescribed for those before you, so that you may be mindful of God (*tattaqūn*). (2:183)
>
> You who believe (*āmanū*), be mindful (*'ittaqū*) of God. Give up any outstanding dues from usury, if you are true believers (*mu'minīn*). (2:278)
>
> You who believe (*āmanū*), be steadfast, more steadfast than others. Be ready. Always be mindful (*'ittaqū*) of God, so that you may prosper. (3:200)
>
> You who believe (āmanū), be mindful (*'ittaqū*) of God. Seek ways to come closer to God and strive for God's cause, so that you may prosper. (5:35)
>
> Those who believe (*āmanū*) and do good deeds will not be blamed for what they may have consumed as long as they are mindful of God (*'ittaqū*), believe (*āmanū*) and do good deeds, then are mindful of God (*'ittaqū*) and believe (*āmanū*), then are mindful of God (*'ittaqū*) and do good. God loves those who do good. (5:93)

The last two *āyāt* highlight that there is always a way to move closer to God, to increase one's level or degree of *taqwā*. Qur'ān 5:93, in particular, describes iterations of this ongoing process: be mindful of God; believe; do good deeds; then become more mindful and develop more belief; then become more mindful and do more good deeds; and on and on. It is a cycle that knows no limit and continues until the point of death.

While many *āyāt* related to *taqwā* are addressed to the *mu'minūn*, the general command to strive for *taqwā* is directed indiscriminately to all *nās*, to all of humanity:

> O People (*nās*), be mindful (*'ittaqū*) of your Lord, for the earthquake of the Last Hour will be a mighty thing. (22:1)

Moreover, as both Barlas and Wadud indicate, *taqwā* is the primary criterion by which humanity is judged; the most honored people in the sight of God are those who are the most mindful:

> People (*nās*), we created you all from a single man and a single woman and made you into races and tribes so that you should recognize one another. In God's eyes, the most honored of you are the ones most mindful of God (*'atqākum*). God is all knowing, all aware. (49:13)

This *āya* is highly significant not only because it identifies *taqwā* as the criterion by which God judges between people but also because it juxtaposes *taqwā* with other forms of difference. The *āya* directly states that humanity is divided by God into nations and tribes but that these divisions are not the basis of evaluation. The only basis of evaluation is *taqwā*. While lateral difference is the subject of the subsequent section of this chapter, it is vital to highlight that the distinction between nations/tribes and *taqwā* is a patent example of the distinction between lateral and hierarchical difference. Lateral difference exists by God's intention and is not the basis of evaluation; hierarchical difference is the only evaluative standard.

Wadud draws attention to the fact that Qur'ān 49:13 is preceded by two *āyāt* that criticize groups that jeer at one another, taunting each other on the basis of group affiliation:

> Believers (*ya 'ayyuhā alladhīna āmanū*), no one group of men should jeer at another, who may after all be better than them. No one group

> of women should jeer at another, who may after all be better than them. Do not speak ill of one another. Do not use offensive nick-names for one another. How bad it is to be called a mischief-maker after accepting faith! Those who do not repent from this behavior are evildoers. Believers (*ya ʾayyuhā alladhīna āmanū*), avoid making too many assumptions—some assumptions are sinful—and do not spy on one another or speak ill of people behind their back. Would any of you like to eat the flesh of your dead brother? No, you would hate it. So be mindful (*ʾittaqū*) of God. God is ever relenting, most merciful. (49:11-12)

Wadud argues that when Qurʾān 49:13 is read in the context of these *āyāt*, *taqwā* as the decisive criterion is distinguished not only from national or tribal difference but also from all sorts of group difference. Value is ascribed only to *taqwā*, not group identity. Wadud contends that "one might attribute greater or lesser value to another on the basis of gender, wealth, nationality, religion or race, but from Allah's perspective, these do not form a valuable basis for distinction between individuals (or groups)."[12]

Following her assertion, it is not surprising that judgment on the basis of *taqwā* is carried out only on the individual level:

> People (*nās*), be mindful (*ʾittaqū*) of your Lord and fear a Day when no parent will take the place of their child, nor a child take the place of their parent, in any way. God's promise is true, so do not let the present life delude you, nor let the Deceiver delude you about God. (31:33)

On the Day of Judgment, not even a child or parent—the closest of human relations—will be able to trade places with each other; no person will be able to save another, nor will any person be held accountable for another. The invocation of kinship relationships in this *āya* reiterates the fact that, while *taqwā* connects the vertical (human-to-God) and horizontal (human-to-human) relationships, ultimately the human-to-God relationship—or more precisely the individual-to-God relationship—will be the decisive factor. The emphasis on individual accountability and assessment is confirmed in many other Qurʾānic *āyāt*:

> You who believe (*ya ʾayyuhā alladhīna āmanū*), you are responsible for your own souls. If anyone else goes astray it will not harm you

> as long as you follow the guidance. You will all return to God, and God will make you realize what you have done. (5:105)
>
> ... Each soul is responsible for its own actions. No soul will bear the burden of another. You will all return to your Lord in the end, and God will tell you the truth about your differences. (6:164, excerpt)
>
> The Hour is coming—though I choose to keep it hidden—for each soul to be rewarded for its labor. (20:15)
>
> Every soul is held in pledge for its deeds. (74:38)

The convergence of the universal and egalitarian command to have *taqwā* with the emphasis on individual accountability indicates that every individual has both the potential and the responsibility to manifest *taqwā*. Those who constantly strive to fulfill this potential and responsibility are promised the Garden, and those who do not are promised the Fire:

> Here is a picture of the Garden that those mindful of God (*muttaqūn*) have been promised: flowing streams, perpetual food, and shade. This is the reward that awaits those who are mindful of God. The disbelievers' (*kāfirūn*) reward is the Fire. (13:35)

The eschatological endpoints outlined in this *āya* also indicate that *taqwā* is situated in a positive relationship with certain concepts that fall within its semantic field and in a negative relationship with others. This *āya* itself contrasts the *muttaqūn* with the *kāfirūn*. Qurʾān 31:15, which has already been discussed, similarly contrasts *taqwā* with *shirk* when it states that children should not obey their parents "if they strive to make you associate" anything with God. Conversely, *taqwā* is positively connected to concepts such as *īmān* and *islām*. This is evident in the preceding *āyāt* directed to the *muʾminūn* as well as in other *āyāt* that connect *taqwā* directly to those concepts or indirectly through references to actions and beliefs that are characteristic of *taqwā*:

> You who believe (*āmanū*), be mindful (*ʾittaqū*) of God, as is God's due, and do not die except as one who has submitted him or herself to God (*muslimūn*). (3:102)
>
> For men and women who are devoted to God (*muslimūn* and *muslimāt*), believing men and women (muʾ*minūn* and *muʾmināt*), obedient men and women, truthful men and women, steadfast men and women, humble men and women, charitable men and

women, fasting men and women, chaste men and women, men and women who remember God often, God has prepared forgiveness and a rich reward. (33:35)

In Qur'ān 30:30-30:32, *taqwā* is linked with the concept of *ḥanīf*:

So as one of pure faith, stand firm and true (*ḥanīfan*) in your devotion to the religion. This is the natural disposition (*fiṭra*) God instilled in humankind—there is no altering God's creation—and this is the right religion, though most people do not realize it. Turn to God alone, all of you. Be mindful (*'ittaqū*) of God, keep up the prayer, do not join those who ascribe partners to God, those who divide their unity into factions, with each party rejoicing in their own.

In addition to demonstrating that *ḥanīf* is situated in a positive relationship with *taqwā* (i.e., being *ḥanīf* is a manifestation of *taqwā*), this *āya* also reiterates the critique that is lodged against those that prioritize group divisions above all else. It classifies those who divide into *ḥizb* (factions) with those who engage in *shirk* (ascribing partners to God). Significantly, this *āya* also connects *taqwā* with *fiṭra*, or human nature. The natural disposition instilled in each person by God is to be *ḥanīf*, to be fully devoted to and conscious of God. This disposition is confirmed by a description of the human soul as having knowledge of *taqwā*:

By the soul and how God formed it and inspired it [to know] its own rebellion and piety (*taqwā*)! (91:7–8)

Knowledge of *taqwā* and a natural disposition toward God are therefore characteristics of all humanity, or every soul. However, as stressed, *taqwā* is something that is dynamic and active, something that must be constantly and consciously actualized. To facilitate this actualization, the Qur'ān states that God provides natural *āyāt* (signs) and revelation delivered through messengers.[13] *Sūrat al-dhāriyāt*, for example, relates the rewards of the *muttaqūn* with the *yaqīn* (certainty of faith) that results from contemplating natural *āyāt*:

Those who are mindful of God (*muttaqūn*) will be in Gardens with springs. They will receive their Lord's gifts because of the good they

> did before: sleeping only little at night, praying at dawn for God's forgiveness, giving a rightful share of their wealth to the beggar and the deprived. On earth there are signs (*āyāt*) for those with sure faith (*mūqinīn*). And in yourselves too, do you not see? In the sky is your sustenance and all that you are promised. (51:15–22)

In another instance where *yaqīn* (certainty of faith) is linked with natural *āyāt*, it is made explicit that such signs are intended for people to reflect upon and contemplate using reason:

> There are signs (*āyāt*) in the heavens and the earth for those who believe. In the creation of you, in the creatures God scattered on earth, there are signs for people of sure faith (*mūqinīn*). In the alternation of night and day, in the rain God provides, sending it down from the sky and reviving the dead earth with it, and in God's shifting of the winds there are signs for those who use their reason (*ya'qilūn*). (45:3–5)

Reason, of course, as a human faculty is something that is instilled by God in all humanity through creation; thus, it is integrally associated with *fiṭra* (human nature). Every human is created not only with a soul that knows *taqwā* and a *fiṭra* that is disposed toward *taqwā* but also with the capacity to reflect rationally upon the signs (*āyāt*) of God that are readily available in the natural world.

Yet this is not the end of the story. God provides still another means by which humans are called to manifest *taqwā*: exhortations and guidance from revelation and messengers. *Sūrat al-shu'arā'* makes this clear. The chapter offers brief accounts of many messengers, and each account ends with the respective prophets calling their people to manifest *taqwā*:

> Their brother Noah said to them, "Will you not be mindful of God (*tattaqūn*)? I am a faithful messenger sent to you. Be mindful of God (*'attaqū*) and obey me." (26:106–108)
>
> Their brother Hud said to them, "Will you not be mindful of God (*tattaqūn*)? I am a faithful messenger sent to you. Be mindful of God (*'attaqū*) and obey me." (26:124–126)
>
> Their brother Salih said to them, "Will you not be mindful of God (*tattaqūn*)? I am a faithful messenger to you. Be mindful of God (*'attaqū*) and obey me." (26:142–144)

> Their brother Lot said to them, "Will you not be mindful of God (*tattaqūn*)? I am a faithful messenger to you. Be mindful of God (*ʾattaqū*) and obey me." (26:161–163)

God designs humans with an orientation toward *taqwā* and the capacity to actualize *taqwā* and then provides reminders of and guidance toward *taqwā*. It is imperative to recognize that *taqwā* derives not only from one of these means. In other words, *taqwā* is not something that can be arrived at only through revelation. The example of Abraham, which I will examine in detail the next chapter, is also indicative of this. Nonetheless, the fact that *taqwā* is associated with creation and *fiṭra* should not lead to the erroneous and relativist conclusion that all humans have *taqwā*. All humans have an equal capacity with respect to *taqwā*, but not all humans manifest *taqwā* equally.[14] There is equality of potentiality but diversity of actualization.

Based on the preceding exploration, two conclusions are patent. First, *taqwā* is a concept of great significance within the Qur'ān. Second, *taqwā* displays the defining characteristics of hierarchical difference; it is evaluative, assessed individually, and manifest in the social context as well in relation to God.

Lateral Religious Difference: The Semantic Field of Umma

In addition to the concepts that inhabit the semantic field of *taqwā*, the Qurʾānic discourse on religious difference also involves numerous references to various groups, including the Sabians (*al-ṣābiʾūn*), Magians (*al-majūs*, commonly understood to refer to Zoroastrians), Jews (*alladhīna hādū*, or *al-yahūd*), Children of Israel (*Banī Isrāʾīl*), Nazarenes (*al-naṣārā*), and the People of the Scripture (*ahl al-kitāb*):

> As for the believers, those who follow the Jewish faith, the Sabians, the Nazarenes, the Magians, and those who ascribe partners to God, God will judge between them on the Day of Resurrection. God witnesses all things. (22:27)[15]

> Those who believe, the Jews, the Nazarenes, and the Sabians—all those who believe in God and the Last Day and do good—will have their reward with their Lord. No fear for them, nor will they grieve. (2:62)

> We told the Children of Israel, "Live in the land, and when the promise of the Hereafter is fulfilled, We shall bring you to the assembly of all people." (17:104)
>
> Some of the People of the Scripture believe in God, in what has been sent down to you and in what was sent down to them: humbling themselves before God, they would never sell God's revelation for a small price. These people will have their reward with their Lord. God is swift in reckoning. (3:199)

Although these *āyāt* demonstrate that the Qur'ān is concerned with such groups, the exact referents of some of the groups are contested. For example, there exists historical and contemporary debate over the exact referents of the labels Sabians, Magians, and People of the Scripture.[16] Additionally, the Arabic term *al-naṣārā* is commonly translated as "Christians." This translation, however, deproblematizes and obscures debates that surround the identity of this community, which include whether the term *al-naṣārā* derives from the name of a geographical locale (i.e., Nazareth) or from the description of Jesus' disciples as his helpers (i.e., the *anṣār*, those who *naṣara*, those who help). While there is a definite connection between the Qur'ānic Nazarenes and the group called Christians, it is not wholly synonymous and, consequently, I use the term *Nazarenes* throughout as a translation of the Arabic *al-naṣārā*.

It is also necessary to explicitly distinguish from this juncture forward between the usage of Islam and Muslim to denote a particular community (the community of Muḥammad) and a member of that community and the usage of *islām* (submission) and *muslim* (submitter) to denote the Qur'ānic concepts associated with *taqwā*. I further explore the intersections of this community and the concept throughout the remainder of this analysis, but I retain the distinction using capitalized, unitalicized letters for the communal references and lowercase, italicized transliterations for the conceptual references.

In examining the Qur'ānic discourse, many scholars have attempted to argue that the *taqwā*-related concepts are associated completely and exclusively with specific groups. For instance, Ibn Kathīr's exegesis of the concept of *islām* (submission) unequivocally links the concept only with the historical community of Muḥammad.[17] Izutsu makes a similar move when he presents the conceptual opposition between *īmān* (faith) and *kufr* (disbelief) as corresponding exactly to the conceptual opposition between the Muslim community (the followers of Muḥammad) and non-Muslim Others.[18]

A few scholars, however, have sought to challenge the idea that Qur'ānic concepts are applicable to particular identifiable groups. Following W. C. Smith, Mahmut Aydin argues that the term *islām* refers not to the "concrete forms" of a particular religious community but to a more general notion of faith.[19] However, he does not maintain this distinction between the Qur'ānic terms and groups that they might identify, since he states that the concept of *īmān* is expressive of the particular concrete forms and practices of the Muslim community. Farid Esack makes a more thorough and intentional distinction when he rails against the depiction of these concepts, both positive and negative, as "entrenched qualities" of specific communities:

> One cannot hold hostage to the ethos of *kufr* which characterized their forebears, those who, by accident of birth, are a part of any group, nor others who subsequently emerge from it; nor can we do this to individuals who existed within that group, but were non-participants in *kufr*. Similarly, one cannot attribute the faith commitment and faith of preceding generations of *muslims* to contemporary Muslims.[20]

Esack's critique resonates with Barlas's argument about the distinction between categories of hierarchical evaluation and those of lateral differentiation. Esack stresses that the evaluations associated with *kufr* and *islām* are not organically and permanently connected with particular groups and that individuals within groups may variously manifest *kufr* or *islām*. Building upon his distinction, I contend that these groups are manifestations of lateral religious difference. Not only are they of a different genre than the concepts signifying hierarchical religious difference, but they are also associated with a distinct semantic field, the semantic field of *umma*.

As groups, the Sabians, Magians, Jews, Children of Israel, Nazarenes, and the People of the Scripture plainly fulfill the first characteristic of lateral difference; they denote difference that exists on a collective level rather than on the individual level. Yet these groups are not all of the same sort, nor are they all mutually exclusive. Some, for example, overlap with one another. Qur'ānic descriptions of the Children of Israel primarily revolve around Moses, the Israelites of his time, his interactions with Pharaoh, and the Exodus.[21] As such, they form the theological and historical backdrop of the communities referred to in the Qur'ān as Jews and Nazarenes. They also in many ways form the theological and historical backdrop of the Qur'ānic revelation itself. These interconnections and overlaps are also made explicit in a number of references to Jesus' interaction and relationship to the Children of Israel. Jesus is depicted as being sent to the Children of Israel and as receiving various responses:

> You who believe, be God's helpers. As Jesus, son of Mary, said to the disciples, "Who will come with me to help God?" The disciples said, "We shall be God's helpers." Some of the Children of Israel believed and some disbelieved. We supported the believers against their enemy, and they were the ones who came out on top. (61:14)

Jesus' prophetic mission is also presented as a confirmation of the Torah (*al-Tawrāt*)—the scripture of the Children of Israel and the Jews—and the introduction of a new scripture, the Gospel (*al-'Injīl*):

> We sent Jesus, son of Mary, in their footsteps, to confirm the Torah that had been sent before him. We gave him the Gospel with guidance, light, and confirmation of the Torah already revealed. A guide and lesson for those who are mindful of God (*muttaqīn*). (5:46)

Similarly, the label People of Scripture (*ahl al-kitāb*) does not refer to just one group; it is a collective term for multiple groups that have received divine revelation prior to the advent of the Qur'ānic revelation. This inclusive character is manifest in Qur'ān 5:65–66, which, like the preceding mention of Jesus, urges the People of Scripture to uphold the Torah, the Gospel, and what God has "sent down to them:"

> If only the People of the Scripture would believe and be mindful of God (*'ittaqau*), We would take away their sins and bring them into the Gardens of Delight. If they had upheld the Torah and the Gospel and what was sent down to them from their Lord, they would have been given abundance from above and from below. Some of them are on the right course, but many of them do evil. (5:65–66)

The fact that the Torah and the Gospel are mentioned explicitly indicates that the collective designation *People of the Scripture* at least refers to the Children of Israel, the Jews, and the Nazarenes. Many have aimed to restrict the designation People of the Scripture to these groups alone.[22] However, there have been vigorous debates over this restriction and, as

Esack notes, in "none of the disciplines of exegesis, Islamic history or legal scholarship have Muslims known anything approximating consensus about the identity of the People of the Book."[23] The lack of consensus has resulted from unresolved questions related to the identity of the Sabians who appear to be included among the *ahl al-kitāb*, related to Qur'ānic references to other scriptures besides the Torah and Gospel,[24] and related to the possibility of other religions being included among *ahl al-kitāb*.[25]

Daniel Madigan's semantic analysis of the concept *kitāb* (literally "book" but indicating scripture or revelation) adds additional layers of complexity to the discussion of the referents of the label People of the Scripture. If, as he argues, *kitāb* represents not a physical book but rather a process and symbol, then this has serious implications for understanding the collective label. Madigan himself states that in light of his larger study the label *ahl al-kitāb* should be "understood as those who have been given not *possession of* but rather *access to* and *insight into* the knowledge, wisdom and sovereignty of God for which the very fluid term *kitāb* serves as a symbol."[26] If the criteria for inclusion in this group become access and insight rather than a possession of a physical book, then the boundaries of the People of the Scripture most certainly expand. It is not my objective to definitively redefine those boundaries, but it is vital to acknowledge that such questions do arise.

While debates over the identity of the People of the Scripture and other groups continue, one thing that is known about all of these groups is that they are communities defined by their encounter with divine revelation. This is clear in the preceding *āyāt* that mention various scriptures and messengers of God in relation to the People of Scripture, Nazarenes, Jews, and the Children of Israel. In the case of the Sabians and the Magians, the connection with revelation is made indirectly because they, along with others, are described as being subject to divine judgment:

> As for the believers, those who follow the Jewish faith, the Sabians, the Christians, the Magians, and those who ascribe partners to God, God will judge between them on the Day of Resurrection. God witnesses all things. (22:27)

Elsewhere, the Qur'ān indicates that no individual will be subject to judgment unless he or she has received warning in the form of revelation delivered through a messenger:

> Whoever accepts guidance does so for his or her own good. Whoever strays does so at his or her own peril. No soul will bear another's burden, nor do We punish until We have sent a messenger. (17:15)

Sabians and Magians must have received revelation and messengers as well, or else the people that comprise these communities would not be subject to judgment. The fact that Sabians and Magians have received revelation is also confirmed in a series of *āyāt* depicting revelation and messengers as universal phenomena. God has not deprived any community of revelation:

> We have sent you [Prophet] with the Truth as a bearer of good news and warning. Every community (*umma*) has been sent a warner. (35:24)

> We sent a messenger to every community (*umma*), saying, "Worship God and shun false gods." Among the communities were some God guided; error took hold of others. So travel through the earth and see what was the fate of those who denied the truth. (16:36)

> For every community (*umma*) there is a messenger, and when their messenger comes, they will be judged justly. They will not be wronged. (10:47)

These *āyāt* proclaim the universal nature of revelation and messengers and also introduce the central concept of *umma* (community). God's communication is delivered to various *umam* (communities) to guide and warn the individuals of those *umam*. *Umam* are the communal recipients of God's revelation. Some of these *umam* and their messengers are mentioned explicitly by name—such as, the Sabians, Magians, Jews, Children of Israel, Nazarenes, and the People of the Scripture—while others are not:

> We have sent other messengers before you, some We have mentioned to you and some We have not. And no messenger could bring about a sign except with God's permission. When [the Day] God ordained comes, just judgment will be passed between them. There and then, those who followed falsehood will be lost. (40:78)

Even Muḥammad is described as being sent to an *umma*:[27]

> So We have sent you [Prophet] to a community (*umma*)—other communities (*umam*) passed away long before them—to recite to them

> what We reveal to you. Yet they disbelieve in the Lord of Mercy. Say, "God is my Lord: there is no god but God. I put my trust in God and to God is my return." (13:30)

Moreover, the centrality of the concept of *umma* is confirmed in *āyāt* that, similar to the already mentioned Qur'ān 10:47, state that on the Day of Judgment messengers will be called as witnesses for their respective *umam*:

> What will they do when We bring a witness from each community (*umma*), with you [Muḥammad] as a witness against these people? (4:41)
>
> The day will come when We raise up a witness from every community (*umma*), when the disbelievers will not be allowed to make excuses or amends. (16:84)
>
> The day will come when We raise up in each community (*umma*) a witness against them, and We shall bring you [Prophet] as a witness against these people, for We have sent the Scripture down to you explaining everything, and as guidance and mercy and good news to those who submit themselves to God. (16:89)
>
> We shall call a witness from every community (*umma*), and say, "Produce your evidence." And then they will know that truth belongs to God alone. The gods they invented will forsake them. (28:75)

When taken as a whole, the preceding Qur'ānic *āyāt* indicate that in its most general form the term *umma* denotes a community that is sent revelation and messengers and then held accountable on the Day of Judgment. It is crucial to highlight that, although revelation is delivered to a community as a whole and thus every member of that community will be subject to judgment, judgment will not be carried out on a group-by-group basis. Only revelation and the resultant "eligibility" for judgment are assigned communally; judgment—on the basis of *taqwā*—is carried out individually, *nafs* (soul) by *nafs*, not *umma* by *umma*:

> On the Day when every soul (*nafs*) finds all the good it has done present before it, it will wish all the bad it has done to be far, far away. God warns you to beware of God, but God is compassionate towards God's servants. (3:30)

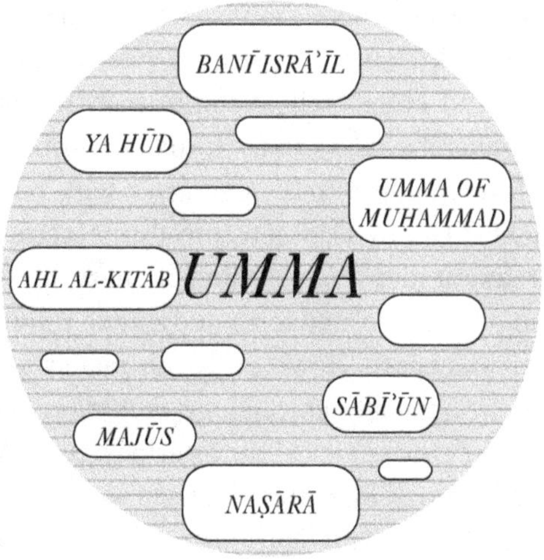

FIGURE 6.2 Lateral Religious Difference: Semantic Field of *Umma*

Note: Unlabeled shapes represent anonymous *umam*. Diagram does not depict overlapping among various *umam*.

> Beware (*'ittaqū*) of a Day when you will be returned to God. Every soul (*nafs*) will be paid in full for what it has earned, and no one will be wronged. (2:281)

In light of the general meaning of *umma* and its connection to revelation and judgment, it is possible to envision the Sabians, Magians, Jews, Children of Israel, Nazarenes, People of the Scripture, the *umma* of Muḥammad, and the myriad anonymous *umam* as various key terms that reside in the semantic field surrounding the focus word *umma* (Figure 6.2).

This is a semantic or conceptual relationship, not a relationship of exact symmetry. As already discussed, some of these terms may refer to specific discrete communities, others overlap, and others are collective terms. Moreover, some of these key terms appear to be ex post facto labels for communities that have received revelation (that is, *ahl al-kitāb*), while others may be labels that were connected with the communities even prior to the advent of revelation. This would, for example, be the case with Nazarenes if the label were based upon the geographical locale of Jesus. Despite these differences, they are all conceptually woven together through their common association as *umam* of revelation and judgment.

The connection between these groups and the concept of *umma* is not entirely novel. Frederick Denny has written extensively on the Qur'ānic meaning of *umma* and other "religio-communal" terms.[28] He acknowledges that *umma* generally refers to a "human community in a religious sense," that is, a human community associated with revelation, messengers, and judgment.[29] Denny also perceptively connects the term *umma* with a variety of relevant themes, including oneness, messengers and revelation, the notion of an appointed term, judgment, religion, and *manāsik* (particular rites or practices). However, he ultimately grounds his argument in the Nöldeke-Schwally chronology that classifies Qur'ānic *āyāt* and chapters into four chronological time periods: three Makkan and one Madinan.[30] This chronology, like others, is used as a basis to track changes in and development of Qur'ānic concepts and themes over time. Upon this hermeneutic, he contends that the general meaning of *umma* is characteristic only of the earliest chronological stages of the Qur'ān's revelation. Thereafter, the term *umma* progressively develops, first into a specific reference to a community that is unified in beliefs and practices (*umma waḥida*) and then into the specific reference to the ideal unified community of Muḥammad (*umma muslima,* the *khayr umma*).[31] As the chronological culmination, this latter meaning of *umma*, according to Denny, becomes the primary meaning of the term within the Qur'ān: "although nowhere does the Qur'ān explicitly state this, it is not inaccurate to assert that the Muslim *umma* is seen in Islam's scripture as the 'qur'ānic *umma*.' "[32] His conclusion does represent the common, extra-Qur'ānic understanding of *umma* as a term that specifically designates the Muslim community, but it also detrimentally colors his examination of some crucial themes. This is evident, for instance, in his limited treatment of the fact that God has in some way willed the disunity of humankind through diverse revelations. If unity were the ideal, then why would God will disunity or difference? Denny attempts no explanation of this but refers to it only as a mystery and as part of Qur'ānic ambiguity.

In outlining the structure of his study, Denny states that he has purposely excluded the analysis of the more general connotation of the term *umma*. His rationale behind this exclusion is noteworthy; according to Denny, such analysis "would not add to our understanding, because all of the examples would fall under the same heading."[33] What Denny has dismissed here as insignificant is what I assert to be most significant about the Qur'ānic concept of *umma*. It is precisely the general and comprehensive connotation of *umma* as a human community associated with revelation, messengers, and judgment that defines it as the focus word of the semantic field of lateral religious difference. As such, it is this connotation on which I focus. I will, however, later in this chapter return to some of Denny's contentions about reification as expressed in nongeneral usages of *umma*, such as *umma waḥida* and *umma muslima*.

In line with the general connotation, God sends revelation and messengers to different *umam*. This is a universal fact, although only some communities are mentioned specifically in the Qurʾān. The connection between the *umam* and revelation raises a number of important questions related to divine intention and will (i.e., the second defining characteristic of lateral difference). Where do *umma* come from? Are they the products of revelation or the targets of revelation? If they are targets—as they appear to be—then how did they come into existence? Are they the result of human degeneration? Or are they the result of something else? Also, what is the intended outcome of the revelation sent to various *umam*? Should they all become one *umma* united without any differentiation, as Denny contends? Or has God willed certain particularities in each *umma*?

To begin, revelation does not create the various *umam*. Revelation is sent via a messenger to a community that already exists:

> We have sent you [Prophet] with the Truth as a bearer of good news and warning. Every community (*umma*) has been sent a warner. (35:24)

Thus, *umma* should not be considered as religious communities in the sense of a community that arises from a particular experience of revelation. The communities will be affected and possibly changed by revelation, but they are not called into existence through revelation.

From where then do these different communities emerge? What is their origin? As discussed by Muslim women interpreters, the Qurʾān describes God's creation of humankind as the initial creation of a singular *nafs* (soul) that was later, and intentionally, differentiated:

> People, be mindful of your Lord, who created you from a single soul, and from the same essence created its mate, and from the pair of them spread countless men and women far and wide. Be mindful of God, in whose name you make requests of one another. Beware of severing the ties of kinship. God is always watching over you. (4:1)

While Muslim women interpreters highlight intentional differentiation into the male and female biological sexes, the Qur'ān is equally explicit about intentional linguistic, racial, and ethnic differentiation of the original creation:

> One of God's signs is that God created you from dust and—lo and behold!—you became human and scattered far and wide. Another of God's signs is that God created spouses from among yourselves for you to live with in tranquility. God ordained love and kindness between you. There truly are signs in this for those who reflect. Another of God's signs is the creation of the heavens and earth, and the diversity of your languages and colors. There truly are signs in this for those who know. (30:20–22)
>
> Have you not considered how God sends water down from the sky and that We produce with it fruits of varied colors; that there are in the mountains tracks of white and red of various hues and black; that there are various colors among human beings, wild animals, and livestock too? It is those of God's servants who have knowledge who stand in awe of God. God is almighty, most forgiving. (35:27–28)

The various human languages and colors that God has created and scattered throughout the world are described as *āyāt* (natural signs) of God. As emphasized in the preceding discussion of *taqwā*, *āyāt* are things that God intentionally creates to prompt human reflection on God's existence, majesty, and power. The communal aspect of this intentional diversification of humanity is made even more explicit in a familiar *āya*:

> People, we created you all from a male and a female and made you into races and tribes so that you should recognize one another. In God's eyes, the most honored of you are the ones most mindful of God (*'atqākum*). God is all knowing, all aware. (49:13)

This *āya* is the same one Barlas and others invoke to argue that *taqwā* is the sole basis of evaluation. God intentionally creates communal diversity in the form of races and tribes. However, individuals are assessed not based on that type of difference but only in reference to *taqwā*. This *āya* also confirms another aspect of lateral difference. The intentional communal differences are created for a purpose: "so that you should recognize one another." While I examine the meaning of this phrase in the concluding chapter, at this point it is enough to acknowledge that there is some purpose behind the difference. The existence of a purpose confirms the divine intentionality of this communal diversification, and it also introduces the fact that such differences are not supposed to be homogenized or eradicated.

If communal difference arises at least in part from creation, as willed by God, what is the goal of the revelation that is sent to these communities? Before endeavoring to answer this, I acknowledge that I am deliberately simplifying the question to a degree since I am not grappling with the historical change and processes that transpire between the moment of creation and the moment of revelation. Nonetheless, I am not implying that God creates communities that are statically bound and unchanging, and then those communities are the exact ones to which revelation is sent. What I am suggesting is that two things are made explicit in the Qur'ānic discourse: creation of communal difference; and revelation sent to communities. There are a vast number of intervening processes, including group interaction, the formation of new communities, and the disappearance of other communities. However, at some juncture there is a necessary convergence between God's willing communal diversification in creation and God sending revelation to communities. Therefore, it is legitimate to ask what type of change does revelation come to effect within these communities? The simple answer is that all revelation and messengers share a common goal of teaching people about God, of guiding them to correct practice, and of warning them of individual accountability and the Day of Judgment. It is important, though, to recall that revelation and messengers are only some of the vehicles by which God intends to carry out this mission; the *fiṭra* (human nature) and natural *āyāt* (signs) are also created to facilitate these insights.

Strikingly, while Qur'ānic references to *umma* plainly indicate this overarching mission of teaching, guiding, and warning, they simultaneously indicate that every *umma* has deliberately been appointed particular rites and practices, or acts of devotion (*manāsik*) by God:

> We have appointed acts of devotion (*mansak*) for every community (*umma*) to observe. So do not let them argue with you about this matter. Call them to your Lord. You are on the right path. And if they argue with you, say, "God is well aware of what you are doing." (22:67)

> We appointed acts of devotion (*mansak*) for every community (*umma*), for them to celebrate God's name over the livestock God provided for them. Your God is One, so devote yourselves to God. Give good news to the humble whose hearts fill with awe whenever God is mentioned, who endure whatever happens to them with patience, who keep up the prayer, who give to others out of Our provision to them. (22:34–35)

Connecting *manāsik* closely with the rituals of the *ḥajj* (pilgrimage), Denny contends that the term *manāsik* refers not to daily or routine religious practices but to more specialized or intensive rituals, rituals that comprise only a small part of any religion including Islam.[34] In doing so, he downplays the significance of this form of divinely intended difference. However, Qur'ān 5:48 reiterates the idea that God has willed *ummatic* particularities through revelation:

> ...We have assigned a law (*shir'a*) and a path (*minhāj*) to each of you. If God had so willed, God would have made you one community (*umma waḥida*), but God wanted to test you through that which God has given you, so race to do good. You will all return to God and God will make clear to you the matters you differed about. (5:48, excerpt)

Unlike *manāsik*, the terms *shir'a* (ordained way or law) and *minhāj* (path) are not as easy to confine or relegate, despite their limited frequency within the text; there is only one other Qur'ānic reference to *sharī'a* ("Now We have set you (Muhammad) on the path/way of religion (*sharīatin*), so follow it. Do not follow the desires of those who lack knowledge" [45:18]), and no other references to *minhāj*. The inability to confine or relegate these terms is due to the generally held view that the specific law associated with the Muslim community is the only acceptable *shir'a*; it is seen as abrogating and superseding all others. However, this *āya* states that God has intentionally given diverse laws and paths. It also emphasizes that despite God's ability to do otherwise God did not create an *umma waḥida* (a single community). Thus, God not only appoints particularities but also deliberately withholds uniformity.

Moreover, this *āya* specifies a purpose for God's diversification through revelation: "to test you... so race to do good." As with the purpose of diversification mentioned in reference to creation ("so that you may recognize one another"), I will later explore the potential meanings of this purpose, but again its existence alone confirms the divine intention behind these differences. For that reason, it raises a whole host of challenging questions about how diverse communities of revelation should understand those differences. The general perception of this within the Islamic tradition is that other ways were appointed in the past but now have been superseded. In many ways this is a shortcut out of the maze of complexities raised by the clear depiction of *umam*—in both their origins in creation and their relationship to revelation—as communities that are intentionally and therefore purposefully differentiated.

The final defining characteristic of lateral difference is that it does not serve as the basis of evaluation. This means not that lateral groups are completely free of evaluation but rather that evaluation will always be partial and differentiated. If there is evaluation of lateral groups, a single evaluation will not be uniformly ascribed to an entire group solely on the basis of membership in that group. Consequently, in attempting to demonstrate that the Sabians, Magians, Jews, Children of Israel, Nazarenes, People of the Scripture, the *umma* of Muḥammad, and the anonymous *umam* are lateral religious groups, it is necessary only to show that they are partially and diversely evaluated, not that they are never evaluated.

Partial evaluation is reasonably easy to discover within the Qurʾānic text; many *āyāt* distinguish a portion or section within a particular *umma*:

> Some Jews distort words from their contexts. They say, "We hear and disobey," and "Listen," "May you not hear," and "*Raʿina* [Look after us]," twisting it abusively with their tongues so as to disparage religion. If they had said, "We hear and obey," "Listen," and "*Unzurna* [Look towards us]," that would have been better and more proper for them. But God has spurned them for their defiance. They believe very little. (4:46)

> Some of the People of the Scripture would dearly love to lead you astray, but they only lead themselves astray, though they do not realize it. (3:69)

In their partial evaluation, these *āyāt* demonstrate that the behaviors of distorting the meaning of revelation and leading astray are not ascribed to these *umam* in their entirety. Only "some of" the individuals within these *umam* engage in such actions. By inference, this means that some within those *umam* uphold the meaning of revelation and do not lead others astray. Qur'ān 3:75–76, however, does not require any inference as it describes two different types of behavior among the People of the Scripture:

> There are People of the Scripture who, if you entrust them with a heap of gold, will return it to you intact, but there are others of them who, if you entrust them with a single dinar, will not return it to you unless you keep standing over them, because they say, "We are under no obligation towards the gentiles." They tell a lie against God and they know it. No indeed! God loves those who keep their pledges and are mindful of God (*muttaqīn*).

It is critical to underscore the basis upon which the preceding evaluations are lodged. They are not an assessment of the particularities of the *umam* but of qualities and actions that have a negative or positive relationship with *taqwā*. In other words, they are not criticized because they are Jews or People of the Scripture but because *taqwā* demands recognition and consciousness of God as well as social interactions that align with and encourage such consciousness. Qur'ān 3:75–76 confirms this, when after distinguishing between the two types of people it connects the keeping of pledges with being *muttaqūn*, being among those that manifest *taqwā*.

The fact that it is *taqwā* determining these assessments is made even clearer in *āyāt* that juxtapose the various lateral religious communities with the hierarchical religious concepts:

> Some of the People of the Scripture believe (*yu'minu*) in God, in what has been sent down to you and in what was sent down to them. Humbling themselves before God, they would never sell God's revelation for a small price. These people will have their reward with their Lord. God is swift in reckoning. (3:199)

> Those who disbelieve (*kafarū*) among the People of the Scripture and those who ascribe partners to God were not about to change their ways until they were sent clear evidence. (98:1)

> Those who disbelieve (*kafarū*) among the People of the Scripture and the associators will have the Fire of Hell, there to remain. They are the worst of creation. (98:6)

Here, *īmān* and *kufr* (two of the key terms in the semantic field of *taqwā*) are ascribed to portions of the People of the Scripture (a key term in the semantic field of *umma*). Many exegetes have attempted to evade the apparent meaning of *āyāt* such as 3:199 that praise other communities outside of the Muslim community, the *umma* of Muḥammad. They have endeavored to argue that such *āyāt* refer to minimal or highly specific contingents of those *umam* or that they refer to People of the Scripture who actually converted to Islam.[35] Other scholars have appealed to the theory of *naskh* (abrogation) and have stated that these *āyāt* have been replaced by other, less affirmative Qurʾānic *āyāt*. A similar amount of effort has been given to arguing that negative, yet partial, depictions (e.g., Qurʾān 98:1 and 98:6) should be extended holistically to entire groups. The endeavors to both circumscribe and extend the explicit meaning of these *āyāt* result from the failure to distinguish between lateral and hierarchical religious difference. When the two are conflated or treated as being synonymous—as with Ibn Kathīr, Izutsu, and Denny—intricate exegetical efforts must be made to demonstrate that every positive evaluation is associated with the Muslim community and that every negative evaluation is associated with other *umam*.

Still, some *āyāt* appear to make more inclusive and intrinsic evaluations of groups. For example, Qurʾān 9:30–31 describes the Jews and Nazarenes, without explicit qualification, as engaged in some form of ascribing partners to God (*shirk*):

> The Jews said, "Ezra is the son of God," and the Nazarenes said, "The Messiah is the son of God." They said this with their own mouths, repeating what earlier disbelievers had said. May God confound them! How far astray they have been led! They take their rabbis and their monks as lords, as well as the Messiah, the son of Mary. But they were commanded to serve only one God. There is no god but God. God is far above whatever they set up as God's partners!

Based on the *āyāt* that unambiguously state the evaluations are not all-inclusive and on the differentiation between lateral and hierarchical religious difference, it is not possible to interpret the critiques in this *āya* as applying to all. Nor is it possible to say that, from the Qurʾānic perspective, there is an automatic or ubiquitous connection between *shirk* and the communities of the Jews and the Nazarenes. To do so would be to conflate lateral and hierarchical religious difference. Furthermore, conflation must be avoided with *āyāt* that depict other *umam* both negatively and favorably:

> The believers, the Jews, the Nazarenes, and the Sabians—all those who believe in God and the Last Day and do good—will have their rewards with their Lord. No fear for them, nor will they grieve. (2:62)

Commonly invoked as a blanket affirmation of other communities outside of the *umma* of Muḥammad (the Muslim community), this *āya* cannot be read as such for the same reasons that *shirk* cannot be inclusively or inherently tied to all Jews or all Nazarenes. This *āya* is not an affirmation of lateral communities, which do not need to be affirmed or critiqued but are divinely willed and nonevaluative entities. This *āya*, rather, is an affirmation of *taqwā* (God consciousness) and *īmān* (belief). If people within those communities—and apparently within any community—manifest *taqwā*, they will be rewarded. If they do not, they will not. This *āya* does not imply that those communities in their entirety manifest *taqwā* any more than the preceding *āya* implies that all Jews and Nazarenes in their entirety engage in *shirk*. Some do; others do not.

While it is specifically stated as not being the case in reference to the Jews, the Nazarenes, and the People of the Scripture, the possibility always exists that an entire lateral *umma* could be characterized by a specific hierarchical manifestation of *taqwā*. For example, an entire *umma* might manifest *īmān* (belief) or *kufr* (disbelief). Improbable as this may be, even in such a situation the assessment would still be based upon *taqwā* and would still be carried out on an individual level. One illustration of this is found in Qur'ānic accounts of previous *umam* that received messengers but did not heed their guidance. The Qur'ān occasionally describes their lack of *taqwā* and punishment in communal terms:

> How many towns We have destroyed! Our punishment came to them by night or while they slept in the afternoon. (7:4)

However, the Qur'ānic account of the prophet Hud, for example, clarifies that judgment is always based on *taqwā* and always carried out on the individual level. In this account, not everyone was destroyed, and those who were denied and did not believe, that is, did not manifest *taqwā*:

> We saved him, and those who were with him, through Our mercy. We destroyed those who denied Our revelations and would not believe. (7:72)

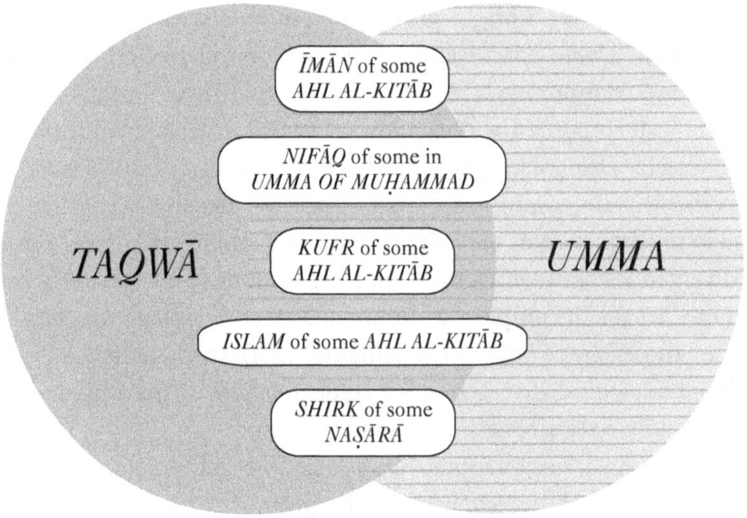

FIGURE 6.3 Dynamic Intersections of Hierarchical and Lateral Religious Difference
Note: Diagram does not depict all possible combinations that result from the intersection of the two semantic fields.

In sum, the key to understanding Qur'ānic evaluations of religious difference is to recognize them as intersections of the semantic field of hierarchical religious difference with that of lateral religious difference, as intersections of the semantic field of *taqwā* with that of *umma*. (Figure 6.3).

The two fields intersect, thereby producing evaluations, but the intersections are dynamic, multiple, and partial. The fields do not merge and so lose their unique characteristics. Nor do they intersect once and for all. They dynamically intersect in a number of possible ways and in an ongoing fashion. This is why, for instance, there are various assessments of the People of the Scripture. It is not an inconsistency to be argued away through specification or abrogation. It is the result of the fact that the semantic fields of *taqwā* and *umma* are distinct yet related.

Umma *and Reification?*

While my primary focus is the general usage of *umma*, it is essential to consider some unique Qur'ānic occurrences of the term. In these occurrences, the word *umma* itself is modified, resulting in designations such as *umma qāʾima* (an upright group), *umma muqtaṣida* (a group on the right course), *umma muslima* (a group that submits to God), and *umma waḥida* (one community). Denny maintains that these various formulations indicate progressive reification in the term *umma*, moving from references to a singular, generalized religious community to ultimately a specific Muslim community. His perspective presents a possible challenge to my depiction of *umma* as designating lateral difference. Some of the divergences between Denny's and my own analyses inevitably result from the fact that he employs a chronological methodology whereas I utilize a methodology of synchronic semantic analysis. Nonetheless, beyond this methodological divergence his interpretation of the unique occurrences of *umma* requires examination.

The first two designations, *umma qāʾima* and *umma muqtaṣida*, describe portions of the People of the Scripture:

> But they are not all alike. There are some among the People of the Scripture who are upright (*umma qāʾima*), who recite God's revelations during the night, who bow down in worship, who believe in God and the Last Day, who order what is right and forbid what is wrong, who are quick to do good deeds. These people are among the righteous and they will not be denied [the reward] for whatever good deeds they do. God knows exactly who is mindful of God (*muttaqīn*). (3:113-115)

> If only the People of the Scripture would believe and be mindful of God (*ʾittaqū*), We would take away their sins and bring them into the Gardens of Delight. If they had upheld the Torah and the Gospel and what was sent down to them from their Lord, they would have been given abundance from above and from below. Some of them are on the right course (*umma muqtaṣida*), but many of them do evil. (5:65–66)

While the word *umma* here is uniquely used to describe a group within a lateral *umma*, the resulting meaning is no different from the previously discussed partial evaluations. These two designations describe some of the People of the Scripture who are upright and on the right course in the same manner that other *āyāt* described some of the People of the Scripture as believing. The usage of the word *umma* is unique, but the connotation is not. Denny admits that *umma qāʾima* has some "religious" meaning but does not mean a specific religion. He describes it as "the portion of an *ummah* which is actually living up to its calling."[36] This description aligns with what I have already stated: it is a *taqwā*-related evaluation of a portion of a lateral *umma*. Strangely, after acknowledging this Denny nevertheless proceeds to contend that the "term applies ideally to the Muslims [*umma* of Muḥammad]."[37] He does not explain how he arrives at this conclusion. In relation to the designation *umma muqtaṣida*, Denny describes Qur'ān 5:66 as perplexing and ponders whether this designation refers to Jews or Christians who had become Muslims through conversion. What confuses him is not whether it refers to Muslims in the lateral sense; rather, he struggles to determine from which group the converts came. Since Denny equates the Qur'ānic ideal of *umma* with the Muslim community alone, he does not read the *āya* for its apparent meaning, that is, that some of the People of the Scripture are on the right course. Rather, he reads it, without question, as referring to a group of people who joined the reified Muslim community.

The designation *umma muslima* (a group that submits to God) appears in the context of a prayer made by Abraham and Ishmael:

> Our Lord, make us devoted to You. Make our descendants into a community that submits to You (*umma muslima*). Show us how to worship and accept our repentance, for You are the Ever Relenting, the Most Merciful. (2:128)

Denny interprets this *āya* as depicting Abraham praying for a particular and novel type of lateral community that is distinct from the Jews and the Nazarenes. In other words, he contends that the prayer of Abraham is a prayer for the emergence of the reified Muslim community. Denny seems to overlook the straightforward meaning of the designation *umma muslima*. Abraham is praying for his descendants to submit and be devoted to God, that is, to manifest *taqwā* through *islām* (submission). Abraham is not praying for the emergence of a particular lateral community, the *umma* of Muḥammad. It may be true that other lateral *umam* have failed as a whole to live up to this prayer, and it may even be true that Abraham is praying for a lateral community to do so in its entirety. However, the mere occurrence of the Arabic word *muslim* (submitter) does not automatically substantiate his claim that this is a unique and exclusive allusion to the Muslim community. According to the Qur'ān, every individual in every community has been commanded by God to manifest *taqwā*, and part of *taqwā* is *islām*.

Denny attempts to substantiate his contention about the reified and exclusive nature of *umma muslima* by citing Qur'ān 3:110, which appears to describe the lateral Muslim *umma* as *khayr umma* (the best community):

> You are the best community (*khayr umma*) singled out for people. You order what is right, forbid what is wrong, and believe in God. If the People of the Scripture had also believed, it would have been better for them. For, although some of them do believe, most of them are lawbreakers. (3:110)

Denny's explanation of the characteristics of the best *umma* is unquestionable: according to the Qur'ān, its members would order what is right, forbid what is wrong, and believe. In others words, the best *umma* would be one in which all its members manifested *taqwā*. Yet he interprets this *āya* as stating that the *taqwā*-related evaluation of being "the best" is inherently ascribed to the lateral Muslim community as a whole. This is an unacceptable conclusion in light of what has been argued throughout this chapter. While it is conceivable that all members of the lateral Muslim community could manifest *taqwā* and thus be the *khayr umma*, it would never be automatically ascribed. Therefore, although the language of the *āya* states "you are the best community," this designation must be contextualized to garner a better appreciation of its meaning.

Situated in the context of a critique of some of the People of the Scripture who split into factions, fell into disputes, and did not believe,[38] Qur'ān 3:110 is preceded by 3:104–105, which issues an exhortation to *be* a community that does the same things as the *khayr umma*:

> Be a community (*umma*) that calls for what is good, urges what is right, and forbids what is wrong. Those who do this are the successful ones. Do not be like those who, after they have been given clear revelation, split into factions and fall into disputes. A terrible punishment awaits such people. (3:104–105)

If the Muslim community is automatically ascribed the status of *khayr umma* (the best community)—as Denny's theory of reification advocates—then what is the purpose of this exhortation? Additionally, Qur'ān 3:113–115 distinguishes between individuals within the People of the Scripture. This is significant in and of itself, but in relation to Qur'ān 3:110 it is significant due to the way some of the People of Scripture are described:

> But they are not all alike. There are some among the People of the Scripture who are an upright community (*umma qāʾima*), who recite God's revelations during the night, who bow down in worship, who believe in God and the Last Day, who order what is right and forbid what is wrong, who are quick to do good deeds. These people are among the righteous and they will not be denied [the reward] for whatever good deeds they do. God knows exactly who is mindful of God (*muttaqīn*). (3:113–115)

This *umma qāʾima* is described in exactly the same way as the *khayr umma*; among other things, they believe, order what is right, and forbid what is wrong. Moreover, like all the *muttaqūn* (those who manifest *taqwā*), irrespective of their lateral communal affiliation they will be rewarded. When Qurʾān 3:110 is placed in its intratextual context, what initially appears as an automatic ascription must be reinterpreted as a contingent assessment: if you do these things, if all of you do these things, then you are the *khayr umma*. The original Arabic does not contain the "if" or "then," but the context of the *āya* and the overarching Qurʾānic perspective on *taqwā* demand it.

The final distinctive usage of *umma* is the phrase *umma waḥida* (one community). As mentioned, Denny struggles with the idea that God wills disunity, that is, that God has not made humans into an *umma waḥida*. He acknowledges the *āyāt* that state this, but nevertheless argues that *umma waḥida* is a midpoint in the progress of chronological reification, which describes the intended "single religious community of the People of the Book."[39] He bases this on Qurʾān 21:92–94 and Qurʾān 23:52–54:

> This community of yours is one single community (*umma waḥida*), and I am your Lord, so serve Me. They have torn their unity apart, but they will all return to Us. (21:92–93)
>
> This community of yours is one (*umma waḥida*), and I am your Lord. Be mindful of Me (*ʾattaqūn*). But they have split their affair into factions, each rejoicing in their own. (23:52–53)

Denny argues that these *āyāt* state that the People of the Scripture are supposed to be an *umma waḥida* but that "they" divide themselves into factions. However, his presentation of these *āyāt* is not straightforward. The *umma waḥida* referred to is not an *umma waḥida* of the People of the Scripture. As Denny acknowledges (markedly without any resultant modification to his theory of reification), the Qur'ān is explicit that this has not been willed:

> ... We have assigned a law and a path to each of you. If God had so willed, God would have made you one community (*umma waḥida*), but God wanted to test you through that which God has given you, so race to do good. You will all return to God and God will make clear to you the matters you differed about. (5:48, excerpt)

> If God so willed, God would have made you all one community (*umma waḥida*), but God leaves to stray whoever God will and guides whoever God will. You will be questioned about your deeds. (16:93)

> If God had so pleased, God could have made them a single community (*umma waḥida*), but God admits to God's mercy whoever God will. The evildoers will have no one to protect or help them. (42:8)

> If your Lord had pleased, God would have made all people a single community (*umma waḥida*), but they continue to have their differences—except those on whom your Lord has mercy—for God created them to be this way, and the word of your Lord is final: "I shall definitely fill Hell with both jinn and humankind." (11:118–119)

Whatever this *umma waḥida* is, it is not something for humankind in general or lateral *umam*. In fact, this is also evident in the very verses cited by Denny to make this claim. Denny conveniently commences his quotation of these *āyāt* without acknowledging their explicit addressees. Both of the *āyāt* that say "this community of yours is an *umma waḥida*" are specifically addressed to the collective of God's messengers. Intriguingly, he does acknowledge this meaning in his other writings, but this does not impact his interpretation.[40] In Qur'ān 21:92–93, the immediate context is not just the story of the Virgin birth. Rather, the forty-four *āyāt* that precede those cited by Denny recount the missions and trials of messengers, including Moses, Aaron, Abraham, Lot, Noah, David, Solomon, Job, Ishmael, and Jonah. God gave all of these messengers the same mission: to teach about *taqwā*, to guide people to it, and to warn people. And they were all met with accusations of falsehood and people who refused their mission. The *āyāt* of Qur'ān 23:51–53 are situated similarly in a discussion of Noah's and Moses' missions. Yet, in this case, it is necessary only to cite the preceding *āya* to clarify the intended addressees:

> Messengers, eat good things and do good deeds. I am well aware of what you do. This community of yours is one (*umma waḥida*), and

> I am your Lord. Be mindful of Me. But they have split their unity into factions, each rejoicing in their own. (23:51–53)

Therefore, the *āyāt*, which Denny presents as being indicative of progressive reification, refer not to a particular lateral religious community but to the collective of messengers God sent to various *umam*. God's messengers form an *umma waḥida*. Recognizing that it is messengers that are designated as an *umma waḥida* and that God has deliberately not made humankind in general into an *umma waḥida* prompts an important question: what does *umma waḥida* signify? What is it that messengers as a group share that God intentionally denies humankind? Are messengers a reified religious community, as Denny understands the phrase? His interpretation of it as such prevents him not only from acknowledging that the phrase refers to messengers—not People of the Scripture as a single lateral *umma*—but also from seeing another important and integrated possibility.

In addition to those already cited, there are three other Qur'ānic references to *umma waḥida*: Qur'ān 2:113, 10:19, and 43:33. The first two state that humankind in general (*nās*) was originally an *umma waḥida* but then differed:

> Humankind (*nās*) was a single community (*umma waḥida*), then God sent prophets to bring good news and warning, and with them God sent the Scripture with the Truth, to judge between people in their disagreements. It was only those to whom it was given who disagreed about it after clear signs had come to them because of rivalry between them. So by God's leave God guided the believers to the truth they had differed about. God guides whoever God will to a straight path. (2:213)

> Humankind (*nās*) was originally one single community (*umma waḥida*), but later they differed. If it had not been for a word from your Lord, judgment would already have been passed between them regarding their differences. (10:19)

Three aspects of these *āyāt* are significant. First, *nās* (humankind) was once an *umma waḥida*. Second, the differences—the divergences from that state of being an *umma waḥida*—are caused by people and so are considered blameworthy, that is, subject to evaluation and judgment. This same sentiment is also expressed in the already quoted Qur'ān 16:93,

42:8, and 11:118–119, which likewise tie differences to the themes of guidance, straying, mercy, and judgment. Third, the differences mentioned in these *āyāt* are considered resolvable through revelation and messengers. Thus, the question becomes what kind of unity did humankind have originally that they are negatively evaluated for losing and for which they are sent revelation and messengers to regain?

Lateral religious difference is not the basis of evaluation or judgment; only hierarchical religious difference is the basis of evaluation. If humans are being evaluated in these *āyāt*—which they are—then it must be due to hierarchical differences in terms of *taqwā*. This is supported by the fact that it is only the differences in *taqwā* that humans cause. God intentionally introduces lateral religious differences both through the creation of nations and tribes (Qur'ān 30:20–22, 35:27–28, and 49:13) and through the various rites, laws, and ways that God ordains through revelation (Qur'ān 5:48, 22:34–35, and 22:67).

Moreover, the fact that God ordains diverse religious rites, laws, and ways through revelation means that the unity that revelation and messengers are sent to restore cannot possibly be uniformity that negates lateral religious difference. Revelation and messengers are one of the intentional means by which God creates such difference. Therefore, the type of unity that people have lost and messengers are sent to restore is unity of *taqwā*, or hierarchically evaluated religious unity. Going back to the first aspect of these *āyāt*, can it be said that humankind originally had a unity in terms of *taqwā*? Is there a form of unity that God created in all of humankind? It appears that this unity of *taqwā*—the *umma waḥida* that humankind was—refers to the universal *fiṭra* (natural disposition, human nature) of all humankind, which God forms and inspires to know the distinction between "rebellion and *taqwā*."[41]

In light of this interpretation, *āyāt* stating that God could have made humankind into an *umma waḥida* but has deliberately refrained from doing so (Qur'ān 5:48, 16:93, 42:8, 11:118–119) become less ambiguous than Denny acknowledges. God does not compel individuals to manifest *taqwā*; God does not compel unity of hierarchical difference. Rather, God provides various guides (in *fiṭra*, natural signs, revelation, and messengers), and individuals are held accountable for freely and persistently choosing to follow those guides.

The *āyāt* that describe messengers as an *umma waḥida* (Qur'ān 23:52–54 and 21:92–94) are also consistent with and better explicated by the interpretation of *umma waḥida* as a unity of *taqwā*. Messengers are not a unity in terms of the various rites, laws, and ways that they bring to their people. They are, however, united—perhaps even somewhat compelled—in their consciousness of God.[42] They all manifest *taqwā* and carry out their prophetic missions.

Moreover, the interpretation of *umma waḥida* as referring to a unity of *taqwā* and not a unity of lateral communal difference is manifest in the last Qur'ānic occurrence of the designation:

> If it were not that all humankind might have become a single group (*umma waḥida*), We could have given all those who disbelieve in the Lord of Mercy houses with roofs of silver, sweeping staircases to ascend. (43:33)

This *āya* states that God would have given disbelievers an abundance of worldly goods but did not because it would have resulted in all human beings becoming an *umma waḥida* of disbelievers. They would have all become unified in their lack of *taqwā*.

Based on the foregoing analysis of these unique occurrences of *umma* within the Qur'ān, there is little indication that they depict progressive reification toward an ideal, unified, and singular lateral religious community. These occurrences are better accounted for in light of the distinction between hierarchical and lateral religious difference.

Taqwā *and Denotative Stability?*

In the context of critiquing Izutsu's comparison of the Qur'ānic and Khārijite worldviews, I raised the question of whether it was possible for *īmān* (belief) to lose its denotative stability and fixedness in the same manner in which *kufr* (disbelief) had lost its denotative stability within the Khārijite worldview. In the Khārijite worldview, *kufr* was no longer something kept at bay outside the wall of the Muslim community; rather, it had become something mobile and freely roaming within the wall. Based upon the distinction between lateral and hierarchical religious difference, it is now possible to answer this question.

All of the concepts that inhabit the semantic field of *taqwā*, including *kufr* and *īmān*, are uniquely defined by their lack of denotative stability.

They do not denote or correspond exactly and statically with specific lateral religious communities. These hierarchical concepts are mobile and able to roam within, outside, and across the boundaries of lateral communities (*umam*). As such, they are precisely the type of difference, or Otherness, described by J. Z. Smith: a form of difference that is always relational, dynamic, and provocative.

The lack of denotative stability in reference to lateral communities, though, should not be misconstrued as indicating that *taqwā* and its related concepts lack definite content. As shown, hierarchical concepts are specific, evaluative, and social; certain actions, behaviors, and beliefs in relation to God and other humans are positively evaluated and others are negatively evaluated. In fact, it is precisely by distinguishing between the two distinct yet dynamically intersecting semantic fields that it is possible to navigate between two objectionable extremes: exclusivism and relativism. By distinguishing between hierarchical and lateral religious difference, it is possible to avoid the depiction of *taqwā* as captive within one reified, lateral religious community and also to avoid the depiction of *taqwā* as some sort of relativistic and amorphous form of belief.

It is also by distinguishing between hierarchical and lateral religious difference that it becomes feasible to account for the full complexity of the proximate religious Other, the Other-who-can-never-be-wholly-other. Difference is no longer conceived of as dividing humanity through the erection of clear, static, and impermeable boundaries; it is now the dynamic intersection between two semantic fields that produces various (perhaps even infinite) combinations of proximity (sameness) and Otherness (difference). As a result, the choice is no longer between prioritizing sameness and proximity to the detriment of Otherness or neglecting the intricacies of proximity through isolation and linear hierarchies. The only choice is to focus on the intersections themselves and to examine the diverse convergences of proximity and Otherness without collapsing the two or depicting them in a static or exclusive relationship.

If the boundaries of lateral communities can no longer be seen as corresponding exactly with the hierarchical concepts, then it is essential to develop a much more complex appreciation of the *taqwā*-related hierarchical concepts themselves. Since both the positive and negative hierarchical concepts are mobile, it is not possible to rely upon simple, static threshold criteria intended to designate boundaries. Moreover, if the aim is to identify and comprehend *taqwā* or the lack thereof, a more intricate understanding is needed, an understanding that goes beyond Izutsu's conceptual opposition and subsumption to explicate the nuances of and relationships among the hierarchical concepts themselves.

7

Relational Mapping of the Semantic Field of Taqwā*: Concepts of Hierarchical Religious Difference*

FAILURE TO ACCOUNT effectively for the proximate religious Other is not only a result of the conflation or undifferentiated aligning of Qur'ānic concepts of hierarchical religious difference with lateral religious communities. It is also a result of the manner in which hierarchical religious concepts (those concepts that inhabit the semantic field of *taqwā*) themselves have been understood and analyzed. Toshihiko Izutsu exemplifies this in his overriding conceptual opposition and his subsumption of evaluative concepts under other evaluative concepts. Additionally, in the historical Islamic discourse, great emphasis was placed on distinguishing between the various concepts and identifying simple threshold criteria with which to mark those distinctions unambiguously.

In reconceptualizing the Qur'ānic concepts of hierarchical religious difference as all being situated in the semantic field of *taqwā*, I have intended to deconstruct the presentation of *īmān* (belief) and *kufr* (disbelief) as exact conceptual opposites and to emphasize the importance and complexity of other previously subsumed concepts. In this new schematization, the primary question is not how *īmān* is distinguished from *kufr* or even the historical preoccupation with how *īmān* is or is not distinguished from *islām* (submission or devotion to God). Instead, the central question becomes how each concept relates directly to the core facets of *taqwā*. This does not mean that the concepts themselves are not related but rather that it is through reference to and in comparison with the central concept of *taqwā* that the complexities and the nuances of both the individual concepts and their interrelationships are most effectively grasped.

In this chapter, therefore, I explore the concepts of *īmān, islām, ḥanīf* (commonly translated as nondenominational monotheist), *kufr, shirk* (ascribing partners to God), and *nifāq* (hypocrisy) in reference to central aspects of *taqwā* on three pivotal themes: recognition of and attitude toward God; response to God's guidance; and type and nature of actions. In relation to each theme, essential characteristics of these concepts and interconnections among them are illuminated.

Throughout the subsequent exploration, I draw upon some of the analysis of these concepts offered by both Izutsu and Farid Esack. While I do not embrace Izutsu's conclusions or depiction of the overarching Qur'ānic worldview, his method of semantic analysis and certain observations are invaluable. Moreover, Izutsu's focus on salvation is somewhat similar to the project I undertake in this chapter in that he compares various Qur'ānic concepts to the theme of salvation to illuminate similarities and dissimilarities between the concepts. However, his analysis falls short in that he ultimately structures his entire depiction of the Qur'ānic worldview on the basis of this singular point of thematic intersection. I diverge from Izutsu's singular focus and explore the concepts in relation to multiple points of intersection, aiming to highlight—without eventual subsumption—similarities, differences, overlaps, and gradations. In reference to Esack, I build upon and expand his challenge to the depiction of *īmān, kufr*, and other concepts as static and reified entities, and I share his commitment to problematizing boundaries and underscoring complexity. However, rather than exploring the nuances and complexities of each concept in relative isolation from the others, I explore their nuances and complexities in relation to one another by discussing them in reference to the central themes derived from *taqwā*. My analysis thus expands upon Esack's work by exploring additional concepts and by focusing on the complex relationality that exists among the concepts.

As previously alluded to in reference to the concept of *ḥanīf*, the number of occurrences of each of the hierarchical *taqwā*-related concepts within the Qur'ān varies greatly. The concepts are also expressed in a variety of grammatical structures, such as nouns, verbs, and adjectives. While some interpreters have endeavored to specify distinct meanings for the various grammatical structures,[1] throughout the following I have chosen to use the phrase "those who manifest" (e.g., "those who manifest *islām*") when

Table 7.1

Frequency and Form of Occurrence within the Qur'ān

Concept	Root	Total	Noun	Verb	Participle/Adjective
ḥanīf	*Ḥ-N-F*	12	12		
islām	*S-L-M* (form IV)	72	8	22	42
īmān	*'-M-N* (form IV)	827	45	550	232
nifāq	*N-F-Q* (form III)	37	3	2	32
shirk	*SH-R-K* (form I, IV)	165	45	71	29
kufr	*K-F-R* (form I)	504	37	289	158/17

analyzing all of the various occurrences and structures. This deliberate interpretative choice is intended to underscore the dynamic nature of the concepts and to impede the depiction of the concepts as referring to reified communal groups. Table 7.1 indicates the frequency and structures of occurrence for each concept.[2]

From this table it is evident that *īmān* and *kufr* far exceed the other concepts in terms of frequency. While this variance can be read as an indication of the relative importance of concepts, this is not always the case. A conspicuous example of this is the concept of *islām*. Although the term *islām* itself appears only eight times in the Qur'ān, it plays a profound role in the Qur'ānic discourse on religious difference and in historical and contemporary interpretations of that discourse.

Recognition of and Attitude toward God

The manifestation of *taqwā* in relation to God is a combination of mindfulness, awe, fear, belief, and worship. The *muttaqūn* (those who manifest *taqwā*) recognize God's existence and understand God's power. Intimately tied to this recognition of God is certainty about the Hereafter and God's ultimate judgment of all humankind. How are the various forms of hierarchical difference (i.e., the concepts) related to these aspects of *taqwā*? Does the Qur'ān depict all individuals as recognizing the existence of God? What is the nature of that recognition? Do individuals who manifest these various forms of hierarchical difference recognize God in different ways? Do they fear God and understand God's power? What is their perspective on the Hereafter?

One of most striking aspects of the Qur'ānic discourse is that it does not discuss people who do not recognize the existence of God. In other words, there is no discourse aimed at atheism or a group of people that could be considered atheists. This is an especially important point in reference to common English translations of some of the hierarchical concepts. For example, *kāfir* (disbeliever) is commonly translated as "unbeliever," thereby implying the utter absence of belief.[3] The Qur'ān, however, depicts all of humanity as acknowledging the existence of God.

Part of the reason that the Qur'ānic discourse does not address atheism is tied to the presentation therein of human nature, the *fiṭra*, which is created to know *taqwā*:

> By the soul and how God formed it and inspired it [to know] its own rebellion and piety (*taqwā*)! (91:7–8)

This is the initial and essential state of every human being. Moreover, the Qur'ān depicts every individual as testifying at the moment of creation to the existence and status of God:

> When your Lord took out the offspring from the loins of the Children of Adam and made them bear witness about themselves, God said, "Am I not your Lord?" and they replied, "Yes, we bear witness." So you cannot say on the Day of Resurrection, "We were not aware of this." (7:172)

The Qur'ānic discourse is primarily concerned not with impelling the basic acknowledgment of the existence of God, but rather with guiding people to acknowledge God in a "correct" and sustained fashion, that is, in a fashion consistent with *taqwā*:

> If you ask them who created the heavens and earth and who harnessed the sun and moon, they are sure to say, "God." Then how are they deluded? It is God who gives abundantly to whichever of God's servants God will, and sparingly to whichever God will: God has full knowledge of everything. If you ask them, "Who sends water down from the sky and gives life with it to the earth after it has died?," they are sure to say, "God." Say, "Praise belongs to God!" Truly, most of them do not use their reason (*ta'qilūn*). (29:61–63)

As the preceding *āyāt* indicate, people acknowledge God, especially in terms of God's role as creator and sustainer. However, this acknowledgment is not constant; people become deluded, fail to be grateful, and fail to use their reason (ʿ*aql*) to understand the true status and power of God. Qurʾān 10:22–23 depicts a similar oscillation between recognition and ingratitude:

> It is God who enables you to travel on land and sea until, when you are sailing on ships and rejoicing in the favoring wind, a storm arrives. Waves come at those on board from all sides and they feel there is no escape. Then they pray to God, professing sincere and exclusive devotion to God (*mukhliṣīna*), "If You save us from this we shall be truly thankful." Yet no sooner does God save them than, back on land, they behave outrageously against all that is right. People! Your outrageous behavior only works against yourselves. Take your little enjoyment in this present life. In the end you will return to Us, and We shall confront you with everything you have done.

In moments of dire crisis, people call upon God, knowing that it is God alone who can save them. They promise gratitude in return, yet when they are safe they forget God and behave in a manner inconsistent with *taqwā*. These *āyāt* illustrate the primary Qurʾānic concern with actively and appropriately sustaining the acknowledgment of God. *Taqwā* is something that must be constantly striven for and sustained, not simply achieved or professed. The people described in these *āyāt* profess sincere devotion (*mukhliṣīna*), but then they falter in that devotion and divert from it.

This depiction of humankind—as knowing that God exists yet being challenged in their ability to sustain and manifest *taqwā*—forms the backdrop of the entire Qurʾānic discourse on hierarchical religious difference. The various concepts thus denote not whether people acknowledge God but rather the manner in which they do so. Do they recognize God's power? Do they fear God? Do they take God as their only protector?

Īmān

The concept of *īmān* exists, unsurprisingly, in a positive relationship with *taqwā*. This is partly the case because it is associated with individuals who fear God and put their full trust (*tawakkul*) in God alone:

> True believers (*muʾminūn*) are those whose hearts tremble with awe when God is mentioned, whose faith increases when God's revelations are recited to them, who put their trust in their Lord. (8:2)

> God! There is no god but God, so let the faithful (*mu'minūn*) put their trust in God. (64:13)

Their fear and trust in God is intimately connected to their recognition of God's unique status; they recognize that there is no power except the power of God. This also implies that they do not place fear of other beings before their fear of God:

> It is Satan who urges you to fear his followers. Do not fear them, but fear Me, if you are true believers (*mu'minīn*). (3:175)
>
> Those whose faith (*īmān*) only increased when people said, "Fear your enemy. They have amassed a great army against you," and who replied, "God is enough for us. God is the best protector." (3:173)

The preceding *āya* describes their conception of God's power and role as protector, but it also depicts the behavior that those who manifest *īmān* display when faced with difficulties. In the face of human threats, their *īmān* increases. This is notable because it emphasizes that *īmān*, like *taqwā*, has levels and can always be increased. It is also significant because it indicates that those with *īmān* will not be exempted from trials and hardships. In fact, the Qur'ān explicitly states that those with *īmān*—along with all other humans—will be tested:

> We shall certainly test you with fear and hunger, and loss of property, lives, and crops. But give good news to those who are steadfast (*ṣābirīn*), those who say, when afflicted with a calamity, "We belong to God and to God we shall return." These will be given blessings and mercy from their Lord, and it is they who are rightly guided. (2:155–157)
>
> Did you think you would enter the Garden without God first proving which of you would struggle for God's cause and remain steadfast (*ṣābirīn*)? (3:142)

Humans will be tested and assessed by God based upon their responses to those tests. As these *āyāt* state, the most appropriate response is to remain steadfast, that is, to consistently demonstrate *ṣabr* (patience perseverance). Once again, this aligns with the active and continuous nature of *taqwā*. Neither *taqwā* nor *īmān* is about profession alone, and neither is something an individual can simply claim to have. Rather, both must be continuously and deliberately enacted.[4]

As a result of the recognition of God's singular status and power, those who manifest *īmān* do not mix or combine their belief in and worship of God with other beliefs and practices that may compromise that recognition:

> It is those who have faith (*alladhīna āmanū*), and do not mix their faith with wrongdoing, who will be secure, and it is they who are rightly guided. (6:82)
>
> Say, "Disbelievers (*kāfirūn*), I do not worship what you worship. You do not worship what I worship. I will never worship what you worship. You will never worship what I worship. You have your religion and I have mine." (109:1–6)

Qur'ān chapter 109, *Sūrat al-kāfirūn*, also indicates that those who manifest *īmān* are forthcoming about their perspective and the distinction between it and other perspectives. Another crucial feature of this chapter is that although it involves an inherent evaluation of *kufr* it does not append any automatic action to that evaluation. The evaluation does not necessitate action to eliminate the negatively evaluated form of hierarchical difference. *Kufr* is not regarded positively, but people who manifest *īmān* are not charged with the responsibility of eradicating *kufr*. This is confirmed in the Qur'ānic depiction of the role of messengers. Even messengers, including Muḥammad, are sent only to warn, not to compel *īmān*:

> "And [I am commanded] to recite the Qur'ān." Whoever chooses to follow the right path does so for his or her own good. Say to whoever deviates from it, "I am only here to warn." (27:92)
>
> We know best what they say. You are not there to force them, so remind with this Qur'ān those who fear My warning. (50:45)

Three other prominent characteristics of those who manifest *īmān* are that they do not have doubt, they are thankful for God's blessings, and they are humble in their relationship to God:

> The true believers (*mu'minūn*) are the ones who have faith (*āmanū*) in God and God's Messenger and leave all doubt behind . . . (49:15, excerpt)
>
> You who believe (*alladhīna āmanū*), eat the good things We have provided for you and be grateful to God if it is God that you worship. (2:172)

> But those who believed (*alladhīna āmanū*), did good deeds, and humbled (*ʾakhbatū*) themselves before their Lord will be companions in Paradise, and there they will stay. (11:23)
>
> Prosperous are the believers (*muʾminūn*)! Those who pray humbly (*khāshiʿūn*) . . . (23:1–2)

The particular significance of gratitude and humility will become more evident in the subsequent discussions of other concepts. At this juncture, though, it is important to note that the humility that those who manifest *īmān* display in this world is the same posture assumed by all humans on the Day of Judgment:

> On that Day, people will follow the summoner from whom there is no escape. Every voice will be humbled (*khashaʿat*) for the Lord of Mercy. Only whispers will be heard. (20:108)
>
> On the Day when the blast reverberates and the second blast follows, hearts will tremble and eyes will be cast down in humility (*khāshiʿatun*). (79:6–9)

On that day, the trait that those who manifest *īmān* have adopted *by choice* in this world will be the one all people assume *by necessity*. It is not surprising, therefore, to find that the Qurʾān describes those with *īmān* as those who also believe in the Hereafter:

> The believers (*alladhīna āmanū*), the Jews, the Nazarenes, and the Sabians—all those who believe (*āmana*) in God and the Last Day and do good—will have their rewards with their Lord. No fear for them, nor will they grieve. (2:62)

This belief is integrally connected to their acknowledgment of God's power; they stand in awe of God, and their hearts tremble in the face of God's power. Moreover, the fact that those who manifest *īmān* have firm conviction in the Judgment and Hereafter is corroborated by descriptions of their future discussions with others on the Day of the Resurrection:

> On the Day the Hour comes, the guilty will swear they lingered no more than an hour. They have always been deluded. But those endowed with knowledge and faith (*īmān*) will say, "In accordance with God's decree, you actually lingered till the Day of Resurrection. This is the Day of Resurrection, yet you did not know." (30:55–56)

Those who had knowledge and manifested *īmān* in the world will recognize the Day of Resurrection as the fulfillment of God's promise.

Shirk

Shirk is commonly translated as either idolatry or polytheism,[5] but the term can also be translated more broadly as associationism or ascription. Those who manifest *shirk* are those who associate things with God or ascribe partners to God. As Gerald Hawting argues, the concept of *shirk* in the Qurʾān is not confined to literal idolatry (i.e., the worship of idols) or polytheism (i.e., the worship of multiple Gods).[6] These may be some of the concrete manifestations of *shirk*, but the Qurʾān does not limit *shirk* to these forms:

> Sometimes the nature of the thing thus venerated is left unspecified and anonymous in phrases such as: those who are worshipped/called upon before/other than God, those who are taken as patrons/friends (*awliyaʾ*) before God, and those who are taken as 'equals/peers' (*andād*) before God.[7]

The unspecified nature of the discourse means that *shirk* must be envisioned as any act of ascribing partners to God. This includes following one's desires in a slavish fashion as well as envisioning human power to be on par with God's power (e.g., Qurʾān 25:43, 2:258).[8]

Although those who manifest *shirk* ascribe partners to God—seeking assistance and protection from those partners—this does not indicate that they do not recognize God's power. Many *āyāt* testify to the contrary:

> When a human suffers some affliction, he prays to his Lord and turns to God, but once he has been granted a favor from God, he forgets the One he had been praying to and sets up rivals to God, to make others stray from God's path. Say, "Enjoy your ingratitude (*kufr*) for a little while. You will be one of the inhabitants of the Fire." (39:8)

When tested with affliction, those who manifest *shirk* initially behave similarly to those with *īmān*; they turn to God and seek God's protection and favors. Turning to God in times of crisis is a clear indication that they recognize and do not deny God's power. They turn to God for help because they know God can help them. However, when their affliction subsides or when they are granted favors, they forget God and set up rivals. As such, they are not steadfast in their recognition of and dependence on God; they do not manifest *ṣabr* (patient perseverance). They also lack appreciation for the favors they are granted. It is essential to highlight the term used to indicate their ingratitude: *kufr*. As Izutsu notes, the concept of *kufr* can imply either ingratitude or disbelief.[9] In the context of Qur'ān 39:8, the concept is utilized to underscore the ingratitude of those who manifest *shirk*.

It is possible, therefore, to argue that the main Qur'ānic contention with those who manifest *shirk* is not that they have no appreciation of God's status and power but rather that they have a limited appreciation and flawed conception of that power. They do not recognize every aspect of God's power. Hawting makes a similar assertion:

> The gist of the koranic criticism is that although the opponents know that God is the creator and regulator of the universe, and although they appeal to God in times of distress, regularly they fall back into something that it views as less than total monotheism.[10]

Hawting expounds this lack of total monotheism, or complete recognition of God's power, by discussing the distinction between *tawḥīd al-rubūbiyya* (oneness of God as Lord) and *tawḥīd al-ulūhiyya* (oneness of God as God). Those who manifest *shirk* have the former; they recognize God as Lord, that is, as the Creator and Sustainer. But they do not have the latter; they do not have a comprehensive conception of God as the only God. This is clarified with reference to the description of God presented in Qur'ān 59:22–24:

> God is God. There is no god other than God. It is God who knows what is hidden as well as what is in the open. God is the Lord of Mercy, the Giver of Mercy. God is God. There is no god other than God, the Controller, the Holy One, Source of Peace, Granter of Security, Guardian over all, the Almighty, the Compeller, the Truly Great. God is far above anything they consider to be God's partner (*yushrikūn*). God is God. The Creator, the Originator, the Shaper. The best names belong to God. Everything in the heavens and earth glorifies God. God is the Almighty, the Wise.

As these *āyāt* indicate, God is much more than the Creator and Sustainer; God is also the only protector, the only granter mercy, and the one with complete knowledge.

These *āyāt* also introduce another facet of the Qur'ānic critique of those who manifest *shirk*. Not only do they have a partial conception of God's power and ascribe partners to God, but they also fail to recognize that the chosen partners and false protectors have no real power whatsoever:

> It is God who created you and provided for you, who will cause you to die and then give you life again. Which of your partners can do any one of these things? Glory be to God, and exalted be God above the partners they ascribe to God (*yushrikūna*). (30:40)
>
> They worship alongside God things that can neither harm nor benefit them, and say, "These are our intercessors with God." Say, "Do you think you can tell God about something God knows not to exist in the heavens or earth?" Glory be to God! God is far above the partner-gods they ascribe to God (*yushrikūna*)! (10:18)

Qur'ān 10:18 again emphasizes that those who manifest *shirk* do have some conception of God's power. They say that the other things they worship will be their intercessors with God. While the Qur'ān denies the reality of such intercession elsewhere (e.g., Qur'ān 6:70, 6:94, 7:53, 10:3, 32:4.), their acknowledgment of the need for intercession is an implicit acknowledgment of God's status and power.

Their misconception of God's power is also evident in their contention that God could have prevented them from ascribing partners if God had so desired:

> Those who associate others with God (*alladhīna 'ashrakū*) say, "If God had willed, we would not have worshipped anything but God, nor would our forebears. We would not have declared anything forbidden without God's sanction" ... (16:35, excerpt)

Certainly God as All-Powerful *could* prevent such a thing, but those who manifest *shirk* lack true understanding of God's relationship with humanity. As discussed in Chapter 6, God does not compel *taqwā*; rather, God orders *taqwā* and humans choose whether or not to strive for it. What is intriguing is that other *āyāt* indicate that those who manifest *shirk* actually do so in order to move closer to God:

> Sincere devotion (*al-dīn al-khāliṣ*) is due to God alone. Those who choose other protectors beside God, saying, "We only worship them

> because they bring us nearer to God," God will judge between them regarding their differences. God does not guide any ungrateful liar. (39:3)

This creates a more complex scenario than the simple equation of *shirk* with utter disbelief. While the claim that they worship other things to move closer to God can be understood as an excuse, it can also be interpreted as a forthright statement. Both possibilities exist within the Qur'ānic depiction of *shirk*. There may be those whose primary allegiance is to the "partners" or things they associate with God. There may also be those who truly believe that they need intermediaries to establish a relationship with God. The Qur'ān's response to both possibilities, though, is clear: devotion should be to God alone, and devotion to God should be sincere and exclusive (*ikhlaṣ*).

Thus, the Qur'ān does not primarily juxtapose *shirk* with monotheism but rather with *ikhlaṣ*, a form of monotheistic devotion that is devoid of any and all intermediaries.[11] There is, however, another significant nuance to the comparison between *shirk* and *ikhlaṣ*. It is not the case that those who manifest *shirk* never manifest *ikhlaṣ*. In fact, there are times when they do:

> Whenever they go on board a ship they call on God, and dedicate their faith to God alone (*mukhliṣīn*), but once God has delivered them safely back to land, see how they ascribe partners to God (*yushrikūn*)! (29:65)

This *āya* indicates—similar to Qur'ān 39:8—that they are capable of manifesting *ikhlaṣ*, but they are critiqued for failing to sustain that manifestation.

Those who manifest *shirk* are also described as denying the reality of the Hereafter:

> Say [Prophet], "I am only a mortal like you. It has been revealed to me that your God is One. Take the straight path to God and seek God's forgiveness. Woe to those who ascribe partners (*mushrikūn*), who do not pay the prescribed alms and refuse to believe (*kāfirūn*) in the world to come! (41:6–7)

Although the precise reason for denial (*kufr*) of the Hereafter is not made explicit, based on what has been discussed thus far certain conclusions can be drawn. They do not deny the Hereafter as an automatic consequence of denying God or God's power. They deny neither. Their denial, therefore, must be attributed to their flawed conception of God's power. Whereas they recognize God's power and dominion in certain arenas—such as creation and sustaining of the creation—they do not extend that recognition to the power to resurrect humankind after death. This view is confirmed in other *āyāt* that ask humans to reflect on creation as a proof of God's ability to effect the resurrection:

> They also say, "What? When we are turned to bones and dust, shall we really be raised up in a new act of creation?" Say, "Even if you were stone, or iron, or any other substance you think hard to bring to life." Then they will say, "Who will bring us back?" Say, "The One who created you the first time" . . . (7:49–51, excerpt)

It is also confirmed through descriptions of the Day of Judgment, when those who manifested *shirk* will learn that all and every power belongs to God:

> Even so, there are some who choose to worship others besides God as rivals to God, loving them with the love due to God, but the believers have greater love for God. If only those who did wrong could see—as they will see when they face the torment—that all power belongs to God, and that God punishes severely. (2:165)

Ḥanīf

The exact meaning of the term *ḥanīf* is a matter of vigorous debate. Scholars have variously suggested that it is related to the Syriac term for "pagan," that it derives its meaning from pre-Qurʾānic Jewish and Christian literature, or that it means "to incline" toward something.[12] The Qurʾānic concept of *ḥanīf*, however, is best illuminated relationally, that is, with reference to the manner in which it is distinguished from and affiliated with other Qurʾānic concepts and themes. In this vein, *ḥanīf* is frequently invoked in contrast to *shirk*:

> Be true in faith (*ḥunafāʾ*) to God and assign God no partners (*mushrikīn*), for the person who does so (*yushrik*) is like someone

> who has been hurled down from the skies and snatched up by the birds or flung to a distant place by the wind. (22:31)

This contrast is further asserted through the affirmative connection of *ḥanīf* with *ikhlaṣ* (sincere, exclusive devotion to God):

> Though all they are ordered to do is worship God alone, sincerely devoting (*mukhliṣīn*) their religion to God as people of true and pure faith (*ḥunafā'*), keep up the prayer (*yuqīmū al-ṣalāt*), and pay the prescribed alms. For that is the religion right and straight (*dīn al-qayyima*). (98:4–5)

Recollecting the concept of *shirk*, it is notable that a *ḥanīf* is not simply someone who manifests *ikhlaṣ* while those who manifest *shirk* do not. As indicated, those who manifest *shirk* display *ikhlaṣ* on some occasions and in certain circumstances. Therefore, the contrast between *ḥanīf* and those who manifest *shirk* relates to the manner in which *ikhlaṣ* is or is not sustained. A *ḥanīf* is someone who consistently sustains *ikhlaṣ* in relation to God, whereas one who manifests *shirk* falters in the expression of *ikhlaṣ*. Moreover, the sustained manifestation of *ikhlaṣ* characteristic of the *ḥanīf* is described as *dīn al-qayyima* (the correct or true religion).

The notion of sustained *ikhlaṣ* is further emphasized in other *āyāt* that use the expression "to turn one's face" toward something:

> [Prophet], set your face towards religion as one of true and pure faith (*'aqim wajhaka lil-dīni ḥanīfan*). Do not be one of those who join partners with God (*mushrikīn*). (10:105)

> So as one of pure faith, stand firm and true in your devotion to the religion (*'aqim wajhaka lil-dīni ḥanīfan*). This is the natural disposition (*fiṭra*) God instilled in humankind. There is no altering God's creation. And this is the right religion (*al-dīn al-qayyim*), though most people do not realize it. (30:30)

> "I have turned my face (*wajjahtu wajhiya*) as one of true and pure faith (*ḥanīf*) towards God who created the heavens and the earth. I am not one of those who ascribe partners (*mushrikīn*)." (6:69)

There are a variety of significant aspects of these *āyāt*. First, the expression "to turn one's face" means to devote oneself wholly and constantly to something, to orient one's whole being toward a singular object, that is,

God. This is exactly what those who manifest *shirk* fail to do: they turn occasionally toward God, but then they turn away. This is further illuminated in reference to the definition of *birr* (goodness) provided in Qurʾān 2:177:

> Goodness (*al-birr*) does not consist in turning your face towards East or West . . . (excerpt)

Birr, taqwā, and *ḥanīf*—in contrast with *shirk*—are linked with turning one's face in a singular direction in a consistent fashion. The emphasis on sustained devotion that characterizes the *ḥanīf* is also evoked through the imperative *ʾaqim*. This verb means to establish something and then to perform that action in an ongoing manner. Notably, the most frequent occurrence of this verb is in the context of prayer. As in the previously cited Qurʾān 98:4–5, people are told to "*yuqīmū al-ṣalāt*" (to establish or keep up prayer). This does not mean to simply pray but rather to pray in an ongoing and constant manner, to establish prayer as a habitual pattern of behavior. Therefore, in the context of these verses about *ḥanīf,* the appearance of the imperative *ʾaqim* underscores the emphasis on upholding and sustaining devotion to God.

Qurʾān 30:30 also introduces the connection between *ḥanīf* and *fiṭra* (human nature or natural disposition). As the only occurrence of the noun *fiṭra* within the entire Qurʾān, it is conspicuous. To be *ḥanīf* is the natural disposition of humans, who are created to incline toward and turn their faces toward God. This confirms the intimate relation between *ḥanīf* and *taqwā* because, as discussed, the human soul is created to know *taqwā*.

The concept of *ḥanīf* is also closely associated with the figure of Abraham:

> [Prophet] say, "God speaks the truth, so follow Abraham's way. He was true and pure in faith (*ḥanīf*), and he was never one who ascribed partners (*mushrikīn*)." (3:95)

> Who could be better in religion than those who submit themselves wholly (*ʾaslama wajhahu*) to God, do good, and follow the way of Abraham, who was true and pure in faith (*ḥanīf*)? . . . (4:125, excerpt)

> Abraham was neither a Jew nor a Nazarene. He was upright and devoted to God (*ḥanīf muslim*), never one who ascribes partners (*mushrikīn*). (3:67)

Abraham is depicted as the archetypal *ḥanīf*, and to follow Abraham's way is the ideal path, even for Muḥammad. This ideal path is illuminated through the depiction of Abraham's relationship with his father and his community, all of whom engaged in *shirk*, even literal idolatry. Abraham is presented as someone who had no interest in engaging in *shirk*, and he vigorously argued with his people against such practices:

> His people argued with him, and he said, "How can you argue with me about God when God has guided me? I do not fear anything you ascribe (*tushrikūna*) to God. Unless my Lord wills [nothing can happen]. My Lord's knowledge encompasses everything. How can you not take heed? Why should I fear what you ascribe (*ʾashraktum*) to God? Why do you not fear to associate (*ʾashraktum*) with God things for which God has sent you no authority? Tell me, if you know the answer, which side has more right to feel secure?" (6:80–81)

This exchange is in many ways a recapitulation of the Qurʾānic critique of those who manifest *shirk*. Abraham underscores the true nature of God's power and the impotence of those things that are associated with God. Abraham also stresses that as a result fear should be of nothing but God.

The preceding *āyāt* (Qurʾān 4:125 and 3:67) also connect the concept of *ḥanīf* with the concept of *islām* (submission or devotion). Abraham is described as submitting "his face"—his whole self—to God. Moreover, he is placed in contrast not only with those who manifest *shirk* but also with the Jews and Nazarenes. This juxtaposition will be explored later in this chapter.

Kufr

As discussed in reference to the concept of *shirk*, the concept of *kufr* is associated in part with ingratitude. Individuals manifest *kufr* when they display a lack of appreciation for God's abundant favors upon them:

> If you tried to count God's favors, you could never calculate them. Humankind is truly unjust and ungrateful (*kaffār*). (14:34, excerpt)

Kufr, however, is also associated with disbelief. In fact, Izutsu argues that this dual association renders *kufr* semantically ambiguous. As such, in many circumstances it becomes "difficult to draw a sharp line of demarcation between them...the two are connected with each other in Qur'anic thought by a firm conceptual link."[13] Izutsu's observation is provocative, especially in light of the strict demarcation that he draws between *kufr* and other concepts. If *kufr* is semantically ambiguous, then this would seem to imply that such distinctions may be less than apparent. While Izutsu claims that both ingratitude and disbelief can end only in the denial of the oneness of God, this does not appear to hold true in all situations. Certainly ingratitude is a negative trait. However, it also manifests periodically in much of humanity, and is potentially even displayed bythose who manifest *īmān*:

> You who believe (*alladhīna āmanū*), eat the good things We have provided for you and be grateful to God, if it is God that you worship. (2:172)

This *āya* is a reminder to those who manifest *īmān* to remain grateful if they truly worship God and thus indicates the potential for any person to display ingratitude. No person rests in a position of security from this possibility.

With respect to *kufr* as disbelief, it is also necessary to unpack further the meaning of disbelief. Since the Qur'ān does not discuss any people who do not recognize the existence of God, *kufr* cannot be understood as a simple absence of belief. This is confirmed in *āyāt* that critique individuals for rejecting and denying God's signs. These individuals are described as displaying *kufr* yet as believing to some degree. They may believe only a little, but they do manifest some belief:

> They say, "Our hearts are impenetrably wrapped." But God has rejected them for their disbelief (*kufrihim*). They have little faith (*yu'minūn*). (2:88)[14]
>
> And so for breaking their pledge, for rejecting God's revelations, for unjustly killing their prophets, for saying "Our hearts [minds] are closed." No! God has sealed them in their disbelief (*kufrihim*), so they believe (*yu'minūna*) only a little. (4:155)

The preceding *āyāt* also introduce the Qur'ānic depiction of the hearts of those who manifest *kufr*. Izutsu examines these descriptions in detail,[15] and therefore I will offer only a few comments on this aspect of the concept of *kufr*. The Qur'ān variously describes their hearts as wrapped, hard, sealed, veiled, and arrogant (e.g., Qur'ān 2:88, 4:155, 6:43, 2:74, 5:13, 2:6–7, 9:93, 17:45–46, 6:25, 6:43). These descriptions should be considered in reference to the descriptions of the hearts of those who manifest *īmān;* they have hearts that tremble in response to God and that are calm and humble (e.g., Qur'ān 8:2, 22:35, 13:20, 13:28, 57:16, 22:54). One notable contrast that emerges through this comparison is that the hearts of those with *īmān* are defined through their relationship with God: whether it be fear, security, or humility, each of these involves a relational element. The hearts of those who manifest *kufr*, however, are described as isolated and distant from the relationship with God. This can be the result of the action of both humans (i.e., veiling and hardening) and God (i.e., sealing). Another significant observation regarding these descriptions is that they should not all be assumed to indicate a singular situation or form of *kufr*. Rather, they appear to be indications of different manifestations of *kufr*, of diverse ways individuals manifest disbelief.

One of the best approaches to comprehending the intricacies of the concept of *kufr* is through exploration of the figure of Iblis, or Satan. Iblis is presented as a prototypical example of the manifestation of *kufr*:

> When We told the angels, "Bow down before Adam," they all bowed. But not Iblis, who refused and was arrogant. He was one of those who deny the truth (*kāfirīn*). (2:34)[16]

While the story of Iblis is recounted in various places throughout the Qur'ān, one of the most illuminating accounts appears in chapter 7, *Sūrat al-'a'rāf*:

> We created you, We gave you shape, and then We said to the angels, "Bow down before Adam," and they did. But not Iblis. He was not one of those who bowed down. God said, "What prevented you from bowing down as I commanded you?" And he said, "I am better than him [Adam]. You created me from fire and him from clay." God said, "Get down from here! This is no place for your arrogance. Get out! You are contemptible!" (7:11–13)

Iblis is here depicted as existing before humankind was created and then being asked by God to bow down to the human creation. Iblis refuses to do so, and when asked why his rationale is that he is better than humanity. This reveals a number of essential characteristics of those who manifest *kufr*. First, they know God. Just like Iblis, they are well aware of God's existence and even God's power. Iblis, for example, witnesses the creation of humankind. Thus, *kufr* does not emerge from lack of belief strictly speaking. Second, Iblis disobeys the command of God. Once again, the nuances are important. It is not that Iblis is ignorant of the commands of God but that he deliberately and consciously refuses to follow them. Third, Iblis's rationale for not obeying is due to arrogance and an inflated sense of self, which derives from a distinct source. He considers himself to be better based upon the manner and substance of his creation: he was created from fire, and humans were created from only clay (see also Qur'ān 15:33). In other words, he assesses his own worth and the worth of other creations on the basis of divinely intended difference (i.e., lateral difference) rather than on the basis of *taqwā* as indicated in Qur'ān 49:13.

With regard to the Hereafter, the Qur'ān describes the views of those who manifest *kufr* in multiple ways. As with the multiple portrayals of their hearts, it is tempting to collapse these descriptions into a generalized negative appraisal. However, this strategy is not well suited to illuminating or comprehending complexities. Three particular perspectives on the Hereafter are associated with the concept of *kufr*: doubt; denial; and exclusivism. In reference to the first, those who manifest *kufr* are depicted as having doubt about the Day of Judgment until the moment that it actually arrives:

> The disbelievers (*alladhīna kafarū*) will remain in doubt about it until the Hour suddenly overpowers them or until torment descends on them on a Day devoid of all hope. (22:55)

While doubt is the result of a lack of full conviction,[17] it is not the same as outright denial of the Hereafter. Other *āyāt*, though, do describe those who manifest *kufr* as denying the resurrection and the Day of Judgment:

> They say, "There is nothing beyond our life in this world. We shall not be raised from the dead." If you could only see, when they are made to stand before their Lord, how God will say, "Is this not real?" They will say, "Yes indeed, by our Lord." God will say, "Then taste the torment for having disbelieved (*takfurūna*)." Lost indeed are

> those who deny the meeting with their Lord until, when the Hour suddenly arrives, they say, "Alas for us that we disregarded this!" They will bear their burdens on their backs. How terrible those burdens will be! (6:29–31)

Remarkably, although some of those who manifest *kufr* flatly deny the Hereafter in this world, when questioned by God they will readily admit that they were wrong. In attempting to explicate the reason for their denial, Izutsu contends that those who manifest *kufr* deny the Hereafter and judgment due to their reliance on reason. He states that their rationalism in particular leads them to reject the resurrection as "absurd and fantastic."[18] Yet this assertion does not seem to comply with the overarching depiction of reason (*ʿaql*) in the Qurʾān. As discussed in relation to human nature, reason is seen as a faculty instilled in humans so they may reflect on God's natural signs and thereby gain a true appreciation of God (e.g., Qurʾān 2:164). Therefore, while the explanation for this denial is not made explicit it does not seem to be caused by an excessive dependence on reason.

The third perspective associated with those who manifest *kufr* is the assertion that the rewards of the Hereafter will be for them, or their group, exclusively:

> They also say, "No one will enter Paradise unless he or she is a Jew or a Nazarene." This is their own wishful thinking. Say, "Produce your evidence, if you are telling the truth." In fact, any who devote themselves wholly to God (*ʾaslama wajhahu*) and do good will have their reward with their Lord. No fear for them, nor will they grieve. (2:111–112)

> Say, "If the last home with God is to be for you alone and no one else, then you should long for death, if your claim is true." But they will never long for death because of what they have stored up with their own hands. God is fully aware of the evildoers. (2:94–95)

Qurʾān 2:111–112, which should be understood as referring to those among the Jews and Nazarenes who engage in *kufr*, not only shows the exclusive claim to rewards but also contrasts this claim with the concept of *islām*. The reward is not for these groups exclusively but rather for all individuals who devote themselves wholly to God. Moreover, these *āyāt* parallel Iblis's assertion that he is better than humans, as the assertion of those who manifest *kufr* is also an example of attempting to evaluate based on communal identity and lateral difference. The response to this is a reassertion that evaluation will be carried out only on the basis of hierarchical difference, only on the basis of whether one manifests *taqwā* and *islām*.

Qurʾān 2:94–95, which refers to a group of people among the followers of Moses that manifested *kufr*, indicates a similar exclusive claim to rewards. It also reveals that, although they make such claims, they do not wish for the Day of Judgment. The Qurʾān is highlighting an incongruity in their thought. If they are automatically privileged in the Hereafter, why would they not wish for the Hereafter to arrive immediately? The reason is made clear: they know they are at fault, and they know they will be judged. Once again, this confirms that those who manifest *kufr* recognize God's existence and God's power.

Islām

The concept of *islām* has already been encountered a number of times in this section. As seen, it has a very close relationship with *ḥanīf* and the figure of Abraham. Therefore it is not surprising to find *islām* commonly juxtaposed with *shirk* and closely connected with *ikhlaṣ*:

> Say, "Instead of God, are we to call on what neither profits nor harms us? To turn on our heels after God has guided us, like someone bewildered, having been tempted by devils into a desert ravine, though his companions call him to guidance, 'Come to us'?" Say, "God's guidance is the true guidance. We are commanded to devote ourselves (*nuslima*) to the Lord of the Worlds." (6:71)
>
> Say, "I have been commanded to serve God, dedicating my worship entirely (*mukhliṣ*) to God. I have been commanded to be the first to submit (*muslimīn*)." (39:11–12)

Additionally, as in Qurʾān 4:125, the expression *ʾaslama wajhahu* appears numerous times to denote the absolute and steady nature of the submission of those who manifest *islām*:

> In fact, any who devote themselves wholly to God (*ʾaslama wajhahu*) and do good will have their reward with their Lord. No fear for them, nor will they grieve. (2:112)[19]

> Whoever directs themself wholly (*yuslim wajhahu*) to God and does good work has grasped the surest handhold (*istamsaka bil-ʿurwati al-wuthqā*), for the outcome of everything is with God. (31:22)

To submit one's face or self in this manner is described in Qurʾān 31:22 as "grasping the surest handhold." Thus, to submit one's self fully and consistently is the most secure and stable position in relation to God. The expression *istamsaka bil-ʿurwati al-wuthqā* is further elucidated by the only other occurrence of it in the Qurʾān:

> There is no compulsion in religion (*dīn*). True guidance has become distinct from error, so whoever rejects evil and believes in God has grasped the firmest handhold (*istamsaka bil-ʿurwati al-wuthqā*), one that will never break. God is all hearing and all knowing. (2:256)

This *āya* specifies that the grasping of the surest handhold, associated with the concept of *islām*, is something that cannot be compelled. It is a decision that every individual must make freely and that results from recognition of the clear distinction between guidance and error. Moreover, as long as an individual grasps this surest handhold, the relationship between God and the one who manifests *islām* will never break. People, though, certainly can sever—or at least disrupt—this relationship if they cease to strive in the manner described.

Similar to those who manifest *īmān*, those who manifest *islām* are described as recognizing God's power and oneness and being humble and steadfast:

> "...Creator of the heavens and the earth, You are my protector in this world and in the Hereafter. Let me die in true devotion to You (*muslim*). Join me with the righteous." (12:101, excerpt)

> Say, "What is revealed to me is that your God is one God. Will you submit to God (*muslimūn*)?" (21:108)

> We appointed acts of devotion (*mansak*) for every community, for them to celebrate God's name over the livestock God provided for them. But your God is One, so devote yourselves to God (ʾ*aslimu*). Give good news to the humble whose hearts fill with awe whenever God is mentioned, who endure whatever happens to them with

> patience (*ṣabirīn*), who keep up the prayer, who give to others out of Our provision to them. (22:34–35)

Qur'ān 22:34–35 revisits the topic of *manāsik* (religious rites or practices) that was explored in relation to lateral religious difference and the concept of *umma*. These *āyāt* state that God has intentionally appointed these diverse rites, but then they quickly recall that, despite this divinely intended lateral difference, there is only one God and that the correct relationship with God is *islām*.

Those who manifest *islām* are also portrayed as fearing and having no doubt about the Hereafter. Certainty and fear are the result of their comprehensive understanding of God's true status and power:

> Say, "To whom belongs all that is in the heavens and the earth?" Say, "To God. God has self-prescribed mercy. God will certainly gather you on the Day of Resurrection, which is beyond all doubt. Those who deceive themselves will not believe. All that rests by night or by day belongs to God. God is the All Hearing, the All Knowing." Say, "Shall I take for myself a protector other than God, the Creator of the heavens and the earth, who feeds but is not fed?" Say, "I am commanded to be the first to devote myself [to God] (*'aslama*)." Do not be one of those who ascribe partners (*mushrikīn*). Say, "I fear (*'akhāfu*) the punishment of a dreadful Day if I disobey my Lord." (6:12–15)

Other well-known *āyāt* about *islām* should be understood in light of the preceding description of those who manifest *islām*:

> Religion, in God's eyes, is devotion to God alone (*islām*) . . . (3:19, excerpt)

> If anyone seeks a religion other than complete devotion to God (*islām*), it will not be accepted from him or her. He or she will be one of the losers in the Hereafter. (3:85)

In line with Chapter 6, these *āyāt* cannot be read as referring exclusively to the community of people who follow Muḥammad. They refer to those who manifest *ikhlaṣ*, who follow Abraham, who submit their entire selves, who freely grasp the surest handhold, and who fear God's power. Moreover, in light of Qur'ān 22:34–35 and 2:111–112 (discussed in reference to *kufr*), these *āyāt* also refer to those who are not distracted by lateral difference but who remain steadfast in the manifestation of *taqwā* despite such differences.

Nifāq

In reference to the general attitude toward God, the concept of *nifāq* is associated with three dominant characteristics. The first is that individuals who manifest *nifāq* are described as ignoring and forgetting God:

> The hypocrites, both men and women (*munāfiqūn* and *munāfiqāt*), are all the same. They order what is wrong and forbid what is right. They are tight-fisted. They have ignored God, so God has ignored them. The hypocrites (*munāfiqīn*) are the disobedient ones. (9:67)
>
> Satan has gained control over them and made them forget God. They are on Satan's side, and those on Satan's side will be the losers. (58:19)

Similar to those who manifest *kufr*, the flawed relationship in the case of *nifāq* is connected to Satan. The *munafiqūn* are described as being members of the *ḥizb* (faction, party) of Satan.

The second key characteristic of those who manifest *nifāq* is that they fear people more than God. Whereas it is God who makes the hearts of the *muʾminūn* tremble, the *munāfiqūn* display more fear of the hardships that people may inflict:

> Fear of you is more intense in their hearts than fear of God because they are people devoid of understanding. (59:13)
>
> ...They think every cry they hear is against them. And they are the enemy. Beware of them. May God confound them! How devious they are! (63:4, excerpt)
>
> There are some people who say, "We believe in God," but, when they suffer for God's cause, they think that human persecution is as severe as God's punishment. Yet, if any help comes to you from your Lord, they will say, "We have always been with you." Does God not know best what is in everyone's hearts? (29:10)

The primary concern of those who manifest *nifāq* is to protect and benefit themselves in the world irrespective of their actions and irrespective of the fact that God knows what is truly in their hearts. The fact that they are primarily concerned with their status before humans rather than their status before God is also evident in their willingness to oscillate between groups dependent solely upon which group has power or experiences success:

> They wait to see what happens to you and, if God brings you success, they say, "Were we not on your side?" But if the disbelievers (*kāfirīn*) have some success, they say to them, "Did we not have the upper hand over you, and [yet] protect you from the believers (*mu'minīn*)?" ... (4:141, excerpt)

A similar description of their fear of other humans and their attempt to negotiate their position is found in Qur'ān 9:64–66:

> The hypocrites (*munāfiqūn*) fear that a chapter will be revealed exposing what is in their hearts. Say, "Carry on with your jokes. God will bring about what you fear!" Yet if you were to question them, they would be sure to say, "We were just chatting, just amusing ourselves." Say, "Were you making jokes about God, God's Revelations, and God's Messenger? Do not try to justify yourselves. You have gone from belief (*īmān*) to disbelief (*kafartum*)." We may forgive some of you, but We will punish others. They are evildoers.

These *āyāt* bring two subtler yet significant ideas to the fore. To begin, if those who manifest *nifāq* fear that a chapter of revelation (*sūra*) will be revealed, thus informing people of their true nature, this implies that they acknowledge God's power to some extent. They would not fear the revelation of a *sūra* if they did not ascribe any power or knowledge to God. Those who manifest *nifāq* know that God has power, but they fear and covet human power more. Additionally, these *āyāt* describe those who manifest *nifāq* as moving from *īmān* to *kufr*. Other *āyāt* describe them as being closer to *kufr* than *īmān* in particular circumstances:

> ... On that day they were closer to disbelief (*kufr*) than belief (*īmān*). They say with their tongues what is not in their hearts. God knows exactly what they conceal. (3:167, excerpt)

These various depictions lead Izutsu to astutely observe that *nifāq* is not a watertight compartment but rather has a "conspicuously dynamic nature, that may extend with elasticity towards either direction to shade off almost imperceptibly into *kufr* or *īmān*."[20] The dynamic nature of *nifāq* is also suggested in a description that is commonly associated with the concept, that is, "sickness in the heart" (e.g., Qur'ān 24:50, 5:41, 3:167, 47:20, 2:8–10).[21] The analogy of sickness, while not flattering, does evoke the possibility of positive change, of regaining health, and of being cured. In fact, this ability is affirmed in Qur'ān 4:145–146, which states that those who manifest *nifāq* can repent, mend their ways, and thereby be joined with those who manifest *īmān*:

> The hypocrites (*munāfiqīn*) will be in the lowest depths of Hell, and you will find no one to help them. Except those who repent, mend their ways, hold fast to God, and purify their religion for God. These will be joined with the believers (*mu'minīn*), and God will give the believers (*mu'minīn*) a mighty reward. (4:145–146)

The third prominent characteristic that those who manifest *nifāq* display in their acknowledgment of God is deception; they fruitlessly attempt to deceive God in the same manner that they strive to deceive other humans:

> The hypocrites (*munāfiqīn*) try to deceive God, but it is God who causes them to be deceived . . . (4:142, excerpt)
>
> Some people say, "We believe in God and the Last Day," when really they do not believe. They seek to deceive God and the believers but they only deceive themselves, though they do not realize it. (2:8–9)[22]

While these *āyāt* indicate that they are not successful in their endeavor to deceive God, this characteristic must be further explicated in light of some of the other traits that have already been explored. If those who manifest *nifāq* fear God's revelation of a chapter (*sūra*), then they also know that their attempt to deceive God, their attempt to hide what is truly in their hearts, has failed. There is some sort of inconsistency, not a textual inconsistency, but an inconsistency in behavior. Those who manifest *nifāq* appear similar to compulsive liars; they lie or attempt to deceive even when they know they have been caught. This is pointedly confirmed in the depiction of their comportment on the Day of Resurrection:

> On the Day God raises them all from the dead, they will swear before God as they swear before you now, thinking that it will help them.

> What liars they are! Satan has gained control over them and made them forget God. They are on Satan's side, and those on Satan's side will be the losers. (58:19)

On that day—the day that even those who manifest *kufr* and *shirk* will submit to and acknowledge God—the *munāfiqūn* will stand in the very face of God and attempt to use their worldly tactics to ingratiate themselves with God. This behavior sheds additional light on the analogy of sickness.

Response to God's Guidance

Another facet of *taqwā* is humankind's response to God's guidance. God's guidance assumes a variety of forms, including a *nafs* (soul) and *fiṭra* (natural disposition) that know *taqwā*; natural *āyāt* (signs) that provoke thought, leading to *taqwā*; and revelation delivered through messengers. What is the connection of each of the hierarchical concepts to these sources of guidance? Do people who manifest these concepts actualize their *fiṭra*? Do they properly reflect upon natural *āyāt*? Do they accept the revelation sent through messengers?

Īmān

The response of those who manifest *īmān* to God's guidance is encapsulated in four primary characteristics. The first characteristic is that they hear and obey revelation:

> ...They say, "We hear and obey. Grant us Your forgiveness, our Lord. To You we all return!" (2:285, excerpt)
>
> When the true believers (*mu'minīn*) are summoned to God and God's Messenger in order to judge between them, they say, "We hear and we obey." These are the ones who will prosper. (24:51)

This indicates not simply the faculty of hearing but also the notion of comprehension. Those who manifest *īmān* truly grasp the message that they are sent, and their response in light of that clear comprehension is to obey God, the message, and the messenger:

> You who believe (*alladhīna āmanū*), obey God and the Messenger, and those in authority among you. If you are in dispute over any

> matter, refer it to God and the Messenger, if you truly believe (*tu'minūna*) in God and the Last Day. That is better and fairer in the end. (4:59)
>
> Believers (*alladhīna āmanū*), obey God and God's Messenger. Do not turn away when you are listening to him. (8:20)

It should be reiterated that the order to "obey" the message and messenger is not unique to Muḥammad. It is universally given with each revelation and messenger (e.g., Qur'ān 26:106–108). However, it does raise an important question: what does such obedience entail, especially in light of the diversity of rites and practices (*manāsik*) sent with each messenger? According to theories of supersession, this question is easily resolved in favor of the chronologically latest revelation—that is, the revelation of Muḥammad—and it is suggested that all obedience is now due to Muḥammad alone. I will return to this question, but at this juncture it is enough to acknowledge that obedience is commanded and is an integral part of the manifestation of *īmān*.

The second characteristic of those who manifest *īmān* is that revelation increases their *īmān*:

> True believers (*mu'minūn*) are those whose hearts tremble with awe when God is mentioned, whose faith (*īmān*) increases when God's revelations are recited to them, who put their trust in their Lord. (8:2)
>
> When a chapter is revealed, some say, "Have any of you been strengthened in faith (*īmān*) by it?" It certainly does strengthen in faith (*īmān*) those who believe (*alladhīna āmanū*), and they rejoice. (9:124)

Qur'ān 9:124 stands in stark contrast to the description of those who manifest *nifāq*. As noted in reference to Qur'ān 9:64–66, those who manifest *nifāq* fear the revelation because of the impact it may have on their social position. Here, however, the conviction of those who manifest *īmān* is only strengthened through revelation. This also highlights that *īmān* can be strengthened or increased and underscores the depiction of *īmān* as dynamic and composed of diverse levels and degrees. Moreover, if *īmān* is something that can increase, it would also have to be something that can decrease.

Humility in response to revelation is the third trait that defines those who manifest *īmān*:

> Say, "Whether you believe it or not, those who were given knowledge earlier fall down on their faces when it is recited to them, and say, 'Glory to our Lord! Our Lord's promise has been fulfilled.' They fall down on their faces, weeping, and it increases them in humility (*khushūʿ*)." (17:108–109)

> Some of the People of the Scripture believe (*yuʾmin*) in God, in what has been sent down to you and in what was sent down to them. Humbling themselves (*khāshiʿīn*) before God, they would never sell God's revelation for a small price (*thamanan qalīlan*). These people will have their rewards with their Lord. God is swift in reckoning. (3:199)

> The only people who truly believe (*yuʾminu*) in Our messages are those who, when they are reminded of them, bow down in worship, celebrate their Lord's praises, and are not arrogant (*lā yastakbirūn*). (32:15)

Those who manifest *īmān* are described as humbling themselves, even assuming the physical posture of prostration in response to the revelation of God. Also, similar to the preceding depiction of *īmān* itself, these *āyāt* indicate that humility as well can be increased. This results in the same implications: humility is dynamic, has degrees, and can fluctuate. Qurʾān 3:199 juxtaposes the humility of those who manifest *īmān* with the notion of selling God's revelation for *thamanan qalīlan* (a small price), the response of those who manifest *kufr*. Qurʾān 32:15 states that those who manifest *īmān* are willing to humble themselves in prostration because they do not think they are above doing so; they are not arrogant (*lā yastakbirūn*). Suggestively, what those who manifest *īmān* lack is exactly what Iblis displays. As seen in Qurʾān 7:13, Iblis, in response to God's guidance, was *takabbara* (arrogant)[23] and thus refused to obey God.

It is also noteworthy that in Qurʾān 17:108–109 and 3:199 the people described as manifesting these essential traits of *īmān* are from earlier communities of revelation and the People of Scripture. While much exegesis has tended to explain these references through the assumption of implied conversion, which is based on the problematic view of religious difference as creating static boundaries, the references are more straightforwardly understood as the manifestation of the hierarchical concept of *īmān* in other lateral religious communities.

The characteristic of humility is also provocatively attributed to nature:

> If We had sent this Qur'ān down to a mountain, you would have seen it humbled (*khāshi'a*) and split apart in its awe of God. We offer people such illustrations so that they may reflect. (59:21)
>
> Another of God's signs is this, you see the earth lying desolate (*khāshi'a*), but when We send water down on to it, it stirs and grows ... (41:39, excerpt)

The first *āya* states that a mountain would respond to the Qur'ān in a manner similar to those who manifest *īmān*: it would be humbled and awed. This establishes a connection between the freely chosen behavior of some people and the natural behavior of other aspects of God's creation. In other words, the behavior of those who manifest *īmān* is depicted as a natural response. While the concept of *fiṭra* is not invoked in this *āya*, it is possible to draw a connection between the *āya* and the depiction of *fiṭra* as being inherently oriented toward God. Qur'ān 41:39 states that God's blessings are sent in the form of water to the "humble" earth, which then responds and grows. Again, this natural analogy is a parallel of the response of those who manifest *īmān* to God's revelation. They are humble, and when God sends revelation it stirs them to respond and causes them to grow in faith.

The final characteristic of those who manifest *īmān* is that they do not draw distinctions among God's revelations or messengers:

> The Messenger believes (*āmana*) in what has been sent down to him from his Lord, as do the faithful (*mu'minūn*). They all believe (*āmana*) in God, God's angels, God's scriptures, and God's messengers. "We make no distinction (*lā nufarriqu*) between any of God's messengers," they say. "We hear and obey. Grant us Your forgiveness, our Lord. To You we all return!" (2:285)

A similar assertion is made in Qur'ān 3:199 in reference to the People of the Scripture who believe in "what has been sent down to you and in what was sent down to them." However, Qur'ān 2:285 not only details the type of behavior those who manifest *īmān* avoid but also states the type of behavior they display. Those who manifest *īmān* do not make distinctions (*lā nufarriqu*) among revelations and messengers. On the contrary, they hear and obey.

Shirk

As noted in the discussion of their recognition of God, those who manifest *shirk* fail to comprehend the true nature of God's power. This failure in understanding is also evident in their response to God's guidance. To begin, they do not reflect upon natural *āyāt* in a manner that produces pure belief. Although God has provided a multitude of natural signs that attest to God's stature, those who manifest *shirk* fail to use their reason (*ʿaql*) to understand the implications of these signs:

> In the creation of the heavens and earth; in the alternation of night and day; in the ships that sail the seas with goods for people; in the water which God sends down from the sky to give life to the earth when it has been barren, scattering all kinds of creatures over it; in the changing of the winds and clouds that run their appointed courses between the sky and earth: there are signs in all these for those who use their reason (*yaʿqilūn*). Even so, there are some who choose to take others as rivals to God ... (2:164–165, excerpt 165)

They also fail to use reason to reflect on the inconsistencies of their practices. Qur'ān 21:51–67 recounts the story of Abraham and the idols of his people. Abraham breaks all of the idols except the largest one. When his people find the idols in this state and inquire as to what transpired, Abraham tells them that they should question the largest idol. Abraham knows that the idol is incapable of responding:

> He said, "No, it was done by the biggest of them. This one. Ask them, if they can talk." They turned to one another, saying, "It is you who are in the wrong," but then they lapsed again and said, "You know very well these gods cannot speak." Abraham said, "How can you worship what can neither benefit nor harm you, instead of God? Shame on you and on the things you worship instead of God. Will you not use your reason (*taʿqilūn*)?" (21:63–67)

When forced into a logical corner, however, Abraham's people readily admit that the idols cannot speak. They are aware of their lack of power, but this does not change their devotion to those idols. Therefore, their beliefs and practices are not based upon the natural capacity for reason or upon consideration of God's natural *āyāt*. Other Qur'ānic *āyāt* confirm this when they critique those who manifest *shirk* for inventing beliefs and practices without any firm basis, that is, without any connection to God's guidance or grounding in reason:

> Consider al-Lat and al-ʿUzza, and the third one, Manat. Are you to have the male and God the female? That would be a most unjust distribution! These are nothing but names you have invented yourselves, you and your forebears. God has sent no authority for them. These people merely follow conjecture (*ẓann*) and the whims of their souls, even though guidance has come to them from their Lord. (53:19-23)[24]

As Izutsu argues, the concept of *ẓann* denotes "a groundless, unwarranted type of thinking, uncertain or doubtful knowledge, unreliable opinion, or mere conjecture."[25] This type of baseless knowledge is contrasted in the Qurʾān with *ʿilm*, which is sound knowledge derived from God's guidance.

Those who manifest *shirk* are also described as following what their ancestors or forebears followed in lieu of following God's guidance:

> They found their forebears astray and rushed to follow in their footsteps. Before them most people in the past went astray, even though We sent messengers to warn them. (37:69–72)
>
> No indeed! They say, "We saw our forebears following this tradition. We are guided by their footsteps." (43:22)

They persist in their allegiance to their inherited ways, regardless of whether or not divine guidance differs from those ways. Qurʾān 7:172 depicts all individuals as testifying at the moment of creation to the existence and status of God. In reference to those who manifest *shirk*, the *āya* that directly follows 7:172 assumes great consequence as well:

> When your Lord took out the offspring from the loins of the Children of Adam and made them bear witness about themselves, God said, "Am I not your Lord?" and they replied, "Yes, we bear witness." So you cannot say on the Day of Resurrection, "We were not aware of this." Or, "It was our forebears who, before us, ascribed partners to God, and we are only the descendants who came after them. Will you destroy us because of falsehoods they invented?" (7:172–173)

The children of Adam are made to testify for two reasons: so that they cannot claim ignorance of God; and so that they cannot claim blind adherence to the ways of their forebears. As is blatantly evident in example of Abraham, the ideal is for someone to follow what is right and clear irrespective of the practices and context in which they find themselves situated. The Qur'ān's optimism about such a possibility is directly connected to the depiction of the *fiṭra* as inclining toward God and being created to distinguish between rebellion and *taqwā*.

The Qur'ān also states that those who manifest *shirk* do not accept the message of revelation because it is delivered by a mere human being:

> ... But they said, "You are only human like us. You want to turn us away from what our forebears used to worship. Bring us clear proof then." (14:10, excerpt)
>
> The disbelievers (*kāfirūn*) think it strange that a prophet of their own people has come to warn them. They say, "He is just a lying sorcerer. How can he claim that all the gods are but one God? What an astonishing thing!" (38:4–5)
>
> The only thing that kept these people from believing, when guidance came to them, was that they said, "How could God have sent a human being as a messenger?" (17:94)

They refuse to accept that God would choose a human being to deliver divine revelation. Instead, they cling to the ways of their forebears and demand miracles and other forms of proof. For them, the message is not sufficient proof in and of itself. This contrasts with those who manifest *īmān*, those who become humble upon hearing the revelation. These *āyāt* also reveal another area of overlap between *shirk* and *kufr*; Qur'ān 38:4–5 describes those who manifest *kufr* as associating partners with God.

Ḥanīf

In terms of recognition of God, the concept of *ḥanīf* was semantically related to the themes of *ikhlaṣ* (sincerity, exclusive devotion), *fiṭra*, and Abraham. These same themes recur in reference to God's guidance. The Qur'ān indicates that *ikhlaṣ* can be provoked by both natural *āyāt* and revelation:

> It is God who shows you God's signs (*āyāt*) and sends water down from the sky to sustain you, though only those who turn to God

> will take heed. So call upon God and dedicate your religion to God alone (*mukhliṣīn*), however hateful this may be to the disbelievers (*kāfirūn*). (40:13–14)

> It is We who sent down the Scripture to you with the Truth, so worship God with your sincere devotion (*mukhliṣ*). (39:2)

Sincere and exclusive devotion thus is not restricted to a particular form of God's communication or disclosure alone. Moreover, the arrival at a proper understanding of and sincere devotion to God as a result of reflection on natural signs is connected to both *fiṭra* and Abraham. Qur'ān 6:75–79 describes the process whereby Abraham arrived at a negative evaluation of the *shirk* of his people and certainty regarding God's singular status:

> In this way We showed Abraham [God's] mighty dominion over the heavens and the earth, so that he might be among those who arrive at certainty (*mūqinīn*). When the night grew dark over him he saw a star and said, "This is my Lord," but when it set, he said, "I do not like things that set." And when he saw the moon rising he said, "This is my Lord," but when it too set, he said, "If my Lord does not guide me, I shall be one of those who go astray." Then he saw the sun rising and cried, "This is my Lord! This is greater." But when the sun set, he said, "My people, I disown all that you worship beside God (*tushrikūna*). I have turned my face (*wajjahtu wajhiya*) as a true believer (*ḥanīf*) towards God who created the heavens and the earth. I am not one of those who ascribe partners (*mushrikīn*)."

Abraham is awed by the natural *āyāt*.[26] This is, after all, the purpose of natural *āyāt*; they are created to stir wonder in human beings. Where Abraham as *ḥanīf* differs from those who manifest *shirk* is that he does not stop at the stage of awe. He probes deeper, examining the behavior of the natural signs. This leads him to the observation that each of these creations eventually "sets"; each of the natural *āyāt* appears powerful and overwhelming, yet that stature is transient. Thus, Abraham reasons that such things are not worthy of worship. What *is* worthy of worship is the Creator of those *āyāt*. The conclusion at which Abraham arrives is confirmed in Qur'ān 41:37:

> The night, the day, the sun, the moon are only a few of God's signs (*āyāt*). Do not bow down in worship to the sun or the moon, but

> bow down to God who created them, if it is truly God that you worship. (41:37)

In reference to this account of Abraham, it is also important to underscore that through this type of reflection Abraham arrives at *yaqīn* (certainty of knowledge). Therefore, revelation in the strict sense cannot be the only means of arriving at certainty about God and God's will.

Occasionally, the term *ḥanīf* has been understood to denote someone who has never been exposed to revelation.[27] In this depiction, the *ḥanīf* is one who has arrived at an understanding of God through *fiṭra* alone. While the preceding account of Abraham achieving *yaqīn* indicates the possibility of such, it is challenging to support this depiction. First, the Qur'ān describes revelation as universal; it has been sent to all communities. Second, the Qur'ān also depicts Abraham as responding to God's order to submit (Qur'ān 2:131) and refers to the *ṣuḥuf* (scriptures, literally "sheets") of Abraham and Moses (Qur'ān 87:19). Moreover, Muḥammad is instructed in the Qur'ān—that is, through revelation—to emulate the way of Abraham the *ḥanīf*:

> Then We revealed to you [Muḥammad], "Follow the way of Abraham, as one of true and pure faith (*ḥanīf*) who was not one of those who ascribe partners (*mushrikīn*)." (16:123)

If the way of Abraham is solely based upon *fiṭra*, reason, and reflection on natural *āyāt*, how could Muḥammad emulate such a way while simultaneously receiving revelation? The attempt to depict the *ḥanīf* as someone with no experience of revelation appears to be an attempt to limit its applicability and importance and to present it as an exception rather than the norm. In this scenario, the norm, of course, would be explicit alignment with the revelation of Muḥammad; only those who were never exposed to revelation would be exempted from this obligation. Yet this does not appear to be the Qur'ānic position at all. Not only is Abraham connected with revelation, but also Abraham the *ḥanīf* is presented as the ideal. *Ḥanīf* is the ideal in part due to its distinction from *shirk*, but it is also presented as the ideal in relation to other communities of revelation:

> People of the Scripture, why do you argue about Abraham when the Torah and the Gospels were not revealed until after his time? Do you not understand (*ta'qilūn*)? You argue about some things

> of which you have some knowledge (*ʿilm*), but why do you argue about things of which you know nothing? God knows, and you do not. Abraham was neither a Jew nor a Nazarene. He was upright and devoted to God (*ḥanīf muslim*), never one who ascribes partners (*mushrikīn*), and the people who are closest to him are those who truly follow his ways, and this Prophet, and the believers (*alladhīna āmanū*). God is a protector of the believers (*muʾminīn*). (3:65–68)

These *āyāt* state that although Abraham preceded both the Jews and the Nazarenes, both communities nevertheless attempt to claim Abraham as their own. However, the mere claiming of affiliation is not the point of contention in these *āyāt*. The Qur'ān, rather, is critiquing their attempt to lay *exclusive* claim to Abraham. Significantly, the ideal way of Abraham is placed in direct contrast with such divisive behavior:

> So as one of pure faith, stand firm and true in your devotion to the religion (*ʾaqim wajhaka lil-dīni ḥanīfan*). This is the natural disposition (*fiṭra*) God instilled in humankind. There is no altering God's creation. And this is the right religion (*al-dīn al-qayyim*), though most people do not realize it. Turn to God alone, all of you. Be mindful (*ʾittaqū*) of God; keep up the prayer; do not join those who ascribe partners to God (*mushrikīn*), those who divide (*farraqū*) their religion and become sects (*shiyaʿ*) with each faction (*ḥizb*) rejoicing in what they have. (30:30–32)

The use here of the verb *farraqū* (to divide) recalls the description of those who manifest *īmān*; they do not make distinctions (*lā tafarriqu*). Moreover, the attempt to make exclusive and divisive claims is one of the behaviors of those who manifest *kufr*. As seen, they make exclusive claims to the Hereafter. Drawing together these various elements, it is possible to define *ḥanīf* as one who understands God through the *fiṭra*, through the *āyāt* of nature and revelation, who does not associate any partners with God, and who does not divide the one religion into factions (*shīʿa, ḥizb*) based upon exclusive claims.

Kufr

Many of the Qur'ānic references to the concept of *kufr* are related to those people who had previously been granted revelation. As such, the majority of the critiques of those who manifest *kufr* relate to their treatment of those revelations and to their receptivity to the revelation to Muḥammad. People of the Scripture in general are reminded to hold fast to their own revelation:

> Say, "People of the Scripture, you have no true basis unless you uphold the Torah, the Gospel, and that which has been sent down to you from your Lord." But what has been sent down to you [Prophet] from your Lord is sure to increase many of them in their insolence and defiance. Do not worry about those who defy. (5:68)

This reminder should be compared with the critiques of those who manifest *shirk*, who do not have any basis for their religion but follow only their own suppositions and the ways of their forebears. The reminder issued here differs. People of the Scripture have a sound basis for their beliefs and practices, yet some of them fail to uphold that revelation.

The failure to uphold the revelation assumes a variety of forms. Similar to the concept of *kufr* in relation to the other themes, it is vital not to lump these forms together, thus obscuring their nuances. The first way those who manifest *kufr* fail to uphold the revelation is through concealment. Those who previously received revelation swore to share the revelation with others, yet some failed to do so:

> God took a pledge from those who were given the Scripture, "Make it known to people. Do not conceal it." But they tossed the pledge over their shoulders. They bartered it for a small price (*thamanan qalīlan*). What a bad bargain they made! (3:187)

The second manner in which those who manifest *kufr* fail to uphold the revelation is through invention and ascription. They fabricate ideas, practices, and beliefs and then claim that they are part of the revelation:

> So woe to those who write something down with their own hands and then claim, "This is from God," in order to make some small gain (*thamanan qalīlan*). Woe to them for what their hands have written! Woe to them for all that they have earned! (2:79)

The third manner in which they fail to uphold revelation is through distortion. They attribute different meanings to the words or change the words all together:

> Some Jews distort words from their contexts. They say, "We hear and disobey," and "Listen," [adding the insult] "May you not hear," and "Raʿina [Look after us]," twisting it abusively with their tongues so as to disparage religion. If they had said, "We hear and obey" ... (4:46, excerpt)

The nature of the specific distortion depicted in this *āya* is especially significant in reference to the description of those who manifest *īmān*, who respond to revelation by saying, "We hear and we obey." In contrast, those who manifest *kufr* hear but do not obey. As already stated, to "hear" implies comprehension and understanding not the mere faculty of hearing. Thus, those who manifest *kufr* do not lack an understanding of the revelation, but rather they fail to behave in line with the revelation. Izutsu confirms this when he depicts the essence of *kufr* as the fact that "man denies ... the blessing of God, although he recognizes it clearly."[28]

In fact, all three ways those who manifest *kufr* fail to uphold revelation share a common trait: they are all based on recognition of the authority of revelation. In fact, they are all various attempts to co-opt that authority. This presents another interesting distinction from those who manifest *shirk*. Those who manifest *shirk* have a flawed conception of God, acknowledging God's power in some respects but not in all. They do not understand the natural *āyāt* in an appropriate manner, and when confronted with revelation through a messenger they do not accept it because the messenger is only a mortal. Those who manifest *kufr*, however, do recognize the truth.[29] They know the revelation and that the messenger is a messenger, yet they still engage in *kufr*.[30]

> People of the Scripture, why do you deny (*takfurūna*) God's signs when you yourselves witness them? People of the Scripture, why do you cover up truth with falsehood? Why do you hide the truth when you recognize it? (3:70–71)

> Those to whom We have given the Scripture know this as well as they know their own sons. Those who have lost their souls will not believe. (6:25)

The Qurʾān also provides a specific explanation for their refusal to acknowledge the revelation of Muḥammad:

> ... [They say], "Do not believe that anyone else could be given a revelation similar to what you were given, or that they could use it

> to argue against you in your Lord's presence." Say [to them], "All grace is in God's hands. God grants it to whoever God will. God is all embracing, all knowing. (3:73, excerpt)[31]

> Do they envy people for the bounty God has granted them? We gave the descendants of Abraham the Scripture and wisdom, and We gave them a great kingdom. (4:54)

Parallel with the story of Iblis, those who manifest *kufr* display a sense of privilege based on lateral difference; they believe that revelation will be sent only to their group. This sense of privilege leads them to deny and envy other revelations. They deny other revelations explicitly yet recognize and envy them implicitly. The sense of privilege, as seen in reference to the Hereafter, also leads them to make exclusive claims. As a result, they are placed in contrast with those who manifest *īmān*, who do not make distinctions among revelations and do not sell the revelation for the small price (*thamanan qalīlan*) of falsely exulting their own lateral group:

> As for those who deny (*yakfurūna*) God and God's messengers and want to make a distinction between (*tufarriqū*) them, saying, "We believe in some but not in others," seeking a middle way. They are really disbelievers (*kāfirūn*). We have prepared a humiliating punishment for those who disbelieve (*kāfirīn*). But God will give rewards to those who believe (*alladhīna āmanū*) in God and God's messengers and make no distinction between (*lam tufarriqū*) any of them. God is most forgiving and merciful. (4:150–152)

These *āyāt* also present a provocative coupling, pairing the imperative to make no distinctions with the imperative to believe. In critiquing those who manifest *kufr*, the dual imperatives indicate that *īmān* involves believing in all messengers, including Muḥammad, and making no distinctions among them. This implies that the recognition of Muḥammad would be one facet of the manifestation of *īmān*. However, the commands also and equally imply that Muḥammad should not be distinguished from or privileged in respect to other messengers. These two seemingly contending implications provoke questions about threshold criteria (Is belief in Muḥammad a prerequisite for *īmān*?); about the necessity of enacting the particularities of the message of Muḥammad (Must every person follow the specific acts and practices outlined in the message of Muḥammad?); and about the specific meaning of terms such as *believe, recognize,* and *obey* when used in reference to messengers (Are they synonymous? Are they progressive, meaning that recognition leads to belief which leads to obedience?). I will revisit these questions in Chapter 8.

Islām

The concept of *islām* is connected to the *fiṭra* through its relationship with the concept of *ḥanīf.* I will not reexamine these connections, since they have already been explored in reference to *ḥanīf.* The Qur'ān also depicts *islām* as the appropriate response to the evidence of God's existence that is presented in natural *āyāt*:

> Say, "Since clear evidence (*bayyināt*) has come to me from my Lord, I am forbidden to serve those you call upon besides God. I am commanded to submit (*'aslima*) to the Lord of the Worlds." It is God who created you from dust, then from a drop of fluid, then from a tiny, clinging form, then God brought you forth as infants, then God allowed you to reach maturity, then God let you grow old—though some of you die sooner—and reach your appointed term so that you might use your reason (*ta'qilūn*). (40:66–67)

The reference to reason reiterates the connection between the concept of *islām* and the concepts of *fiṭra* and *ḥanīf.* The manifestation of *islām*, however, is not only associated with *fiṭra* and natural *āyāt*, but it is also closely tied to revelation. The second chapter of the Qur'ān, *Sūrat al-baqara*, describes Abraham's interaction with God. God commands Abraham to surrender himself in devotion:

> His Lord said to him, "Devote yourself to Me (*'aslim*)." Abraham replied, "I devote myself (*'aslamtu*) to the Lord of the Universe." And commanded his progeny to do the same, as did Jacob: "My children, God has chosen [your] religion for you, so make sure you devote yourselves to God (*muslimūn*), to your dying moment." Were you there to see when death came upon Jacob? When he said to his progeny, "What will you worship after I am gone?" They replied, "We shall worship your God and the God of your forebears, Abraham, Ishmael, and Isaac, one single God. We devote ourselves to God (*muslimūn*)." (2:131–133)

Abraham responds obediently to God's command, enjoining his descendants to do the same. This obedience is similar to that displayed by those who manifest *īmān*. As this *āya* also indicates, the expression of *islām* is not unique to Abraham. In fact, all prophets and messengers are depicted as being individuals who manifest *islām*. Furthermore, those who respond to God's revelations—the previous ones and the one given through Muḥammad—have always been *muslimūn*:

> ...God has called you those who are devoted to God (*muslimīn*) both in the past and in this [revelation] ... (22:78, excerpt)
>
> Those to whom We gave the Scripture before believe in it (*mu'minūn*) and, when it is recited to them, they say, "We believe in it (*āmannā*). It is the truth from our Lord. Before it came we had already devoted ourselves to God (*muslimīn*). (28:52–53)

These two *āyāt* underscore the fact that the concept of *islām* is not aligned automatically with Islam, that is, the historical community of Muḥammad. The concept of *islām* is rather a thread that weaves together all messengers and all communities of revelation. This is evident in Qur'ān 2:135–136, which issues a response to another exclusive and proprietary claim of those who manifest *kufr* among the Jews and the Nazarenes:

> They say, "Become Jews or Nazarenes, and you will be rightly guided." Say, "No, [ours is] the way of Abraham, who was upright and true in faith (*ḥanīf*), who was not among those who ascribe partners to God (*mushrikīn*)." So, say, "We believe (*āmannā*) in God and in what was sent down to us and what was sent down to Abraham, Ishmael, Isaac, Jacob, and the Tribes, and what was given to Moses, Jesus, and all the prophets by their Lord. We make no distinction between (*lā nufarriqū*) any of them, and we devote ourselves to God (*muslimūn*)." (2:135–136)

Similar to the concept of *īmān* in reference to Qur'ān 2:285, these *āyāt* place divisive and exclusive claims based on lateral difference in direct contrast to the concept of *islām*, which emphasizes unity amid difference.

Those who manifest *kufr* and those who manifest *islām* are further contrasted in light of the manner in which they approach each other.

Those who manifest *kufr* display arrogance, envy, and rivalry. They also claim a special status in relationship to God, emphasizing the particularities of their lateral group. In contrast, those who manifest *islām* call others to acknowledge commonalities related to hierarchical difference, to *taqwā*:

> Argue only in the best way with the People of the Scripture, except with those of them who act unjustly. Say, "We believe (*āmannā*) in what was revealed to us and in what was revealed to you. Our God and your God are one [and the same]. We are devoted to God (*muslimūn*)." (29:46)

> Say, "People of the Scripture, come to an equitable word between us and you. We worship God alone, we ascribe no partners (*lā nushrika*) to God, and none of us takes others beside God as lords." If they turn away, say, "Witness our devotion to God (*muslimūn*)." (3:64)

Nifāq

Those who manifest *nifāq* fear revelation because it could compromise their position in relation to other humans (Qur'ān 9:64–66); it could reveal their true nature and true beliefs, thus making them unable to seek benefits from multiple groups. Other *āyāt* describe those who manifest *nifāq* as claiming to believe in the revelation. However, this is deemed insincere since they are not willing to be judged in accordance with the revelation. Rather, they prefer to be judged by those who are unjust but proffer a potential—and undeserved—benefit:

> Do you not see those who claim to believe in what has been sent down to you, and in what was sent down before you, yet still want to turn to unjust tyrants for judgment, although they have been ordered to reject them? Satan wants to lead them far astray. When they are told, "Turn to God's revelations and the Messenger," you see the hypocrites (*munāfiqīn*) turn right away from you. (4:60–61)

The response to God's guidance on the part of those who manifest *nifāq* is also compared with the response of those who manifest *īmān*:

> When a chapter is revealed, some [hypocrites] say, "Have any of you been strengthened in faith (*īmān*) by it?" It certainly does

> strengthen the faith (*īmān*) of those who believe (*alladhīna āmanū*) and they rejoice, but as for those with disease in their hearts, each new chapter adds further to their perversity. They die disbelieving (*kāfirūn*). Can they not see that they are afflicted once or twice a year? Yet they neither repent nor take heed. Whenever a chapter is revealed, they look at each other and say, "Is anyone watching you?," and then they turn away. God has turned their hearts away because they are people who do not use their reason. (9:124–127)

Unlike those whose *īmān* is strengthened through revelation, those who manifest *nifāq* grow in perversity. They even express wonder at the possibility that revelation could increase *īmān*. Moreover, they demonstrate no desire to claim revelation. As in Qur'ān 4:60, they will claim to believe if it benefits them, but they do not display the same proprietary concern as those who manifest *kufr*. Their concern is not to claim special or exclusive status in respect to *God*; their primary and perpetual concern is claiming status with respect to other *humans*. As a result, they are equally amenable to claiming status through hollow affirmations of belief or through denial of belief:

> When they meet the believers (*alladhīna āmanū*), they say, "We believe." But when they are alone with their evil ones, they say, "We're really with you. We were only joking." (2:14)

Type and Nature of Actions

Taqwā is not only related to belief in the general sense of the term but is also about actions in relation to God and in relation to other humans. In particular, *taqwā* is associated with praying, giving charity, performing good deeds, and demonstrating kindness in social and familial relations. Furthermore, *taqwā* is described as something that must be actively pursued and sustained and as something that can fluctuate. Therefore, there is great emphasis placed on constancy and perseverance in the required actions. Do individuals who manifest the hierarchical characteristics perform the actions associated with *taqwā*? How do they perform them? Do they do so in a constant manner? What is their motivation?

Īmān

The actions of those who manifest *īmān* essentially parallel the actions associated with *taqwā*. They are described as praying, paying alms, being chaste, and fulfilling their pledges:

> Prosperous are the believers (*mu'minūn*)! Those who pray humbly (*khāshi'ūn*), who shun idle talk, who pay the prescribed alms, who guard their chastity except with their spouses, those whom they rightfully possess—with these they are blameless, but anyone who seeks more than this is exceeding the limits—who are faithful to their trusts and pledges and who keep up their prayers, will rightly be given Paradise as their own, there to remain. (23:1–11)

Their actions are also frequently depicted in the more general expression "those who believe and do good works (*ṣāliḥāt*)" (e.g., Qur'ān 29:58). This pairing, however, should not lead to the erroneous conclusion that *īmān* is something separate from actions. As Qur'ān 23:1–11 highlights, they are people who manifest *īmān* because they engage in those actions; the actions are an integral part of *īmān*. The manner in which these actions are performed is particularly noteworthy. Those who manifest *īmān* perform actions with humility and constancy. As with the concepts of *ḥanīf* and *islām*, constancy is indicated in the verb *yuqīmūna*. Those who manifest *īmān* engage in these actions on a routine basis; they establish a pattern of performing the actions. Moreover, they also manifest perseverance (*ṣabr*); that is, they struggle to maintain the constancy of their actions even in difficulties:

> Seek help with steadfastness (*ṣabr*) and prayer. Though this is hard indeed for anyone but the humble (*khāshi'īn*), who know that they will meet their Lord and that it is to God they will return. (2:45–46)[32]

This specific *āya* provides a striking example of the interlacing of specific actions (e.g., seeking help and praying) with the specific dispositions (e.g., steadfastness, humility, knowledge of the meeting) that characterize the concept of *īmān*. Those who manifest *īmān* do not simply profess belief but also demonstrate constancy and perform specific actions.

In other *āyāt*, those who manifest *īmān* are portrayed as "ordering what is right and forbidding what is wrong":

> The believers, both men and women, (*muʾminūn* and *muʾmināt*) support each other. They order what is right (*maʿrūf*) and forbid what is wrong. They keep up (*yuqīmūna*) the prayer and pay the prescribed alms. They obey God and God's Messenger. God will grant mercy to such people. God is almighty and wise. (9:71)

This generalized depiction of their action is connected with a description of those who manifest *īmān* as being supporters of one another. However, while they support and help each other, they do not privilege *any* horizontal (human-to-human) relationship over the vertical relationship with God:

> You who believe (*alladhīna āmanū*) do not take your fathers and brothers as allies if they prefer disbelief (*kufr*) to faith (*īmān*). Those of you who do so are doing wrong. (9:23)

To take allies from their families if they prefer *kufr* would be to prioritize social relationships over the relationship with God, to seek some sort of benefit from people rather than God:

> Do those who ally themselves with the disbelievers (*kāfirīn*) rather than the believers (*muʾminīn*) seek power through them? In reality all power is God's to give. (4:139)

Significantly, *āyāt* that advise against taking allies from among the Jews or Nazarenes (e.g., Qurʾān 5:51) should be understood in the same manner as Qurʾān 9:23. Such allegiances are not prohibited either automatically or without any distinction; rather, they are restricted only due to *kufr* or *shirk*. There is nothing inherently wrong with having close ties with one's family, nor is there anything inherently wrong with having ties with these other lateral religious groups. It becomes an issue only when *kufr* or *shirk* is introduced. Furthermore, the presence of *kufr*, *shirk*, or even *nifāq* does not necessitate or even permit an absolute and holistic severing of relationships:

> ... If you hear people denying (*yukfaru*) and ridiculing God's revelation, do not sit with them unless they start to talk of other things,

> or else you yourselves will become like them. God will gather all the hypocrites (*munāfiqīn*) and disbelievers (*kāfirīn*) together into Hell. (4:140, excerpt)

Those who manifest *īmān* should not sit with people who are engaging in *kufr until* they cease doing so. When and if they cease, interaction is acceptable.

As Qurʾān 4:135 makes abundantly clear, the priority for those who manifest *īmān* should always be to pursue justice in respect to other humans, even if this entails testifying against one's family or one's own self:

> You who believe (*alladhīna āmanū*), be steadfast in upholding justice (*qawwāmīn bil-qisṭ*) and bear witness to God, even if it is against yourselves, your parents, or your close relatives. Whether the person is rich or poor, God can best take care of both. Refrain from following your own desire, so that you can act justly. If you distort or neglect justice, God is fully aware of what you do. (4:135)

The pursuit of justice, moreover, is not a singular act but a habitual orientation, as indicated in the term *qawwāmūn*, which is derived from the same root as *yuqīmū* (to establish as a routine). A similar emphasis on justice is found in Qurʾān 49:9, which discusses the actions that should be taken when two groups of *muʾminūn* fall into conflict:

> If two groups of the believers (*muʾminīn*) fight, you should try to reconcile them. If one of them acts wrongly (*baghat*) towards the other, fight the group that acts wrongly (*tabghī*) until they submit to God's command. Then reconcile them justly (*bi-l-ʿadl*) and be even-handed between the two of them. God loves those who are even-handed (*muqsiṭīn*).

In both the use of *ʿadl* and *qisṭ*, this *āya* again elevates the concept of justice—that is, a concept associated with *taqwā*—over social or group affiliations. Another interesting aspect of this *āya* is that the wrongful action perpetrated by one group is expressed through the verb *B-GH-Y*. This term has many nuances, but it is the same root used to describe the rivalry and envy that lead people who have previously received revelation to divide their unity and to reject the revelation of Muḥammad (e.g.,

Qur'ān 2:213, 42:14, 2:90–91). *B-GH-Y* also appears in another *āya* where it is juxtaposed with the most central components of *taqwā*:

> God commands justice (*ʿadl*), doing good, and generosity towards relatives, and God forbids what is shameful, blameworthy, and oppressive (*baghyī*). God explains things to you, so that you may remember. (16:90)

This juxtaposition indicates that it is a serious offense, which runs contrary to the essential characteristics of *taqwā*. This term certainly means to oppress or treat wrongly. However, in light of its contextual situatedness with the Qur'ān, it also refers to a particular type of oppression that arises out of mutual rivalry and the erection of boundaries along the lines of lateral difference.

Shirk

Two central actions of those who manifest *shirk* have already been encountered: they worship partners alongside of God; and they invent practices based upon their own suppositions. In relation to these, the Qur'ān offers multiple critiques of fabricated practices, such as apportioning produce and livestock to God and to their partners:

> They apportion to God a share of the produce and the livestock God created, saying, "This is for God"—so they claim!—"and this is for our partners (*shurakāʾinā*)." Their partners' (*shurakāʾihim*) share does not reach God, but God's share does reach their partners (*shurakāʾihim*). How badly they judge! (6:136)

This practice is not only condemned as an invention but also as a vivid and concrete illustration of their misconception of God. They apportion shares to God without understanding that God has no need of such things. This is confirmed in other *āyāt* that discuss the sacrificial rites connected to the *ḥajj* (pilgrimage):

> It is neither their meat nor their blood that reaches God but your piety (*taqwā*). God has subjected them to you in this way so that you may glorify God for having guided you ... (22:37, excerpt)

Even in the practices (*manāsik*) that God has ordained, the only thing that reaches God is *taqwā*.

The invention of practices is also grouped with other negatively evaluated actions, such as killing children and fabricating lies:

> Lost indeed are those who kill their own children out of folly, with no basis in knowledge, forbidding what God has provided for them, fabricating lies against God. They have gone far astray and have heeded no guidance. (6:140)

As with the apportioning of shares, the killing of children should be understood not only as a violation of God's explicit commands but also as a lack of understanding of and reliance upon God. As part of a much longer articulation of correct actions in the sight of God, the manifestation of *shirk* is again grouped with the practice of killing one's children:

> Say, "Come! I will tell you what your Lord has really forbidden you. Do not ascribe anything as a partner (*tushrikū*) to God; be good to your parents; do not kill your children in fear of poverty." We will provide for you and for them ... (6:151, excerpt)

While it is surely possible that certain groups or people have engaged in ritual activities that would involve such horrific actions, this *āya* provides another explanation. It states that people should not kill their children based on the fear that having to care for them could lead to poverty. The *āya* then reminds that God is capable of providing for everyone. As such, those who engage in the killing of children for fear of poverty are seen as those who do not have complete trust in or appreciation of God.[33]

Two other *āyāt* are of particular interest in terms of explicating the nature and types of actions performed by those who manifest *shirk*:

> ... Woe to those who ascribe partners (*mushrikīn*), who do not pay the prescribed alms and refuse to believe in the world to come! (41:6–7, excerpt of 6)

> "He might almost have led us astray from our gods if we had not stood so firmly (*ṣabarnā*) by them." When they see the punishment, they will know who is furthest from the path. (25:42)[34]

Qur'ān 41:6–7 describes those who manifest *shirk* as refraining from two of the most important actions associated with *taqwā*: paying alms and believing in the Hereafter. Moreover, these two actions are typically grouped with belief in God and prayer (e.g., Qur'ān 2:2–5 and 2:177, which provide definitions of *taqwā* and *birr*). The Qur'ānic silence on belief in God and prayer in this *āya* confirms what has already been demonstrated. Those who manifest *shirk* believe in God, albeit without *ikhlaṣ* (sincere and exclusive devotion) and they pray to God, albeit without constancy.

Qur'ān 25:42 describes those who manifest *shirk* as clinging closely to the partners they associate with God. This clinging has already been indicated. However, what is striking about this *āya* is that it underscores the nature of their adherence to partners. Those who manifest *shirk* demonstrate *ṣabr* in their clinging; they demonstrate the same patient perseverance that those who manifest *īmān* and *islām* demonstrate. Only they persevere in actions that are negatively evaluated.

Ḥanīf

The concept of *ḥanīf* is associated with the same type of constancy affiliated with *īmān* and *islām*. This was explored in relation to the term *'aqīm* (e.g., Qur'ān 10:105, 30:30): Abraham as *ḥanīf* is constant in turning his whole self toward God alone. Similarly, *ḥanīf* is connected in two places to the specific action of praying to God alone (Qur'ān 10:105–106, 30:30–31).

In multiple other occurrences, the concept *ḥanīf* is contextualized within discussions of *ḥajj* (pilgrimage). These accounts detail Abraham's and Ishmael's construction of God's House (the Kaaba) as well as the specific rituals associated with *ḥajj*:

> We showed Abraham the site of the House, saying, "Do not ascribe partners to Me. Purify My House for those who circle around it, those who stand to pray, and those who bow and prostrate themselves. Proclaim the pilgrimage to people. They will come to you on foot and on every kind of swift mount, emerging from every deep mountain pass to attain benefits and celebrate God's name, on specified days, over the livestock God has provided for them. Feed yourselves and the poor and unfortunate. So let the pilgrims complete their acts of cleansing, fulfill their vows, and circle around the Ancient House." All this, anyone who honors the sacred rites of God will have good rewards from his Lord ... (22:26–30, excerpt of 22:30)

In a similar account, the *ḥajj* is described as a duty owed to God:

> ...Pilgrimage to the House is a duty owed to God by people who are able to undertake it. To those who reject this, God has no need of anyone. (3:97, excerpt)

These *āyāt* appear to indicate that the concept of *ḥanīf* has an inherent connection with the rights of *ḥajj*. Moreover, they appear to state that *ḥajj* is a universal obligation for all people. This, however, is not the case. The concept of *ḥanīf* is situated in descriptions of the *ḥajj* in three places in the Qur'ān (Qur'ān 2:125–130, 3:96–97, 22:26–31). In two of these three, the descriptions conclude with references to *manāsik*, that is, to the diverse divinely intended rites of each lateral *umma*:

> Our Lord, make us devoted (*muslimīn*) to You. Make our descendants into a community that submits to You (*umma muslima*). Show us our rites (*manāsik*) and accept our repentance, for You are the Ever Relenting, the Most Merciful. (2:128)
>
> We appointed acts of devotion (*mansak*) for every community (*umma*) ... (22:34, excerpt)

The rites of the *ḥajj* are the *manāsik* of the *umma* of Muḥammad and perhaps of the *umma* of Abraham. Thus, while Abraham is inherently connected to the *ḥajj*, the concept of *ḥanīf* is not. Rather, the concept of *ḥanīf* is inherently connected to the acknowledgment that lateral religious difference among *umam* is not the basis of evaluation or privilege. This conclusion is reinforced by the fact that the concept of *ḥanīf* is repeatedly juxtaposed with attempts to claim status based upon lateral difference. This has already been discussed in relation to various exclusive claims of those who manifest *kufr*. However, the response to those who attempt to do so is worthy of reiteration:

> It will not be according to your hopes or those of the People of the Scripture. Anyone who does wrong will be requited for it and will find no one to protect or help them against God. Anyone, male or female, who does good deeds (*ṣālihāt*) and is a believer (*mu'minūn*) will enter Paradise and will not be wronged by as much as the dip in a date stone. Who could be better in religion than those who submit themselves wholly (*'aslama wajhahu*) to God, do good,

> and follow the way of Abraham, who was true and pure in faith (*ḥanīf*)? ... (4:123–125, excerpt)

To those who attempt to use lateral religious difference as the basis of evaluation, the Qur'ān responds unequivocally. Evaluation will be based not on lateral particularities or group affliation. It will be based, rather, on *taqwā*, *ṣāliḥāt*, and *īmān*; to recognize such is to truly align oneself with the *dīn al-qayyim* (the correct religion), the *dīn* of the *ḥanīf*, the *dīn* of *al-islām*.

Kufr

In addition to the actions detailed in other sections, those who manifest *kufr* are generally described as those who ignore the laws or limits that God has established:

> ...These are the limits set by God. Grievous torment awaits those who ignore (*kāfirūn*) them. (58:4, excerpt)

These limits or bounds are related to ritual actions, such as fasting, as well as to interpersonal interactions, such as inheritance, marriage, and divorce (e.g., Qur'ān 2:187, 4:12, 2:229, 65:1). Those who manifest *kufr* are also described as violating other prescribed actions, such as upholding pledges and agreements:

> The worst creatures in the sight of God are those who reject (*alladhīna kafarū*) God and will not believe (*lā yu'minūna*), who, whenever you make an agreement with them, break it, for they are not mindful of God (*lā tattaqūna*). (8:55–56)

The explanation that these *āyāt* provide for the failure to uphold agreements is also noteworthy: those who manifest *kufr* fail to do so because they do not have *taqwā*.

However, the most significant characteristic of those who manifest *kufr* is their active opposition to those who manifest *īmān*. This is clarified by returning to the story of Iblis:

> And then Iblis said, "Because You have put me in the wrong, I will lie in wait for them all on Your straight path. I will come at them

> from their front and their back, from their right and their left, and You will find most of them ungrateful." God said, "Get out! You are disgraced and banished! I swear I shall fill Hell with you and all who follow you!" (7:16–18)

These *āyāt* recount Iblis's deliberate and conscious plan to lead people away from the path of God, and they directly follow his refusal to bow to the human creation. Therefore, Iblis's pledge to lead astray is a product of his arrogance and wounded pride. Iblis holds himself to be better than humankind. Thus, when God gives blessings to humanity, Iblis is angered. However, he does not simply refuse to obey and then harbor anger. Rather, he pledges to work actively and persistently against those whom he feels have compromised his status. It is this active opposition that also characterizes those who manifest *kufr*:

> ...Those who turned others away from God's path and tried to make it crooked, those who denied (*kāfirūn*) the Hereafter. (7:45)

> But those who strive to oppose Our messages and try in vain to defeat Us are destined for the Blaze. (22:51)

> But as for those who work against Our Revelations, seeking to undermine them, there will be a torment of painful suffering. (34:5)

As Esack perceptively argues, *kufr* is therefore "something conscious, deliberate and active rather than a casual ignoring or disregard of the existence of God."[35] Those who manifest *kufr* are cognizant of their actions, intend to lead others astray, and demonstrate persistence in their negative actions.[36]

Islām

Many characteristics related to the actions of those who manifest *islām* have already been highlighted. For example, they display a constant and consistent turning toward God. The active nature of this turning is emphasized in other *āyāt* indicating that one should strive to maintain *islām* until the moment of death:

> ..."Let me die in true devotion to You (*musliman*). Join me with the righteous." (12:101, excerpt)

> You who believe (*alladhīna āmanū*), be mindful (*'ittaqū*) of God, as is God's due, and make sure you devote yourselves to God (*muslimūn*) until your dying moment. (3:102)

The fact that Qur'ān 3:102 is addressed to those who manifest *īmān* further indicates the necessity for every individual to strive to maintain *islām* in every moment.

The concept of *islām* is also invoked in descriptions of the divinely intended *manāsik* (rites/practice) of each lateral *umma*. Like the concept of *ḥanīf*, *islām* acts as a reassertion of evaluation based only on *taqwā* (Qur'ān 22:34).[37] Not surprisingly, it is also linked with the central actions of *taqwā*, including praying, paying alms, acknowledging God, and doing good works:

> ... So keep up the prayer, give the prescribed alms, and seek refuge in God. God is your protector, an excellent protector and an excellent helper. (22:78)

> In fact, any who devote themselves wholly to God (*'aslama wajhahu*) and do good will have their reward with their Lord. No fear for them, nor will they grieve. (2:112)

> Who speaks better than someone who calls people to God, does what is right (*ṣāliha*), and says, "I am one of those devoted to God (*muslimīn*)"? (41:33)

However, as stated in Qur'ān 41:33, those who manifest *islām* not only perform these *taqwā*-related actions but also call others to God and explicitly identify themselves as people devoted to God. This type of explicit identification was also noted in reference to those who manifest *īmān*. In both cases, it serves as a point of contrast with those who manifest *nifāq*—those who fear people more than God—and therefore never reveal their true convictions for fear that it would compromise their social and economic position. In distinction, the explicit statement of those who manifest *islām* or *īmān* is a sign of their primary dependence upon and allegiance to the vertical relationship with God, a dependence and allegiance that dictates their actions on the horizontal level.

Nifāq

Those who manifest *nifāq* display discordance between their words and deeds;[38] they make statements that do not align with their actions. This is evident both in their relationship to God and response to God's guidance and in their social actions and interactions. Qur'ān 59:11–12, for instance, describes the empty pledges of support they make to other people:

> Have you considered the hypocrites (*munāfiqūn*) who say to their fellows, the disbelievers (*alladhīna kafarū*) among the People of the Scripture, "If you are driven out, we shall go with you. We would never listen to anyone who sought to harm you. And if you are attacked, we shall certainly come to your aid"? God bears witness that they are in fact liars. If they are driven out, they will never leave with them. If they are attacked, they will never help them. Even if they did come to their aid, they would soon turn tail and flee. In the end, they would have no help. (59:11–12)

Although those who manifest *nifāq* adamantly promise to assist others, they will never follow through in action. Moreover, these *āyāt* also indicate that their words and deeds are discordant with respect not only to those who manifest *īmān* (e.g., Qur'ān 9:56–59) but also with respect to other groups. In fact, those who manifest *nifāq* are not even united or dependable among themselves:

> . . . There is much hostility between them. You think they are united but their hearts are divided because they are people devoid of reason. (59:14, excerpt)

They are free agents; they float from group to group seeking individual benefit. The discordance they manifest is also compared to the actions of Iblis, who entices people to stray from the path of God, and then disowns them in the face of God:

> Like Satan, who says to humankind, "Do not believe!" But when humankind disbelieves, says, "I disown you. I fear God, the Lord of the Worlds." (59:16)

This comparison also highlights that those who manifest *nifāq* display discordance between their own belief and actions and encourage others to do the same:

> They have used their oaths to cover up, and barred others from the path of God . . . (58:16, excerpt)

> The hypocrites, both men and women (*munāfiqūn* and *munāfiqāt*), are all the same. They order what is wrong and forbid what is right. They are tight-fisted. They have ignored God, so God has ignored them. The hypocrites (*munāfiqīn*) are the disobedient ones. (9:67)

Pointedly, Qur'ān 9:67 directly contrasts those who manifest *nifāq* with those who manifest *īmān*. Those who manifest *nifāq* order the wrong and forbid the right and refuse to give from their wealth or to pay alms. These actions are central elements of *taqwā*. However, when they do engage in actions associated with *taqwā*—and they do—they perform them only to be seen by others and even then as if they are under duress:

> The hypocrites (*munāfiqūn*) try to deceive God, but it is God who causes them to be deceived. When they stand up to pray, they do so sluggishly, showing off in front of people, and remember God only a little, wavering all the time between this and that, belonging neither to one side nor the other … (4:142–143, excerpt)

The Qur'ān also emphasizes that those who manifest *nifāq* frequently appear impressive in their words and material possessions. Though, in reality they are superficial and devoid of any true convictions or allegiances:

> When you see them, their outward appearance pleases you. When they speak, you listen to what they say. But they are like propped-up timbers; they think every cry they hear is against them. And they are the enemy … (63:4, excerpt)[39]

The nature of those who manifest *nifāq* is vividly illuminated in juxtaposition with a description of those who manifest *taqwā*, the *muttaqūn*:

> Those who are steadfast (*ṣābirīn*), truthful, truly devout, who give and pray before dawn for forgiveness. (3:17)

Those who manifest *nifāq* diverge from each component of this description. They are not steadfast; rather, they waver constantly. They are not truthful but always say what benefits them in any particular situation. They are not devout but fear people more than God. If they give, they give only a little and remind others of their gifts (Qur'ān 2:264). If they pray, they pray only to be seen and not to seek forgiveness in the seclusion of the night. They may pray the five daily obligatory prayers, which are done in a congregational (i.e., public) format, but they do not engage privately or inwardly in supererogatory prayers or supplications for forgiveness.

Observations and Implications

In light of the preceding exploration of the concepts of hierarchical religious difference, it is vital to underscore a few analytical observations about the nature of these concepts and to note some of the resultant implications thereof. To begin, it is evident that each concept is complex and multifaceted; each is defined by an intricate array of central characteristics in terms of the belief, responses, actions, and interactions.

Second, all of the concepts are characterized by an active and deliberate nature. Not one is defined based upon the simple neglect of belief or action, whether it be those who manifest *shirk* and unfalteringly cling to the ways of their forebears or those who manifest *īmān* and strive constantly to maintain *ṣabr*.

Third, and closely related to the fact that these concepts signify active postures, the concepts themselves are dynamic. They do not denote fixed or static positions but rather dynamic manifestations that can increase and decrease. This is apparent in the description of revelation increasing the *īmān* of some and the hostility and rejection of others. This is also evident in the multitude of reminders to display *taqwā* that are issued even to those who already manifest *īmān*.

Fourth, even though the concepts have unique facets, they overlap with one another. Those who manifest *shirk* are depicted as engaging in *kufr* and vice versa. Those who manifest *nifāq* engage in some of the actions associated with *īmān* and *islām*. These overlaps challenge the notion of discrete boundaries and clearly delineated distinctions. However, this does not indicate that these traits are subsumed under others, since the Qur'ān deliberately maintains the distinct concepts. For example, *shirk* and *kufr* do overlap, but they are maintained as distinct in *āyāt* such as Qur'ān 98:1.

Fifth, a central aspect of each of these concepts relates to their negotiation of the horizontal (human-to-human) and vertical (human-to-God) relationships. *Shirk*, *kufr*, and *nifāq* represent diverse infringements upon the prioritization of the relationship with God. Those who manifest *shirk* prioritize their social relationships through clinging to inherited practices.

Those who manifest *kufr* prioritize lateral religious affiliation through claims of exclusive and special status. Those who manifest *nifāq* prioritize individual and material welfare on the horizontal level over all else. The concepts of *īmān, ḥanīf* and *islām* demonstrate the inverse of this: placing the relationship with God and the emphasis on *taqwā* above all else. More significantly, they also offer incisive and diverse critiques of the other concepts. For instance, the behavior of the *ḥanīf* is a counterpoint to the blind adherence to inherited practices and allegiance to social groups associated with *shirk; īmān,* with its emphasis on consistency and justice, rails against the wavering and injustice of *nifāq*; and all three—*īmān, ḥanīf,* and *islām*—contend with the lateral exclusivism of *kufr*.

These observations about the nature of the Qur'ānic discourse on hierarchical religious difference have many implications. One of the most prominent relates to the notion of threshold criteria. As seen in the historical Islamic discourse, there have been many attempts to establish simple and singular threshold criteria by which to indicate an individual's alignment with these concepts. This has been part of the effort to erect unambiguous and enforceable boundaries between groups. While I have already argued against the indiscriminate alignment of these concepts with any historical lateral community, the issue of threshold criteria remains. One may admit that *taqwā* is not automatically confined or holistically attributed to a particular historical group while still maintaining the singular necessity of explicitly recognizing Muḥammad. This indirectly results in the same confinement of *taqwā* to the historical community of Muḥammad. The importance of recognizing Muḥammad *is* supported by the Qur'ānic command not to distinguish between any messengers. Since the Muslim community recognizes some other messengers as well as Muḥammad, they become the only ones who manifest *taqwā*, whereas others fall short. There is a certain amount of irony in the fact that this position is supported with reference to the same Qur'ānic *āyāt* (those that state "*lā nufarriqū*," "make no distinctions") that rail against automatic privileging of lateral groups. I do not dispute that these *āyāt* and many others order people to recognize Muḥammad and critique them for failing to do so. The question is whether this is the primary and prerequisite criterion that defines a supposed boundary between *taqwā* and all else.

In light of the complexity and dynamism of the concepts, it is almost impossible to prioritize only one aspect above the all others. This does not mean that recognition of Muḥammad is not part of *īmān* or *islām*. It clearly is. However, is it the singular prerequisite? It is crucial to unpack the implications of such an assertion. To present it as such is to place all other aspects including good works, praying, paying alms, believing in God, and believing in judgment in a secondary role. If explicit acknowledgment of Muḥammad is a prerequisite or threshold criterion, then it implies that these actions have no salvific value if they are performed in the absence of the explicit recognition. I specify salvific value here to indicate value in the sight of God. Some scholars accept such actions as having social or worldly value but no value in the Hereafter.[40] This is a difficult argument to make in the face of repeated Qur'ānic assertions about those who believe in God and perform good deeds being rewarded (e.g., Qur'ān 16:97, 18:2, 18:88). Moreover, in the majority of these *āyāt*, there is no explicit indication that the reward is differentiated—that is, worldly or otherworldly—contingent upon recognition of Muḥammad. While it is tempting to simplify this discourse by reading a distinction into the text, it is also of upmost importance to listen to and grapple with the apparent message.

Even if it were possible (or beneficial) to select one criterion to demarcate the threshold, it would have to be recognition of God. There is no way to elevate the recognition of Muḥammad over the recognition of God as a singular threshold criterion. What is interesting about this is that the Qur'ān depicts every human being as recognizing God, though they may have various misconceptions in that regard. They may periodically be forgetful. They may join others with God. However, they all recognize God, and in doing so they could all be depicted as manifesting at least a miniscule amount of *taqwā*.[41] The argument could be made that these are not correct ways of recognizing God and therefore they are devoid of all value. However, since the Qur'ānic discourse depicts dynamic levels and degrees of *taqwā*, it is hard to determine what would count as the lowest level or the cutoff point.

Many other possible criteria or combinations thereof could be identified to demarcate boundaries. The real question, though, is whether boundaries are even the issue. The Qur'ānic discourse on hierarchical religious difference does not appear to be consumed with boundary delineation but rather with complexity, dynamism, and relationality. The discourse presents the possibility of different individuals manifesting the same concept in diverse ways, to diverse degrees, and with diverse constancy. Once complexity, dynamism, and degrees of actualization are admitted within any one concept, it becomes almost impossible to confine those elements within discrete and static boundaries.

Moreover, the discourse indicates that one individual could manifest multiple concepts simultaneously. Izutsu flatly denies this possibility, acknowledging only, for example, that people could have *īmān* and *kufr* in succession.[42] Izutsu's position is made possible because of his conceptual opposition, but it is also based on an overly simplified view of these concepts. If people believe in God and the Hereafter, are good to their parents, pay alms, pray, and remain steadfast but think that their historical religious community is an automatically privileged community in the eyes of God, what are they manifesting? Are they not manifesting *īmān* and *kufr* simultaneously? It may be more *īmān* than *kufr*, but it is both.

Moving away from the emphasis on boundary delineation, though, should not be misconstrued as relativism. It is not an attempt to universally and automatically validate all people, all actions, or all beliefs. As explicated, the various concepts depict concrete beliefs, responses, actions, and interactions that are positively and negatively evaluated. The fact that boundaries are not clearly defined does not mean that content is not ascertainable. In fact, it is precisely by shifting the focus away from static and discrete boundaries that the true nuances and intricacies of the Qurʾānic discourse—the evaluative discourse—are illuminated.

8

Never Wholly Other: Sameness, Difference, and Relationality

IN CRITIQUING THE contemporary Islamic discourse on religious difference, I identified two interconnected shortcomings: the shared conception of religious difference as that which divides humanity through the erection of clear, static, and impermeable boundaries; and the resultant failure to account in an integrated manner for both religious sameness and religious difference without resorting either to isolation or hierarchy. In the preceding two chapters, I have aimed to address the first by distinguishing between lateral and hierarchical religious difference and by reinterpreting the concepts of hierarchical difference as complex, dynamic, and interrelated. In this concluding chapter, I build upon this dual reconceptualization of difference to reweave sameness, lateral religious difference, and hierarchal religious difference into a coherent—although complex and at times ambiguous—account.

In doing so, I explore creation, the relationship between creation and revelation, the relationship between revelations, and the purpose of lateral difference. While some of these topics have already been introduced, my present goal is to bring them together and to begin to unpack the implications of the reconceptualization of difference for each. This reweaving will demonstrate that religious diversity demands that we think differently not only about difference but also about the Qur'ān itself.

Creation and Theological Anthropology

The Qur'ān affirms God as the Creator of all humanity. God creates the singular *nafs* (soul) and then the *zawj* (pair, mate). From this shared origin emerge all human beings, who are described as being scattered far and wide.[1] The Qur'ān also states that all humans were created with a singular purpose, that is, to worship God and act as God's vicegerents on Earth.[2] To fulfill this purpose, humanity has been equipped with the necessary tools.[3] Humanity has been created in the best form—that is, the form most suitable to its purpose—and has been equipped with faculties such as hearing, sight, and minds.[4] These aspects of human creation refer not only to the literal physical faculties but also to a more general capacity for comprehension and receptivity to God's guidance. This nonliteral interpretation is confirmed in repeated Qur'ānic descriptions in which those who reject guidance, who do not believe correctly, or who fail to reflect upon God's natural *āyāt* are described as having sealed hearts, being deaf, or being blind.[5]

In addition to these faculties, God has endowed all of humanity with knowledge of God and *taqwā*. All the Children of Adam are depicted as testifying to their recognition of God as their Lord and sustainer,[6] and the *nafs* is depicted as having an innate awareness of *taqwā*.[7] It is in this sense that humanity as whole was once a single community (*umma waḥida*); at the time of creation all of humanity was unified in terms of *taqwā*.[8] The existence of such knowledge, however, is not a guarantee that humanity will sustain awareness or act in accordance with that awareness. Humans can choose, or more accurately will have to choose, whether to grow in *taqwā* or to bury it. The allusion to burying is significant as it implies that this nature of the soul—the knowledge of *taqwā*—is something that can be hidden but not eradicated. The testimony of the Children of Adam similarly indicates the potential of humans to act counter to their innate knowledge of God (*fiṭra*); on the Day of Judgment, some humans will find themselves having to make excuses for their failures.

Humanity therefore is also universally endowed with another quality: freedom. Humans are created both "capable of action as well as free to act or not to act."[9] While this freedom permits the possibility of acting in discordance with their purpose, it is in actuality only through free acquiescence that worship of God has any meaning. Moreover, it is only through the combination of capacity—in faculties and knowledge—and freedom that humans become moral subjects, that they are held accountable and are subject to God's judgment. This is confirmed by the fact that individuals who either lack certain mental, physical, or material capacities, or lack freedom are exempted from central Qur'ānic obligations, responsibility, and accountability.

It is this depiction of the universal capacity, freedom, and accountability of all humanity that forms the foundation of the Qur'ānic discourse. At the moment of creation, every individual stands in the exact same relationship with God; they are the capable creations of God and the objects of God's concern.[10] Yet it is vital to underscore that the universal and positive affirmation of all humanity that results from this depiction is simultaneously an affirmation of equal responsibility and equal liability to judgment. In other words, since what is bestowed through creation is sufficient to fulfill one's purpose, no individual will be exempted from fulfilling that purpose. Although other forms of guidance will come after creation, the ability to fulfill one's purpose is not exclusively dependent upon those forms. This creates a unique characteristic of the Qur'ānic discourse: from the most basic level, the Qur'ān affirms all people, though it never affirms all actions.

The aspects of creation discussed thus far revolve around sameness, but creation also involves difference, that is, divinely intended lateral difference. This is indicated in the creation of the *zawj* from the one *nafs*[11] as well as in the deliberate creation of diverse nations, tribes,[12] languages, and colors among humanity.[13] Notably, none of these forms of lateral difference impinges upon the status, capacity, purpose, or responsibility of all humans. Descriptions of lateral difference are quickly followed by exhortations to manifest *taqwā* or explicit statements that divine assessment will be based only on *taqwā* rather than on any of these lateral forms of difference.

Moreover, these forms of lateral difference serve a purpose, which the Qur'ān describes in two ways. In Qur'ān 30:20–22, lateral difference is an *āya* (sign) of God; it is something designed to cause awe and provoke reflection, thus leading to recognition and glorification of God. In Qur'ān 49:13, lateral difference is described as something that is created so that people may recognize one another or become acquainted with one another. What is the value of recognizing one another? The text does not expound in any further detail, but certain deductions can be made. First, whatever the value is, it cannot be achieved in isolation; becoming acquainted with each other requires engagement. Therefore, it is safe to assume that God is encouraging interaction across the boundaries of lateral difference. Second, a reflective and engaged encounter with the lateral Other reveals something about God. This is similar to the often reiterated value of reflecting on other natural *āyāt*. Specifically, the *āya* of lateral difference reveals that the lateral Other—despite his or her lateral particularities—is also the creation, concern, and subject of God. This underscores the singular status and infinite capacity of God as Creator, but it also reveals something about the self: that the self and the Other both stand in the same relationship with God. Lateral difference does not place one in a privileged status before God or reduce the other simply to a marginal or derivative status.

Creation and Revelation

What are the implications of the preceding depiction of created sameness and divinely intended difference for understanding revelation? Revelation here does not only refer to the physical scriptures of various communities but more generally also denotes God's interaction with humanity. Given that humanity is not situated in an initial position of incapacity but rather one of capacity, what is the purpose of revelation?

Before attempting to answer these questions, it is vital to reiterate the hermeneutical importance of theological interconnections. Frequently, the value of revelation is discussed from the predetermined standpoint that one specific revelation has ultimate value. Thus, if other revelations are acknowledged as valid, they are to be interpreted in a manner that sustains the ultimate value of that specific revelation. Other revelations are variously presented as partial, particular to a limited context, or corrupted. While some consideration may be given to the implications of such assessments for other aspects of theology, the primary issue at stake is to maintain the preeminence of the specific revelation. Though it is possible that one specific revelation does have ultimate value, the discussion of such must begin with and remain connected to an understanding of God and theological anthropology. Therefore, in this section I aim to situate the phenomenon of general revelation in relationship to what was previously outlined in respect to God's creation of humanity.

Creation, natural *āyāt,* and revelation are not sequential steps in a linear hierarchy but rather are entangled and mutually reinforcing aspects of one process aimed at assisting humans to fulfill their singular purpose, that is, to worship God and manifest *taqwā*. Humans are created with the capacity to achieve their purpose, and this has not been definitively compromised through any event. This is why scholars including Ismāʿīl al-Fārūqī, Riffat Hassan, and even Muhammad Legenhausen adamantly argue against the insinuation of the concept of the Fall into the Qurʾān.[14]

As al-Fārūqī contends, "Islam entertains no idea of fall, of original sin, or of a predicament from which man may not extricate himself by his own effort."[15] The nuances of what al-Fārūqī is arguing are important. God has created humans capable, but God has also created them free. Humans will find themselves in "predicaments"; they will forget, be deceived, and be led astray due to rivalry and arrogance. However, with exertion and actualization of the inherent created capacities—the *fiṭra*—they are able to extricate themselves. The efficacy of exertion and actualization, though, does not imply that humans are self-sufficient; rather, employment of these capacities is an engagement in the ongoing relationship between God and humankind. Furthermore, the predicaments in which humans may find themselves do not obliterate the created human capacities. Knowledge and capacities can be buried but not destroyed,[16] and God's creation of the human *fiṭra* can never be altered.[17]

Moreover, exertion and actualization of the *fiṭra* take place in relation to the rest of the creation (i.e., God's natural *āyāt*) and in relation to revelation. As the example of Abraham demonstrates, it is possible to reflect on creation alone and gain thereby an understanding of God, but not all humans will exert themselves in this manner. As also discussed, humans in general, even those who manifest *īmān*, perpetually struggle with sustaining the recognition of God and the expression of *taqwā*. In fact, this was the predicament even of Adam and Eve; they had been given knowledge, had made a pledge or covenant with God, but forgot and were deceived.[18] It is here that one of the most significant roles of revelation becomes evident. Like water that falls upon the earth and stirs it to grow,[19] revelation stirs the innate *fiṭra* of human beings. The seed that will grow is already there, but the seed benefits from cultivation and nurture. In this way, it is possible to conceive of the relationship between creation and revelation as the relationship between God as creator and God as sustainer.[20] God creates with perfection and demonstrates mercy in perpetually sustaining—or recreating—that creation. The acts of creating and sustaining are not discretely distinguished; God does not create and then recede. Rather, God is depicted as being engaged in a process of ongoing creation. Moreover, God sustains not only through revelation but also through ongoing natural *āyāt*, signs designed to evoke awe and rouse the *fiṭra*.

In light of this, revelation in general should be considered as something gratuitous[21]: in the technical sense of not being the only means by which humans can arrive at an understanding of God; and in the theological sense of being a freely given mercy and blessing from God. Revelation is something that comes not to remedy inherent deficiencies in capacity. Rather, it illuminates the same knowledge that was instilled in humanity from the beginning and that, with exertion, humanity is capable of discovering through created faculties and contemplation of natural *āyāt*. In this sense, revelation is a reiteration, a reminder, a guide, and a warning. It does not bring something new but highlights and reasserts the same message of *taqwā*. The fact that revelation reiterates what is instilled through creation is also evident in the Qur'ān's questioning of people who will not accept the revelation; they are questioned as to why they will not believe when they already made a pledge to God.[22] As *nafs*, they already testified that God was their creator and Lord, but they still refuse to believe. The Qur'ān calls them not to affirm something new but rather to reaffirm, to dig up, what is latent.

While revelation may be conceived of as gratuitous in the technical and theological senses, the Qur'ān also presents it as being universal.[23] There is no *umma* that has not been sent revelation. While this Qur'ānic assertion is widely accepted at face value, its implications have not been fully unpacked. The first implication of universal revelation is similar to one of the implications of a universal and capable *fiṭra*: all humanity is accountable to God and subject to judgment. The second implication is that it reasserts God's concern with all of humanity, not just a select group. The third is that it raises important questions about the boundaries of concepts, such as the People of the Scripture, that is, those who have received God's revelation. Scholarly discourse has tended to restrict this denotation to Jews and Christians, maybe Sabians and Zoroastrians. Given what is known about human history and geography, it seems difficult to make the case that these groups comprise the totality of those who have received revelation. Thus, there are two options. One is to restrict this denotation to these few groups and accept a relative silence on the part of Qur'ān with respect to a multitude of other communities. The other choice is to reconceive this term as more inclusive and even possibly wholly inclusive. The latter may seem to be a radical supposition, but if revelation is truly universal and the term *kitāb* refers to both a physical book of scripture[24] and also to revelation in general, then this conclusion is viable.

Moreover, inclusion within this category cannot be based upon perfect adherence to *taqwā* or absolute monotheism, since the Qur'ān criticizes some of the People of the Scripture for failing in both of these regards. The purpose of reinterpreting this category, therefore, is not to automatically raise the value of religious Others but to gain more insight into the Qur'ānic message. The value of religious Others could not be assessed based on their inclusion in or exclusion from the group People of the Scripture anyhow, since it is a category of lateral nonevaluative religious difference. Though I will not endeavor to definitely answer this question, what new insights may be gleaned if this category were reread in light of the Qur'ān's own teaching about the universality of revelation? Moreover, might not the borders of the category People of the Scripture not only expand outward but also fold inward? Would it not be possible, after the Qur'ānic revelation, to understand even the recipients of the Qur'ān to be People of the Scripture? I am not contending that the Qur'ān employs the denotation with this referent. However, I am suggesting that once the Qur'ānic revelation occurs those that follow it find themselves in many of the same situations as other People of the Scripture.

Revelation also has a unique relationship with lateral difference. Revelation is sent to *umam* (communities), which in some fashion are the products of the lateral difference introduced in creation. Moreover, revelation also introduces new forms of lateral religious difference in terms of diverse rites, practices, ways, and laws. Intriguingly, even though it is closely connected to and productive of lateral difference, the primary goal of revelation is related to hierarchical difference. The goal is to reiterate the message of *taqwā*; to foster its manifestation; and to address differences that have arisen in terms of *taqwā*. Revelation therefore urges and stresses *taqwā* (i.e., unity in hierarchical difference) but simultaneously introduces lateral religious difference. Connecting this observation to broader theological suppositions is imperative. If revelation is the intentional product of God, as it is depicted in the Qur'ān, then there must be a rationale behind this seemingly incongruous pairing. There are multiple possibilities, but when stress is placed on divine intentionally it indicates that the purpose of revelation (the urging of *taqwā*) is facilitated through responsiveness to and production of lateral difference. In other words, one of the primary means by which revelation aims to eradicate hierarchical religious difference (i.e., difference in terms of *taqwā*) is through the introduction of lateral religious particularities.

Revelation and Revelation

Since there have been multiple revelations, the next question that arises relates to the relationship between the various revelations. Does one revelation complete another? Do they change each other? What is the appropriate response on the part of those who have already received revelation to the arrival of a new revelation?

Before addressing these specific questions, it is necessary to reflect back momentarily on the universality of revelation. Discussions of the relationship between revelations usually focus only on those associated with Judaism, Christianity, and Islam. These revelations may be more closely related than others, and they are the background against and part of the intertextual context within which the Qur'ān speaks. However, they are not the entirety of revelation.[25] By simply considering this fact, the effort to depict revelations as occurring in a neat line of supersession is greatly complexified. If the universality of revelation is taken seriously, then it is possible that multiple revelations were communicated simultaneously. While I will not explore this possibility in detail, it does prompt new questions and challenge the typical depiction of sequential and supersessional revelation.

In distinguishing between lateral and hierarchical religious difference, I discussed the relationship between revelations fairly extensively, arguing that the hierarchical exhortation to *taqwā* is something common in all revelations whereas the lateral laws, rites, and ways are particular to each revelation. In connection to *taqwā*, the exhortation is common to every revelation and is also fully communicated in every revelation. No Qur'ānic *āya* describes specific revelations of God as being partial. As a result, there can be no conception of a partial or incomplete revelation. Inversely, there can be no conception of a revelation that comes to complete another revelation. If revelations are not partial, they do not need to be completed by subsequent revelations. This position is supported by the Qur'ānic description of later revelations as *muṣaddiq* (confirming) of earlier revelations. This depiction is explicitly applied, for example, to the relationship between the Gospel and the Torah,[26] as well as between the Qur'ān and earlier revelations.[27]

What about the question of change? Can one revelation come to change another? In reference to hierarchical difference, this is a moot point. If the same message of *taqwā* is completely communicated in every revelation, then there is nothing to change. However, revelations can act as reminders in reference to other revelations or communities of revelation. This is why numerous Qur'ānic *āyāt* exhort those who had already received revelation to uphold it and critique them for failing to do so.[28] Additionally, revelations are described as explaining or making things clear to people who had previously received revelation.[29] Making things clear, however, should not be understood as changing or supplementing the original message. Clarification is necessary and appropriate only once an original and complete message has been delivered. It is not needed because of any deficiency in the original revelation but may be necessary because the recipients have neglected their revelation or have fallen into disagreements over it. However, when a revelation acts as a reminder or clarification to another, it does so in terms of hierarchical religious difference alone; it reemphasizes and restates the message of *taqwā*. In this way, there is a certain parallel between the relationship of revelations to one another and the relationship of creation to revelation. The full and perfect message of *taqwā* is available, but humans as individuals benefit from and need constant reminders.

The fact that the Qur'ān understands all revelations to contain the same, complete, and unchanging message of *taqwā* is evident in the descriptions of the appropriate response to new revelations and messengers. Those who previously received revelation are described as recognizing (*ʿ-R-F*) and bearing witness (*SH-Ḥ-D*) to the new revelation.[30] What they recognize is the singular message of *taqwā*, the same message contained in their revelation and confirmed in the new one. The notion of recognition is also intimately connected with *mīthāq al-nabiyyīn* (the pledge of the prophets).[31] In this pledge, the recipients of revelation promise that if another messenger comes and confirms the message they have already received (i.e., the message of *taqwā*) then they must believe (*ʾ-M-N*) in and support (*N-Ṣ-R*) that messenger. To do otherwise would be to turn away from *islām* or true devotion to God and to draw distinctions between the various messengers and messages. I have already discussed the harsh critiques lodged against those who make such distinctions due to rivalry and envy and who divide themselves into factions (*aḥzāb*). In contrast, those who do not make such distinctions (*lā tafarriqu*) recognize and affirm the continuity of all revelations; they believe in them and support them.

In Chapter 7, I also discussed another response to revelation: obedience. Those who manifest *īmān* were described as hearing and obeying the revelation and messenger. The question that arises is whether there is a difference between believing and supporting (i.e., the responses demanded of those who previously received revelation) and obeying (i.e., the appropriate response of the primary recipients of a specific revelation). It is clear that obedience is not something unique to any one messenger; it is the command of every messenger.[32] Significantly, the call to obedience is typically paired with a call to *taqwā*: "Fear (*ʾittaqū*) God and obey me."[33]

The fact that the display of *taqwā* and obedience are paired yet distinct, suggests that obedience to a messenger is connected to lateral religious particularities. This is supported by the fact that many Qur'ānic exhortations to obey Muḥammad are semantically linked with descriptions of particular religious practices and laws (*manāsik*), including those related to inheritance, fighting, usury, gambling, and intoxicants.[34] Therefore, in the Qur'ān all people are called to obey a messenger but they are not all called to obey the same messenger.

Returning to the notions of believing and supporting, these two responses define the act of not distinguishing between messengers and revelation. To not distinguish means to believe in and recognize the truth of another revelation because it confirms the universal message of *taqwā*. The concept of support goes a step beyond mere recognition and requires that those who believe in God's revelations aid and assist each other. This is evident in the general descriptions of those who manifest *īmān*—irrespective of lateral religious particularities—as supporters and protectors of one another.[35] It is also vividly illustrated in Qur'ān 22:39–41, which authorizes fighting to protect the various houses—churches, synagogues, and mosques—within which God is worshiped.[36] Those who worship in and protect these houses are described as those who help (*N-Ṣ-R*) God's cause, those who establish prayer, pay alms, command the right, and forbid the wrong—in other words, those who do these things are described as those who manifest *taqwā*, the *muttaqūn*.

It is here vital not to collapse, simplify, or subsume these various responses. Belief, recognition, help, and obedience are not the same, nor are they used randomly or synonymously in the Qur'ānic discourse. When tracing the appearances of these responses throughout the discourse and relating them to recurring themes, their unique nuances are revealed. And with the illumination of those nuances comes a provocative challenge and a profound resource: the discourse indicates that it is possible for individuals to fully manifest *taqwā* (through belief, recognition, and help) without following (without obedience to) the lateral particularities revealed in the revelation to Muḥammad.

Purpose of Lateral Religious Difference

If this is indeed indicated in the Qur'ānic discourse, then what is the purpose of lateral religious difference? If a specific set of lateral religious particularities is not the sole path to *taqwā*, then what is their import and role?

Qur'ānic *āyāt* that affirm the divinely intended status of lateral religious particularities (rites, laws, ways) describe the appropriate response to those particularities as racing or vying (*'istabiqū*) with one another in pursuit of what is good (*khayrāt*).[37] While the nature of this "good" can appear at first to be rather amorphous, it is essential to recognize the connection between *khayrāt* and *taqwā*. Those who manifest *taqwā* are those who race after the *khayrāt*.[38] Therefore, *khayrāt* refers not simply to any good but rather to the good as specifically defined through *taqwā*. It is the good that is manifest in belief, prayer, almsgiving, social interactions, and the prioritization of the vertical relationship with God over horizontal human relationships. Moreover, as with *taqwā*, this is a good that must be pursued actively, constantly, and socially.

What is the relationship of lateral religious difference to this commanded pursuit of *khayrāt*, to the striving for *taqwā*? Is it just an obstacle to be overlooked or ignored? Or does it have another purpose? I have already argued that revelation is both responsive to and productive of lateral difference and that it is through lateral difference that the purpose of revelation—communicating the message of and fostering the expression *taqwā*—is best achieved. In other words, revelation is sent to particular *umam* and is responsive to the particular contexts. This is confirmed in the description of revelation being delivered by a messenger from among the nation that is to receive revelation and in the description of revelation as being delivered in the people's own language.[39] It is logical therefore to assume that another facet of the contextual responsiveness of God's message would be to tailor specific rites and practices that would facilitate the manifestation of *taqwā* in particular contexts.

However, contextual purpose is a slippery slope. If lateral religious difference is *only* a matter of contextual responsiveness, then what does that entail for those who follow the lateral religious particularities of revelations that came to geographically and temporally distant contexts? This is no small question. According to the Islamic tradition and the common view that prophetic revelation has ceased, this is the situation in which all of humanity finds itself today. Every person who adheres to a particular religious tradition follows lateral religious particularities that were introduced in and tailored for other contexts. Moreover, despite some attempts to claim the contrary, every religious tradition undergoes change in terms of rites and practices. Muslim communities today do not follow every single practice of Muḥammad. Some practices have been modified deliberately, some have been discontinued, and others have been adapted to suit new contexts. Additionally, there exists great diversity even within religious traditions. Lateral religious communities are neither static nor homogeneous. I will not here tackle the multitudes of intricacies related to questions of change and diversity within lateral religious communities, but it is vital to note that the issue of change can also raise the question of corruption. If things change, which they do, that does not necessarily mean that every change is a change for the better or a change that encourages *taqwā*.

I will make only two observations in this regard. First, no religious community, including the Muslim community, is exempt from corruption. Even if the Qur'ān has divine protection for its textual integrity, this does not prevent its message from being interpreted and enacted in ways inconsistent with *taqwā*. In fact, reflecting back to the historical Islamic discourse on *taḥrif* (corruption), one of the more common definitions of *taḥrif* was corruption in terms of interpretation. Second, corruption is not synonymous with change. Every change is not automatically corruption or *bid'a* (negative innovation). There is no inherent value in blind imitation. In fact, great consequences can be associated with blind imitation, especially when it leads to or perpetuates injustice or oppression. Thus, corruption should be understood as that which impedes the manifestation of *taqwā*, not as any and all change within religious communities. Based on these brief observations, the purpose of lateral religious difference must transcend contextual responsiveness alone.

It is helpful, in light of this, to reflect back to the depiction of another form of lateral difference, which is introduced through creation. It was not responsive to context but was designed to create a situation of relational engagement that would provoke ongoing reflection on the status of the Other, the self, and God. In addition to some degree of contextual responsiveness, lateral religious difference is similarly designed to provoke ongoing reflection. It is intricately and ingeniously designed in its tensive and simultaneous demands for both obedience and nondistinction to perpetually challenge individuals, to continually raise questions about boundaries, difference, and sameness. In other words, it is designed to simultaneously maintain both proximity and otherness. The combination of lateral and hierarchical religious difference produces the Other-who-can-never-be-wholly-other. However, this Other is not simply a byproduct of the convergence of lateral and hierarchical religious difference. This Other is the means by which God sustains God's challenge to humanity. The Other-who-can-never-be-wholly-other becomes an *āya* of God, something that when reflectively engaged facilitates the singular human purpose: worship of God and manifestation of *taqwā*. It does so not through exact correspondence and assertion of sameness alone but *only* by being both irreducibly and dynamically familiar and distinct.

The Religious Other and the Qur'ān

This exploration of the Qur'ānic depiction of the religious Other has been premised upon the notion that existing interpretations of the religious Other display shortcomings that result from a specific underlying conception of difference. As a result, I have offered another interpretation of the discourse and also have identified an alternative conception of difference and an alternative method of interpretation appropriate to that conception.

The impact of rethinking difference in this manner, however, is not only confined to the depiction of the religious Other but also has implications for how we understand the Qur'ān itself. If the tension between lateral and hierarchical religious difference cannot be dissipated and the dynamism and complexity of hierarchical religious difference cannot be reduced or confined, then it is impossible to present the Qur'ān as being primarily concerned with classifying and unambiguously distinguishing between religious groups. The Qur'ān cannot be envisioned as a taxonomy of religious difference, nor can it be conceived of as a verdict on religious difference or a yardstick by which humans may definitively judge each other on the basis of this difference. Such judgment is the province of God alone on the Day of Resurrection.[40] Rather, the Qur'ān must be conceived of as an exhortation, a challenge to humanity, a challenge to believe, act, and relate in certain ways. As it labels itself, it is guidance, and provocative guidance at that. It challenges clear boundaries, complacency, and blind adherence. As with the Other-who-can-never-be-wholly-other, this challenge is sustained through irreducible complexities and tensions. These complexities and tensions, however, are not barriers or deficiencies. They are the precise means by which the Qur'ān, as God's Word, continues to speak. If complexity is reduced and dynamism contained, then the revelation assumes one meaning and desists from communicating. The divine and universal nature of this revelation is bound to its ability to continuously engage, speak, guide, and challenge and to the human ability to continuously embrace and grapple with its illuminative complexity.

Notes

INTRODUCTION

1. Veli-Matti Kärkkäinen, *An Introduction to the Theology of Religions: Biblical, Historical & Contemporary Perspectives* (Downers Grove, IL: InterVarsity, 2003), 20.
2. Kärkkäinen, *Introduction*, 26.
3. For example, Emile Brunner, "Revelation and Religion," in *Christianity and Other Religions*, ed. John Hick and Brian Hebblethwaite (Philadelphia: Fortress, 1980), 113–132. See also Paul F. Knitter, *Introducing Theologies of Religions* (Maryknoll, NY: Orbis Books, 2002), 33–36.
4. For example, Chester Gillis, *Pluralism: A New Paradigm for Theology* (Louvain: Peeters, Eerdmans, 1998), 133–164. See also Knitter, *Introducing Theologies*, 134–148.
5. For example, Mohammad Hassan Khalil, *Islam and the Fate of Others: The Salvation Question* (New York: Oxford University, 2012); Jane Dammen McAuliffe, *Qur'anic Christians: An Analysis of Classical and Modern Exegesis* (Cambridge: Cambridge University, 1991); Mahmoud Ayoub, *A Muslim View of Christianity: Essays on Dialogue by Mahmoud Ayoub*, ed. Irfan A. Omar (Maryknoll, NY: Orbis, 2007); Reza Shah-Kazemi, *The Other in the Light of the One: The Universality of the Qur'an and Interfaith Dialogue* (Cambridge: Islamic Texts Society, 2006); Muhammad Legenhausen, *Islam and Religious Pluralism* (London: Al Hoda Publishing, 1999).
6. Muhammad Legenhausen, "A Muslim's Non-reductive Religious Pluralism," in *Islam and Global Dialogue: Religious Pluralism and the Pursuit of Peace*, ed. Roger Boase (Surrey: Ashgate, 2005), 51–73, here 65.
7. Shah-Kazemi, *The Other*, xxiv–xxvi.
8. See John Hick, *An Interpretation of Religion: Human Responses to the Transcendent* (New Haven, CT: Yale University, 2004).

9. For example, see Ursula King, "Feminism: The Missing Dimension in the Dialogue of Religions," in *Pluralism and the Religions: The Theological and Political Dimensions*, ed. John D'Arcy May (Herndon, VA: Cassell/Wellington House, 1998), 40–58; Kwok Pui-lan, "Beyond Pluralism," in *Postcolonial Imagination and Feminist Theology* (Louisville, KY: Westminster John Knox, 2005), 186–208; Rosemary Radford Ruether, *Sexism and God-Talk: Toward a Feminist Theology* (Boston: Beacon, 1993); Jeannine Hill Fletcher, *Monopoly on Salvation?: A Feminist Approach to Religious Pluralism* (New York: Continuum, 2005).
10. For example, see Haideh Moghissi, *Feminism and Islamic Fundamentalism: The Limits of Postmodern Analysis* (London: Zed Books, 1999); Valentine M. Moghadam, "Islamic Feminism and Its Discontents: Toward a Resolution of the Debate," *Signs* 27, no. 4 (Summer 2002): 1135–1171.
11. For example, see Margot Badran, *Feminism in Islam: Secular and Religious Convergences* (Oxford: Oneworld, 2009); miriam cooke, *Women Claim Islam: Creating Islamic Feminism through Literature* (New York: Routledge, 2001).
12. See Riffat Hassan, "Feminist Theology: The Challenges for Muslim Women," in *Women and Islam: Critical Concepts in Sociology*, ed. Haideh Moghissi (London: Routledge, 2005), 195–208.

CHAPTER 1

1. Daniel Boyarin, *Border Lines: The Partition of Judaeo-Christianity* (Philadelphia: University of Pennsylvania, 2004), 1, xi.
2. Boyarin, *Border Lines*, 9–11.
3. In fact, Boyarin holds that the concept of "religion" in and of itself is a reproduction of this particular Christian worldview (Boyarin, *Border Lines*, 8). Religion as a concept comes to denote a distinct entity with clear boundaries that is "disembedded" from other aspects of experience (11). He cites W. C. Smith (*The Meaning and End of Religion* [Minneapolis: Fortress, 1991]) and Talal Asad (*Genealogies of Religion: Discipline and Reasons of Power in Christianity and Islam* [Baltimore: Johns Hopkins University, 1993]) as confirming this theory.
4. The lowercase "h" is an abbreviation for *hijri*. It indicates the date according to the Islamic lunar calendar, which commenced with Muḥammad's emigration (*hijra*) from Mecca to Medina. When two dates are provided, for example, 247/861, the former refers to the *hijri* date and the latter to the Common Era (C.E.) date.
5. Abū ʿĪsā Muḥammad ibn Hārūn al-Warrāq, *Kitāb al-radd ʿalā l-thalāth firaq min al-Naṣārā*, ed. and trans. David Thomas, *Anti-Christian Polemic in Early Islam: Abū ʿĪsá al-Warrāq's "Against the Trinity,"* University of Cambridge Oriental Publications, no. 45 (Cambridge: University of Cambridge, 1992); idem, *Early Muslim Polemic Against Christianity: Abū ʿĪsá al-Warrāq's "Against the Incarnation,"* University of Cambridge Oriental Publications, no. 59 (Cambridge: Cambridge

University, 2002). See Chapter 3, "Early Islamic Refutations of Christianity," in *Anti-Christian* for a detailed survey of various other early polemical writings, including those authored by ʿAlī b. Rabbān al-Ṭabarī, Abū ʿUthmān al-Jāḥiz, Abū Yūsuf al-Kindī, al-Qāsim ibn Ibrāhīm al-Ḥasanī, and Abū ʿAlī Muḥammad b. ʿAbd al-Wahhāb al-Jubbāʾī and their intersections with the arguments and approach of Abū ʿĪsā.

6. Thomas, *Anti-Christian*, 12, 42–43. See also S. M. Stern, "Abū ʿĪsā Muḥammad b. Hārūn al-Warrāḳ," in *Encyclopaedia of Islam, Second Edition*, ed. P. Bearman, Th. Bianquis, C.E. Bosworth, E. van Donzel, and W.P. Heinrichs (Leiden: Brill, 1960–2005), vol. 1, 130.
7. Thomas, *Anti-Christian*, 9, 12; David Thomas, *Early Muslim Polemic against Christianity: Abū ʿĪsá al-Warrāq's "Against the Incarnation,"* University of Cambridge Oriental Publications, no. 59 (Cambridge: Cambridge University, 2002), 3, 19–20. See also David Thomas, "Abū ʿĪsā al-Warrāq and the History of Religions," *Journal of Semitic Studies* 41 (1996): 275–290.
8. Abū ʿĪsā's discussions of Islamic doctrines are focused on the view that prophetic status could not be affirmed based upon miracles; on the need for conformity between prophetic claims and reason; and on the role and status of revelation. Intriguingly, his critiques of Islam, similar to his critiques of other religions, stemmed from his prioritization of divine unity, *tawḥīd*, and reason. See Thomas, *Early Muslim*, 28–29; Thomas, *Anti-Christian*, 25–29.
9. Thomas, *Anti-Christian*, 59.
10. Thomas, *Early Muslim*, 263.
11. Thomas, *Early Muslim*, 18.
12. Abū Bakr Muḥammad b. al-Ṭayyib al-Bāqillānī, *Kitāb al-tamhīd*, ed. Richard J. McCarthy, S.J. (Beirut: al-Maktaba al-Sharqiyya, 1957). *Al-Radd ʿalā l-Naṣārā* (The Refutation of the Christians), which is part of this larger work, also appears in David Thomas, *Christian Doctrines in Islamic Theology* (Leiden: Brill, 2008), 143–203.
13. Thomas, *Christian Doctrines*, 122–124; Wadi Z. Haddad, "A Tenth-Century Speculative Theologian's Refutation of the Basic Doctrines of Christianity: Al-Bāqillānī (d. A.D. 1013)," in *Christian-Muslim Encounters*, ed. Yvonne Yazbeck Haddad and Wadi Zaidan Haddad (Gainesville: University Press of Florida, 1995), 83–94, here 87.
14. Thomas, *Christian Doctrines*, 124–125.
15. Thomas, *Christian Doctrines*, 139. Cf. Thomas, *Early Muslim*, 81.
16. Haddad, "A Tenth-Century Speculative Theologian's Refutation," 84–85; Thomas, *Christian Doctrines*, 121.
17. Ghulām Ḥaider Āasī, *Muslim Understanding of Other Religions: An Analytical Study of Ibn Ḥazm's* Kitāb al-faṣl fī al-milal wa-aḥwāʾ wa al-niḥal (Ann Arbor: University Microfilms International, 1986), 13.

18. See, for example, Theodore Pulcini, *Exegesis as Polemical Discourse: Ibn Ḥazm on Jewish and Christian Scriptures,* American Academy of Religion, The Religions Series, no. 2 (Atlanta: Scholars, 1998), 42; Āasī, *Muslim Understanding,* 39.
19. ʿAlī ibn Aḥmad ibn Ḥazm, *Kitāb al-faṣl fī al-milal wa al-aḥwāʾ wa al-niḥal,* 5 vols. (Jeddah: ʿUqaẓ, 1982).
20. See Robert G. Hoyland, *Muslims and Others in Early Islamic Society,* The Formation of the Classical Islamic World, vol. 18 (Burlington, VT: Ashgate, 2004), 225; Pulcini, *Exegesis as Polemical Discourse,* 44.
21. Reynolds and Samir, *Critique of Christian Origins,* xlvi.
22. Gabriel Said Reynolds, *A Muslim Theologian in a Sectarian Milieu: ʿAbd al-Jabbār and the Critique of Christian Origins,* Islamic History and Civilization, vol. 56 (Leiden: Brill, 2004), xlviii, liii, 85.
23. Thomas, *Christian Doctrines,* 216.
24. For more information on abrogation, including abrogation within and between the Qurʾān and Ḥadīth, see John Burton, "Abrogation," in *Encyclopaedia of the Qurʾān,* ed. Jane Dammen McAuliffe, vol. 1 (Leiden: Brill, 2001, vol. 1), 11–19.
25. Ibn Ḥazm, *Kitāb al-fiṣal,* 1:138.
26. Ibn Ḥazm, *Kitāb al-fiṣal,* 2:5.
27. Reynolds and Samir, *Critique of Christian Origins,* 53, 57, 61, 225, 261, 304.
28. For information on these works, in particular *Al-Sarim al-maslul ʿalā shatim al-Rasūl, al-Risāla al-Qubrusiyya, Masʾalāt al-Kanaʾis,* and *Iqtidaʾ al-ṣirāt al-mustaqīm,* see Aḥmad ibn ʿAbd al-Ḥalīm ibn Taymiyya, *A Muslim Theologian's Response to Christianity: Ibn Taymiyya's* al-Jawab al-Sahih, ed. and trans. Thomas F. Michel (Delmar, NY: Caravan Books, 1999), 68–86.
29. Aḥmad ibn ʿAbd al-Ḥalīm ibn Taymiyya, *Ibn Taimīya's Struggle Against Popular Religion with an Annotated Translation of His* Kitāb iqtiḍāʾ aṣ-ṣirāṭ al-mustaqīm mukhālafat aṣḥāb al-Jaḥīm, ed. and trans. Muhammad Umar Memon (The Hague: Mouton, 1976), 86. For more on his hermeneutical approach, see Walid A. Saleh, "Ibn Taymiyyah and the Rise of Radical Hermeneutics: An Analysis of An Introduction to the Foundations of Qurʾānic Exegesis," in *Ibn Taymiyya and His Times,* ed. Yossef Rapoport and Shahab Ahmed (Karachi: Oxford University, 2010), 123–162.
30. Aḥmad ibn ʿAbd al-Ḥalīm ibn Taymiyya, *Jawāb al-ṣaḥīḥ li-man baddala dīn al-Masīḥ* (Egypt: Maṭbaʿat al-Nīl, 1905); Michel, *Muslim Theologian's Response.*
31. David Thomas, "Apologetic and Polemic in the *Letter from Cyprus* and Ibn Taymiyya's *Jawāb al-Ṣaḥīḥ li-man Baddala Dīn al-Masīḥ,*" in Rapoport and Ahmed, *Ibn Taymiyya,* 247–265, here 249–251. Cf. Michel, *Muslim Theologian's Response,* 87–98.
32. Thomas, "Apologetic," 258.
33. Tariq al-Jamil, "Ibn Taymiyya and Ibn al-Muṭahhar al-Ḥillī: Shiʿi Polemics and the Struggle for Religious Authority in Medieval Islam," in Rapoport and Ahmed, *Ibn Taymiyya,* 229–246, here 232.

34. Memon, *Ibn Taimīya's Struggle*, 5.
35. Memon, *Ibn Taimīya's Struggle*, 86.
36. Thomas, "Apologetic," 256.
37. Memon, *Ibn Taimīya's Struggle*, 97–99, 118.
38. While I here focus on these three concepts, other similar concepts are involved in this discourse. These include *shirk/mushrik* (associationism/associator), *nifāq/munāfiq* (hypocrisy/hypocrite), *ahl al-kitāb* (People of the Scripture), and *ḥanīf* (nondenominational monotheist). As part of her examination of exegesis on Qur'ānic Christians, Jane Dammen McAuliffe deals with some of the discourse related to *ahl al-kitāb*. One of the main issues in this body of exegesis is how to understand the Qur'ānic praise of Christians, Jews, and *ahl al-kitāb*. McAuliffe explicates a variety of interpretative maneuvers adopted by exegetes in their efforts to limit the praise to particular—and small—contingents of these groups or to argue that the praised groups were actually converts to the path of Muḥammad. The investment in maintaining distinctions between self and Other should not be overlooked. See Jane Dammen McAuliffe, *Qur'anic Christians*.
39. Jane Smith, *A Historical and Semantic Study of the Term 'Islām' as Seen in a Sequence of Qur'ān Commentaries* (Missoula, MT: Scholars Press, 1975).
40. Abū Ja'far Muḥammad ibn Jarīr al-Ṭabarī, *Jāmi' al-bayān 'an ta'wīl āyāt al-Qur'ān* (Cairo: al-Maṭba'ah al-Kubra al-Amīrīyah, 1900-1911).
41. al-Ṭabarī, *Jāmi' al-bayān*, vol. 2, 510–511, *ad* Qur'ān 2:111–112.
42. Smith, *Historical and Semantic Study*, 63.
43. al-Ṭabarī, *Jāmi' al-bayān*, vol. 6, 274, *ad* Qur'ān 3:19.
44. Abū 'Abd Allāh Muḥammad ibn 'Umar Ibn al-Ḥusayn al-Rāzi, *Mafātīḥ al-ghayb al-mushtahar bi'l-tafsīr al-kabīr* (Istanbul: al-Maṭba'ah al-'Amirah, 1891), vol. 2, 628.
45. Smith, *Historical and Semantic Study*, 117.
46. Smith, *Historical and Semantic Study*, 119–120.
47. Ismā'īl ibn 'Umar ibn Kathīr, *Tafsīr al-Qur'ān al-'aẓīm* (Beirut: Dār al-Fikr, 1987).
48. Ibn Kathīr, *Tafsīr*, vol. 6, 648.
49. See also Mun'im Sirry, "'Compete with One Another in Good Works': Exegesis of Qur'an Verse 5.48 and Contemporary Muslim Discourses on Religious Pluralism," *Islam and Christian-Muslim Relations* 20, no. 4 (2009): 424–438, here 425–428.
50. Smith, *Historical and Semantic Study*, 131.
51. Yaḥyā ibn Sharaf Muḥyī al-Dīn al-Nawawī, "Hadith 2," in *al-Nawawi's Forty Ḥadīth* (Matn al-arba'īn al-Nabawiyya), ed. and trans. Ezzeddin Ibrahim and Denys Johnson-Davies (Cambridge: Islamic Texts Society, 1997), 6.
52. Yaḥyā ibn Sharaf Muḥyī al-Dīn al-Nawawī, *Kitāb al-arba'īn al-Nawawīya wa-sharḥu* (Manshīyat al-bakrā, Egypt: Dār ḥarā' lil-kitāb, 1987), 14–20. For a partial English translation of this commentary, see Yaḥyā ibn Sharaf Muḥyī al-Dīn

al-Nawawī, "Ḥadīth Two," in *Classical Islam: A Sourcebook of Religious Literature*, ed. Norman Calder, J.A. Mojaddedi, and Andrew Rippin (New York: Routledge, 2003), 143–146. For the full commentary in French, see Yaḥyā ibn Sharaf Muḥyī al-Dīn al-Nawawī, *Une herméneutique de la tradition islamique: le commentaire des* Arbaʿūn al-Nawawīya *de Muḥyī al-Dīn Yaḥyā al-Nawawī (m. 676/1277)*, ed. Louis Pouzet, S.J. (Beirut: Dar el-Machreq, 1982).

53. Aḥmad ibn ʿAbd al-Ḥalīm ibn Taymiyya, *al-Īmān* (Cairo: Maktabat Anas Ibn Mālik, 1980); Aḥmad ibn ʿAbd al-Ḥalīm ibn Taymiyya, Kitāb al-īmān: *Book of Faith*, ed. and trans. Salman Hassan al-Ani and Shadia Ahmad Tel (Bloomington, IN: Iman Publishing House, 1999).
54. Al-Ani and Tel, *Kitāb al-īmān*, 24–25.
55. See Al-Ani and Tel, *Kitāb al-īmān*, 181–182.
56. Abū ʿUbayd al-Qāsim ibn Sallām, *Kitāb al-īmān wa-maʿālimihi, wa-sunanihi, wa-istikmālihi, wa-darajātih* (Beirut: al-Maktab al-Islāmī, 1983). See also Abū ʿUbayd al-Qāsim ibn Sallām, "Chapter on the Characteristics of Faith with Regards to Its Perfection and Its Stages," in Calder, Mojaddedi, and Rippin, *Classical Islam*, 135–142.
57. Abū ʿUbayd, *Kitāb al-īmān*, 12; Abū ʿUbayd, "Chapter on the Characteristics of Faith," 137.
58. Abū ʿUbayd, *Kitāb al-īmān*, 19; Abū ʿUbayd, "Chapter on the Characteristics of Faith," 141.
59. D. Sourdel, "al-Ḳādir Biʾllāh," in Bearman, *Encyclopaedia of Islam*, vol. 4, 378.
60. ʿAbd al-Raḥman ibn al-Jawzi, *al-Muntaẓam fī taʾrīkh al-mulūk wa al-umam* (Beirut: Dār al-Kutūb al-ʿIlmīya, 1992). For partial English translation, see ʿAbd al-Raḥman ibn al-Jawzi, "On the Edicts of the Caliph al-Qādir," in Calder, Mojaddedi, and Rippin, *Classical Islam*, 159–162.
61. Ibn al-Jawzi, *al-Muntaẓam*, 280–281; Ibn al-Jawzi, "On the Edicts of the Caliph al-Qādir," 161.
62. Recorded in Ṣaḥīḥ Muslim, one of the two most authoritative compilations of *aḥadīth* for Sunni Muslims.
63. Ibn al-Jawzi, *al-Muntaẓam*, 281; Ibn al-Jawzi, "On the Edicts of the Caliph al-Qādir," 161.
64. Abū Ḥāmid Muḥammad ibn Muḥammad al-Ghazālī, *Fayṣal al-tafriqa bayna al-islām wa al-zandaqa*, ed. Sulaymān Dunyā (Cairo: Dār Iḥyāʾ al-Kutub al-ʿArabīya, 1961); Sherman A. Jackson, ed. and trans., *On the Boundaries of Theological Tolerance in Islam: Abu Hāmid al-Ghazālī's* Fayṣal al-Tafriqa Bayna al-Islām wa al-Zandaqa (Oxford: Oxford University, 2002).
65. Jackson, *On the Boundaries*, 32.
66. Jackson, *On the Boundaries*, 40.
67. Jackson, *On the Boundaries*, 92.
68. Jackson, *On the Boundaries*, 94.
69. See Jackson, *On the Boundaries*, 52, 104.

70. Jackson, *On the Boundaries*, 7.
71. Khalil, *Islam and the Fate of Others*, 30–32.
72. Jackson, *On the Boundaries*, 65, 127. See also Khalil, *Islam and the Fate of Others*, 33–36.
73. Jackson, *On the Boundaries*, 127–128.
74. Khalil, *Islam and the Fate of Others*, 35–37.
75. The majority of his views on this topic are contained in various *fatāwā*. See Taqiyaddīn Aḥmad ibn Taymiyya, *Majmū' fatāwā Shaykh al-islām Aḥmad ibn Taymiyya* (Cairo: al-Shurafā' li-al-Tibā'ah wa Taṣwīr al-Mustanadāt, 1979).
76. Khalil, *Islam and the Fate of Others*, 76. See also Ibn Taymiyya, *Jawāb*, 272.
77. Khalil, *Islam and the Fate of Others*, 77.
78. Khalil, *Islam and the Fate of Others*, 77–78.
79. Khalil, *Islam and the Fate of Others*, 84–85.
80. William C. Chittick, *Imaginal Worlds: Ibn al-'Arabī and the Problem of Religious Diversity* (Albany: State University of New York, 1994), 15.
81. Chittick, *Imaginal Worlds*, 16. See also William C. Chittick, *The Sufi Path of Knowledge: Ibn al-'Arabī's Metaphysics of Imagination* (Albany: State University of New York, 1989), 56–57.
82. Jalāl al-Dīn Rūmī, *The Mathnawī of Jalālu'uddīn Rūmī*, ed. and trans. R. A Nicholson, 8 vols. (London: Luzac, 1925–1940), II, 2124–2127.
83. Rūmī, *Mathnawī*, II, 1280, cited in William C. Chittick, *The Sufi Path of Love: the Spiritual Teachings of Rumi* (Albany: State University of New York, 1983), 24, 175.
84. Chittick, *Sufi Path of Love*, 24.
85. Rūmī, *Mathnawī*, VI, 4747, cited in Chittick, *Sufi Path of Love*, 19.
86. Jalāl al-Dīn Rūmī, *Discourses of Rūmī* (Fīhī mā fīhī), trans. A.J. Arberry (London: John Murray, 1961), 184, cited in Chittick, *Sufi Path of Love*, 48.
87. Chittick, *Imaginal Worlds*, 23.
88. Chittick, *Sufi Path of Love*, 39.
89. Chittick, *Imaginal Worlds*, 44.
90. Rūmī, *Discourses*, 237, cited in Chittick, *Sufi Path of Love*, 122.
91. Chittick, *Imaginal Worlds*, 155.
92. Ibn al-'Arabī, *al-Fūtūhat al-Makkiyya* (Cairo, 1911), II 153.12; Chittick, *Imaginal Worlds*, 125.
93. Chittick, *Imaginal Worlds*, 155.
94. Chittick, *Sufi Path of Love*, 124.
95. Chittick, *Imaginal Worlds*, 145. See also Chittick, *Sufi Path of Knowledge*, 302–303; Ibn al-'Arabī, *al-Fūtūhat*, III 410.24.
96. Chittick, *Sufi Path of Knowledge*, 303.
97. Chittick, *Imaginal Worlds*, 146.
98. Chittick, *Imaginal Worlds*, 8.
99. Chittick, *Imaginal Worlds*, 9.
100. Chittick, *Imaginal Worlds*, 141–142; Chittick, *Sufi Path of Knowledge*, 292–293.

101. See Chittick, *Imaginal Worlds*, 142–144.
102. Rūmī, *Mathnawī*, II, 3439, cited in Chittick, *Sufi Path of Love*, 102.
103. Rūmī, *Discourses*, 236, cited in Chittick, *Sufi Path of Love*, 107.
104. Chittick, *Imaginal Worlds*, 113.
105. Francis Peters, "*Alius* or *Alter*: The Qur᾽ānic Definition of Christians and Christianity," *Islam and Christian–Muslim Relations* 8 (1997): 165–176, here 169–170.
106. Peters, "*Alius* or *Alter*," 174.

CHAPTER 2

1. Asghar Ali Engineer, "Islam and Pluralism," in *The Myth of Religious Superiority: A Multifaith Exploration*, ed. Paul Knitter (Maryknoll, NY: Orbis, 2005), 211–219.
2. See Asghar Ali Engineer, *A Rational Approach to Islam* (New Delhi: Gyan Publishing House, 2001); Asghar Ali Engineer, *On Developing Theology of Peace in Islam* (New Delhi: Sterling Publishers, 2005); Asghar Ali Engineer, *Islam in Contemporary World* (New Delhi: New Dawn, 2007); Asghar Ali Engineer, *Islam in Post-Modern World: Prospects and Problems* (Gurgaon: Hope India, 2009); Asghar Ali Engineer, *Rights of Women in Islam* (New York: St. Martin's, 1996).
3. Engineer, "Islam and Pluralism," 212.
4. Engineer, *Islam in Contemporary World*, 49.
5. Engineer, "Islam and Pluralism," 213.
6. Engineer, "Islam and Pluralism," 215.
7. Engineer, "Islam and Pluralism," 217–218.
8. See Qur᾽ān 4:48: "God does not forgive the joining of partners with God: anything less than that God forgives to whoever God will, but anyone who joins partners with God has concocted a tremendous sin."
9. His other publications include *Human Rights and the Conflicts of Culture*, coauthored with D. Little and J. E. Kelsay (Columbia: University of South Carolina, 1988); *The Just Ruler in Shiite Islam* (New York: Oxford University, 1988); *Islam and the Challenge of Human Rights* (New York: Oxford University, 2009). In 1998, Grand Ayatollah Sistani of Iran issued a ruling that advised Muslims not to invite Sachedina to lecture or to seek guidance from him regarding religious matters. This ruling was a response to multiple issues, including Sachedina's writings on religious pluralism, the equality of the Abrahamic faiths, and his interpretation of the term *islām*.
10. Abdulaziz Sachedina, "The Qur᾽ān and Other Religions," in *The Cambridge Companion to the Qur'an*, ed. Jane Dammen McAuliffe (Cambridge: Cambridge University, 2006), 291–309, here 294; Abdulaziz Sachedina, *The Islamic Roots of Democratic Pluralism* (Oxford: Oxford University, 2001), 23. For a critique of Sachedina's approach, especially his acceptance of liberal democracy and

his hermeneutical theory, see Sajjad H. Rizvi, "A Primordial *e pluribus unum?* Exegeses on Q. 2:213 and Contemporary Muslim Discourses on Religious Pluralism," *Journal of Qur'anic Studies* 6, no. 1 (2004): 21–42.

11. Sachedina, "The Qur᾽ān and Other Religions," 295.
12. Sachedina, "The Qur᾽ān and Other Religions," 298.
13. Sachedina, "The Qur᾽ān and Other Religions," 299.
14. Sachedina, "The Qur᾽ān and Other Religions," 303–304.
15. Mahmut Aydin, "Religious Pluralism: A Challenge for Muslims—A Theological Evaluation," *Journal of Ecumenical Studies* 38, nos. 2–3 (Spring–Summer 2001): 330–352, here 330–334. He has published other books and articles, including his dissertation *Modern Western Christian Theological Understanding of Muslims since the Second Vatican Council* (Washington, DC: Council for Research in Values and Philosophy, 2002).
16. Aydin, "Religious Pluralism," 335.
17. Aydin, "Religious Pluralism," 345–346.
18. Aydin, "Religious Pluralism," 339.
19. Mahmut Aydin, "A Muslim Pluralist: Jalaluddin Rumi," in Knitter, *Myth of Religious Superiority*, 220–236.
20. Aydin, "Muslim Pluralist," 222–223. See also John Hick, *An Interpretation of Religion: Human Responses to the Transcendent (*New Haven, CT: Yale University, 2004), 240-251.
21. Aydin, "Muslim Pluralist," 222.
22. See Roger Boase, "Ecumenical Islam: A Muslim Response to Religious Pluralism," in *Islam and Global Dialogue: Religious Pluralism and the Pursuit of Peace*, ed. Roger Boase (Surrey: Ashgate, 2005), 247–266, here 252.
23. Aydin, "Muslim Pluralist," 232.
24. Aydin, "Muslim Pluralist," 228.
25. In the American context, where Rūmī is widely popular, this is the general interpretation of Rūmī's writings. When his poetry is presented without reference to Islamic thought, this is an understandable—albeit simplified—interpretation.
26. Aydin, "Muslim Pluralist," 223, 225.
27. Aydin, "Muslim Pluralist," 236.
28. Aydin, "Muslim Pluralist," 228, footnote 24, and 232.
29. Aydin, "Muslim Pluralist," 232.
30. Nasr, "Religion and Religions," 59–81. He has authored a multitude of books and articles, including *The Garden of Truth: The Vision and Practice of Sufism, Islam's Mystical Tradition* (New York: HaperOne, 2007); *Islam: Religion, History, and Civilization* (New York: HaperOne, 2002); *Knowledge and the Sacred* (Albany: State University of New York, 1989).
31. Seyyed Hossein Nasr, "Islam and the Encounter of Religions," in *The Religious Other: Towards a Muslim Theology of Other Religions in a Post-Prophetic Age*, ed. Muhammad Suheyl Umar (Lahore: Iqbal Academy Pakistan, 2008), 83–120, here 84–87.

32. Nasr, "Islam and the Encounter of Religions," 86.
33. Nasr, "Islam and the Encounter of Religions," 85.
34. Nasr, "Islam and the Encounter of Religions," 85.
35. Nasr, "Religion and Religions," in Umar, *Religious Other*, 59–81, here 66–68.
36. Seyyed Hossein Nasr, "Comments on a Few Theological Issues in the Islamic–Christian Dialogue," in Haddad and Ḥaddād, *Christian-Muslim Encounters*, 457–465, here 457. In this piece, which is written specifically about Christianity but nonetheless largely relevant to other religions, he identifies seven central issues that need to be explored: the way God manifests God's self (457); Islam's claims to finality of prophethood (459); the meaning and status of sacred scripture (460); sacred language (462); sacred law (462); the life of Christ (463); and modernism (465).
37. Nasr, "Religion and Religions," 64.
38. Nasr, "Religion and Religions," 65.
39. Nasr, "Religion and Religions," 71. See also Seyyed Hossein Nasr, "Islam's Attitude towards Other Religions in History," in Umar, *Religious Other*, 121–134, here 125.
40. According to Nasr, "Islam and the Encounter of Religions," 111, though, only very few people ever gain real knowledge of the Formless: "Not everyone may be able to see the camel on the top of the minaret, much less to distinguish the hair in its mouth. But those who are possessed of such a vision are bound by duty to explain to others to the greatest extent possible what they have seen." Despite the obligation to disseminate insight, this hints at a structure of elitism that places practical limitations on Nasr's approach. See also Aslan, *Religious Pluralism*, 163, 169; Rizvi, "Primordial *e pluribus unum?*," 34.
41. Nasr, "Religion and Religions," 75.
42. Nasr, "Religion and Religions," 75.
43. See Seyyed Hossein Nasr, "Islam's Attitude towards Other Religions," 128–133.
44. Nasr, "Islam and the Encounter of Religions," 86.
45. His other publications include *Paths of Transcendence: According to Shankara, Ibn Arabi and Meister Eckhart on Transcendent Spiritual Realization* (Bloomington, IN: World Wisdom Books, 2006); *Justice and Remembrance: Introducing the Spirituality of Imam Ali* (London: I.B. Tauris, 2007).
46. Shah-Kazemi, *Other*, xvii-xviii, 59–73.
47. Shah-Kazemi, *Other*, xxv.
48. Shah-Kazemi, *Other*, xxv.
49. Shah-Kazemi, *Other*, 266, 276.
50. Shah-Kazemi, *Other*, xxvi.
51. Legenhausen, "Muslim's Non-reductive Religious Pluralism," 65. For a more extensive account of his objections to the approach of John Hick, see Legenhausen, *Islam and Religious Pluralism*, 31–88. In the same volume (107–115), he also proffers a critique of interpretations (such as that of Aydin) that describe Sufism and mysticism as unequivocally affirming religious pluralism.

52. Legenhausen, "Muslim's Non-reductive Religious Pluralism," 58.
53. Legenhausen, "Muslim's Non-reductive Religious Pluralism," 52.
54. Legenhausen, "Muslim's Non-reductive Religious Pluralism," 65.
55. Tim Winter, "The Last Trump Card: Islam and the Supersession of Other Faiths," *Studies in Interreligious Dialogue* 9, no. 2 (1999): 133–155; Tim Winter, "Realism and the Real: Theology and the Problem of Alternative Expressions of God," in *Between Heaven and Hell: Islam, Salvation, and the Fate of Others*, ed. Mohammad Hassan Khalil (New York: Oxford University, 2013), 122–150. Another brief formulation of the prioritization of difference is found in Yasir Qadhi, "The Path of Allah or the Paths of Allah? Revisiting Classical and Medieval Sunni Approaches to the Salvation of Others," in Khalil, *Between Heaven and Hell*, 109–121. Qadhi voices a similar critique of pluralism as Winter and stresses difference, the classical Sunni consensus, discussions of exposure, and treatment of the Other.
56. Winter, "Last Trump Card," 135–136.
57. Winter, "Realism and the Real," 129–133. Aydin is one of the only contemporary scholars to do so.
58. Winter, "Last Trump Card," 136. See also Winter, "Realism and the Real," 122.
59. Winter, "Last Trump Card," 139.
60. Winter, "Realism and the Real," 128.
61. Winter, "Realism and the Real," 122.
62. Winter, "Realism and the Real," 127–128.
63. Winter, "Last Trump Card," 134.
64. Boyarin, *Border Lines*, xv.
65. Boyarin, *Border Lines*, 14, citing David Chidester. See also David Chidester, *Savage Systems: Colonialism and Comparative Religion in Southern Africa* (Charlottesville: University Press of Virginia, 1996), 4.
66. Jonathan Z. Smith, *Relating Religion: Essays in the Study of Religion* (Chicago: University of Chicago, 2004), 27, 230.
67. Farid Esack, "Muslims Engaging the Other and the *Humanum*," in *Proselytization and Communal Self-Determination in Africa*, ed. Abdullahi Ahmed An-Naʿim (Maryknoll, NY: Orbis, 1999), 51–76, here 53. Among his many other publications are *On Being a Muslim: Finding a Religious Path in the World Today* (Oxford: Oneworld, 1999); *The Qurʾān: A Short Introduction* (Oxford: Oneworld, 2002); *The Qurʾan: A User's Guide* (Oxford: Oneworld, 2005).
68. Farid Esack, "Religio-Cultural Diversity: For What and with Whom? Muslim Reflections from a Postapartheid South Africa in the Throes of Globalization," in *Cultural Diversity and Islam*, ed. Abdul Aziz Said and Meena Sharify-Funk (Lanham, MD: University Press of America, 2003), 165–185, here 171.
69. Esack, "Muslims Engaging the Other and the *Humanum*," 60.
70. Farid Esack, *Qurʾān, Liberation, & Pluralism* (Oxford: Oneworld Publications, 1997), 50.

71. Esack, *Qur'ān, Liberation, & Pluralism*, 115.
72. Esack, "Muslims Engaging the Other and the *Humanum*," 62. In fact, many critiques of Esack have centered on his illumination of complexity.
73. Rizvi, "A Primordial *e pluribus unum?*," 31. Rizvi also critiques Esack for rendering the text so "open" that it becomes "meaningless" (32).
74. Among his other works are *Christian Ethics: A Systematic and Historical Analysis of Its Dominant Ideas* (Montreal: McGill University, 1968); *The Cultural Atlas of Islam* (New York: Macmillan, 1986).
75. Ismā'īl Rājī al-Fārūqī, *al Tawḥīd: Its Implications for Thought and Life* (Herndon, VA: International Institute of Islamic Thought, 1992), 9–15; Ismā'īl Rājī al-Fārūqī, *Islam and Other Faiths* (Leicester, UK: Islamic Foundation and International Institute of Islamic Thought, 1998), 131–133.
76. al-Fārūqī, *al Tawḥīd*, 14–15.
77. al-Fārūqī, *Islam and Other Faiths*, 134.
78. Ismā'īl Rājī al-Fārūqī, "The Essence of Religious Experience in Islam," *Numen* 20, no. 3 (1973): 186–201, here 198.
79. al-Fārūqī, *Islam and Other Faiths*, 135.

CHAPTER 3

1. As will become apparent, they argue that the former is addressed within the Qur'ān whereas the latter is not.
2. Margot Badran, *Feminism beyond East and West: New Gender Talk and Practice in Global Islam* (New Delhi: Global Media, 2007), 35–36.
3. Asma Barlas, *"Believing Women" in Islam: Unreading Patriarchal Interpretations of the Qur'an* (Austin: University of Texas Press, 2002), 33. See also Aysha Hidayatullah, "Inspiration and Struggle: Muslim Feminist Theology and the Work of Elizabeth Schüssler Fiorenza," *Journal of Feminist Studies in Religion* 25, no.1 (2009): 162–170, here 167.
4. Amina Wadud, *Qur'an and Woman: Rereading the Sacred Texts from a Woman's Perspective* (New York: Oxford University, 1999), 2.
5. Riffat Hassan, "Feminism in Islam," in *Feminism and World Religions*, ed. Arvind Sharma and Katherine K. Young (Albany: State University of New York Press, 1999), 248–278, here 249.
6. Barlas, *"Believing Women,"* 17.
7. Wadud, *Qur'an and Woman*, 1.
8. Wadud, *Qur'an and Woman*, 3–4, 31; Barlas, *"Believing Women,"* 21. See also Fazlur Rahman, *Islam and Modernity: Transformation of an Intellectual Tradition* (Chicago: University of Chicago, 1982), 5-12; Fazlur Rahman, *Revival and Reform in Islam: A Study of Islamic Fundamentalisms*, ed. Ebrahim Moosa (Oxford: Oneworld, 2000). For a concise overview of the Rahman's approach as utilized by these scholars, see Hidayatullah, "Women Trustees of Allah," 33–38, 126–128.

9. Wadud, *Qur'an and Woman*, 5.
10. Wadud, *Qur'an and Woman*, 5.
11. Wadud, *Qur'an and Woman*, 5. Italics mine.
12. Asma Barlas, "'Holding Fast by the Best in the Precepts'—The Qur'an and Method," in *New Directions in Islamic Thought*, ed. Kari Vogt, Lena Larsen and Christian Moe (New York: I.B. Tauris, 2009), 17–22.
13. Wadud, "Towards a Qur'anic Hermeneutics of Social Justice," 44. The first principle is the prioritization of universals over particulars.
14. Barlas, *"Believing Women,"* 22.
15. Riffat Hassan, "Muslim Women and Post-Patriarchal Islam," in *After Patriarchy: Feminist Transformations of the World Religions*, ed. Paula M. Cooey, William R. Eakin, and Jay B. McDaniel (Maryknoll, NY: Orbis, 1998), 39–64, here 43.
16. Barlas, *"Believing Women,"* 13. Hidayatullah, "Women Trustees of Allah," 215–216, refers to the use of various aspects of divine ontology as hermeneutical principles as the *tawhidic* paradigm.
17. Hassan, "Feminism in Islam," 252.
18. Wadud, *Qur'an and Woman*, 97.
19. Wadud, *Qur'an and Woman*, 98.
20. Barlas, *"Believing Women,"* 129. See also Wadud, "Towards a Qur'anic Hermeneutics of Social Justice," 42.
21. Barlas, *"Believing Women,"* 130.
22. Barlas, *"Believing Women,"* 133.
23. Hassan, "Feminism in Islam," 253.
24. Hassan, "Feminism in Islam," 262.
25. Wadud, *Qur'an and Woman*, 17–20, 23–25, 44–53.
26. Barlas, *"Believing Women,"* 136.
27. Wadud, *Qur'an and Woman*, 21.
28. Barlas, *"Believing Women,"* 132.
29. Barlas, *"Believing Women,"* 132, 11.
30. Barlas, *"Believing Women,"* 5.
31. Barlas, *"Believing Women,"* 148.
32. Barlas, *"Believing Women,"* 132.
33. Wadud, *Qur'an and Woman*, 19–20.
34. Barlas, *"Believing Women,"* 146.
35. Wadud, *Qur'an and Woman*, 65.
36. Wadud, *Qur'an and Woman*, 64–65.
37. Wadud, *Qur'an and Woman*, 64–65.
38. Barlas, *"Believing Women,"* 11.
39. Barlas, *"Believing Women,"* 145.
40. Barlas, *"Believing Women,"* 11.
41. Wadud, *Qur'an and Woman*, 37.

42. Wadud, *Qur'an and Woman*, 96. Italics mine. See also Wadud, "Towards a Qur'anic Hermeneutics of Social Justice," 41.
43. Wadud, "Towards a Qur'anic Hermeneutics of Social Justice," 38.
44. Riffat Hassan, "The Qur'anic Perspective on Religious Pluralism," in *Peace-Building by, between, and beyond Muslims and Evangelical Christians*, ed. Mohammed Abu-Nimer and David Augsburger (Lanham, MD: Lexington Books, 2009), 91–101, here 91–92.
45. Hassan, "Qur'anic Perspective," 98.
46. Barlas cites this verse as being Qur'ān 5:51.
47. Barlas, *"Believing Women,"* 146.
48. Asma Barlas, "Reviving Islamic Universalism: East/s, West/s, and Coexistence" (paper presented at the Conference on Contemporary Islamic Synthesis, Alexandria, Egypt, October 2003), 7.
49. This is an allusion to Qur'ān 49:13.
50. Asma Barlas, "Hearing the Word, as a Muslim: Thirteen Passages of the Qur'ān and Religious Difference" (paper presented at Cornell University Vespers, November 2007), 6.
51. Barlas, "Reviving Islamic Universalism," 8.
52. Barlas, "Hearing the Word," 6; Barlas, "Reviving Islamic Universalism," 8. She is referring to Qur'ān 5:3 (excerpt): "...Today I have perfected your religion for you, completed My blessing upon you, and chosen as your religion *al-islām* (total devotion to God)...."

CHAPTER 4

1. Jeannine Hill Fletcher, "Shifting Identity: The Contribution of Feminist Thought to Theologies of Religious Pluralism," *Journal of Feminist Studies in Religion*, 19, no. 2 (Fall 2003): 5–24, here 5.
2. The latter concern relates directly to Muslim women scholars' ambivalence toward the label *feminism*. It is a concern that has also been broached by others who highlight the lack of cultural and religious diversity within feminist theology. One result of the critiques and concerns related to lack of diversity and the universalization of a middle-class, 'white,' Euro-American female norm has been the emergence of various specified forms of theology, including womanist theology, mujerista theology, and even, *Muslima* theology. See Kwok Pui Lan, "Feminist Theology as Intercultural Discourse," in *The Cambridge Companion to Feminist Theology*, ed. Susan Parsons (New York: Cambridge University, 2002); Rita Gross and respondents, "Roundtable Discussion: Feminist Theology and Religious Diversity," *Journal of Feminist Studies in Religion* 16, no. 2 (2000): 73–131; Rita Gross, "Where Have We Been? Where Do We Need to Go?: Women's Studies and Gender in Religion and Feminist Theology," in *Gender, Religion and Diversity: Cross-Cultural Perspectives*, ed. Ursula King and Tina Beattie

(New York: Continuum, 2005), 17–27. For more information, including excerpts from representative scholars, on these various forms, see Rosemary Radford Ruether, "Growing Pluralism, New Dialogue," in *In Our Own Voices: Four Centuries of American Women's Religious Writing*, ed. Rosemary Skinner Keller and Rosemary Radford Ruether (San Francisco: HarperSanFrancisco, 1995), 425–468; McGarvey, *Muslim and Christian Women:The Case of Northern Nigeria* (Oxford: Peter Lang, 2009), 64–66.

3. Rosemary Radford Ruether, "The Emergence of Christian Feminist Theology," in Parsons, *Cambridge Companion to Feminist Theology*, 3.
4. Ruether, "Emergence of Christian Feminist Theology," 4.
5. Rosemary Radford Ruether, *Sexism and God-Talk: Toward a Feminist Theology* (Boston: Beacon, 1993), 12.
6. Ruether, *Sexism and God-Talk*, 14.
7. Ruether, *Sexism and God-Talk*, 16.
8. Ruether, *Sexism and God-Talk*, 17.
9. Ruether, *Sexism and God-Talk*, 18–19.
10. Elizabeth Johnson draws a similar parallel when she argues that exclusive, literal, and patriarchal speech about God negatively impacts not only women but also conceptions of the divine and of divine mystery: "Inauthentic ways of treating other human beings go hand-in-glove with falsifications of the idea of God." Elizabeth Johnson, *She Who Is: The Mystery of God in Feminist Theological Discourse* (New York: Crossroad Publishing Company, 2002), 36.
11. Ruether, *Sexism and God-Talk*, 20.
12. Ruether, *Sexism and God-Talk*, 20.
13. Rosemary Radford Ruether, "Feminism and Jewish–Christian Dialogue: Particularism and Universalism in the Search for Truth," in *The Myth of Christian Uniqueness: Toward a Pluralistic Theology of Religion*, ed. John Hick and Paul Knitter (Eugene, OR: Wipf & Stock, 1987), 137–148, here 141.
14. Ruether, "Feminism and Jewish–Christian Dialogue," 143.
15. Rosemary Radford Ruether, "The Future of Feminist Theology in the Academy," *Journal of the American Academy of Religion* 53, no. 4, 75th Anniversary Meeting of the American Academy of Religion (December 1985): 703–713, here 710.
16. Marjorie Hewitt Suchocki, "In Search of Justice: Religious Pluralism from a Feminist Perspective" in Hick and Knitter, *Myth of Christian Uniqueness*, 149–161, here 149.
17. Suchocki, "In Search of Justice," 150.
18. Suchocki, "In Search of Justice," 155.
19. Michael Oppenheim, "Feminism, Jewish Philosophy, and Religious Pluralism," *Modern Judaism* 16, no. 2 (May 1996): 147–160, here 151.
20. Judith Plaskow, *Standing Again at Sinai: Judaism from a Feminist Perspective* (San Francisco: HarperSanFrancisco, 1991), 105.

21. Kate McCarthy, "Women's Experience as a Hermeneutical Key to a Christian Theology of Religions," *Studies in Interreligious Dialogue* 6, no. 2 (1996): 163–173, here 163.
22. McCarthy, "Women's Experience," 165–166.
23. McCarthy, "Women's Experience," 167.
24. McCarthy, "Women's Experience," 170–171.
25. Ursula King, "Feminism: The Missing Dimension in the Dialogue of Religions," in *Pluralism and the Religions: The Theological and Political Dimensions*, ed. John D'Arcy May (Herndon, VA: Cassell/Wellington House, 1998), 40–58, here 45.
26. King, "Feminism: The Missing Dimension," 46–47.
27. King, "Feminism: The Missing Dimension," 52–53.
28. Rita Gross, "Feminist Theology as Theology of Religions," in Parsons, *Cambridge Companion to Feminist Theology*, 60–78, here 63.
29. Gross, "Feminist Theology as Theology of Religions," 65.
30. Rita Gross, "Feminist Theology: Religiously Diverse Neighborhood or Christian Ghetto?," in "Roundtable Discussion: Feminist Theology and Religious Diversity," 77.
31. Rita Gross, "Excuse Me, but What's the Question?," in Knitter, *Myth of Religious Superiority*, 75–87, here 85.
32. Jeannine Hill Fletcher, *Monopoly on Salvation?: A Feminist Approach to Religious Pluralism* (New York: Continuum, 2005), 7.
33. Hill Fletcher, *Monopoly*, 14.
34. Hill Fletcher, *Monopoly*, 19.
35. Hill Fletcher, "Shifting Identity," 7.
36. Hill Fletcher, *Monopoly*, 51–81.
37. Hill Fletcher, "Shifting Identity," 9.
38. Jeannine Hill Fletcher, "Religious Pluralism in an Era of Globalization: The Making of Modern Religious Identity," *Theological Studies* 69 (2008): 397–398. See also Ulrich Beck, *What Is Globalization?*, trans. Patrick Camiller (Malden, MA: Blackwell, 2000).
39. Hill Fletcher, *Monopoly*, 87–88, 95–97. The idea of the web of identity is drawn from Morwenna Griffiths, *Feminisms and the Self: The Web of Identity* (New York: Routledge, 1995). Hill Fletcher also utilizes the concept of relationality when discussing Christology. See Jeannine Hill Fletcher, "Christology between Identity and Difference: On Behalf of a World in Need," in *Frontiers in Catholic Feminist Theology: Shoulder to Shoulder*, ed. Susan Abraham and Elena Procario-Foley (Minneapolis: Fortress, 2009), 79–96, here 80–83.
40. Hill Fletcher, *Monopoly*, 129, 124.
41. See John Hick, *A Christian Theology of Religions: The Rainbow of Faiths* (Louisville, KY: Westminster John Knox, 1995); John Hick, *An Interpretation of Religion: Human Responses to the Transcendent* (New Haven, CT: Yale University, 2004); George Lindbeck, *The Nature of Doctrine: Religion and Theology in a Postliberal Age* (Philadelphia: Westminster, 1984).

42. Kwok Pui Lan, "Beyond Pluralism: Toward a Postcolonial Theology of Religious Difference," in *Postcolonial Imagination and Feminist Theology* (Louisville, KY: Westminster John Knox, 2005), 186–208, here 200.
43. Kwok, "Beyond Pluralism," 202.
44. Kwok, "Beyond Pluralism," 203–204.
45. Kwok, "Beyond Pluralism," 205.
46. McGarvey, *Muslim and Christian Women*, 283.
47. McGarvey, *Muslim and Christian Women*, 299.
48. McGarvey, *Muslim and Christian Women*, 306.
49. Gross, "Feminist Theology as Theology of Religions," 65.

CHAPTER 5

1. The primary verse she is discussing is Qur'ān 4:1: "People, be mindful of your Lord, who created you from a single soul, and from it created its mate, and from the pair of them spread countless men and women far and wide; be mindful of God, in whose name you make requests of one another. Beware of severing the ties of kinship. God is always watching over you."
2. Amina Wadud, *Qur'an and Woman: Rereading the Sacred Texts from a Woman's Perspective* (New York: Oxford University, 1999), 55–57.
3. Among his other English works are *Sufism and Taoism: A Comparative Study of Key Philosophical Concepts* (Berkeley: University of California, 1983); *Creation and the Timeless Order of Things: Essays in Islamic Mystical Philosophy* (Ashland, OR: White Cloud Press, 1994); *Toward a Philosophy of Zen Buddhism* (Boston: Shambhala, 2001).
4. Toshihiko Izutsu, *God and Man in the Qur'an: Semantics of the Qur'anic Weltanschauung* (Kuala Lumpur: Islamic Books Trust, 2008), 3.
5. Izutsu, *God and Man in the Qur'an*, 3.
6. Izutsu, *God and Man in the Qur'an*, 4.
7. Although Izutsu, *God and Man in the Qur'an*, 16, states that basic meaning does not change, he also acknowledges that basic meaning in itself is a methodological postulate that cannot in fact be located in the real world. In the real world, all words are "complex social and cultural phenomena." Cf. Daniel A. Madigan, *The Qur'ān's Self-Image: Writing and Authority in Islam's Scripture* (Princeton, NJ: Princeton University, 2001), 82–83.
8. Izutsu, *God and Man in the Qur'an*, 13.
9. Izutsu, *God and Man in the Qur'an*, 23–24.
10. Izutsu, *God and Man in the Qur'an*, 21–22.
11. See "From Tribal Code to Islamic Ethics," in Toshihiko Izutsu, *Ethico-Religious Concepts in the Qur'an* (Montreal: McGill University, 2002). Reprint Selangor, Malaysia: Islamic Book Trust, 2004), 49–134; Toshihiko Izutsu, *The Concept of Belief in Islamic Theology: A Semantic Analysis of Īmān and Islām* (Kuala Lumpur: Islamic Book Trust, 2006). In these works, Izutsu offers an in-depth

exploration of various positions—including those of the Khārijites, Murji'ites, al-Ghazālī, Ash'arī, and Ibn Taymiyya—on the definitions of and relationship between *īmān* and *islām*. Many of the issues he discusses in this work were introduced in Chapter 1.

12. Toshihiko Izutsu, *God and Man in the Koran: Semantics of the Koranic Weltanschauung* (Tokyo: Keio University, 1964), 40–42. Figure 5.1 appears on page 41. All figures in this chapter are reproductions of Izutsu's own diagrams. They are reproduced with permission from the Keio Institute of Cultural and Linguistic Studies in Tokyo, Japan.
13. Izutsu, *God and Man in the Qur'an*, 75.
14. Izutsu uses the term *man*, for which I have substituted *humankind*.
15. Izutsu, *God and Man in the Qur'an*, 82.
16. Izutsu, *God and Man in the Koran*, 94.
17. Izutsu, *God and Man in the Qur'an*, 49.
18. Izutsu, *Ethico-Religious Concepts*, 118–119.
19. Toshihiko Izutsu, *The Concept of Belief in Islamic Theology: A Semantic Analysis of Īmān and Islām* (Tokyo: Keio University, 1965), 13. (All other citations from this book refer to the Islamic Books Trust reprint edition.) Cf. Izutsu, *God and Man in the Qur'an*, 52. These two figures differ slightly, but Izutsu's main contentions remain the same. I have therefore opted to use the more recent version of the diagram.
20. Izutsu, *Concept of Belief*, 9.
21. Izutsu, *Concept of Belief*, 10.
22. Izutsu, *God and Man in the Qur'an*, 52.
23. Izutsu, *Concept of Belief*, 11–12.
24. Izutsu, *Ethico-Religious Concepts*, 295.
25. Izutsu, *God and Man in the Qur'an*, 1.
26. Izutsu, *God and Man in the Qur'an*, 4.
27. Interestingly, many of the initial reviewers of his books critiqued him for this very lack of attention to chronology within the Qur'ānic text. For example, see Joseph Schacht, "Review of *The Structure of Ethical Terms in the Koran* by Toshihiko Izutsu," *Journal of the American Oriental Society* 83, no. 3 (Aug.–Sept. 1963): 366–367, here 367; Harry B. Partin, "Semantics of the Qur'ān: A Consideration of Izutsu's Studies," *History of Religions* 9, no. 4 (May 1970): 358–362, here 360. Marilyn Waldman goes beyond a critique of Izutsu and attempts to carry out a systematic chronological study of the meaning of *kufr* in the Qur'ān. See Marilyn Robinson Waldman, "The Development of the Concept of *Kufr* in the Qur'ān," *Journal of the American Oriental Society* 88, no. 3 (Jul.–Sep. 1968): 442–455.
28. Izutsu, *Ethico-Religious Concepts*, 42. See also Hill Fletcher, *Monopoly*, 87–88, 95–97.
29. Izutsu, *Ethico-Religious Concepts*, 216.

30. Izutsu, *Ethico-Religious Concepts*, 208. Italics mine.
31. Izutsu, *Ethico-Religious Concepts*, 209.
32. Izutsu, *God and Man in the Qur'an*, 52.

CHAPTER 6

1. Asma Barlas, *"Believing Women" in Islam: Unreading Patriarchal Interpretations of the Qur'an* (Austin: University of Texas Press, 2002), 143; Amina Wadud, *Qur'an and Woman: Rereading the Sacred Texts from a Woman's Perspective* (New York: Oxford University, 1999), 37.
2. From this point forward, I will use the italicized transliteration of these terms as verbal nouns (e.g., *īmān, islām, kufr, nifāq*) or active participles (e.g., *mu'min, muslim, kāfir, munāfiq*). For concepts that are introduced after this juncture, I will indicate the proximate English meaning and alternate form in brackets at the first occurrence. Thereafter, I will utilize only the transliteration.
3. Toshihiko Izutsu, *God and Man in the Qur'an: Semantics of the Qur'anic Weltanschauung (*Kuala Lumpur: Islamic Books Trust, 2008), 22–25.
4. Toshihiko Izutsu, *Ethico-Religious Concepts in the Qur'an* (Montreal: McGill University, 2002), 297.
5. Izutsu, *Ethico-Religious Concepts*, 213.
6. Izutsu, *Ethico-Religious Concepts*, 221-223.
7. *Ḥanīf*, or its plural form *ḥunafā'*, appears only twelve times within the Qur'ān.
8. Izutsu focuses only on this aspect of *taqwā* and explores its relationship with *khashya* and *khawf*. See Izutsu, *Ethico-Religious Concepts*, 223–232.
9. Wadud, *Qur'an and Woman*, 37..
10. Esack, *Qur'ān, Liberation, & Pluralism*, 87.
11. Leah Kinberg, "Piety," in *Encyclopaedia of the Qur'ān*, vol. 1, ed. Jane Dammen McAuliffe (Leiden: Brill, 2001), 9.
12. Wadud, *Qur'an and Woman*, 37.
13. Ismā'īl Rājī al-Fārūqī, *Islam and Other Faiths* (Leicester, UK: Islamic Foundation and International Institute of Islamic Thought, 1998), 83.
14. al-Fārūqī, *Islam and Others Faiths*, 132–133.
15. This is the only Qur'ānic reference to the Magians. There are two other references to the Sabians (Qur'ān 2:62 and 5:69). The other communities are discussed much more extensively and in greater detail.
16. See Jane Dammen McAuliffe, *Qur'anic Christians: An Analysis of Classical and Modern Exegesis* (Cambridge: Cambridge University, 1991), 94–98; Sidney H. Griffith, "Christians and Christianity," in McAuliffe, *Encyclopaedia of the Qur'ān*, vol. 1, 307; François de Blois, "Sabians," in McAuliffe, *Encyclopaedia of the Qur'ān*, vol. 4, 511; William R. Darrow, "Magians," in McAuliffe, *Encyclopaedia of the Qur'ān*, vol. 3, 244.

17. Ibn Kathīr, *Tafsīr, ad* Qur'ān 3:19, 5:3. See also Jane Smith, *A Historical and Semantic Study of the Term 'Islām' as seen in a Sequence of Qur'ān Commentaries* (Montana: Scholars, University of Montana, 1975), 132–133.
18. Izutsu, *God and Man in the Qur'an*, 96.
19. Mahmut Aydin, "Religious Pluralism: A Challenge for Muslims—A Theological Evaluation," *Journal of Ecumenical Studies* 38, no. 2–3 (Spring–Summer 2001), 339.
20. Esack, *Qur'ān, Liberation, & Pluralism*, 144.
21. For example, see Qur'ān 2:246–252, 5: 26, 7:136–141, 7:159–171, 5:26, 32:23, 45:16. See also Uri Rubin, "Children of Israel," in McAuliffe, *Encyclopaedia of the Qur'ān*, vol. 1, 303.
22. For example, M. Sharon, "People of the Book," in McAuliffe, *Encyclopaedia of the Qur'ān*, vol. 4, 36. Sharon states that People of the "Book" refers only to Jews and Christians and that the Qur'ān holistically depicts this group as the "enemies" of the Muslim community.
23. Esack, *Qur'ān, Liberation, & Pluralism*, 153.
24. See Qur'ān 3:163, 4:162, 17:55, 20:133, 21:105, 26:196, 53:36, 80:13, 87:18–19.
25. Yohanan Friedmann provides an overview of these debates as part of his analysis of the manner in which unbelievers have been classified in Islamic exegesis, *ḥadīth*, and *fiqh*. See Yohanan Friedmann, "Classification of Unbelievers," in *Tolerance and Coercion in Islam: Interfaith Relations in the Muslim Tradition* (Cambridge: Cambridge University, 2003), 54–86. See also Esack, *Qur'ān, Liberation, & Pluralism*, 153; François de Blois, "Sabians," in McAuliffe, *Encyclopaedia of the Qur'ān*, vol. 4, 511.
26. Daniel Madigan, "Book," in McAuliffe, *Encyclopaedia of the Qur'ān*, vol. 1, 242. See also *The Qur'ān's Self-Image: Writing and Authority in Islam's Scripture* (Princeton, NJ: Princeton University, 2001).
27. While there are complex and intriguing issues related to the jurisdiction or boundaries of Muḥammad's *umma* (i.e., the recipients of his message), it is generally conceived of by Muslims as being universal and not restricted temporally or geographically.
28. Frederick Mathewson Denny, "The Meaning of *Ummah* in the Qur'ān," *History of Religions* 15, no. 1 (August 1975): 34–70; Frederick Mathewson Denny, "Community and Society in the Qur'ān," in McAuliffe, *Encyclopaedia of the Qur'ān*, vol. 1, 367; Frederick Mathewson Denny, "Some Religio-Communal Terms and Concepts in the Qur'ān," *Numen* 24, no. 1 (April 1977): 26–59; Frederick Mathewson Denny, "Umma," in Bearman, *Encyclopaedia of Islam*, vol. 10, 859.
29. Denny, "Meaning of *Ummah*," 34.
30. See Theodor Nöldeke, *Geschichte des Qorans. Zweite Auflage*, bearbeitet von Friedrich Schwally, 3 vols. (Leipzig: Weicher, 1909–38).
31. Denny, "Meaning of *Ummah*," 64–65, 68–70. See Qur'ān 23:52, 5:48, 2:128, 3:110.

32. Denny, "Community and Society," 367.
33. Denny, "Meaning of *Ummah*," 44.
34. Denny, "Meaning of *Ummah*," 64.
35. Esack, *Qur'ān, Liberation & Pluralism*, 161–164. See also McAuliffe, *Qur'ānic Christians*; Abdulaziz Sachedina, "The Qur'an and Other Religions," in *The Cambridge Companion to the Qur'an*, ed. Jane Dammen McAuliffe (Cambridge: Cambridge University, 2006), 299.
36. Denny, "Meaning of *Ummah*," 65.
37. Denny, "Meaning of *Ummah*," 65.
38. See Qur'ān 3:100–115.
39. Denny, "Meaning of *Ummah*," 48.
40. See Denny, "Umma," 859.
41. Qur'ān 91:7–8.
42. Compelled in that God strengthens them and gives them no choice in carrying out their missions. This is evident, for example, in the Qur'ānic account of Moses (e.g., Qur'ān 20:24–26).

CHAPTER 7

1. See, for example, Farid Esack, *Qur'ān, Liberation and Pluralism* (Oxford: Oneworld Publications, 1997).
2. Arabic words are largely derived from a triliteral or triconsonantal root, for example, *Ḥ-N-F*. These roots then assume a form; vowels and additional consonants are added to the initial triconsonantal root. Most roots have at least ten common forms, which are typically related in meaning yet not synonymous. The particular form of the root for each concept is indicated in the table. For more information on the frequency and grammatical structure of these terms, see Hanna E. Kassis, *A Concordance of the Qur'ān* (Berkeley: University of California, 1983). Another helpful resource is the Qur'ānic Arabic Corpus from the Language Research Group at the University of Leeds, available online at http://corpus.quran.com/.
3. For example, see 'Abdullah Yusuf Alī, *The Meaning of the Holy Qur'an* (Beltsville, MD: Amana Publications, 2004.)
4. Esack, *Qur'ān, Liberation, & Pluralism*, 135.
5. For example, see Alī, *Meaning of the Holy Qur'an*.
6. Gerald R. Hawting, *The Idea of Idolatry and the Emergence of Islam* (Cambridge: Cambridge University, 1999), 48. See also Gerald R. Hawting, "Idolatry and Idolaters," in *Encyclopaedia of the Qur'ān*, vol. 2, ed. Jane Dammen McAuliffe (Leiden: Brill, 2001), 475. While I agree with certain contentions made by Hawting, I do not embrace his argument that the Qur'ānic passages should be understood as polemic. See Hawting, *Idea of Idolatry*, 47.
7. Hawting, *Idea of Idolatry*, 50–51.

8. Mustansir Mir, "Polytheism and Atheism," in McAuliffe, *Encyclopaedia of the Qur'ān*, vol. 4, 158.
9. Toshihiko Izutsu, *Ethico-Religious Concepts in the Qur'an* (Montreal: McGill University, 2002), 135–144.
10. Hawting, *Idea of Idolatry*, 62.
11. Hawting, *Idea of Idolatry*, 61. See also Izutsu, *Ethico-Religious Concepts*, 222.
12. Gabriel Said Reynolds, *The Qur'ān and Its Biblical Subtext* (London: Routledge, 2010), for instance, aims to comprehend the term by exploring the text and subtext of the Qur'ān, meaning the Jewish and Christian literature that was written before the Qur'ān. He discusses various positions taken by translators of the Qur'ān, and he then examines Jewish and Christian accounts of Abraham. Reynolds connects the Qur'ānic discourse on Abraham with Paul's claim that Abraham preceded Mosaic Law and therefore was justified before circumcision. This enabled Paul to claim that Christianity was not an innovation of Judaism but rather "an ancient and primary religion." Reynolds argues that the term *ḥanīf* is thus indicative of the Qur'ānic attempt to make a similar exclusive and polemic claim on Abraham (83). See also Uri Rubin, "Ḥanīf," in McAuliffe, *Encyclopaedia of the Qur'ān*, vol. 2, 402.
13. Izutsu, *Ethico-Religious Concepts*, 141.
14. See also Reynolds, *Qur'ān*, 147–155. Reynolds explains this *āya* in light of the Biblical metaphor "our hearts are uncircumcised." This is presented as a metaphor through which the Jews acknowledged the "impurity" of their hearts.
15. Izutsu, *Ethico-Religious Concepts*, 144–148.
16. While not especially relevant in the context of this study, according to the Qur'ān, Iblis was not an angel but rather another sort of being, a *jinn* (see Qur'ān 18:50).
17. Izutsu, *Ethico-Religious Concepts*, 143.
18. Izutsu, *Ethico-Religious Concepts*, 142–143.
19. See also Qur'ān 3:20 and 4:125.
20. Izutsu, *Ethico-Religious Concepts*, 209.
21. Other *āyāt* (e.g., Qur'ān 8:49 and 33:12) state "the *munāfiqūn* and those with sickness in their hearts" and thus raise some questions about whether this appellation is exclusively applied to those who manifest *nifāq*.
22. In these *āyāt*, the phrase "when really they do not believe" does not indicate that they do not acknowledge the existence of God but that they do not manifest *īmān* correctly or sufficiently.
23. *Takabbara* and *yastakbirūn* both come from the root *K-B-R*, and they mean virtually the same thing.
24. See also Qur'ān 6:148.
25. Izutsu, *Ethico-Religious Concepts*, 151.
26. See also Reynolds, *Qur'ān*, 71–75.

27. For example, see Ismāʿīl Rājī al-Fārūqī, *Islam and Other Faiths* (Leicester, UK: Islamic Foundation and International Institute of Islamic Thought, 1998), 141.
28. Izutsu, *Ethico-Religious Concepts*, 139.
29. Esack, *Qurʾān, Liberation and Pluralism*, 139.
30. In light of the distinction between hierarchical and lateral religious difference, these *āyāt* are read as implicitly referring to only some of the People of the Scripture.
31. See also Qurʾān 2:105.
32. See also Qurʾān 3:200.
33. Islamic legal scholars are not unequivocally opposed to abortion (or to birth control). This *āya* specifies a particular situation (fear of poverty) and should not be generalized to all situations. For example, it cannot be generalized to situations where the health of the mother is endangered.
34. See also Qurʾān 38:6.
35. Esack, *Qurʾān, Liberation and Pluralism*, 136.
36. See also Izutsu, *Ethico-Religious Concepts*, 171.
37. See also Qurʾān 2:128.
38. Izutsu, *Ethico-Religious Concepts*, 207–209.
39. See also Qurʾān 9:54–55.
40. See also Mohammad Fadel, "'No Salvation Outside Islam': Muslim Modernists, Democratic Politics, and Islamic Theological Exclusivism," in Mohammad Hassan Khalil, ed., *Between Heaven and Hell: Islam, Salvation, and the Fate of Others* (New York: Oxford University, 2013), 35–61.
41. See also the section on "uncreated faith" in L. Gardet, "Īmān," in Bearman, P., Th. Bianquis, C. E. Bosworth, E. van Donzel, and W. P. Heinrichs, eds., *Encyclopaedia of Islam, Second Edition*, vol. 3 (Leiden: Brill, 2004), 1170.
42. Izutsu, *Ethico-Religious Concepts*, 217; Esack, *Qurʾān, Liberation, and Pluralism*, 120.

CHAPTER 8

1. Qurʾān 4:1: "People (*nās*), be mindful of your Lord, who created you from a single soul (*nafs*), and from it created its mate (*zawj*), and from the pair of them spread countless men and women far and wide; be conscious of God (ʾ*ittaqū*), in whose name you make requests of one another. Beware of severing the ties of kinship: God is always watching over you."
2. Qurʾān 51:56: "I created jinn and humankind only to worship Me."
   Qurʾān 2:30 (excerpt): "When your Lord told the angels, "I am putting a vicegerent on earth..."
3. Ismāʿīl Rājī al-Fārūqī, *Islam and Other Faiths* (Leicester, UK: Islamic Foundation and International Institute of Islamic Thought, 1998), 135.

4. Qur'ān 95:4–6: "We create humankind in the best form then reduce people to the lowest of the low, except those who believe and do good deeds."
   Qur'ān 32:7–9: "Who gave everything its perfect form. God first created humankind from clay, then made descendants from an extract of underrated fluid. Then God molded humanity; God breathed from God's Spirit into humanity; God gave you hearing, sight, and minds. How seldom you are grateful!"
5. Qur'ān 2:7: "God has sealed their hearts and their ears, and their eyes are covered."
   Qur'ān 27:80–81: "You cannot make the dead hear, you cannot make the deaf listen to your call when they turn their backs and leave, you cannot guide the blind out of their error: you cannot make anyone hear you except those who believe in Our signs and submit (*muslimūn*)."
6. Qur'ān 7:172–173: "When your Lord took out the offspring from the loins of the Children of Adam and made them bear witness about themselves, God said, 'Am I not your Lord?' and they replied, 'Yes, we bear witness.' So you cannot say on the Day of Resurrection, 'We were not aware of this,' or, 'It was our forebears who, before us, ascribed partners to God, and we are only the descendants who came after them. Will you destroy us because of falsehoods they invented?' "
7. Qur'ān 91:7–10: "By the soul (*nafs*) and how God formed it and inspired it [to know] its own rebellion and piety (*taqwā*)! The one who causes it to grow in purity succeeds and the one who buries it fails."
8. Qur'ān 2:213: "Humankind (*nās*) was a single community (*umma waḥida*), then God sent prophets to bring good news and warning, and with them God sent the Scripture with the Truth, to judge between people in their disagreements. It was only those to whom it was given who disagreed about it after clear signs had come to them, because of rivalry between them. So by God's leave God guided the believers to the truth they had differed about: God guides whoever God will to a straight path."
   Qur'ān 10:19: "Humankind (*nās*) was originally one single community (*umma waḥida*), but later they differed. If it had not been for a word from your Lord, judgment would already have been passed between them regarding their differences."
9. al-Fārūqī, *Islam and Other Faiths*, 133.
10. See al-Fārūqī, *Islam and Other Faiths*, 133; Amina Wadud, *Qur'an and Woman: Rereading the Sacred Texts from a Woman's Perspective* (New York: Oxford University, 1999), 15.
11. See Qur'ān 4:1. See note 1.
12. Qur'ān 49:13: "People (*nās*), We created you all from a single man and a single woman, and made you into races and tribes so that you should recognize one

another. In God's eyes, the most honored of you are the ones most mindful of God (*'atqākum*). God is all knowing, all aware."

13. Qur'ān 30:20–22: "One of God's signs (*āyāt*) is that God created you from dust and—lo and behold!—you became human and scattered far and wide. Another of God's signs (*āyāt*) is that God created spouses from among yourselves for you to live with in tranquility. God ordained love and kindness between you. There truly are signs (*āyāt*) in this for those who reflect. Another of God's signs (*āyāt*) is the creation of the heavens and earth, and the diversity of your languages and colors. There truly are signs (*āyāt*) in this for those who know."
14. al-Fārūqī, *Islam and Other Faiths*, 138; Riffat Hassan, "Muslim Women and Post-Patriarchal Islam," in *After Patriarchy: Feminist Transformations of the World Religions*, ed. Paula M. Cooey, William R. Eakin, and Jay B. McDaniel (Maryknoll, NY: Orbis, 1998), 44; Muhammad Legenhausen, "A Muslim's Non-reductive Religious Pluralism," in *Islam and Global Dialogue: Religious Pluralism and the Pursuit of Peace*, ed. Roger Boase (Surrey: Ashgate, 2005), 56.
15. al-Fārūqī, *Islam and Other Faiths*, 138.
16. Qur'ān 91:7–10. See note 7.
17. Qur'ān 30:30 (excerpt): "…This is the natural disposition (*fiṭra*) God instilled in humankind. There is no altering God's creation…"
18. Qur'ān 20:115: "We also took a covenant (*'ahd*) with Adam before you, but he forgot and We found him lacking in constancy."
19. Qur'ān 41:39 (excerpt): "Another of God's signs (*āyāt*) is this: you see the earth lying desolate (*khāshi'atan*), but when We send water down on to it, it stirs and grows…"
20. See also R. Arnaldez, "Khalḳ," in In *Encyclopaedia of Islam, Second Edition*, vol. 4, ed. P. Bearman, Th. Bianquis, C.E. Bosworth, E. van Donzel, and W.P. Heinrichs (Leiden: Brill, 2004), 980.
21. See also al-Fārūqī, *Islam and Other Faiths*, 135–137.
22. Qur'ān 57:8: "Why should you not believe (*tu'minūn*) in God when the Messenger calls you to believe in your Lord, and God has already made a pledge (*mīthāq*) with you, if you have faith (*mu'minīn*)?"
23. Qur'ān 35:24: "We have sent you [Prophet] with the Truth as a bearer of good news and warning. Every community (*umma*) has been sent a warner."
24. Daniel A. Madigan, *The Qur'ān's Self-Image: Writing and Authority in Islam's Scripture* (Princeton, NJ: Princeton University, 2001), 194.
25. Qur'ān 40:78 (excerpt): "We have sent other messengers before you. Some We have mentioned to you and some We have not…"
26. Qur'ān 5:46: "We sent Jesus, son of Mary, in their footsteps, to confirm (*muṣaddiq*) the Torah that had been sent before him. We gave him the Gospel with guidance, light, and confirmation (*muṣaddiq*) of the Torah already revealed, a guide and lesson for those who take heed of God (*muttaqīn*)."

27. Qur'ān 5:48 (excerpt): "We sent to you [Muhammad] the Scripture with the truth, confirming (*muṣaddiq*) the Scriptures that came before it, and with final authority over them..."
28. For example, see Qur'ān 5:68.
29. Qur'ān 5:15: "People of the Book, Our Messenger has come to make clear (*yubayyinu*) to you much of what you have kept hidden of the Scripture, and to overlook much. A light has now come to you from God, and a Scripture making things clear (*mubīn*)."

    Qur'ān 27:76: "Truly, this Qur'ān explains to the Children of Israel most of what they differ about..."
30. Qur'ān 5:83: "And when they listen to what has been sent down to the Messenger, you will see their eyes overflowing with tears because they recognize the Truth [in it]. They say, 'Our Lord, we believe, so count us amongst the witnesses.'"
31. Qur'ān 3:81–85: "God took a pledge through the prophets (*mīthāq al-nabiyyīn*), saying, 'If, after I have bestowed Scripture and wisdom upon you, a messenger comes confirming (*muṣaddiq*) what you have been given, you must believe (*tu'minunna*) in him and support (*tanṣurunna*) him. Do you affirm this and accept My pledge as binding on you?' They said, 'We do.' God said, 'Then bear witness, and I too will bear witness.' Those who turn away after this are the ones who break pledges. Do they seek anything other than submission (*'aslama*) to God? Everything in the heavens and on earth submits to God, willingly or unwillingly. They will all be returned to God. Say, 'We believe (*'āmannā*) in God and in what has been sent down to us and to Abraham, Ishmael, Isaac, Jacob, and the Tribes. We believe (*'āmannā*) in what has been given to Moses, Jesus, and the prophets from their Lord. We do not make a distinction between any of the [prophets]. It is to God that we devote ourselves (*muslimūn*).' If anyone seeks a religion other than complete devotion to God (*islām*), it will not be accepted from him or her: he or she will be one of the losers in the Hereafter."
32. Qur'ān 4:64 (excerpt): "All the messengers We sent were meant to be obeyed..."
33. For example, see Qur'ān 26:106–163.
34. For example, see Qur'ān 3:130, 4:13, 4:80–81, 5:92, and 8:1.
35. Qur'ān 9:71: "The believers, both men and women (*mu'minūn* and *mu'mināt*), support each other; they order what is right and forbid what is wrong; they keep up the prayer and pay the prescribed alms; they obey God and God's Messenger. God will grant mercy to such people. God is almighty and wise."
36. Qur'ān 22:39–41: "Those who have been attacked are permitted to take up arms because they have been wronged—God has the power to help them—those who have been driven unjustly from their homes only for saying, 'Our Lord is God.' If God did not repel some people by means of others, many monasteries, churches, synagogues, and mosques, where God's name is much invoked, would have been destroyed. God is sure to help (*yanṣuranna*) those who help (*yanṣuru*) God's cause—God is strong and mighty—those who, when We

establish them in the land, keep up the prayer, pay the prescribed alms, command what is right, and forbid what is wrong. God controls the outcome of all events."

37. Qur'ān 2:148: "Each community has its own direction to which it turns. Race (*'istabqū*) to do good deeds (*khayrāt*) and wherever you are, God will bring you together. God has power to do everything."
    Qur'ān 5:48: "We sent to you [Muhammad] the Scripture with the truth, confirming (*muṣaddiq*) the Scriptures that came before it, and with final authority over them. So judge between them according to what God has sent down. Do not follow their whims, which deviate from the truth that has come to you. We have assigned a law and a path to each of you. If God had so willed, God would have made you one community (*umma waḥida*), but God wanted to test you through that which God has given you, so race (*'istabqū*) to do good (*khayrāt*). You will all return to God, and God will make clear to you the matters you differed about."
38. Qur'ān 23:57–61: "Those who stand in awe of their Lord, who believe in God's messages, who do not ascribe partners to God, who always give with hearts that tremble at the thought that they must return to God, are the ones who race toward good things (*khayrāt*), and they will be the first to get them (*sābiqūn*)."
39. Qur'ān 14:4: "We have never sent a messenger who did not use his own people's language to make things clear for them. But still God leaves whoever God will to stray, and guides whoever God will. God is the Almighty, the All Wise."
40. Qur'ān 5:48. See note 37.
    Qur'ān 22:67–69: "We have appointed acts of devotion for every community to observe, so do not let them argue with you about this matter. Call them to your Lord. You are on the right path. And if they argue with you, say, 'God is well aware of what you are doing.' On the Day of Resurrection, God will judge between you regarding your differences."

Glossary of Arabic Terms

ahl al-kitāb	People of the Scripture; communities that have received divine revelation
āliha	divinities or gods
Allah	Arabic word for God
ʾaqīm	establish as a routine, perform regularly
ʿaql	reason
Ashʿarī	affiliated with the rationalist school of theology, which traces its origins to Abū al-Ḥasan al-Ashʿarī (d. 935)
ʾaslama wajhahu	lit. submit one's face; direct oneself wholly toward something
āya, pl. āyāt	lit. sign; sign of God; verse of the Qurʾān
baghya	oppression
Banī Isrāʾīl	Children of Israel
baqāʾ	in Sufism, to subsist in God
bidʿa	innovation, with negative connotation
birr	goodness, piety
darajāt	hierarchical levels
dīn	religion; way of life
dīn al-fiṭra	the natural religion
dīn al-qayyima	the correct or true religion
fanāʾ	in Sufism, annihilation of the human ego
fiṭra	natural disposition of humans, human nature
ḥadīth, pl. aḥadīth	narrations of the sayings, actions, and tacit approval of Muḥammad

ḥadīth qudsī	special class of *ḥadīth* that refers to non-Qur'ānic, yet divinely revealed, content
ḥajj	pilgrimage to Mecca
Ḥanbali	affiliated with the most recent of the four Sunni schools of legal thought, which traces its origins to jurist Aḥmad ibn Ḥanbal (d. 767)
ḥanīf	commonly translated as nondenominational monotheist; one who is true and pure in faith, upright
ḥaqīqa	reality, truth; in Sufism, culmination of the path and recognition of the reality of God
hijra	the migration of Muḥammad from Mecca to Medina; marks the beginning of the Islamic lunar calendar
ḥizb, pl. aḥzāb	faction, party
ʿibāda	worship; moral and religious duties
iḥsān	excellence
'ijmāʿ	consensus; in Sunni discourse, specifically denotes consensus of recognized scholars
ikhlaṣ	sincerity, exclusive devotion
ʿilm	knowledge
īmān	generally translated as belief/faith; gratitude
'Injīl	the Gospel
insān al-kāmil	the perfect "man" (person)
iqrār	verbal statement of belief
islām	generally translated as submission, devotion or surrender to God; can also refer to the reified religion of Islam
'ittaqū	command to be mindful or conscious of God; command to manifest *taqwā*
jahannam	the Fire in the Hereafter
janna	the Garden in the Hereafter
kāfir, pl. kāfirūn/kuffār	one who covers, hides, or rejects something; one who manifests *kufr*; generally translated as one who disbelieves
kalām	speculative theology
Khārijites	early and small sect within Islam, noted for their willingness to label other members of the Muslim community as *kuffār*

khushūʿ	humility
kitāb	lit. book; divine scripture, revelation
kufr	rejection, concealment, or ingratitude; generally translated as disbelief
lā tafarriqu	do not make distinctions
majūs	Magians; commonly translated as Zoroastrians
Māliki	affiliated with the second oldest of the four Sunni schools of legal thought, which traces its origins to jurist Mālik ibn Anas (d. 795)
maʿnā	in Sufism, inward reality or "meaning"
manāsik	religious rites or practices, acts of devotion
maqāmāt	in Sufism, stations of spiritual insight
marātib	hierarchical levels
maʿrūf	well-known, equitable
minhāj	path
muʾmin, pl. muʾminūn	generally translated as one who believes; one who is grateful; one who manifests *īmān*
munāfiq, pl. munāfiqūn	generally translated as a hypocrite; one who manifests *nifāq*
mushrik, pl. mushrikūn	generally translated as one who ascribes partners to God; one who manifests *shirk*
muslim, pl. muslimūn	generally translated as one who submits to or is devoted to God; one who manifests *islām*; can also refer to an adherent to the reified religion of Islam, a Muslim
muslima	feminine form of *muslim*; denotes a female who submits to or is devoted to God; a female who manifests *islām*
Muʿtazili(te)	affiliated with the school of theology that prioritized reason, stressed divine oneness and divine justice, and asserted the created nature of the Qurʾān
muttaqīn, pl. muttaqūn	one who is conscious of God; one who manifests *taqwā*
nafs	primordial soul created by God
nās	humankind
naṣārā	Nazarenes; commonly translated as Christians

naskh abrogation; may refer to abrogation of earlier Qur'ānic verses by those revealed later or abrogation of other scriptures by the Qur'ānic revelation

nifāq generally translated as hypocrisy

qiyās analogical reasoning

ṣābi'ūn Sabians

ṣabr patient perseverance, steadfastness

salaf righteous ancestors/predecessors from the early generations of Muslims

ṣalāt ritual prayer

ṣāliḥāt good works

sawm fasting; may refer to obligatory month-long fast of Ramaḍan

Shāfi'ī affiliated with the third oldest of the four Sunni schools of legal thought, which traces its origins to jurist Muḥammad ibn Idrīs al-Shāfi'ī (d. 820)

shahāda verbal profession/testimony of faith consisting of the pronouncement "There is no God worthy of worship but God and Muḥammad is the messenger of God" (*Lā ilāha illā Allāh wa Muḥammadan rasūl Allāh*)

sharī'a law; in Sufism, the obligatory ritual practices

shī'a factions

Shī'a affiliated with *Shī'ism*

Shī'ism second largest branch of Islam, tracing origins to early debates on the legitimate successor of Muḥammad

shir'a law

shirk generally translated as the act of associating partners with God; ascribing partners to God

shukr gratitude

Sufi affiliated with Sufism

Sufism Islamic orientation and system of practices focused on self-purification, transformation and realization of the Truth; commonly described as Islamic mysticism

ṣuḥuf lit. sheets; scriptures

sunna practice or example of Muḥammad

Sunni affiliated with Sunnism

Sunnism largest branch of Islam; deriving its name from the term *sunna*

sūra chapter of the Qur'ān

ṣūrat in Sufism, outward appearance or "form"

tafsīr exegesis of the Qur'ān

tafsīr bi'l-ma'thūr	exegesis of the Qur'ān with primary reference to prophetic *aḥadīth*
tafsīr bi'l-ra'y	exegesis of the Qur'ān based on personal opinion
tafsīr al-Qur'ān bil-Qur'ān	exegesis of the Qur'ān with primary reference to other parts of the Qur'ān
taḥrīf	scriptural falsification or corruption
takfir	pronouncement of *kufr* (disbelief); labeling another as a disbeliever
taqwā	mindfulness or consciousness of God; commonly translated as piety
ṭarīqa	way or path; in Sufism, a school or order
taṣawwuf	Sufism
taṣdīq	conviction of the heart
tawḥīd	unicity or oneness of God
tawḥīd al-rubūbiyya	oneness of God as Lord; conception of God as Creator and Sustainer
tawḥīd al-ulūhiyya	oneness of God as God; holistic and multifaceted conception of the unicity of God
Tawrāt	the Torah
thamanan qalīlan	a small price
umma, pl. umam	community; community of revelation
umma muqtaṣida	a group on the right course
umma muslima	a group that submits to God
umma qā'ima	an upright group
umma waḥida	one community; a unified community
waḥdat al-wujūd	oneness of being
waḥdat-e-dīn	unity of *dīn*; unity of religion
yahūd	Jews
yaqīn	certainty of knowledge
Zabūr	scripture of David; sometimes connected with the Psalms
Ẓāhirī	affiliated with school of Islamic legal thought, which traces its origins to jurist Dawūd ibn Khalaf al-Ẓāhirī (d. 833), and is characterized by a strict prioritization of the literal or well-known meaning of a text
zakāt	obligatory charity, alms
zawj	pair, mate, spouse

Bibliography

Āasī, Ghulām Ḥaider. *Muslim Understanding of Other Religions: An Analytical Study of Ibn Ḥazm's* Kitāb al-faṣl fī al-milal wa-aḥwā' wa al-niḥal. Ann Arbor, MI: University Microfilms International, 1986.

Abugideiri, Hibba. "The Renewed Woman of American Islam: Shifting Lenses toward 'Gender Jihad?'" *Muslim World* 91 (Spring 2001): 1–18.

Abou El Fadl, Khaled. *The Place of Tolerance in Islam*, edited by Joshua Cohen and Ian Lague. Boston: Beacon, 2002.

Adang, Camilla. "Belief and Unbelief." In *Encyclopaedia of the Qur'ān*, edited by Jane Dammen McAuliffe, vol. 1, 218. Leiden: Brill, 2001.

——. "Hypocrites and Hypocrisy." In *Encyclopaedia of the Qur'ān*, edited by Jane Dammen McAuliffe, vol. 2, 468. Leiden: Brill, 2001.

Afsaruddin, Asma. "Celebrating Pluralism and Dialogue: Qur'anic Perspectives." *Journal of Ecumenical Studies* 42, no. 3 (2007): 389–406.

Afshar, Haleh. "Islam and Feminism: An Analysis of Political Strategies." In *Feminism and Islam: Legal and Literary Perspectives*, edited by Mai Yamani, 197–216. Reading, NY: Ithaca, 1996.

Ahmed, Leila. *Women and Gender in Islam*. New Haven, CT: Yale University, 1996.

Alī, 'Abdullah Yusuf. *The Meaning of the Holy Qur'an*. Beltsville, MD: Amana Publications, 2004.

Arkoun, Mohammed. "Islam." In *Encyclopaedia of the Qur'ān*, edited by Jane Dammen McAuliffe, vol. 2, 565. Leiden: Brill, 2001.

Arnaldez, R. "Ibn Ḥazm, Abū Muḥammad 'Alī b. Aḥmad b. Sa'īd." In *Encyclopaedia of Islam, Second Edition*, edited by P. Bearman, Th. Bianquis, C.E. Bosworth, E. van Donzel, and W.P. Heinrichs, vol. 3, 790. Leiden: Brill, 2004.

——. "Khalḳ." In *Encyclopaedia of Islam, Second Edition*, edited by P. Bearman, Th. Bianquis, C.E. Bosworth, E. van Donzel, and W.P. Heinrichs, vol. 4, 980. Leiden: Brill, 2004.

Asad, Talal. *Genealogies of Religion: Discipline and Reasons of Power in Christianity and Islam*. Baltimore: Johns Hopkins University, 1993.

Asani, Ali S. "'So That You May Know One Another': A Muslim American Reflects on Pluralism and Islam." *Annals of the American Academy of Political and Social Science* 588, *Islam: Enduring Myths and Changing Realities* (July 2003): 40–51.

Aslan, Adnan. *Religious Pluralism in Christian and Islamic Philosophy: The Thought of John Hick and Seyyed Hossein Nasr*. Kent: Japan Society Publications, 1994.

Ateş, A. "Ibn al-ʿArabī, Muḥyī'l-Dīn Abū ʿAbd Allāh Muḥammad b. ʿAlī b. Muḥammad b. al-ʿArabī al-Ḥātimī al-Ṭāʾī, known as al-Shaykha al-Akbar." In *Encyclopaedia of Islam, Second Edition*, edited by P. Bearman, Th. Bianquis, C.E. Bosworth, E. van Donzel, and W.P. Heinrichs, vol. 3, 707. Leiden: Brill, 2004.

Aydin, Mahmut. "A Muslim Pluralist: Jalaluddin Rumi." In *The Myth of Religious Superiority: A Multifaith Exploration*, edited by Paul Knitter, 220–236. Maryknoll, NY: Orbis, 2005.

——. "Religious Pluralism: A Challenge for Muslims—A Theological Evaluation." *Journal of Ecumenical Studies* 38, no. 2–3 (Spring–Summer 2001): 330–352.

Ayoub, Mahmoud. *A Muslim View of Christianity: Essays on Dialogue by Mahmoud Ayoub*, edited by Irfan A. Omar. Maryknoll, NY: Orbis, 2007.

——. "Nearest in Amity: Christians in the Qurʾan and Contemporary Exegetical Tradition." *Islam and Christian-Muslim Relations* 8, no. 2 (1997): 145–164.

——. "The Qurʾan and Religious Pluralism." In *Islam and Global Dialogue: Religious Pluralism and the Pursuit of Peace*, edited by Roger Boase, 273–281. Surrey: Ashgate, 2005.

Badawi, Elsaid M., and Muhammad Abdel Haleem. *Arabic-English Dictionary of Qurʾānic Usage*. Leiden: Brill, 2008.

Badran, Margot. "Between Secular and Islamic Feminism/s: Reflections on the Middle East and Beyond." *Journal of Middle East Women's Studies* 1, no. 1 (Winter 2005): 6–28.

——. *Feminism Beyond East and West: New Gender Talk and Practice in Global Islam*. New Delhi: Global Media, 2007.

——. *Feminism in Islam: Secular and Religious Convergences*. Oxford: Oneworld, 2009.

al-Bāqillānī, Abū Bakr Muḥammad b. al-Ṭayyib. *Kitāb al-tamhīd*, edited by Richard J. McCarthy, S.J. Beirut: al-Maktaba al-Sharqiyya, 1957.

Barazangi, Nimat Hafez. *Woman's Identity and the Qurʾan: A New Reading*. Gainesville: University of Florida, 2004.

Barlas, Asma. "Amina Wadud's Hermeneutics of the Qurʾan: Women Rereading Sacred Texts." In *Modern Muslim Intellectuals and the Qur'an*, edited by Suha Taji-Farouki, 97–124. London: Oxford University, 2006.

——. *"Believing Women" in Islam: Unreading Patriarchal Interpretations of the Qur'an*. Austin: University of Texas, 2002.

——. "Four Stages of Denial, or, My On-Again, Off-Again Affair with Feminism: Response to Margot Badran." Paper presented at Ithaca College, October 2006.

——. "Globalizing Equality: Muslim Women, Theology, and Feminism." In *On Shifting Ground: Muslim Women in the Global Era*, edited by Fereshteh Nouraie-Simone, 91–110. New York: Feminist Press at the City of New York, 2005.

——. "Hearing the Word, as a Muslim: Thirteen Passages of the Qurʾān and Religious Difference." Paper presented at Cornell University Vespers, November 2007.

——. "'Holding Fast by the Best in the Precepts'—The Qurʾan and Method." In *New Directions in Islamic Thought*, edited by Kari Vogt, Lena Larsen, and Christian Moe, 17–22. New York: I.B. Tauris, 2009.

——. "Reviving Islamic Universalism: East/s, West/s, and Coexistence." Paper presented at the Conference on Contemporary Islamic Synthesis, Alexandria, Egypt, October 2003.

——. "Women's Readings of the Qurʾān." In *The Cambridge Companion to the Qurʾān*, edited by Jane Dammen McAuliffe, 255–271. Cambridge: Cambridge University, 2006.

Bearman, P., Th. Bianquis, C.E. Bosworth, E. van Donzel, and W.P. Heinrichs, eds. *Encyclopaedia of Islam, Second Edition*, 12 vols. Leiden: Brill, 2004.

Beck, Ulrich. *What Is Globalization?*, translated by Patrick Camiller. Malden, MA: Blackwell, 2000.

Berg, Herbert. "Polysemy in the Qurʾān." In *Encyclopaedia of the Qurʾān*, edited by Jane Dammen McAuliffe, vol. 4, 155. Leiden: Brill, 2001.

Björkman, W. "Kāfir." In *Encyclopaedia of Islam, Second Edition*, edited by P. Bearman, Th. Bianquis, C.E. Bosworth, E. van Donzel, and W.P. Heinrichs, vol. 4, 407. Leiden: Brill, 2004.

Boase, Roger, ed. *Islam and Global Dialogue: Religious Pluralism and the Pursuit of Peace*. Surrey: Ashgate, 2005.

Boyarin, Daniel. *Border Lines: The Partition of Judaeo-Christianity*. Philadelphia: University of Pennsylvania, 2004.

Brockett, A. "al-Munāfiḳūn." In *Encyclopaedia of Islam, Second Edition*, edited by P. Bearman, Th. Bianquis, C.E. Bosworth, E. van Donzel, and W.P. Heinrichs, vol. 7, 561. Leiden: Brill, 2004.

Brunner, Emile. "Revelation and Religion." In *Christianity and Other Religions*, edited by John Hick and Brian Hebblethwaite, 113–132. Philadelphia: Fortress, 1980.

Bullock, Katherine. *Rethinking Muslim Women and the Veil: Challenging Historical & Modern Stereotypes*. Herndon, VA: International Institute of Islamic Thought, 2002.

Burton, John. "Abrogation." In *Encyclopaedia of the Qurʾān*, edited by Jane Dammen McAuliffe, vol. 1, 11–19. Leiden: Brill, 2001.

Calder, Norman, J.A. Mojaddedi, and Andrew Rippin, eds. *Classical Islam: A Sourcebook of Religious Literature*. New York: Routledge, 2003.

Chittick, William C. *Imaginal Worlds: Ibn al-ʿArabī and the Problem of Religious Diversity*. Albany: State University of New York, 1994.

——. *The Sufi Path of Knowledge: Ibn al-ʿArabī's Metaphysics of Imagination*. Albany: State University of New York, 1989.

——. *The Sufi Path of Love: the Spiritual Teachings of Rumi*. Albany: State University of New York, 1983.

cooke, miriam. "Multiple Critique: Islamic Feminist Rhetorical Strategies." In *Postcolonialism, Feminism and Religious Discourse*, edited by Laura E. Donaldson and Kwok Pui-lan, 142–160. New York: Routledge, 2002.

——. *Women Claim Islam: Creating Islamic Feminism through Literature*. New York: Routledge, 2001.

Cornell, Vincent. "Fruit of the Tree of Knowledge: The Relationship between Faith and Practice in Islam." In *The Oxford History of Islam*, edited by John L. Esposito, 63–105. New York: Oxford University, 1999.

Cuypers, Michel. *The Banquet: A Reading of the Fifth Sura of the Qur'an*. Miami: Convivium, 2009.

Davies, Merryl Wyn. *Knowing One Another: Shaping an Islamic Anthropology*. London: Mansell Publishing Limited, 1988.

de Blois, François. "Sabians." In *Encyclopaedia of the Qurʾān*, edited by Jane Dammen McAuliffe, vol. 4, 511. Leiden: Brill, 2001.

Dean, Thomas, ed. *Religious Pluralism and Truth: Essays on Cross-Cultural Philosophy of Religion*. New York: State University of New York, 1995.

Denny, Frederick Mathewson. "Community and Society in the Qurʾān." In *Encyclopaedia of the Qurʾān*, edited by Jane Dammen McAuliffe, vol. 1, 367. Leiden: Brill, 2001.

——. "The Meaning of *Ummah* in the Qurʾān." *History of Religions* 15, no. 1 (August 1975): 34–70.

——. "Some Religio-Communal Terms and Concepts in the Qurʾān." *Numen* 24, no. 1 (April 1977): 26–59.

Donner, Fred M. "From Believers to Muslims: Confessional Self-Identity in the Early Islamic Community." *al-Abhāth* 50–51 (2002–2003): 9–53.

——. *Muhammad and the Believers: At the Origins of Islam*. Cambridge, MA: Belknap, 2010.

Egnell, Helene. "Dialogue for Life: Feminist Approaches to Interfaith Dialogue." In *Theology and the Religions: A Dialogue*, edited by Viggo Mortenson, 249–256. Cambridge: Eerdsmans, 2003.

Engineer, Asghar Ali. *A Rational Approach to Islam*. New Delhi: Gyan Publishing House, 2001.

——. "Islam and Pluralism." In *The Myth of Religious Superiority: A Multifaith Exploration*, edited by Paul Knitter, 211–219. Maryknoll, NY: Orbis, 2005.

——. *Islam in Contemporary World.* New Delhi: New Dawn, 2007.

——. "Islam, Women, and Gender Justice." In *What Men Owe to Women: Men's Voices from World Religions*, edited by John C. Raines and Daniel C. Maguire, 109–128. New York: State University of New York, 2001.

——. *On Developing Theology of Peace in Islam.* New Delhi: Sterling Publishers, 2005.

Esack, Farid. "Islam and Gender Justice: Beyond Simplistic Apologia." In *What Men Owe to Women: Men's Voices from World Religions*, edited by John C. Raines and Daniel C. Maguire, 187–210. New York: State University of New York, 2001.

——. "Muslims Engaging the Other and the *Humanum.*" In *Proselytization and Communal Self-Determination in Africa*, edited by Abdullahi Ahmed An-Na'im, 51–76. Maryknoll, NY: Orbis, 1999.

——. *Qur'ān, Liberation and Pluralism.* Oxford: Oneworld Publications, 1997.

——. "Religio-Cultural Diversity: For What and with Whom? Muslim Reflections from a Postapartheid South Africa in the Throes of Globalization." In *Cultural Diversity and Islam*, edited by Abdul Aziz Said and Meena Sharify-Funk, 165–185. Lanham, MD: University Press of America, 2003.

Fadel, Muhammad. "No Salvation Outside Islam": Muslim Modernists, Democratic Politics, and Islamic Theological Exclusivism." In *Between Heaven and Hell: Islam, Salvation, and the Fate of Others*, edited by Mohammad Hassan Khalil, 35–61. New York: Oxford University, 2013.

al-Fārūqī, Ismā'īl Rājī. "The Essence of Religious Experience in Islam." *Numen* 20, no. 3 (1973): 186–201.

——. "History of Religions: Its Nature and Significance for Christian Education and the Muslim–Christian Dialogue." *Numen* 12, no. 1 (1965): 35–65.

——. *Islam and Other Faiths.* Leicester, UK: Islamic Foundation and International Institute of Islamic Thought, 1998.

——. *al Tawḥīd: Its Implications for Thought and Life.* Herndon, VA: International Institute of Islamic Thought, 1992.

al-Faruqi, Maysam. "Women's Self-Identity in the Qur'an and Islamic Law." In *Windows of Faith: Muslim Women Scholar-Activists in North America*, edited by Gisela Webb, 72–101. Syracuse: Syracuse University, 2000.

Friedmann, Yohanan. *Tolerance and Coercion in Islam: Interfaith Relations in the Muslim Tradition.* Cambridge: Cambridge University, 2003.

Frolov, Dmitry V. "Freedom and Predestination." In *Encyclopaedia of the Qur'ān*, edited by Jane Dammen McAuliffe, vol. 2, 267. Leiden: Brill, 2001.

Gardet, L. "al-Ḳaḍā; Wa 'l-ḳadar." In *Encyclopaedia of Islam, Second Edition*, edited by P. Bearman, Th. Bianquis, C.E. Bosworth, E. van Donzel, and W.P. Heinrichs, vol. 4, 365. Leiden: Brill, 2004.

——. "Īmān."" In *Encyclopaedia of Islam, Second Edition*, edited by P. Bearman, Th. Bianquis, C.E. Bosworth, E. van Donzel, and W.P. Heinrichs, vol. 3, 1170. Leiden: Brill, 2004.

Gaudel, Jean-Marie, ed. *Encounters & Clashes: Islam and Christianity in History*. Collection "Studi arabo-islamici del PISAI," 15. Roma: Pontificio Istituto di Studi Arabi e d'Islamistica, 2000.

al-Ghazālī, Abū Ḥāmid Muḥammad ibn Muḥammad. *Fayṣal al-tafriqa bayna al-islām wa al-zandaqa*, edited by Sulaymān Dunyā. Cairo: Dār Iḥyā' al-Kutub al-'Arabīya, 1961.

Gillis, Chester. *Pluralism: A New Paradigm for Theology*. Louvain: Peeters, Eerdmans, 1998.

Gimaret, D. "SHirk." In *Encyclopaedia of Islam, Second Edition*, edited by P. Bearman, Th. Bianquis, C.E. Bosworth, E. van Donzel, and W.P. Heinrichs, vol. 9, 484. Leiden: Brill, 2004.

Gottschalk, H.L. "Abū 'Ubayd al-Ḳāsim b. Sallām (the *nisba* varies between al-Baghdādī, al-Khurāsāni and al-Anṣārī)." In *Encyclopaedia of Islam, Second Edition*, edited by P. Bearman, Th. Bianquis, C.E. Bosworth, E. van Donzel, and W.P. Heinrichs, vol. 1, 157. Leiden: Brill, 2004.

Griffith, Sidney H. "Christians and Christianity." In *Encyclopaedia of the Qur'ān*, edited by Jane Dammen McAuliffe, vol. 1, 307. Leiden: Brill, 2001.

Griffiths, Morwenna. *Feminisms and the Self: The Web of Identity*. New York: Routledge, 1995.

Griffiths, Paul, ed. *Christianity through Non-Christian Eyes*. Maryknoll, NY: Orbis, 1990.

Gross, Rita. "Excuse Me, but What's the Question?" In *The Myth of Religious Superiority: A Multifaith Exploration*, edited by Paul Knitter, 75–87. Maryknoll, NY: Orbis, 2005.

——. "Feminist Theology as Theology of Religions." In *The Cambridge Companion to Feminist Theology*, edited by Susan Parsons, 60–78. New York: Cambridge University, 2002.

—— and respondents. "Roundtable Discussion: Feminist Theology and Religious Diversity." *Journal of Feminist Studies in Religion* 16, no. 2 (2000): 73–131.

——. "Steps toward Feminine Imagery of Deity in Jewish Theology." In *On Being a Jewish Feminist: A Reader*, edited by Susannah Heschel, 234–247. New York: Schocken Books, 1983.

——. "The Study of Religion as Religious Experience." *Buddhist-Christian Studies* 11 (1991): 254–258.

——. "Where Have We Been? Where Do We Need to Go?: Women's Studies and Gender in Religion and Feminist Theology." In *Gender, Religion and Diversity: Cross-Cultural Perspectives*, edited by Ursula King and Tina Beattie, 17–27. New York: Continuum, 2005.

Ḥaddād, Wadī' Z. "A Tenth-Century Speculative Theologian's Refutation of the Basic Doctrines of Christianity: Al-Bāqillānī (d. A.D. 1013)." In *Christian-Muslim Encounters*, edited by Yvonne Yazbeck Haddad and Wadī' Zaydān Ḥaddād, 83–94. Gainesville: University Press of Florida, 1995.

Haddad, Yvonne Yazbeck, and Wadīʿ Zaydān Ḥaddād, ed. *Christian-Muslim Encounters*. Gainesville: University Press of Florida, 1995.

—— and John L. Esposito, eds. *Daughters of Abraham: Feminist Thought in Judaism, Christianity, and Islam*. Gainesville: University of Florida, 2001.

——, Jane I. Smith, and Kathleen M. Moore, eds. *Muslim Women in America: The Challenge of Islamic Identity Today*. New York: Oxford University, 2006.

Hammer, Juliane. "Identity, Authority, and Activism: American Muslim Women Approach the Qurʾān." *Muslim World* 98 (October 2008): 443–464.

Hassan, Riffat. "Feminism in Islam." In *Feminism and World Religions*, edited by Arvind Sharma and Katherine K. Young, 248–278. Albany: State University of New York, 1999.

——. "Feminist Theology: The Challenges for Muslim Women." In *Women and Islam: Critical Concepts in Sociology*, edited by Haideh Moghissi, 195–208. London: Routledge, 2005.

——. "Human Rights in the Qurʾanic Perspective." In *Windows of Faith: Muslim Women Scholar-Activists in North America*, edited by Gisela Webb, 241–248. Syracuse: Syracuse University, 2000.

——. "Islam." In *Her Voice, Her Faith: Women Speak on World Religions*, edited by Arvind Sharma and Katherine K. Young, 215–242. Boulder, CO: Westview, 2003.

——. "'*Jihād Fī Sabīl Allah*': A Muslim Woman's Faith Journey from Struggle to Struggle to Struggle," and "The Issue of Woman-Man Equality in the Islamic Tradition." In *Women's and Men's Liberation: Testimonies of Spirit*, edited by Leonard Grob, Riffat Hassan, and Haim Gordon, 11–30, 65–82. New York: Greenwood, 1991.

——. "Muslim Women and Post-Patriarchal Islam." In *After Patriarchy: Feminist Transformations of the World Religions*, edited by Paula M. Cooey, William R. Eakin, and Jay B. McDaniel, 39–64. Maryknoll, NY: Orbis, 1998.

——. "The Qurʾanic Perspective on Religious Pluralism." In *Peace-Building by, between, and beyond Muslims and Evangelical Christians*, edited by Mohammed Abu-Nimer and David Augsburger, 91–101. Lanham, MD: Lexington Books, 2009.

——. "Women's Rights in Islam: Normative Teachings versus Practice." In *Islam and Human Rights: Advancing a U.S.–Muslim Dialogue*, edited by Shireen T. Hunter and Huma Malik, 43–66. Washington, DC: Center for Strategic and International Studies, 2005.

Hawting, Gerald R. *The Idea of Idolatry and the Emergence of Islam*. Cambridge: Cambridge University, 1999.

——. "Idolatry and Idolaters." In *Encyclopaedia of the Qurʾān*, edited by Jane Dammen McAuliffe, vol. 2, 475. Leiden: Brill, 2001.

Heim, S. Mark. *The Depth of Riches: A Trinitarian Theology of Religious Ends*. Grand Rapids, MI: Eerdmans, 2001.

——. *Salvations: Truth and Difference in Religion*. Maryknoll, NY: Orbis Books, 1995.

Henzell-Thomas, Jeremy. "The Challenge of Pluralism and the Middle Way of Islam." In *Islam and Global Dialogue: Religious Pluralism and the Pursuit of Peace*, edited by Roger Boase, 267–272. Surrey: Ashgate, 2005.

al-Hibri, Azizah. "Hagar on My Mind." In *Philosophy, Feminism, and Faith*, edited by Ruth E. Groenhaut and Marya 1, 198–212. Bloomington: Indiana University, 2003.

Hick, John. *A Christian Theology of Religions: The Rainbow of Faiths*. Louisville, KY: Westminster John Knox, 1995.

—— and Brian Hebblethwaite, eds. *Christianity and Other Religions*. Philadelphia: Fortress, 1980.

——. *An Interpretation of Religion: Human Responses to the Transcendent*. New Haven, CT: Yale University, 2004.

—— and Paul F. Knitter, eds. *The Myth of Christian Uniqueness: Toward a Pluralistic Theology of Religions*. Eugene, OR: Wipf & Stock, 1987.

——. "Religious Pluralism and Islam." Paper presented at Institute for Islamic Culture and Thought, Tehran, Iran, February 2005.

Hidayatullah, Aysha. "Inspiration and Struggle: Muslim Feminist Theology and the Work of Elizabeth Schüssler Fiorenza." *Journal of Feminist Studies in Religion* 25, no.1 (2009): 162–170.

——. "Women Trustees of Allah: Methods, Limits, and Possibilities of 'Feminist Theology' in Islam." Ph.D. diss., University of California, Santa Barbara, 2009.

Hill Fletcher, Jeannine. "Christology between Identity and Difference: On Behalf of a World in Need." In *Frontiers in Catholic Feminist Theology: Shoulder to Shoulder*, edited by Susan Abraham and Elena Procario-Foley, 79–96. Minneapolis: Fortress, 2009.

——. "Feminisms: Syncretism, Symbiosis, and Synergetic Dance." In *Christian Approaches to Other Faiths*, edited by Alan Race and Paul M. Hedges, 136–154. London: SCM, 2008.

——. "Karl Rahner's Principles of Ecumenism and Contemporary Religious Pluralism." In *Theology and the Social Sciences*, The Annual Publication of the College Theological Society, vol. 46, edited by Michael Horace Barnes, 181–194. Maryknoll, NY: Orbis, 2000.

——. *Monopoly On Salvation?: A Feminist Approach to Religious Pluralism*. New York: Continuum, 2005.

——. "Religious Pluralism in an Era of Globalization: The Making of Modern Religious Identity." *Theological Studies* 69, no. 2 (June 2008): 395–411.

——. "Shifting Identity: The Contribution of Feminist Thought to Theologies of Religious Pluralism." *Journal of Feminist Studies in Religion* 19, no. 2 (Fall 2003): 5–24.

Hofmann, Murad Wilfried. "Religious Pluralism and Islam in a Polarised World." In *Islam and Global Dialogue: Religious Pluralism and the Pursuit of Peace*, edited by Roger Boase, 235–245. Surrey: Ashgate, 2005.

Hoyland, Robert G. *Muslims and Others in Early Islamic Society*, The Formation of the Classical Islamic World, vol. 18. Burlington, VT: Ashgate, 2004.

Huda, Qamar-ul. "Knowledge of Allah and the Islamic View of Other Religions." *Theological Studies* 64 (2003): 278–305.

Ibn al-ʿArabī. *al-Fūtūhat al-Makkiyya*. Cairo, 1911. Reprint Beirut: Dar Sadir, 1968.

Ibn Ḥazm, ʿAlī ibn Aḥmad. *Kitāb al-faṣl fī al-milal wa al-aḥwāʾ wa al-niḥal*, 5 vols. Jeddah: ʿUqaẓ, 1982.

Ibn al-Jawzi, ʿAbd al-Raḥman. *Al-Muntaẓam fī taʾrīkh al-mulūk wa al-umam*. Beirut: Dār al-Kutūb al-ʿIlmīya, 1992.

——. "On the Edicts of the Caliph al-Qādir." In *Classical Islam: A Sourcebook of Religious Literature*, edited by Norman Calder, J.A. Mojaddedi, and Andrew Rippin, 159–162. New York: Routledge, 2003.

Ibn Kathīr, Ismāʿīl ibn ʿUmar. *Tafsīr al-Qurʾān al-ʿaẓīm*. Beirut: Dār al-Fikr, 1987.

Ibn Sallām, Abū ʿUbayd al-Qāsim. "Chapter on the Characteristics of Faith with Regards to Its Perfection and Its Stages." In *Classical Islam: a Sourcebook of Religious Literature*, edited Norman Calder, J.A. Mojaddedi, and Andrew Rippin, 135–142. New York: Routledge, 2003.

——. *Kitāb al-īmān wa-maʿālimihi, wa-sunanihi, wa-istikmālihi, wa-darajātihi*. Beirut: al-Maktab al-Islāmī, 1983.

Ibn Taymiyya, Aḥmad ibn ʿAbd al-Ḥalīm. *al-Īmān*. Cairo: Maktabat Anas Ibn Mālik, 1980.

——. *Jawāb al-ṣaḥīḥ li-man baddala dīn al-masīḥ*. Egypt: Maṭbaʿat al-Nīl, 1905.

——. Kitāb al-īmān: *Book of Faith*, edited and translated by Salman Hassan Al-Ani and Shadia Ahmad Tel. Bloomington, IN: Iman Publishing House, 1999.

—— *Majmūʿ fatāwā shaykh al-islām Aḥmad ibn Taymiyya*. Cairo: al-Shurafāʾ li-al-Tibāʿah wa Taṣwīr al-Mustanadāt, 1979.

——. *A Muslim Theologian's Response to Christianity: Ibn Taymiyya's al-Jawāb al-ṣaḥīḥ*, edited and translated by Thomas F. Michel. Delmar, NY: Caravan, 1999.

Izutsu, Toshihiko. *The Concept of Belief in Islamic Theology: A Semantic Analysis of Īmān and Islām*. Tokyo: Keio University, 1965. Reprint, Kuala Lumpur: Islamic Books Trust, 2006.

——. *Ethico-Religious Concepts in the Qurʾan*. Montreal: McGill University, 2002. Reprint Selangor, Malaysia: Islamic Book Trust, 2004. Originally published as *The Structure of the Ethical Terms in the Koran*. Tokyo: Keio University Institute of Philological Studies, 1959.

——. *God and Man in the Koran: Semantics of the Koranic Weltanschauung*. Tokyo: Keio University, 1964. Reprint, *God and Man in the Qurʾan: Semantics of the Qurʾanic Weltanschauung*. Kuala Lumpur: Islamic Books Trust, 2008.

al-Jabbār, ʿAbd. *Critique of Christian Origins: a Parallel English-Arabic Text*, edited and translated by Gabriel Said Reynolds and Khalil Samir. Provo, UT: Brigham Young University, 2010.

Jackson, Sherman A. *On the Boundaries of Theological Tolerance in Islam: Abu Hāmid al-Ghazālī's* Fayṣal al-Tafriqa Bayna al-Islām wa al-Zandaqa. Oxford: Oxford University, 2002.

al-Jamil, Tariq. "Ibn Taymiyya and Ibn al-Muṭahhar al-Ḥillī: Shi'i Polemics and the Struggle for Religious Authority in Medieval Islam." In *Ibn Taymiyya and His Times*, edited by Yossef Rapoport and Shahab Ahmed, 229–246. Karachi: Oxford University, 2010.

Johnson, Elizabeth. *She Who Is: The Mystery of God in Feminist Theological Discourse.* New York: Crossroad Publishing Company, 2002.

Jones, J. Lynn. *Believing as Ourselves.* Beltsville, MD: Amana Publications, 2002.

Kärkkäinen, Veli-Matti. *An Introduction to the Theology of Religions: Biblical, Historical & Contemporary Perspectives.* Downers Grove, IL: InterVarsity, 2003.

Kassis, Hanna E. *A Concordance of the Qur'ān.* Berkeley: University of California, 1983.

Khalil, Mohammad Hassan, ed. *Between Heaven and Hell: Islam, Salvation, and the Fate of Others.* New York: Oxford University, 2013.

——. *Islam and the Fate of Others: The Salvation Question.* New York: Oxford University, 2012.

——. "Salvation and the 'Other' in Islamic Thought: The Contemporary Pluralism Debate." *Religion Compass* 5, no. 9 (2011): 511–519.

Kinberg, Leah. "Piety." In *Encyclopaedia of the Qur'ān*, edited by Jane Dammen McAuliffe, vol. 4, 90. Leiden: Brill, 2001.

King, Ursula. "Feminism: The Missing Dimension in the Dialogue of Religions." In *Pluralism and the Religions: The Theological and Political Dimensions*, edited by John D'Arcy May, 40–58. Herndon, VA: Cassell/Wellington House, 1998.

—— and Tina Beattie, eds. *Gender, Religion and Diversity: Cross-Cultural Perspectives.* New York: Continuum, 2005.

Knitter, Paul F. *Introducing Theologies of Religions.* Maryknoll, NY: Orbis Books, 2008.

——, ed. *The Myth of Religious Superiority: A Multifaith Exploration.* Maryknoll, NY: Orbis, 2005.

——. *No Other Name?: A Christian Survey of Christian Attitudes toward the World Religions.* Maryknoll, NY: Orbis Books, 2003.

——. "Toward a Liberation Theology of Religions." In *The Myth of Christian Uniqueness: Toward a Pluralistic Theology of Religions*, edited by John Hick and Paul Knitter, 178–200. Eugene, OR: Wipf & Stock, 1987.

Kwok, Pui-lan. "Beyond Pluralism." In *Postcolonial Imagination and Feminist Theology*, 186–208. Louisville, KY: Westminster John Knox, 2005.

————. "Feminist Theology as Intercultural Discourse." In *The Cambridge Companion to Feminist Theology*, edited by Susan Parsons, 23–39. New York: Cambridge University, 2002.

————. *Introducing Asian Feminist Theology.* Cleveland: The Pilgrim, 2000.

Legenhausen, Muhammad. "Islam and Religious Pluralism." *al-Tawhid: A Quarterly Journal of Islamic Thought and Culture* 14 (1997): 115–154.

——. *Islam and Religious Pluralism*. London: Al Hoda Publishing, 1999.

——. "A Muslim's Non-reductive Religious Pluralism." In *Islam and Global Dialogue: Religious Pluralism and the Pursuit of Peace*, edited by Roger Boase, 51–73. Surrey: Ashgate, 2005.

Lindbeck, George. *The Nature of Doctrine: Religion and Theology in a Postliberal Age*. Philadelphia: Westminster, 1984.

Laoust, H. "Ibn Taymiyya, Taḳī al-Dīn Aḥmad Ibn Taymiyya." In *Encyclopaedia of Islam, Second Edition*, edited by P. Bearman, Th. Bianquis, C.E. Bosworth, E. van Donzel, and W.P. Heinrichs, vol. 3, 951. Leiden: Brill, 2004.

Lumbard, Joseph. "Qur'ānic Inclusivism in an Age of Globalization." In *The Religious Other: Towards a Muslim Theology of Other Religions in a Post-Prophetic Age*, edited by Muhammad Suheyl Umar, 151–162. Lahore: Iqbal Academy Pakistan, 2008.

Madigan, Daniel A. "Book." In *Encyclopaedia of the Qur'ān*, edited by Jane Dammen McAuliffe, vol. 1, 242. Leiden: Brill, 2001.

——. *The Qur'ān's Self-Image: Writing and Authority in Islam's Scripture*. Princeton, NJ: Princeton University, 2001.

——. "Revelation and Inspiration." In *Encyclopaedia of the Qur'ān*, edited by Jane Dammen McAuliffe, vol. 4, 437. Leiden: Brill, 2001.

Marshall, Dave. *God, Muhammad, and the Unbelievers: A Qur'anic Study*. Surrey: Curzon, 1999.

Mattson, Ingrid. *The Story of the Qur'an: Its History and Place in Muslim Life*. Malden, MA: Blackwell, 2008.

McAuliffe, Jane Dammen, ed. *The Cambridge Companion to the Qur'ān*. Cambridge: Cambridge University, 2006.

——, ed. *Encyclopaedia of the Qur'ān*, 5 vols. Leiden: Brill, 2001.

——. *Qur'anic Christians: An Analysis of Classical and Modern Exegesis*. Cambridge: Cambridge University, 1991.

——. "Quranic Hermeneutics: The Views of al-Ṭabarī and Ibn Kathīr." In *Approaches to the History of the Interpretation of the Qur'an*, edited by Andrew Rippin, 46–62. Oxford: Clarendon, 1988.

——. "Reading the Qur'an with Fidelity and Freedom." *Journal of the American Academy of Religion* 73, no. 3 (September 2005): 615–635.

McCarthy, Kate. "Women's Experience as a Hermeneutical Key to a Christian Theology of Religions." *Studies in Interreligious Dialogue* 6, no. 2 (1996): 163–173.

McCarthy, R.J. "al-Bāḳillānī (i.e. the greengrocer), the ḳāḍī Abū Bakr Muḥammad b. al-Ṭayyib b. Muḥammad b. Dja'far b. al-Ḳāsim." In *Encyclopaedia of Islam, Second Edition*, edited by P. Bearman, Th. Bianquis, C.E. Bosworth, E. van Donzel, and W.P. Heinrichs, vol. 1, 958. Leiden: Brill, 2004.

McGarvey, Kathleen. *Muslim and Christian Women in Dialogue: The Case of Northern Nigeria*. Oxford: Peter Lang, 2009.

Memon, Muhammad Umar, ed. and trans. *Ibn Taimīya's Struggle Against Popular Religion with an Annotated Translation of His Kitāb iqtiḍā' aṣ-ṣirāṭ al-mustaqīm mukhālafat aṣḥāb al-Jaḥīm*. The Hague: Mouton, 1976.

Min, Anselm Kyongsuk. "Dialectical Pluralism and Solidarity of Others: Towards a New Paradigm." *Journal of the American Academy of Religion* 65, no. 3 (Autumn 1997): 587–604.

Mir, Mustansir. "Polytheism and Atheism." In *Encyclopaedia of the Qur'ān*, edited by Jane Dammen McAuliffe, vol. 4, 158. Leiden: Brill, 2001.

Moghadam, Valentine M. "Islamic Feminism and Its Discontents: Toward a Resolution of the Debate." *Signs* 27, no. 4 (Summer 2002): 1135–1171.

Moghissi, Haideh. *Feminism and Islamic Fundamentalism: The Limits of Postmodern Analysis*. London: Zed Books, 1999.

——, ed. *Women and Islam: Critical Concepts in Sociology*. Volume One: Images and Realities. London: Routledge, 2005.

Mojab, Shahrzad. "Islamic Feminism: Alternative or Contradiction?" *Fireweed*, no. 47 (Winter 1995): 18–25.

——. "Theorizing the Politics of 'Islamic Feminism.'" *Feminist Review* 69 (Winter 2001): 124–146.

Mortenson, Viggo, ed. *Theology and the Religions: A Dialogue*. Cambridge: Eerdsmans, 2003.

Murata, Sachiko, and William C. Chittick. *The Vision of Islam*. New York: Paragon House, 1994.

Mutahhari, Shahid Ayatullah Murtadha. *Islam and Religious Pluralism*. Kitchener, Ontario: Islamic Publishing House, 2004.

al Najjar, 'Abd al Majīd. *The Vicegerency of Man: Between Revelation and Reason: A Critique of the Dialectic of the Text, Reason, and Reality*. Herndon, VA: International Institute of Islamic Thought, 2000.

Nasr, Seyyed Hossein. "The Creation of the World and of Human Beings," "Religion and Religions," "Islam and the Encounter of Religions," and "Islam's Attitude Towards Other Religions in History." In *The Religious Other: Towards a Muslim Theology of Other Religions in a Post-Prophetic Age*, edited by Muhammad Suheyl Umar, 47–58, 59–81, 83–120, 121–134. Lahore: Iqbal Academy Pakistan, 2008.

——. "Comments on a Few Theological Issues in the Islamic-Christian Dialogue." In *Christian-Muslim Encounters*, edited by Yvonne Yazbeck Haddad and Wadī' Zaydān Ḥaddād, 457–465. Gainesville: University Press of Florida, 1995.

——. "The Islamic View of Christianity." In *Christianity through Non-Christian Eyes*, edited by Paul J. Griffiths, 126–134. Maryknoll, NY: Orbis, 1990.

al-Nawawī, Yaḥyā ibn Sharaf Muḥyī al-Dīn. "Ḥadīth Two." In *Classical Islam: A Sourcebook of Religious Literature*, edited by Norman Calder, J. A. Mojaddedi, and Andrew Rippin, 143–146. New York: Routledge, 2003.

——. *Une herméneutique de la tradition islamique: le commentaire des* Arbaʿūn al-Nawawīya *de Muḥyī al-Dīn Yaḥyā al-Nawawī (m. 676/1277)*, edited by Louis Pouzet, S.J. Beirut: Dar el-Machreq, 1982.

——. *Kitāb al-arbaʿīn al-Nawawīya wa-sharḥu*. Manshīyat al-bakrā, Egypt: Dār ḥarāʾ lil-kitāb, 1987.

——. *Al-Nawawi's Forty Ḥadīth* (Matn al-arbaʿīn al-Nabawiyya), edited and translated by Ezzeddin Ibrahim and Denys Johnson-Davies. Cambridge: Islamic Texts Society, 1997.

Netland, Harold. *Encountering Religious Pluralism: The Challenge to Christian Faith & Mission*. Downers Grove, IL: InterVarsity, 2001.

Nöldeke, Theodor. *Geschichte des Qorans. Zweite Auflage*, bearbeitet von Friedrich Schwally, 3 vols. Leipzig: Weicher, 1909–38.

Ogden, Schubert M. "Problems in the Case for a Pluralistic Theology of Religions." *Journal of Religion* 68, no. 4 (October 1988): 493–507.

Oppenheim, Michael. "Feminism, Jewish Philosophy, and Religious Pluralism." *Modern Judaism* 16, no. 2 (May 1996): 147–160.

Osman, Mohamed Fathi. *The Children of Adam: An Islamic Perspective on Pluralism*. Washington, DC: Center for Muslim-Christian Understanding, Georgetown University, 1996.

Panikkar, Raimon. *The Intra-Religious Dialogue*. Mahwah, NJ: Paulist, 1999.

Parsons, Susan, ed. *The Cambridge Companion to Feminist Theology*. New York: Cambridge University, 2002.

Partin, Harry B. "Semantics of the Qurʾān: A Consideration of Izutsu's Studies." *History of Religions* 9, no. 4 (May 1970): 358–362.

Peters, Francis. "*Alius* or *Alter*: The Qurʾānic Definition of Christians and Christianity." *Islam and Christian-Muslim Relations* 8 (1997): 165–176.

——. *A Reader on Classical Islam*. Princeton, NJ: Princeton University, 1994.

Plaskow, Judith. *Standing Again at Sinai: Judaism from a Feminist Perspective*. San Fra ncisco: HarperSanFrancisco, 1991.

Pouzet, Louis, ed. *Une herméneutique de la tradition islamique: le commentaire des Arbaʿūn al-Nawawīya de Muḥyī al-Dīn Yaḥyā al-Nawawī (m. 676/1277)*. Beirut: Dar el-Machreq, 1982.

Pulcini, Theodore. *Exegesis as Polemical Discourse: Ibn Ḥazm on Jewish and Christian Scriptures*, American Academy of Religion, The Religions Series, no. 2. Atlanta: Scholars, 1998.

Qadhi, Yasir. "The Path of Allah or the Paths of Allah? Revisiting Classical and Medieval Sunni Approaches to the Salvation of Others." In *Between Heaven and Hell: Islam, Salvation, and the Fate of Others*, edited by Mohammad Hassan Khalil, 109–121. New York: Oxford University, 2013.

Rahman, Fazlur. *Islam and Modernity: Transformation of an Intellectual Tradition*. Chicago: University of Chicago, 1982.

——. *Islamic Methodology in History*. Karachi: Central Institute of Islamic Research, 1965.

——. "A Muslim Response: Christian Particularity and the Faith of Islam." In *Christian Faith in a Religiously Plural World*, edited by Donald G. Dawe and John B. Carman, 69–82. Maryknoll, NY: Orbis Books, 1978.

——. "The People of the Book and the Diversity of 'Religions.'" In *Christianity through Non-Christian Eyes*, edited by Paul J. Griffiths, 102–110. Maryknoll, NY: Orbis, 1990.

——. *Revival and Reform in Islam: A Study of Islamic Fundamentalisms*, edited by Ebrahim Moosa. Oxford: Oneworld, 2000.

Rapoport, Yossef, and Shahab Ahmed, eds. *Ibn Taymiyya and His Times*. Karachi: Oxford University, 2010.

al-Rāzi, Abū ʿAbd Allāh Muḥammad ibn ʿUmar Ibn al-Ḥusayn. *Mafātīḥ al-ghayb al-mushtahar bi ʾl-tafsīr al-kabīr*. Istanbul: al-Maṭbaʿah al-ʿAmirah, 1891.

Reçber, Mehmet Sait. "Hick, the Real and *al-Ḥaqq*." *Islam and Christian-Muslim Relations* 16, no. 1 (2005): 3–10.

Reynolds, Gabriel Said, and Khalil Samir, eds. and trans. *Critique of Christian Origins: A Parallel English-Arabic Text*. Provo, UT: Brigham Young University, 2010.

——. *A Muslim Theologian in a Sectarian Milieu: ʿAbd al-Jabbār and the Critique of Christian Origins*, Islamic History and Civilization, vol. 56. Leiden: Brill, 2004.

——. *The Qurʾān and Its Biblical Subtext*. London: Routledge, 2010.

Rippin, Andrew, ed. *Approaches to the History of the Interpretation of the Qurʾan*. Oxford: Clarendon, 1988.

Ritter, H., and Bausani, A. "DJalālal-Dīn Rūmī b. Bahāʾ al-Dīn Sulṭān al-ʿulamāʾ Walad b. Ḥusayn b. Aḥmad Khaṭībī." In *Encyclopaedia of Islam, Second Edition*, edited by P. Bearman, Th. Bianquis, C.E. Bosworth, E. van Donzel, and W.P. Heinrichs, vol. 2, 393. Leiden: Brill, 2004.

Rizvi, Sajjad H. "A Primordial e *pluribus unum*? Exegeses on Q. 2:213 and Contemporary Muslim Discourses on Religious Pluralism." *Journal of Qur'anic Studies* 6, no. 1 (2004): 21–42.

Roald, Anne Sofie. "Feminist Reinterpretation of Islamic Sources: Muslim Feminist Theology in the Light of the Christian Tradition of Feminist Thought." In *Women and Islamization: Contemporary Dimensions of Discourse on Gender Relations*, edited by Karin Ask and Marit Tjomsland, 17–44. Oxford: Berg, 1998.

——. *Women in Islam: The Western Experience*. New York: Routledge, 2001.

Rubin, Uri. "Children of Israel." In *Encyclopaedia of the Qurʾān*, edited by Jane Dammen McAuliffe, vol. 1, 303. Leiden: Brill, 2001.

——. "Ḥanīf." In *Encyclopaedia of the Qurʾān*, edited by Jane Dammen McAuliffe, vol. 2, 402. Leiden: Brill, 2001.

Ruether, Rosemary Radford. "The Emergence of Christian Feminist Theology." In *The Cambridge Companion to Feminist Theology*, edited by Susan Parsons, 3–22. New York: Cambridge University, 2002.

——. "Feminism and Jewish–Christian Dialogue: Particularism and Universalism in the Search for Truth." In *The Myth of Christian Uniqueness: Toward a Pluralistic Theology of Religion*, edited by John Hick and Paul Knitter, 137–148. Eugene, OR: Wipf & Stock, 1987.

——. "The Future of Feminist Theology in the Academy." *Journal of the American Academy of Religion* 53, no. 4, 75th Anniversary Meeting of the American Academy of Religion (December 1985): 703–713.

——. "Growing Pluralism, New Dialogue." In *In Our Own Voices: Four Centuries of American Women's Religious Writing*, edited by Rosemary Skinner Keller and Rosemary Radford Ruether, 425–468. San Francisco: HarperSanFranci sco, 1995.

——. *Sexism and God-Talk: Toward a Feminist Theology*. Boston: Beacon, 1993.

Rūmī, Jalāl al-Dīn. *Discourses of Rūmī* (Fīhī mā Fīhī), translated by A.J. Arberry. London: John Murray, 1961.

——. *The Mathnawī of Jalālu'uddīn Rūmī*, 8 vols., edited and translated by R.A. Nicholson. London: Luzac, 1925–1940.

—— and William C. Chittick. *The Sufi Path of Love: The Spiritual Teachings of Rumi*. Albany: State University of New York, 1983.

Ruzgar, Mustapha. "Islam and Deep Religious Pluralism." In *Deep Religious Pluralism*, edited by David Ray Griffin, 158–177. Louisville, KY: Westminster John Knox, 2005.

Sachedina, Abdulaziz. *The Islamic Roots of Democratic Pluralism*. Oxford: Oxford University, 2001.

——. "Islamic Theology of Christian–Muslim Relations." *Islam and Christian-Muslim Relations* 8, no. 1 (1997): 27–38.

——. "The Qur'an and Other Religions." In *The Cambridge Companion to the Qur'an*, edited by Jane Dammen McAuliffe, 291–309. Cambridge: Cambridge University, 2006.

Saeed, Abdullah. *Interpreting the Qur'ān: Towards a Contemporary Approach*. London: Routledge, 2006.

Safi, Omid, ed. *Progressive Muslims: On Justice, Gender and Pluralism*. Oxford: OneWorld, 2003.

Saleh, Walid A. "Ibn Taymiyyah and the Rise of Radical Hermeneutics: An Analysis of An Introduction to the Foundations of Qur'ānic Exegesis." In *Ibn Taymiyya and His Times*, edited by Yossef Rapoport and Shahab Ahmed, 123–162. Karachi: Oxford University, 2010.

Schacht, Joseph. "Review of The Structure of Ethical Terms in the Koran by Toshihiko Izutsu." *Journal of the American Oriental Society* 83, no. 3 (August–September 1963): 366–367.

Schüssler Fiorenza, Elizabeth. *Bread Not Stone: The Challenge of Feminist Biblical Interpretation*. Boston: Beacon, 1984.

——. *But She Said: Feminist Practices of Biblical Interpretation*. Boston: Beacon, 1992.

——. *In Memory of Her: A Feminist Theological Reconstruction of Christian Origins.* New York: Crossroad, 1994.

Shah-Kazemi, Reza. "Illumination and Non-delimitation: Lessons for Inter and Intra Faith Dialogue." In *The Religious Other: Towards a Muslim Theology of Other Religions in a Post-Prophetic Age*, edited by Muhammad Suheyl Umar, 163–178. Lahore: Iqbal Academy Pakistan, 2008.

——. *The Other in the Light of the One: The Universality of the Qur'an and Interfaith Dialogue.* Cambridge: Islamic Texts Society, 2006.

Shahidian, Hammed. "The Politics of the Veil: Reflections on Symbolism, Islam, and Feminism." *Thamyris: Mythmaking from Past to Present* 4, no. 2 (1997): 325–337.

Sharma, Arvind, and Katherine K. Young, eds. *Feminism and World Religions.* Albany: State University of New York, 1999.

——. *Her Voice, Her Faith: Women Speak on World Religions.* Boulder, CO: Westview, 2003.

Sirry, Mun'im. "'Compete with One Another in Good Works': Exegesis of Qur'an Verse 5.48 and Contemporary Muslim Discourses on Religious Pluralism." *Islam and Christian–Muslim Relations* 20, no. 4 (2009): 424–438.

Smith, Wilfred Cantwell. *The Meaning and End of Religion.* Minneapolis: Fortress, 1991. Originally published by New York: Macmillan, 1962, 1963.

——. *Toward a World Theology.* London: Macmillian, 1981.

Smith, Jane. "Faith." In *Encyclopaedia of the Qur'ān*, edited by Jane Dammen McAuliffe, vol. 2, 162. Leiden: Brill, 2001.

——. *A Historical and Semantic Study of the Term 'Islām' as seen in a Sequence of Qur'ān Commentaries.* Montana: Scholars, University of Montana, 1975.

—— and Yvonne Haddad. *The Islamic Understanding of Death and Resurrection.* Albany: State University of New York, 1981.

Sourdel, D. "al-Ḳādir Bi'llāh." In *Encyclopaedia of Islam, Second Edition*, edited by P. Bearman, Th. Bianquis, C.E. Bosworth, E. van Donzel, and W.P. Heinrichs, vol. 4, 378. Leiden: Brill, 2004.

Stern, S.M. "Abū 'Īsā Muḥammad b. Hārūn al-Warrāḳ." In *Encyclopaedia of Islam, Second Edition*, edited by P. Bearman, Th. Bianquis, C.E. Bosworth, E. van Donzel, and W.P. Heinrichs, vol. 1, 130. Leiden: Brill, 1960–2005.

Stowasser, Barbara. "Gender Issues and Contemporary Quran Interpretation." In *Islam, Gender, & Social Change*, edited by Yvonne Yazbeck Haddad and John L. Esposito, 30–44. New York: Oxford University, 1998.

——. *Women in the Qur'an, Traditions, and Interpretation.* New York: Oxford University, 1994.

Suchocki, Marjorie Hewitt. "In Search of Justice: Religious Pluralism from a Feminist Perspective." In *The Myth of Christian Uniqueness: Toward a Pluralistic Theology of Religion*, edited by John Hick and Paul Knitter, 149–161. Eugene, OR: Wipf & Stock, 1987.

al-Ṭabarī, Abū Ja'far Muḥammad ibn Jarīr. *Jāmi' al-bayān 'an ta'wīl āyāt al-Qur'ān.* Cairo: al-Maṭba'ah al-Kubra al-Amīrīyah, 1900–1911.

Taji-Farouki, Suha, ed. *Modern Muslim Intellectuals and the Qur'an*. London: Oxford University and The Institute of Ismaili Studies, 2004.

Talbi, Mohamed. "Dialogue Islamo-Chrétien et Sensibilitités Religieuses" and "A Community of Communities." In *Encounters & Clashes: Islam and Christianity in History*. Collection "Studi arabo-islamici del PISAI," 15, edited by Jean-Marie Gaudel, 113–117, 335–340. Roma: Pontificio Istituto di Studi Arabi e d'Islamistica, 2000.

——. "Dialogue Islamo-Chrétien et Sensibilitités Religieuses." *Islamochristiana*, Rome 1 (1975): 11–25.

——. "Islam and Dialogue—Some Reflections on a Current Topic." In *Christianity through Non-Christian Eyes*, edited by Paul J. Griffiths, 82–101. Maryknoll, NY: Orbis, 1990.

Thomas, David. "ʿAbū ʿĪsā al-Warrāq and the History of Religions." *Journal of Semitic Studies* 41 (1996): 275–290.

——, ed. and trans. *Anti-Christian Polemic in Early Islam: Abū ʿĪsá al-Warrāq's "Against the Trinity,"* University of Cambridge Oriental Publications, no. 45. Cambridge: University of Cambridge, 1992.

——. "Apologetic and Polemic in the *Letter from Cyprus* and Ibn Taymiyya's *Jawāb al-Ṣaḥīḥ li-man Baddala Dīn al-Masīḥ*." In *Ibn Taymiyya and His Times*, edited by Yossef Rapoport and Shahab Ahmed, 247–265. Karachi: Oxford University, 2010.

——. *Christian Doctrines in Islamic Theology*. Leiden: Brill, 2008.

——, ed. and trans. *Early Muslim Polemic against Christianity: Abū ʿĪsá al-Warrāq's "Against the Incarnation,"* University of Cambridge Oriental Publications, no. 59. Cambridge: Cambridge University, 2002.

——. "al-Ṭabarī." In *Encyclopaedia of Islam, Second Edition*, edited by P. Bearman, Th. Bianquis, C.E. Bosworth, E. van Donzel, and W.P. Heinrichs, vol. 10, 17. Leiden: Brill, 2004.

Tracy, David. *Plurality and Ambiguity: Hermeneutics, Religion, Hope*. San Francisco: Harper & Row, 1987.

Umar, Muhammad Suheyl, ed. *The Religious Other: Towards a Muslim Theology of Other Religions in a Post-Prophetic Age*. Lahore: Iqbal Academy Pakistan, 2008.

Van Nieuwkerk, Karin, ed. *Women Embracing Islam: Gender and Conversion in the West*. Austin: University of Texas, 2006.

Veccia Vaglieri, L. "ʿAbd Allāh b. al-ʿAbbās." In *Encyclopaedia of Islam, Second Edition*, edited by P. Bearman, Th. Bianquis, C.E. Bosworth, E. van Donzel, and W.P. Heinrichs, vol. 1, 40. Leiden: Brill, 2004.

Waardenburg, Jacques. "Muslim Studies of Other Religions: The Medieval Period." In *Muslims and Others in Early Islamic Society*, The Formation of the Classical Islamic World, vol. 18, edited by Robert G. Hoyland, 211–239. Burlington, VT: Ashgate, 2004.

Wadud, Amina. "Alternative Qur'anic Interpretation and the Status of Muslim Women." In *Windows of Faith: Muslim Women Scholar-Activists in North America*, edited by Gisela Webb, 3–21. Syracuse: Syracuse University, 2000.

——. *Inside the Gender Jihad: Women's Reform in Islam*. Oxford: Oneworld, 2006.

——. *Qur'an and Woman: Rereading the Sacred Texts from a Woman's Perspective*. New York: Oxford University, 1999.

——. "Response: Roundtable Discussion, Feminist Theology and Religious Diversity." *Journal of Feminist Studies in Religion* 16, no. 2 (2000): 90–100.

——. "Towards a Qur'anic Hermeneutics of Social Justice: Race, Class and Gender." *Journal of Law and Religion* 12, no. 1 (1995–1996): 37–50.

Waldman, Marilyn Robinson. "The Development of the Concept of *Kufr* in the Qur'ān." *Journal of the American Oriental Society* 88, no. 3 (July–September 1968): 442–455.

al-Warrāq, Abū 'Īsā Muḥammad ibn Hārūn. *Kitāb al-radd 'alā l-thalāth firaq min al-Naṣārā*, edited and translated by David Thomas, *Anti-Christian Polemic in Early Islam: Abū 'Īsá al-Warrāq's "Against the Trinity,"* University of Cambridge Oriental Publications, no. 45. Cambridge: University of Cambridge, 1992; *Idem*, *Early Muslim Polemic Against Christianity: Abū 'Īsá al-Warrāq's "Against the Incarnation,"* University of Cambridge Oriental Publications, no. 59. Cambridge: Cambridge University, 2002.

Watt, W. Montgomery. "al-Ghazālī, Abū Ḥāmid Muḥammad b. Muḥammad al-Ṭūsī." In *Encyclopaedia of Islam, Second Edition*, edited by P. Bearman, Th. Bianquis, C.E. Bosworth, E. van Donzel, and W.P. Heinrichs, vol. 2, 1038. Leiden: Brill, 2004.

——. "Ḥanīf." In *Encyclopaedia of Islam, Second Edition*, edited by P. Bearman, Th. Bianquis, C.E. Bosworth, E. van Donzel, and W.P. Heinrichs, vol. 3, 165. Leiden: Brill, 2004.

Webb, Gisela, ed. *Windows of Faith: Muslim Women Scholar-Activists in North America*. Syracuse: Syracuse University, 2000.

Wensinck, A.J. "Muslim." In *Encyclopaedia of Islam, Second Edition*, edited by P. Bearman, Th. Bianquis, C.E. Bosworth, E. van Donzel, and W.P. Heinrichs, vol. 7, 688. Leiden: Brill, 2004.

Winter, Tim. "Realism and the Real: Theology and the Problem of Alternative Expressions of God." In *Between Heaven and Hell: Islam, Salvation, and the Fate of Others*, edited by Mohammad Hassan Khalil, 122–150. New York: Oxford University, 2013.

——. "The Last Trump Card: Islam and the Supersession of Other Faiths." *Studies in Interreligious Dialogue* 9, no. 2 (1999): 133–155.

Yamani, Mai, ed. *Feminism & Islam: Legal and Literary Perspectives*. New York: New York University, 1996.

Young, Iris Marion. *Inclusion and Democracy*. Oxford: Oxford University, 2000.

——. *Intersecting Voices: Dilemmas of Gender, Political Philosophy, and Policy*. Princeton, NJ: Princeton University, 1997.

——. *Justice and the Politics of Difference*. Princeton, NJ: Princeton University, 1990.

Index

iqrār, 27, 30, 32
Isaac (*Tawrāt*), 24
Ishmael, 230
Islam
  and actualization, 43–47
  as "all-inclusive," 42–43
  and *dīn al-fiṭra*, 76
  and feminism, 8–10, 99
  as general faith, 64
  and heretical sects, 24–26
  and human capacity, 244–245
  and *islām*, 155–156, 222
  and *manāsik*, 166
  and norm(s), 64, 67–68
  and reification, 28–29, 171–179
  and superiority, 2–3, 56, 64–71, 95, 173–175
  and violence, 95
islām
  and Abraham, 221–222
  active nature of, 27–28, 233–234
  and conceptual opposition, 129–131
  and *dīn*, 26–28, 57
  dynamism of, 74–75
  and external actions, 27–31
  as general faith, 57
  and *ḥanīf*, 221
  in historical Islamic discourse, 26–31
  and *iḥsan*, 29–31
  and *īmān*, 29–31, 129, 272*n*11
  and interpretation, 262*n*9
  and Islam, 155–156, 222
  and *kufr*, 222–223
  and *manāsik*, 234
  and natural *āyāt*, 221
  occurrence within the Qurʾān, 184*t*
  reification of, 28–29
  and revelation(s), 221–222
  and self-identification, 234
  in semantic field of *taqwā*, 141–144, 144*f*, 196–197, 201–205, 221–223, 233–234
  in semantic field of *umma*, 155–179, 171*f*
  and specific historical communities, 155–156, 171*f*
Islamic feminism, 8–10
Islamic norm(s)
  polemical use of, 19–26
Islamic tradition(s)
  as monolithic, 67–68
  and *Muslima* theology, 7–11
isolation
  and depictions of religious communities, 4, 60–63
  and identity, 110–111
  and Qurʾānic concepts, 54, 124–125, 132–133
  and religious difference, 60–63, 77, 112, 117–118, 180, 243
  and religious sameness, 89–90
  and *taqwā*, 92
Izutsu, Toshihiko, 10, 123–136, 141–144, 155, 169, 182–183, 191, 197–198, 201, 206–207, 213, 219, 240, 271–273*nn*3–32, 273*n*8, 273*nn*3–6, 274*n*18, 276*n*9, 276*n*11, 276*n*13, 276*n*15, 276*n*20, 276*n*25, 276*nn*17–18, 277*n*28, 277*n*36, 277*n*38, 277*n*42
  methodology of, 124–126

Jackson, Sherman A., 260*n*64, 260*n*65, 260*n*66, 260*n*67, 260*n*68, 260*n*69, 260*n*70, 261*n*72, 261*n*73
al-jahannam, 36–38, 44–45, 141–142, 151
  and conceptual opposition, 128–129, 128*f*, 134
al-Jāḥiz, Abū ʿUthmān, 257*n*5
al-Jamil, Tariq, 258*n*33
al-janna, 36–38, 41, 44–45, 151–153
  and conceptual opposition, 128–129, 128*f*, 134

Verse Index